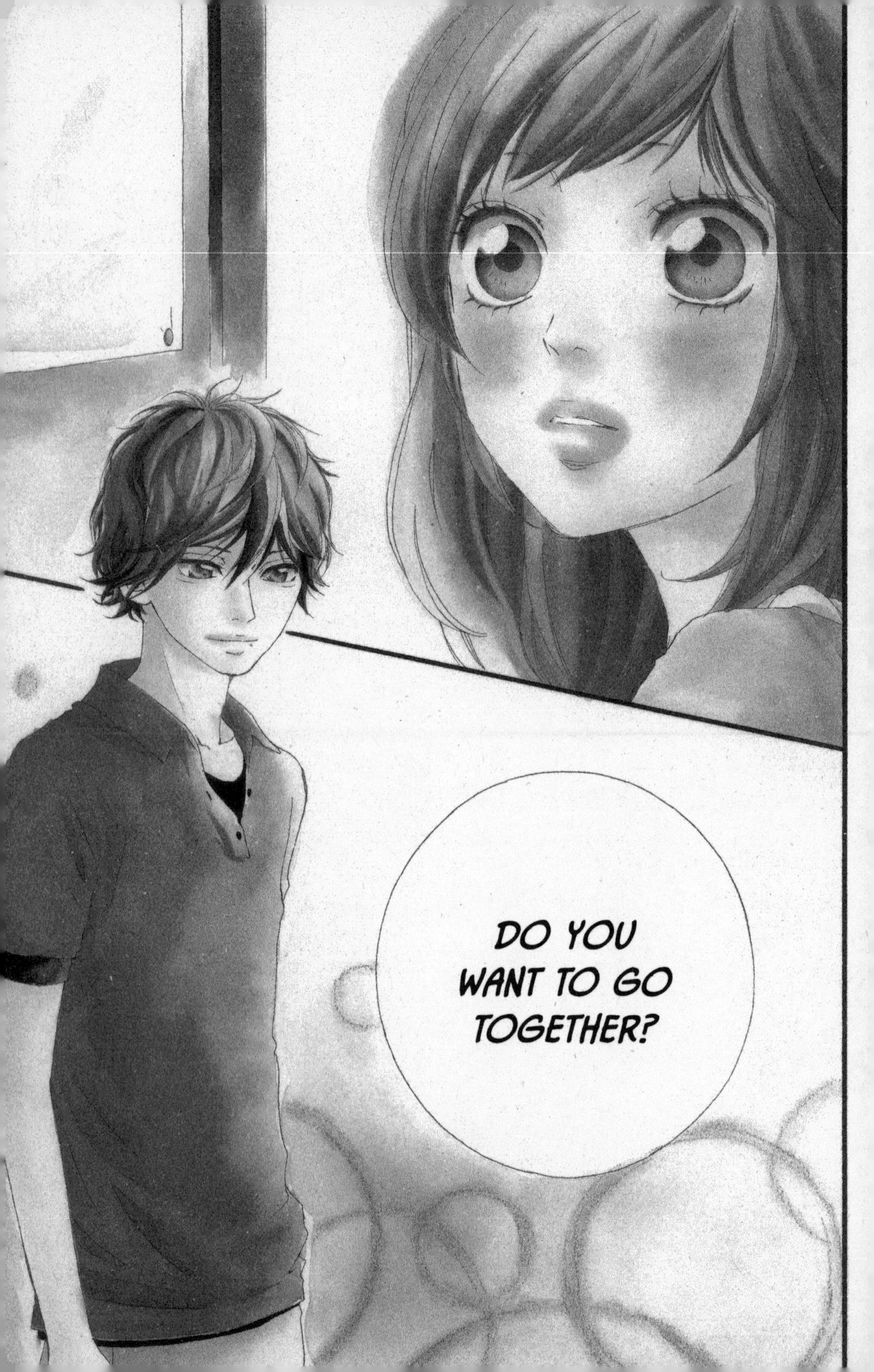
DO YOU WANT TO GO TOGETHER?

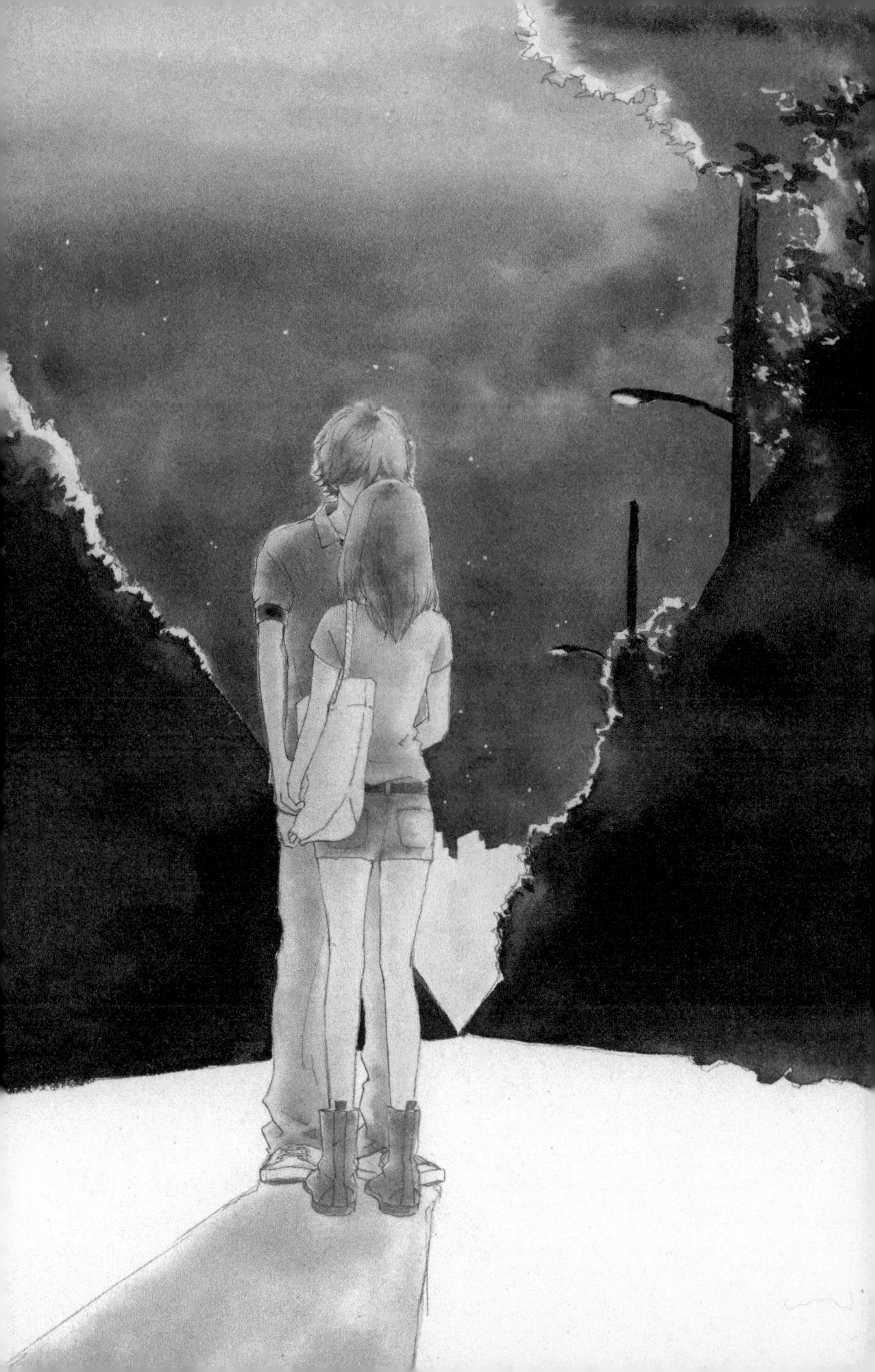

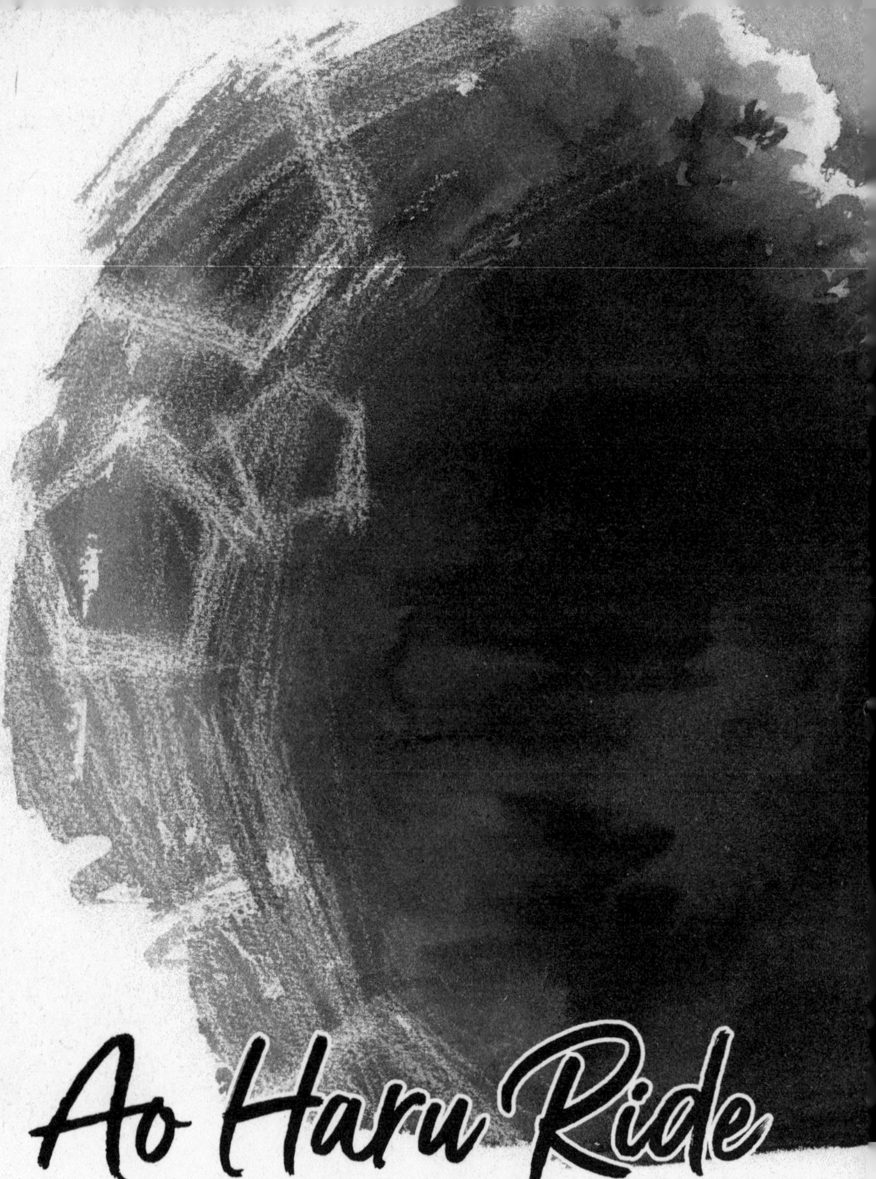

Ao Haru Ride

The scent of air after rain...
In the light around us, I felt your heartbeat.

CHAPTER 16

IO SAKISAKA

GREETINGS

Hi! I'm Io Sakisaka. Thank you for picking up a copy of *Ao Haru Ride* volume 5!

Here I was thinking that volume 4 had just recently come out, and it's time for volume 5 already. That was fast! You know, when *Ao Haru Ride* first started, I felt like time was passing slowly, but lately it flies by—everything is different now. It's a bit frightening. It makes me shiver. Haste makes waste, so I'd rather not rush, but time won't let me! I suppose, if I take a different perspective, this could be a good thing. Although I can't say it'll be good for me mentally. (*laugh*)

Though I'm rushing, I'm doing my best to take care with the story. I want to be sure not to lose the important elements!

With that... Let's go, volume 5! I hope you'll read through to the end! Let's go, go, go!

 Io Sakisaka

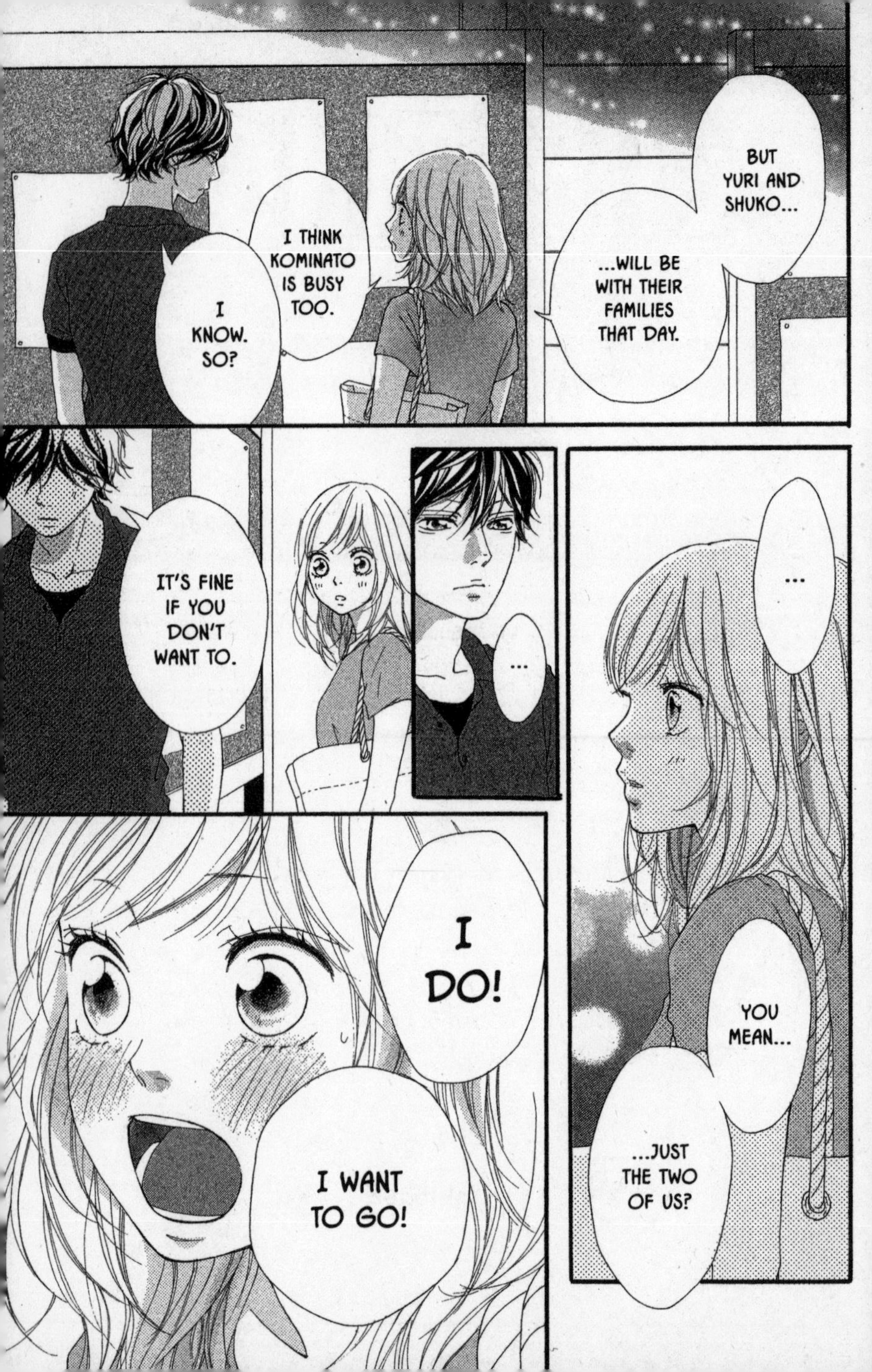
BUT YURI AND SHUKO...
...WILL BE WITH THEIR FAMILIES THAT DAY.
I THINK KOMINATO IS BUSY TOO.
I KNOW. SO?
...
YOU MEAN...
...JUST THE TWO OF US?
...
IT'S FINE IF YOU DON'T WANT TO.
I DO!
I WANT TO GO!

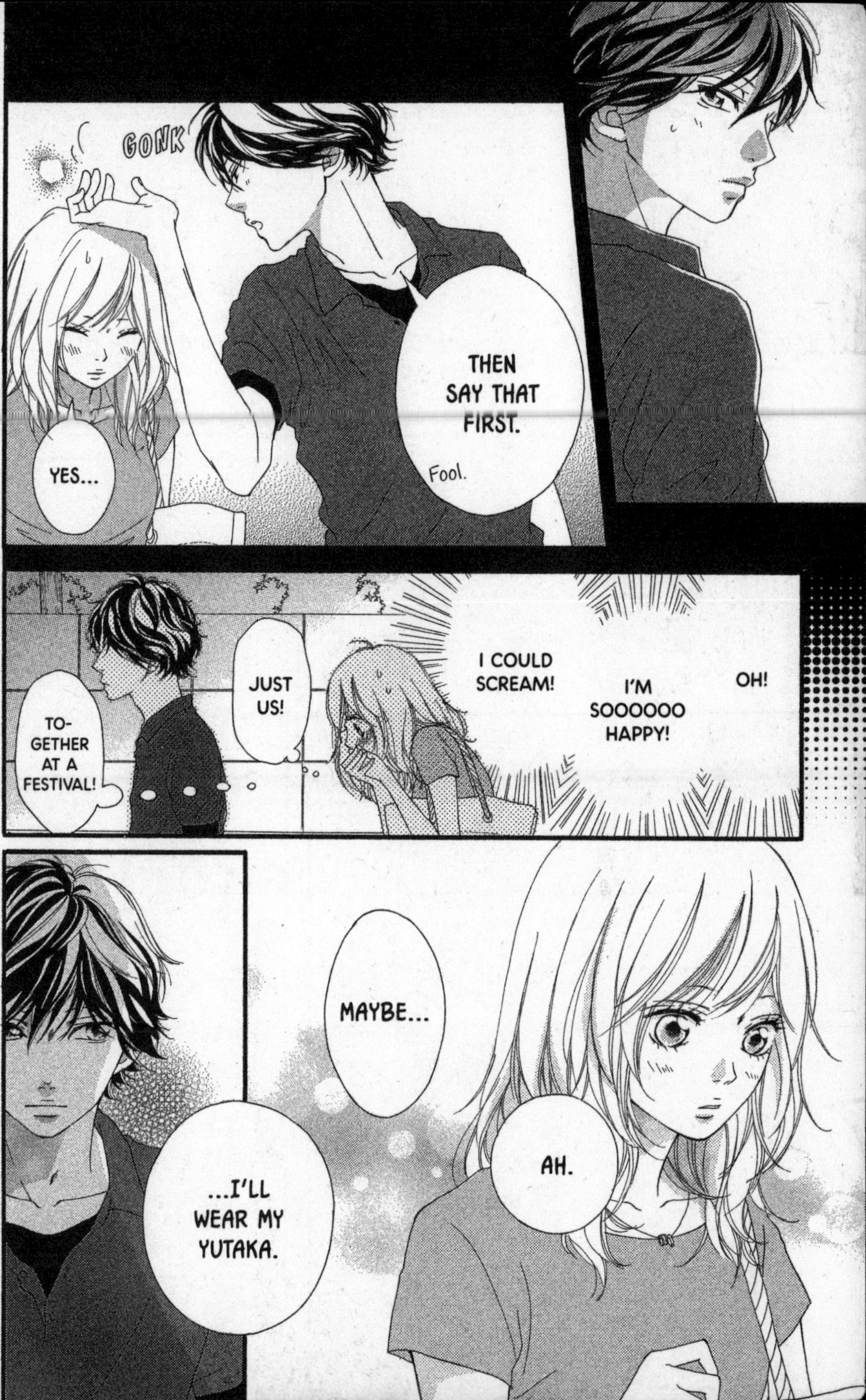
GONK
THEN SAY THAT FIRST.
Fool.
YES...
OH!
I'M SOOOOOO HAPPY!
I COULD SCREAM!
JUST US!
TO-GETHER AT A FESTIVAL!
MAYBE...
AH.
...I'LL WEAR MY YUTAKA.

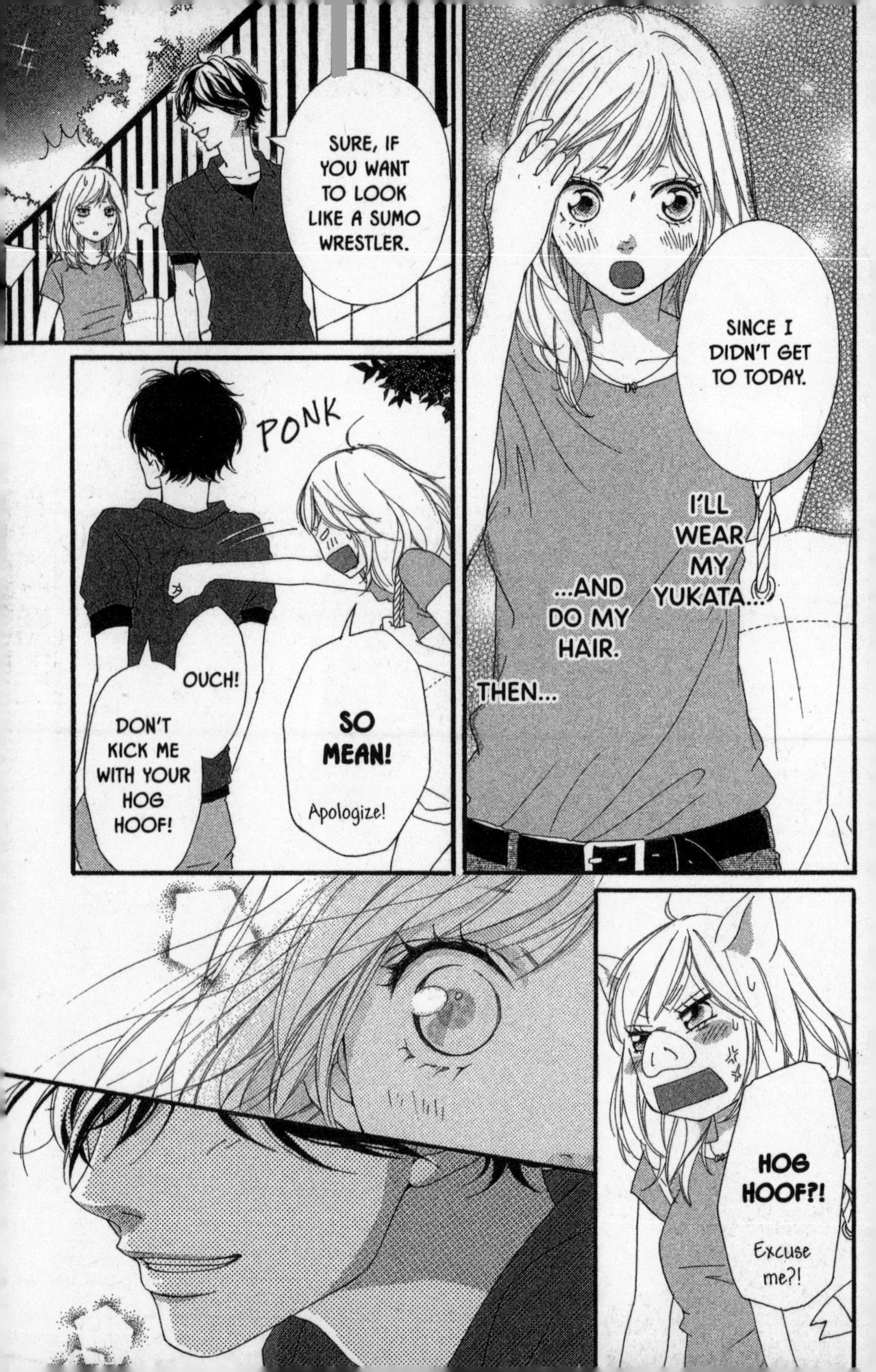
SINCE I DIDN'T GET TO TODAY.
I'LL WEAR MY YUKATA...
...AND DO MY HAIR.
THEN...
SURE, IF YOU WANT TO LOOK LIKE A SUMO WRESTLER.
PONK
SO MEAN!
Apologize!
OUCH!
DON'T KICK ME WITH YOUR HOG HOOF!
HOG HOOF?!
Excuse me?!

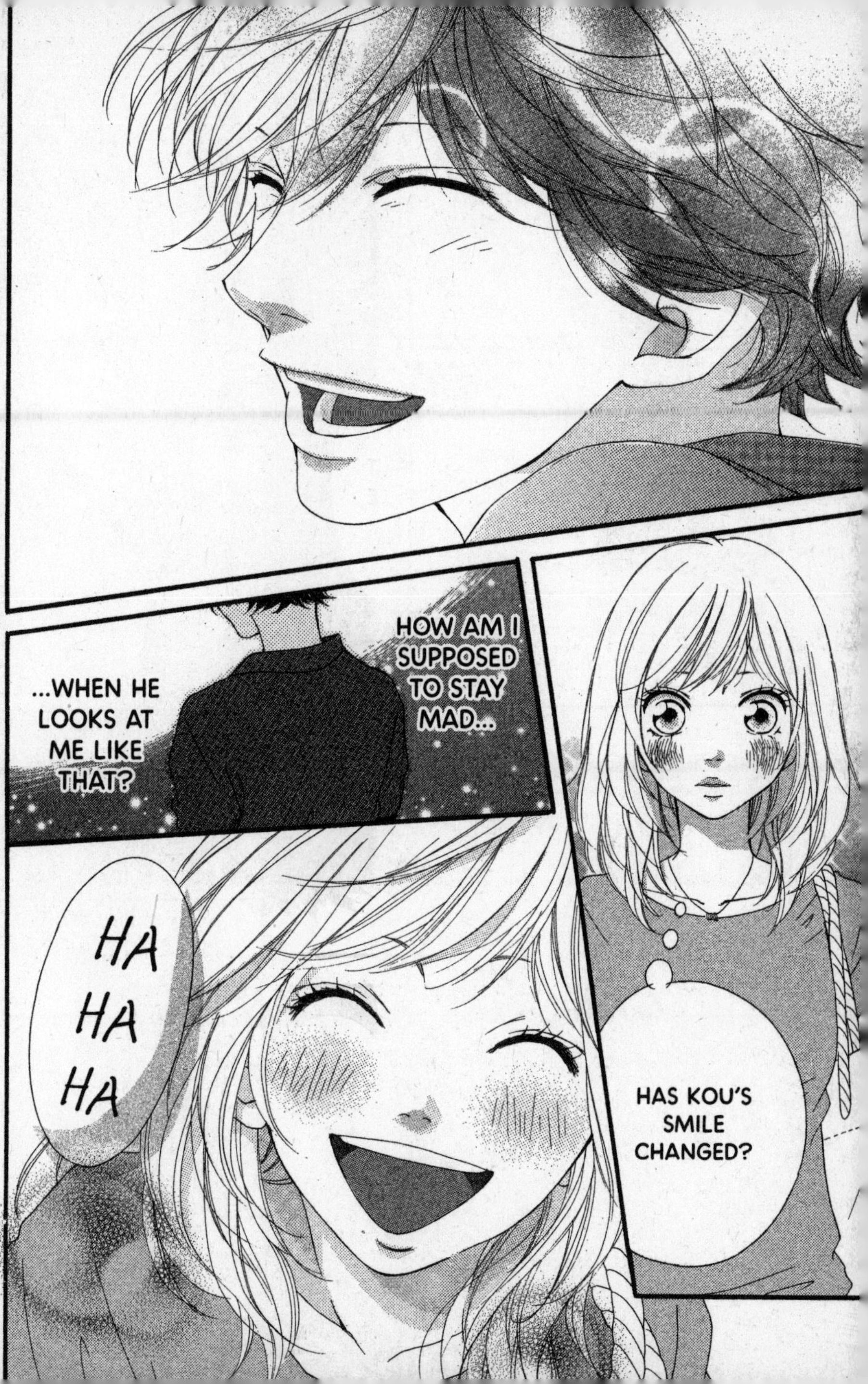
HAS KOU'S SMILE CHANGED?
HOW AM I SUPPOSED TO STAY MAD...
...WHEN HE LOOKS AT ME LIKE THAT?
HA HA HA

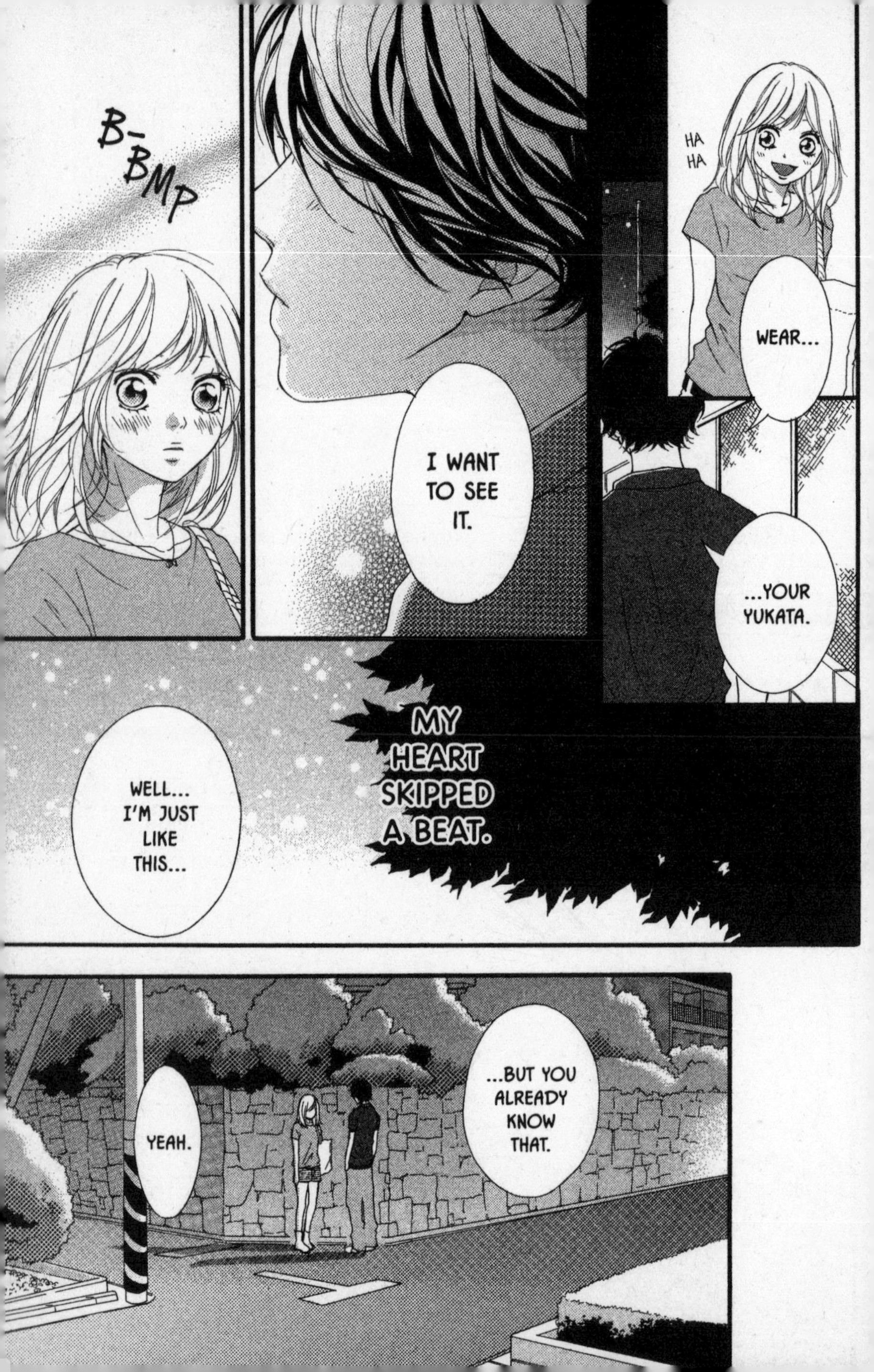
HA HA
WEAR...
...YOUR YUKATA.
I WANT TO SEE IT.
B-BMP
MY HEART SKIPPED A BEAT.
WELL... I'M JUST LIKE THIS...
...BUT YOU ALREADY KNOW THAT.
YEAH.

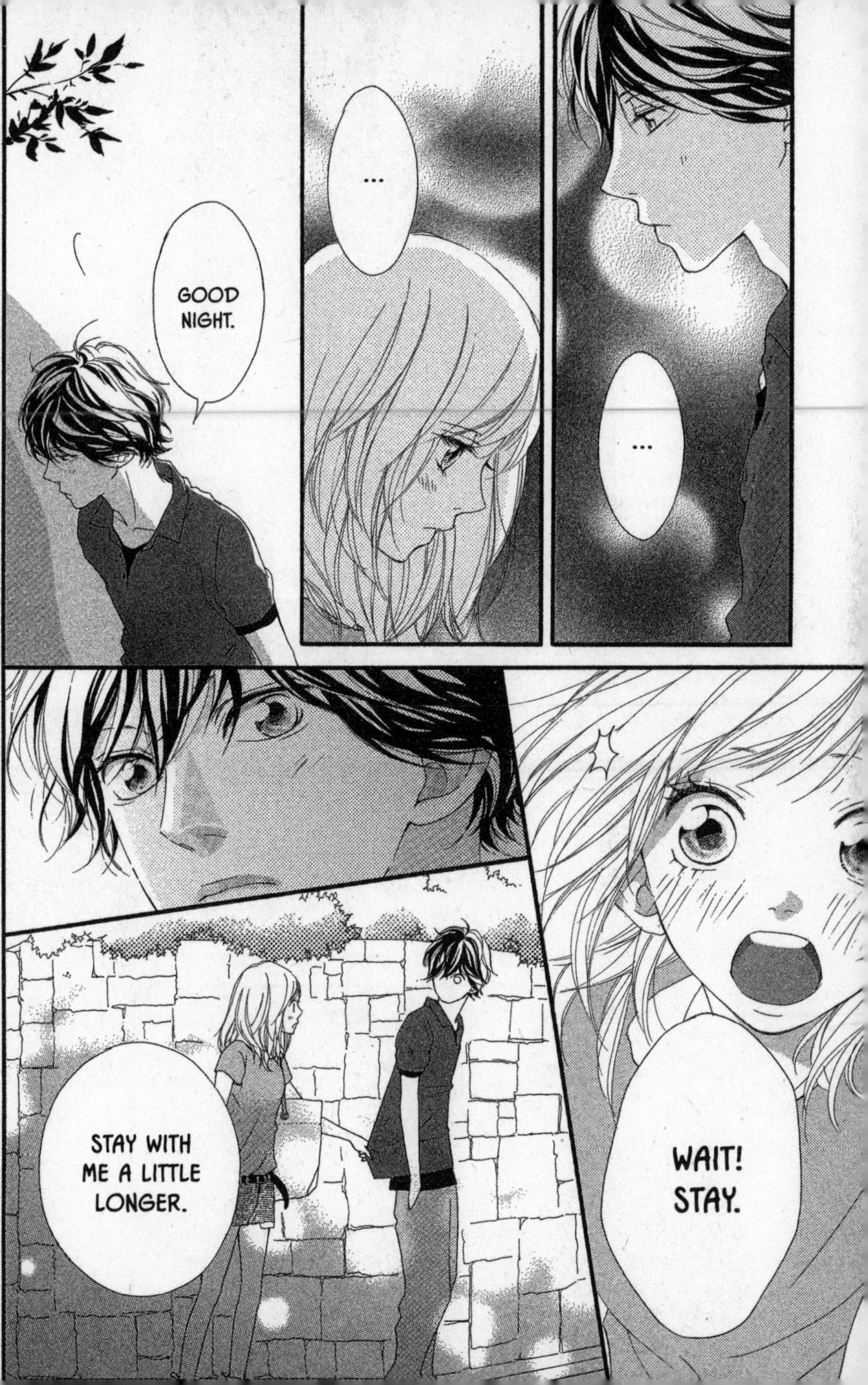
...
...
GOOD NIGHT.
WAIT! STAY.
STAY WITH ME A LITTLE LONGER.

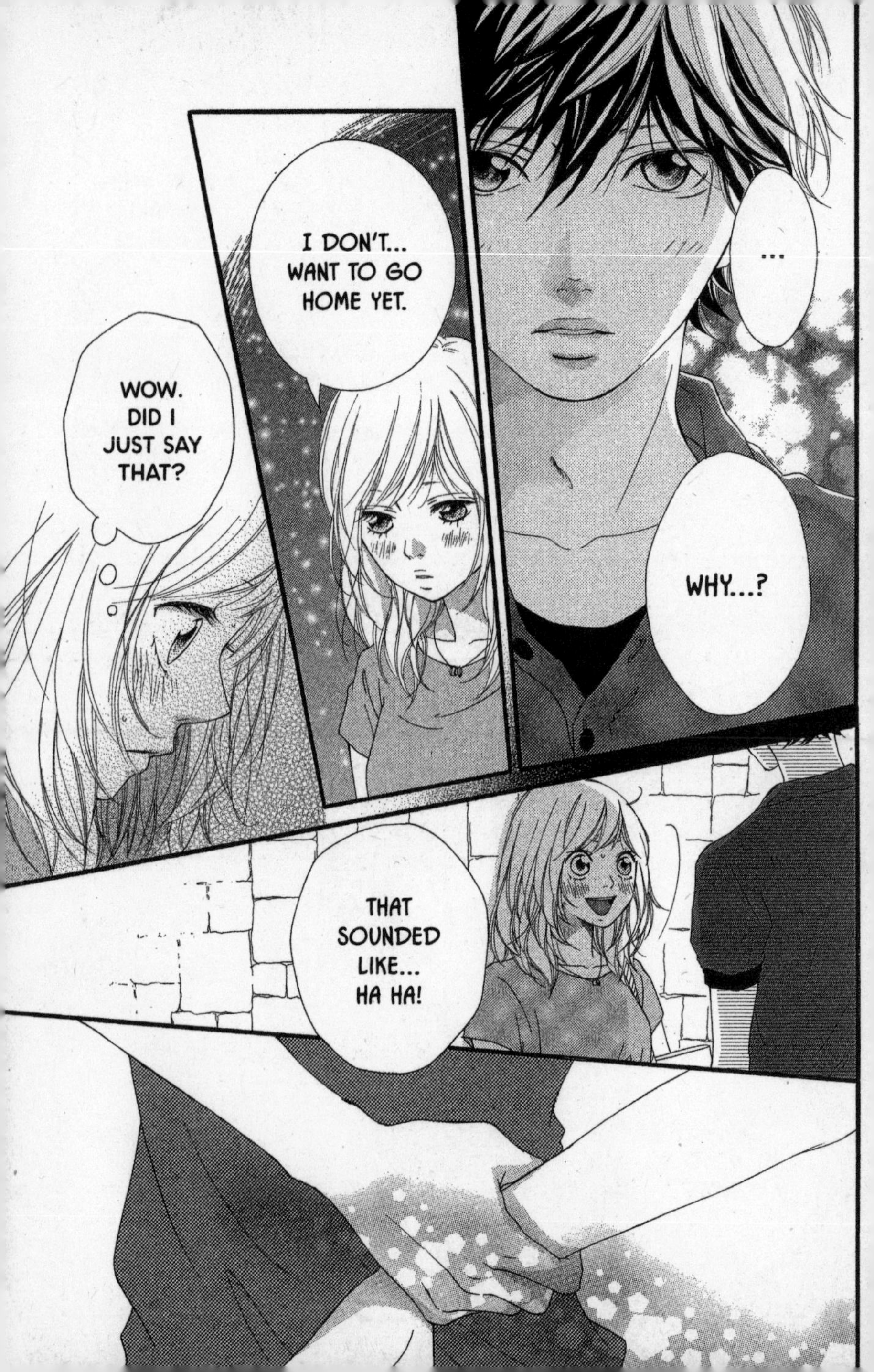
...
WHY...?
I DON'T... WANT TO GO HOME YET.
WOW. DID I JUST SAY THAT?
THAT SOUNDED LIKE... HA HA!

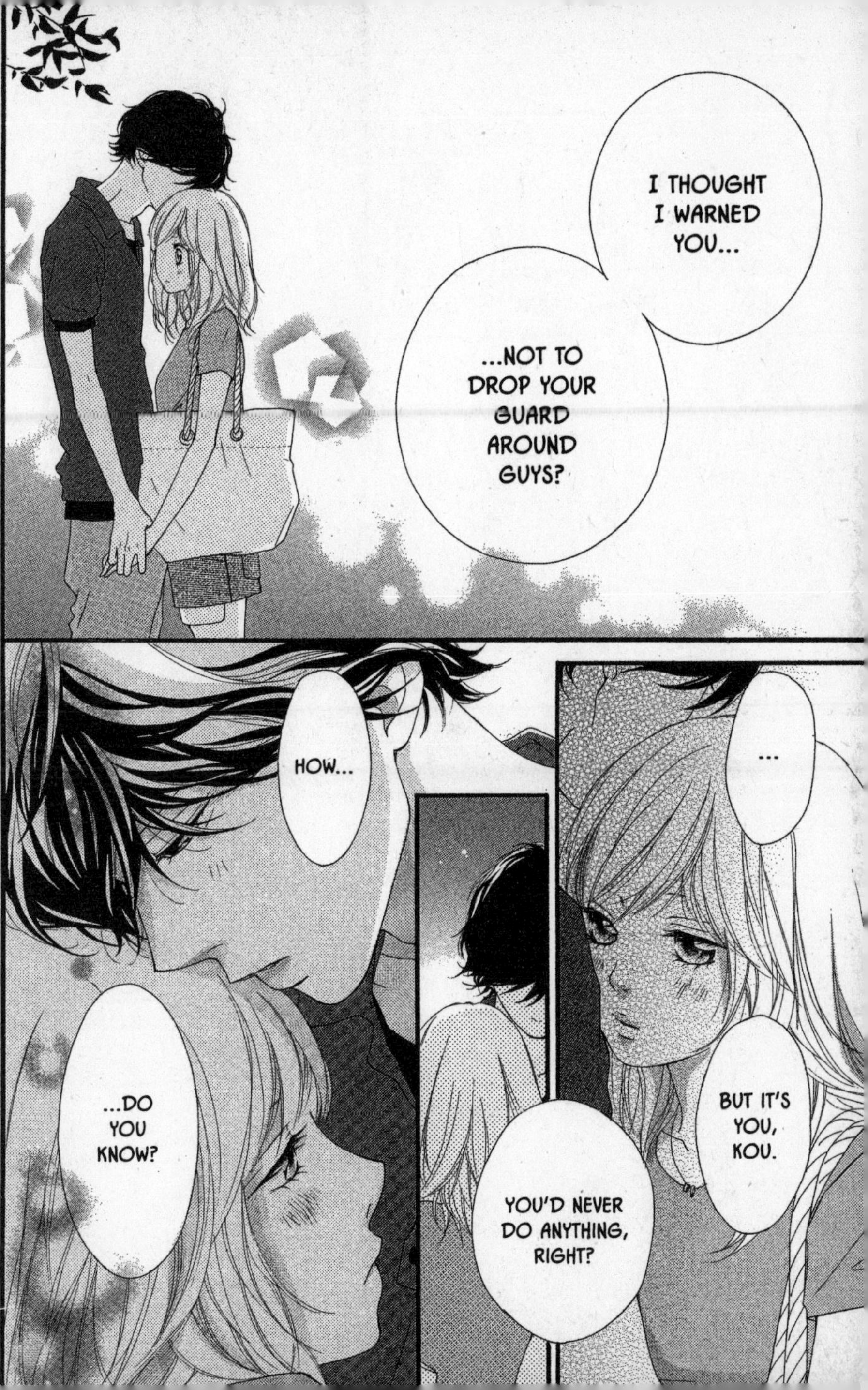
I THOUGHT I WARNED YOU...
...NOT TO DROP YOUR GUARD AROUND GUYS?
...
BUT IT'S YOU, KOU.
YOU'D NEVER DO ANYTHING, RIGHT?
HOW...
...DO YOU KNOW?

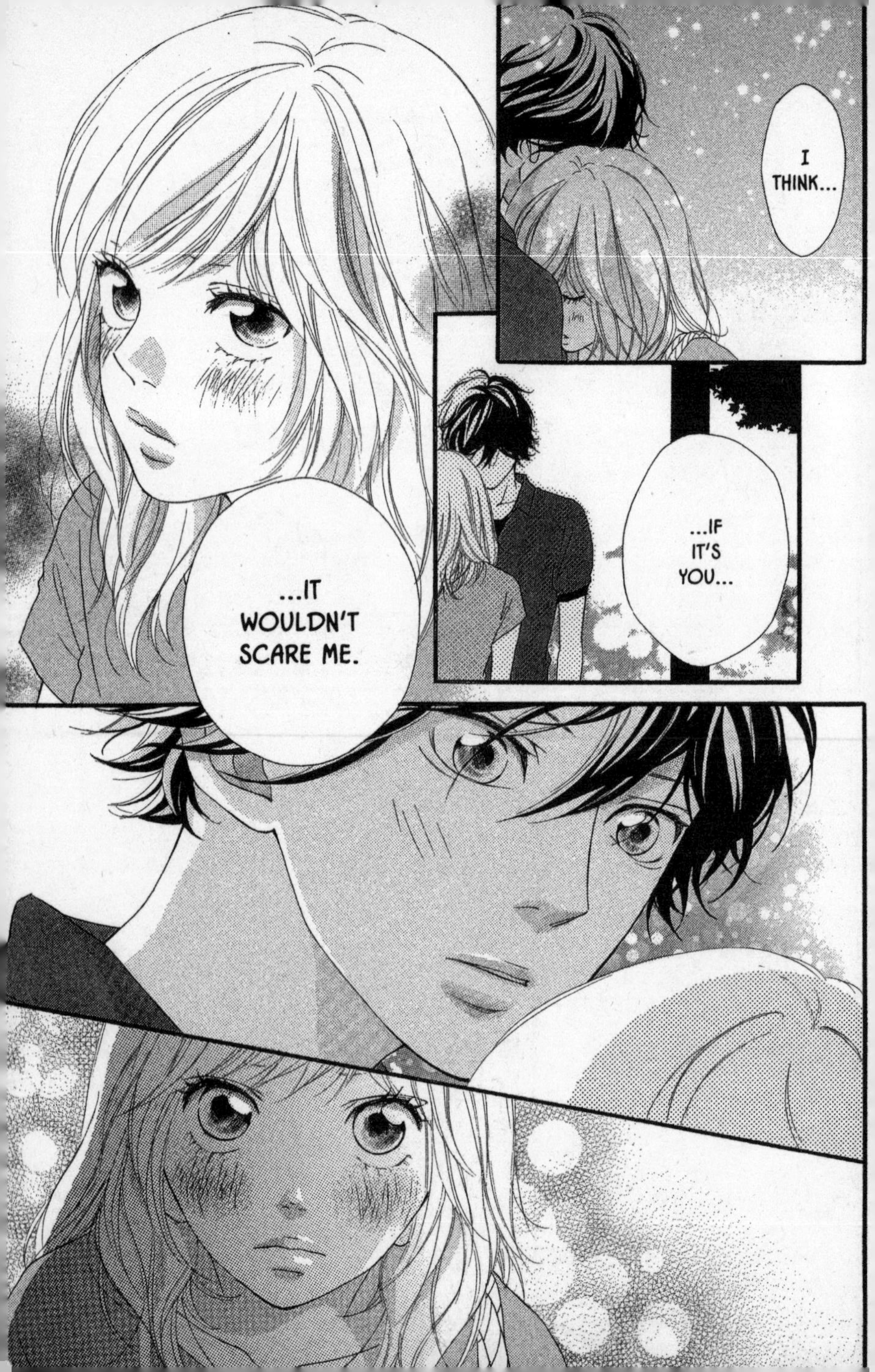
I THINK...
...IF IT'S YOU...
...IT WOULDN'T SCARE ME.

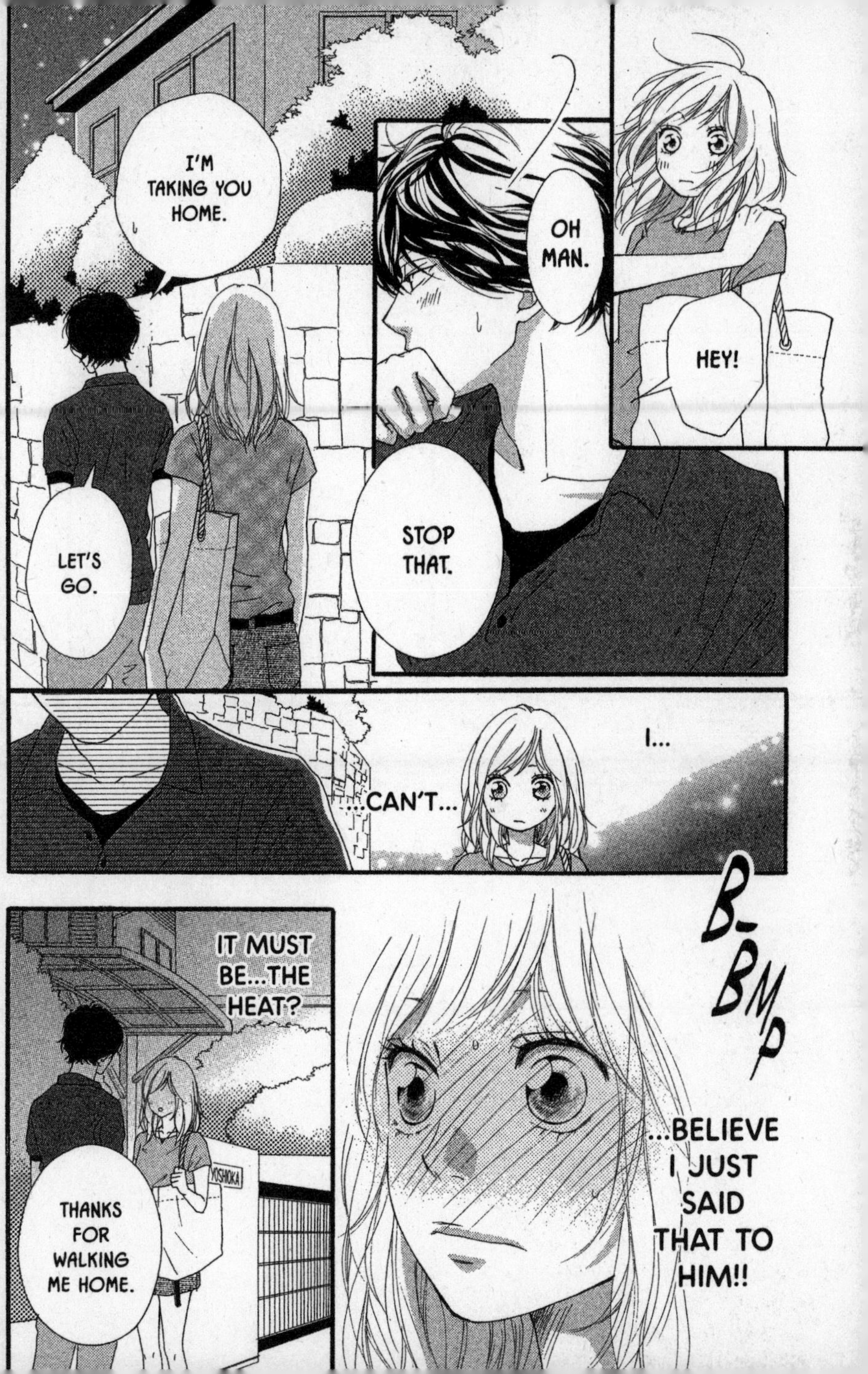
HEY!
OH MAN.
STOP THAT.
I'M TAKING YOU HOME.
LET'S GO.
I...
...CAN'T...
B-BMP
...BELIEVE I JUST SAID THAT TO HIM!!
IT MUST BE...THE HEAT?
THANKS FOR WALKING ME HOME.
YOSHIOKA

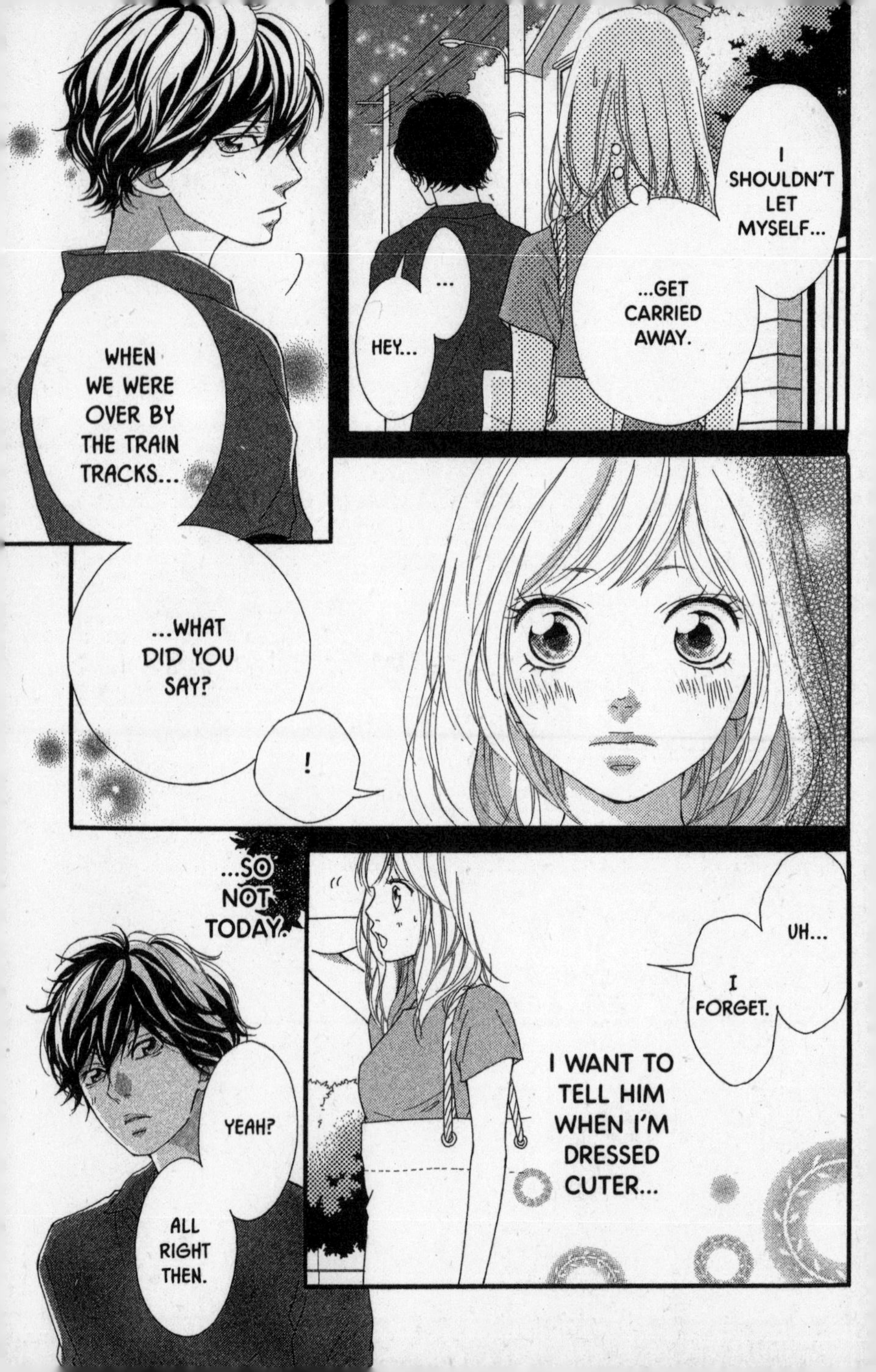

I SHOULDN'T LET MYSELF...
...GET CARRIED AWAY.
...
HEY...
WHEN WE WERE OVER BY THE TRAIN TRACKS...
...WHAT DID YOU SAY?
!
UH...
I FORGET.
I WANT TO TELL HIM WHEN I'M DRESSED CUTER...
...SO NOT TODAY.
YEAH?
ALL RIGHT THEN.

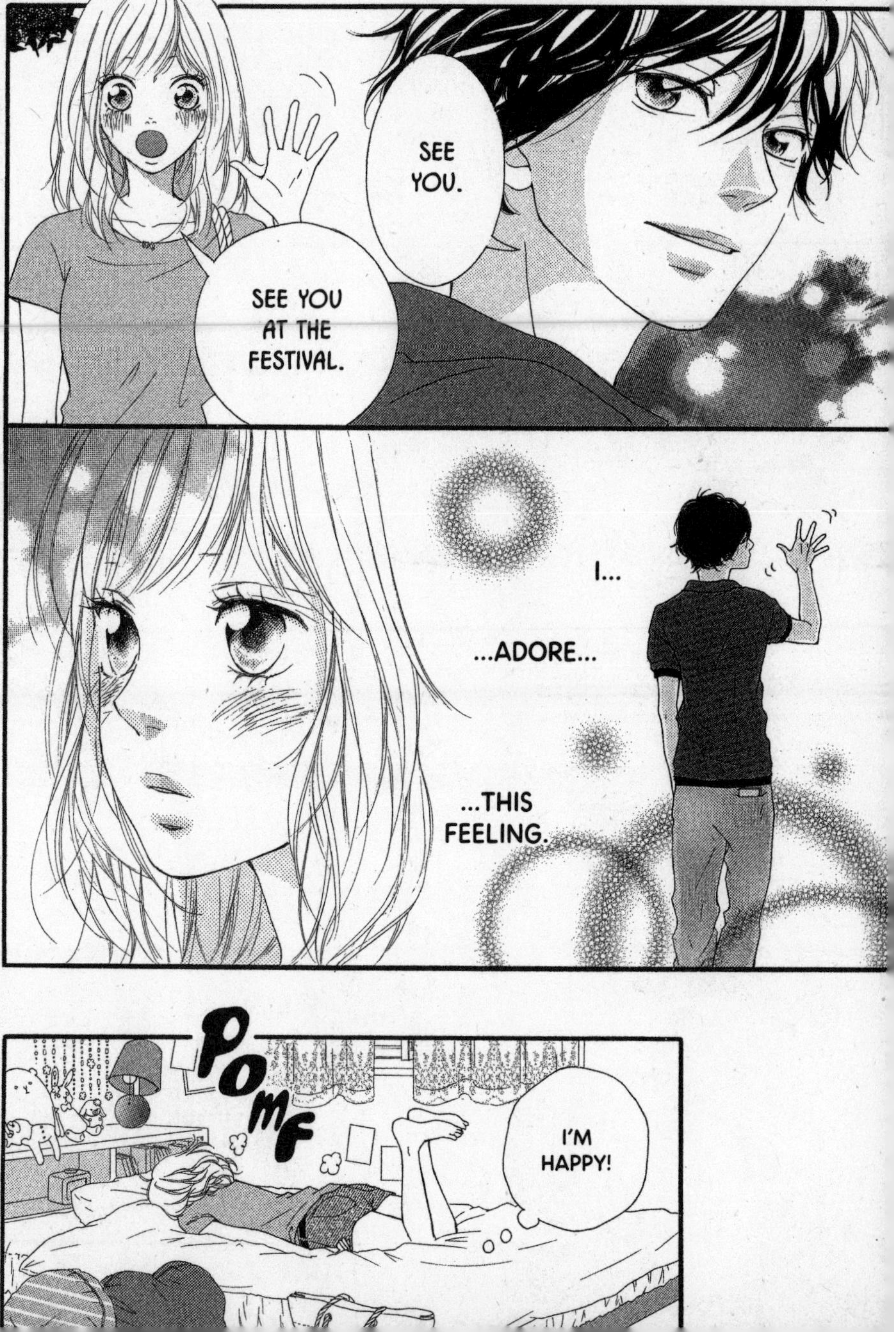
SEE YOU.
SEE YOU AT THE FESTIVAL.
I...
...ADORE...
...THIS FEELING.
POMF
I'M HAPPY!

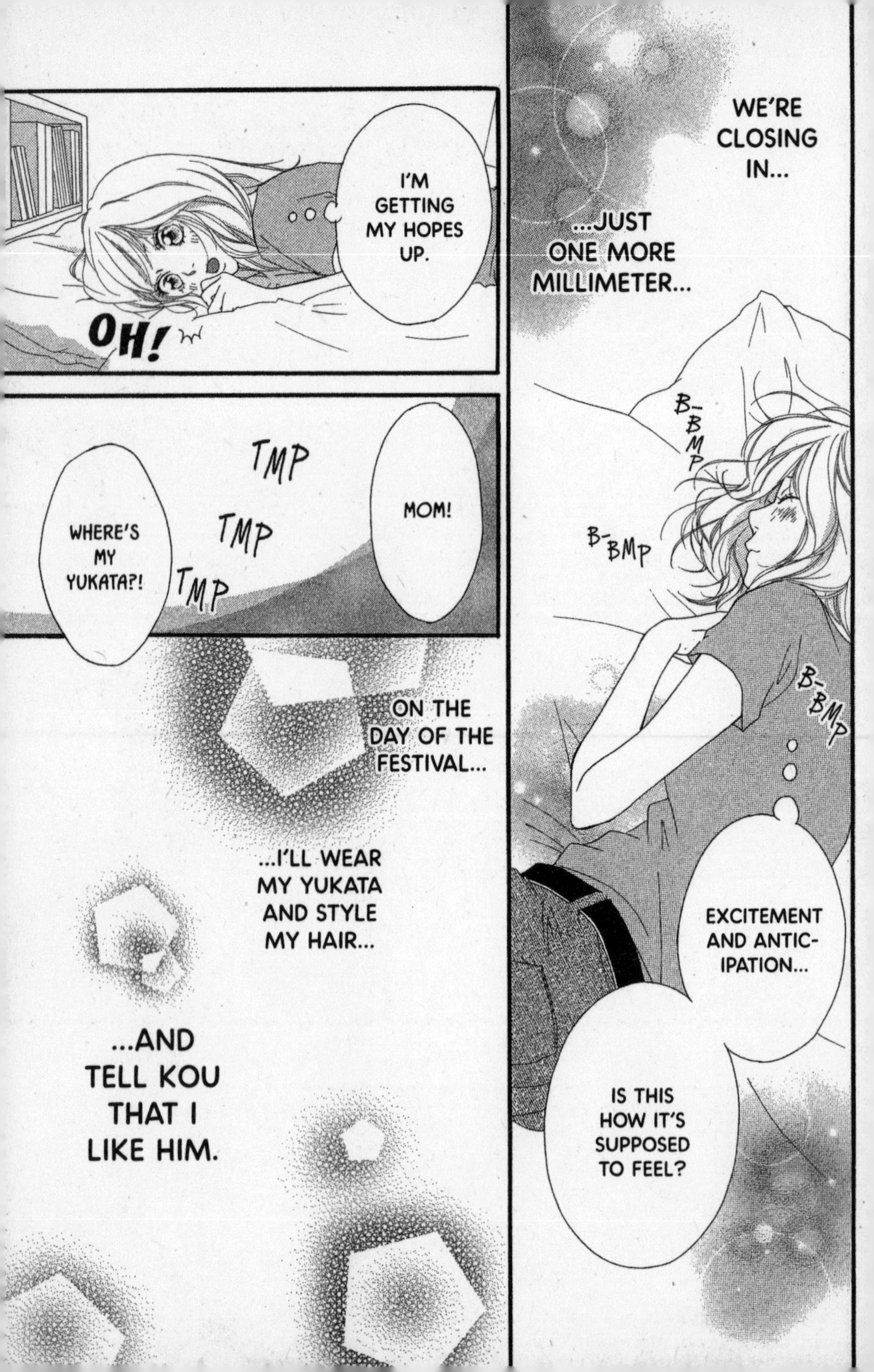
WE'RE CLOSING IN...
...JUST ONE MORE MILLIMETER...
B-BMP
B-BMP
B-BMP
EXCITEMENT AND ANTIC-IPATION...
IS THIS HOW IT'S SUPPOSED TO FEEL?
I'M GETTING MY HOPES UP.
OH!
MOM!
TMP
TMP
TMP
WHERE'S MY YUKATA?!
ON THE DAY OF THE FESTIVAL...
...I'LL WEAR MY YUKATA AND STYLE MY HAIR...
...AND TELL KOU THAT I LIKE HIM.

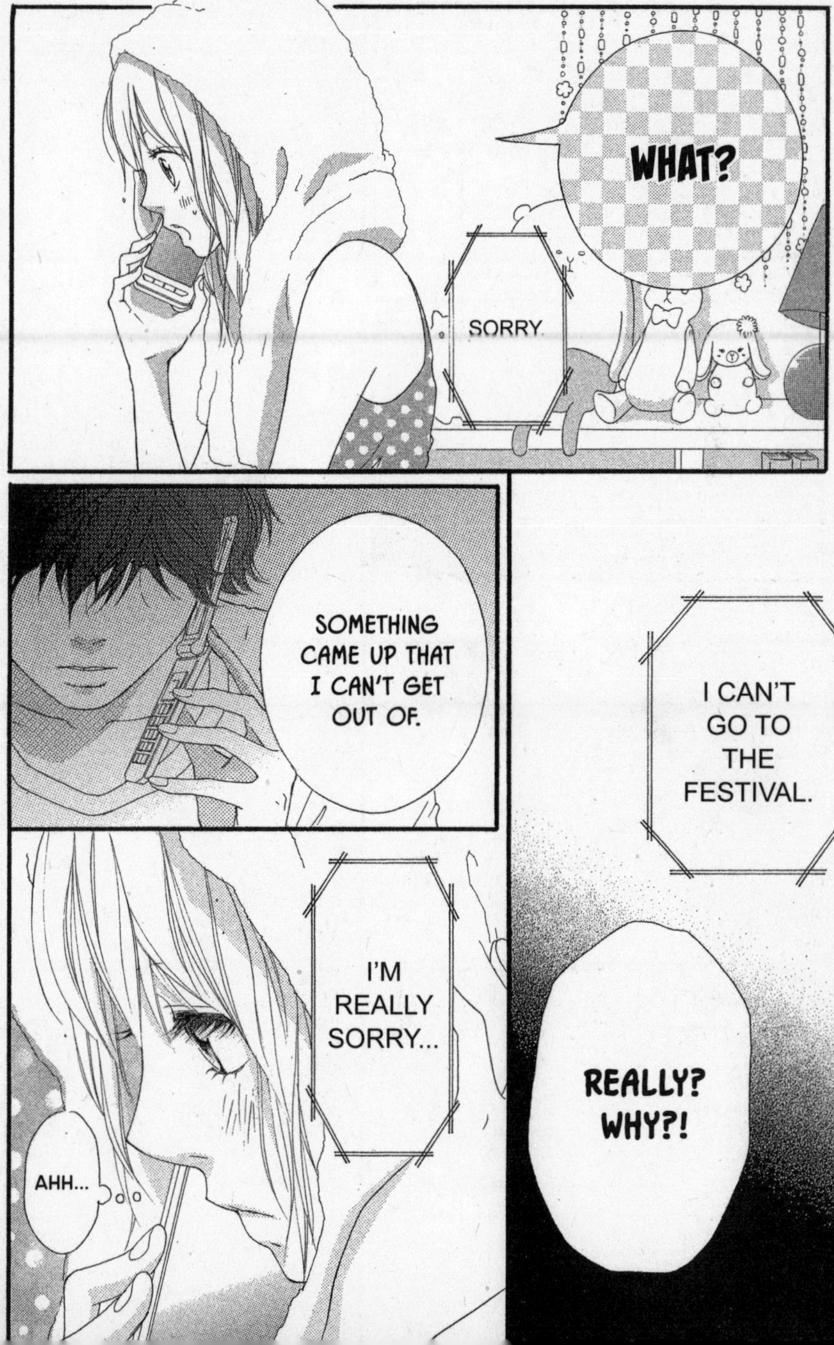
WHAT?
SORRY.
I CAN'T GO TO THE FESTIVAL.
REALLY? WHY?!
SOMETHING CAME UP THAT I CAN'T GET OUT OF.
I'M REALLY SORRY...
AHH...

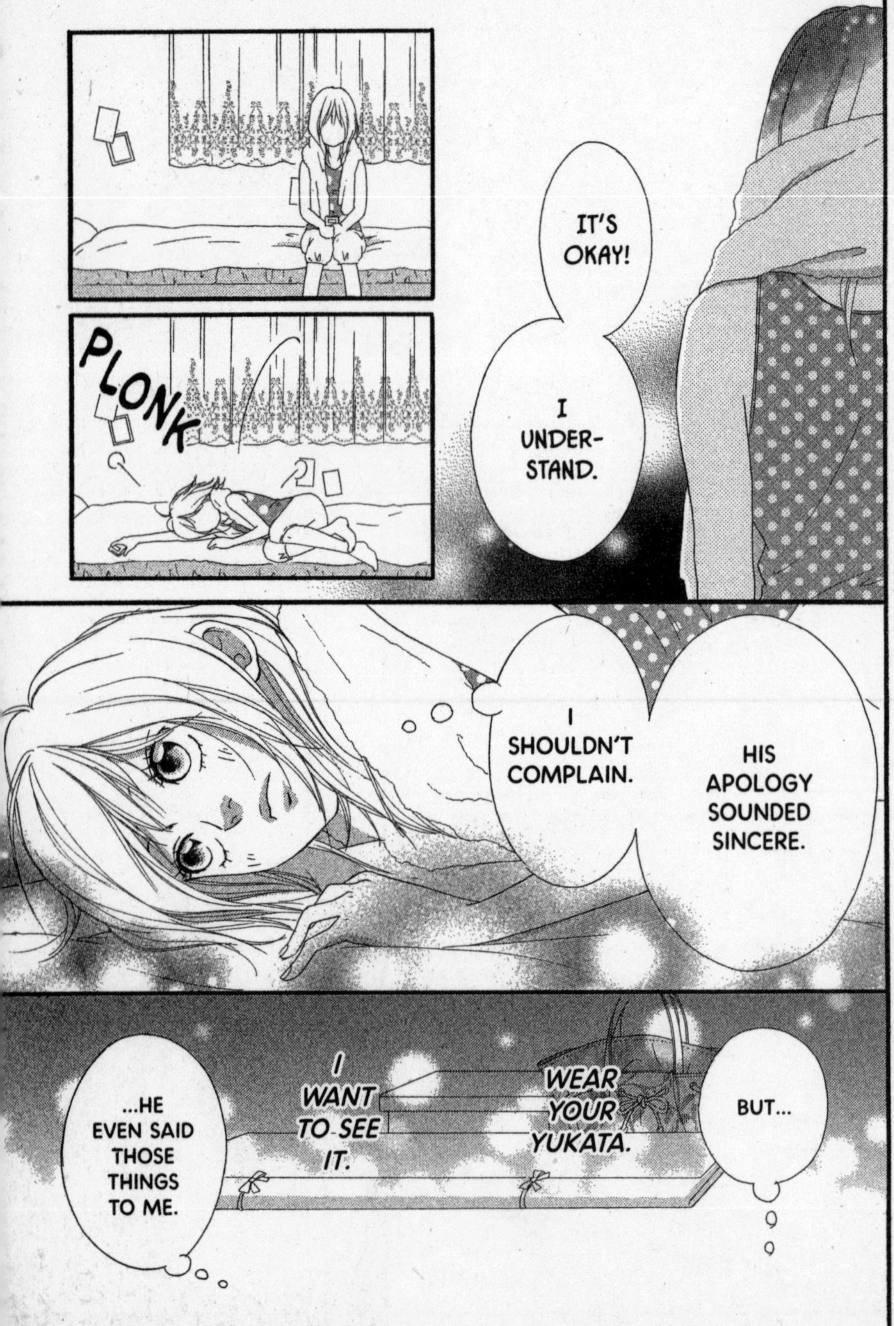
IT'S OKAY!
I UNDERSTAND.
PLONK
HIS APOLOGY SOUNDED SINCERE.
I SHOULDN'T COMPLAIN.
BUT...
WEAR YOUR YUKATA.
I WANT TO SEE IT.
...HE EVEN SAID THOSE THINGS TO ME.

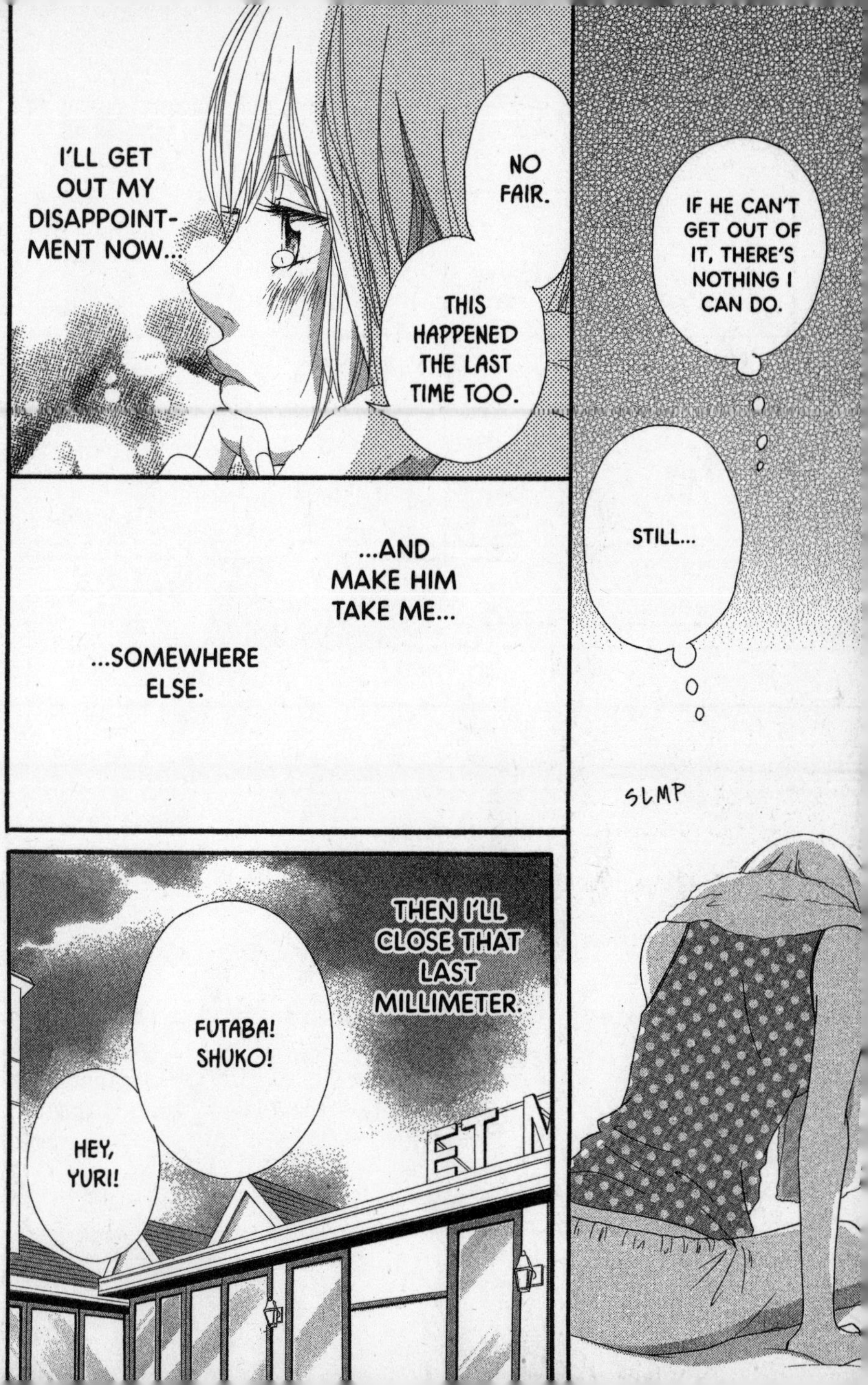
IF HE CAN'T GET OUT OF IT, THERE'S NOTHING I CAN DO.
STILL...
SLMP
NO FAIR.
THIS HAPPENED THE LAST TIME TOO.
I'LL GET OUT MY DISAPPOINT-MENT NOW...
...AND MAKE HIM TAKE ME...
...SOMEWHERE ELSE.
THEN I'LL CLOSE THAT LAST MILLIMETER.
FUTABA! SHUKO!
HEY, YURI!
ET M

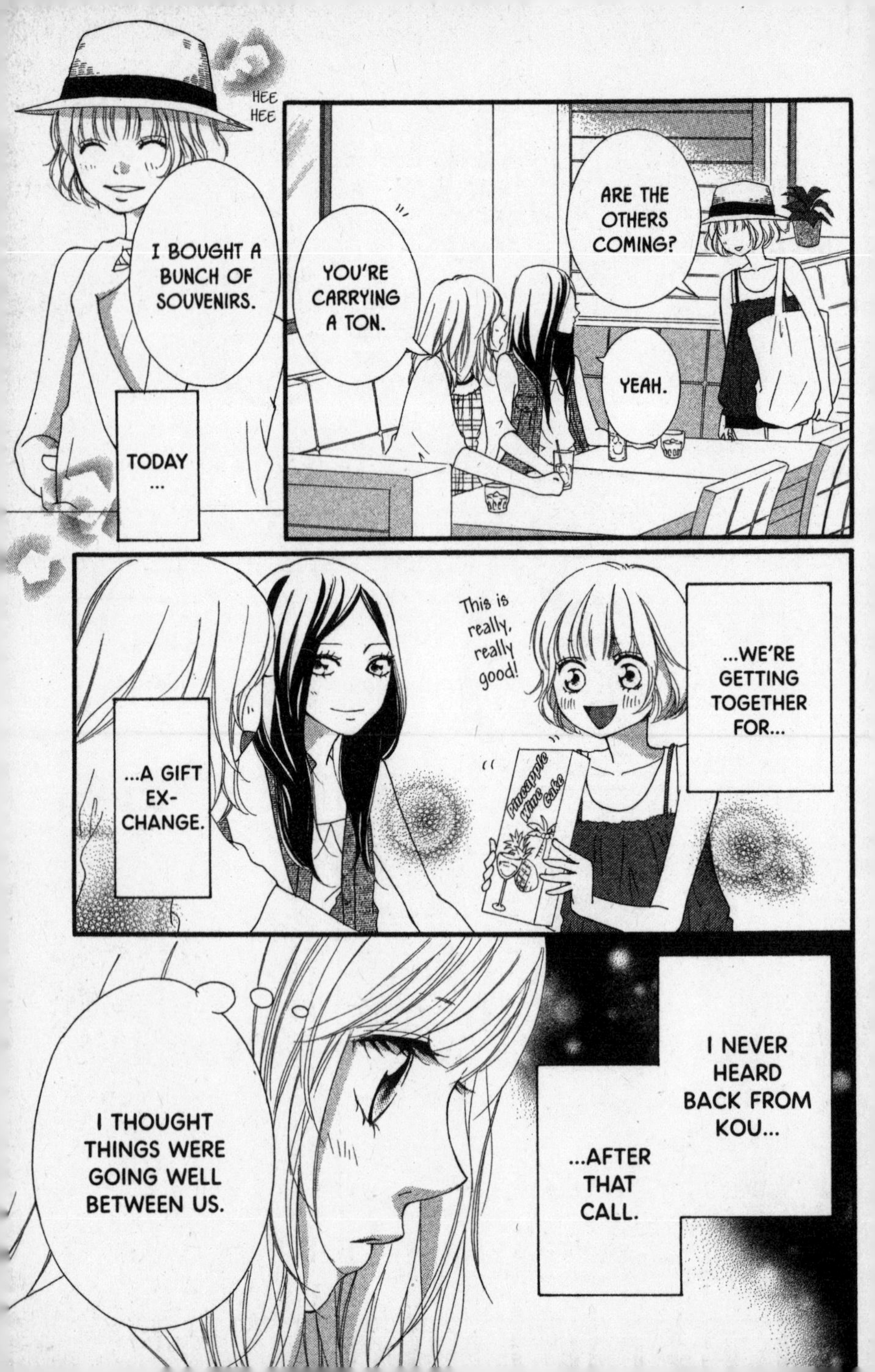
ARE THE OTHERS COMING?
YEAH.
YOU'RE CARRYING A TON.
HEE HEE
I BOUGHT A BUNCH OF SOUVENIRS.
TODAY ...
...WE'RE GETTING TOGETHER FOR...
This is really, really good!
Pineapple Wine Cake
...A GIFT EX-CHANGE.
I NEVER HEARD BACK FROM KOU...
...AFTER THAT CALL.
I THOUGHT THINGS WERE GOING WELL BETWEEN US.

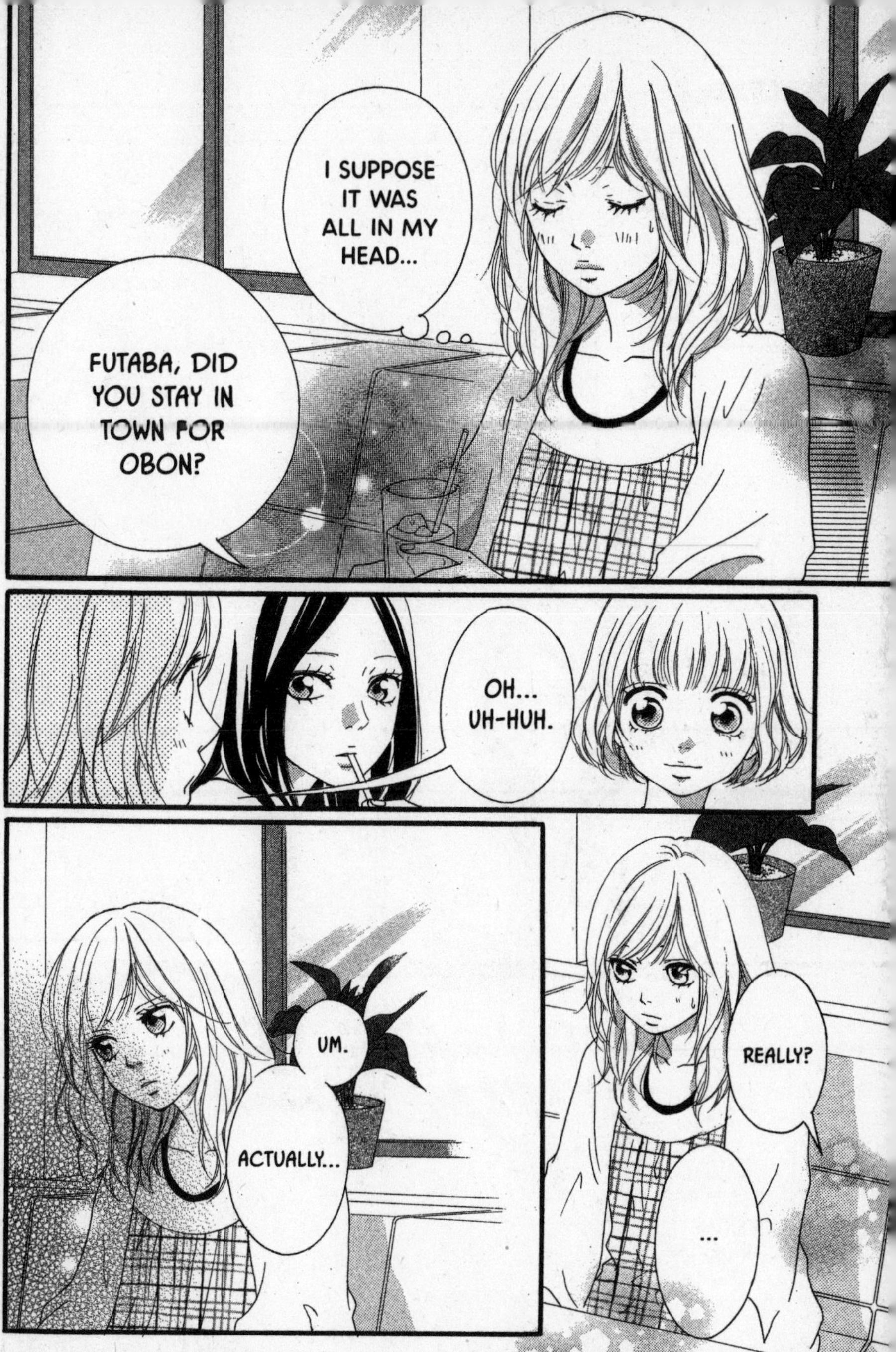
I SUPPOSE IT WAS ALL IN MY HEAD...
FUTABA, DID YOU STAY IN TOWN FOR OBON?
OH... UH-HUH.
REALLY?
...
UM.
ACTUALLY...

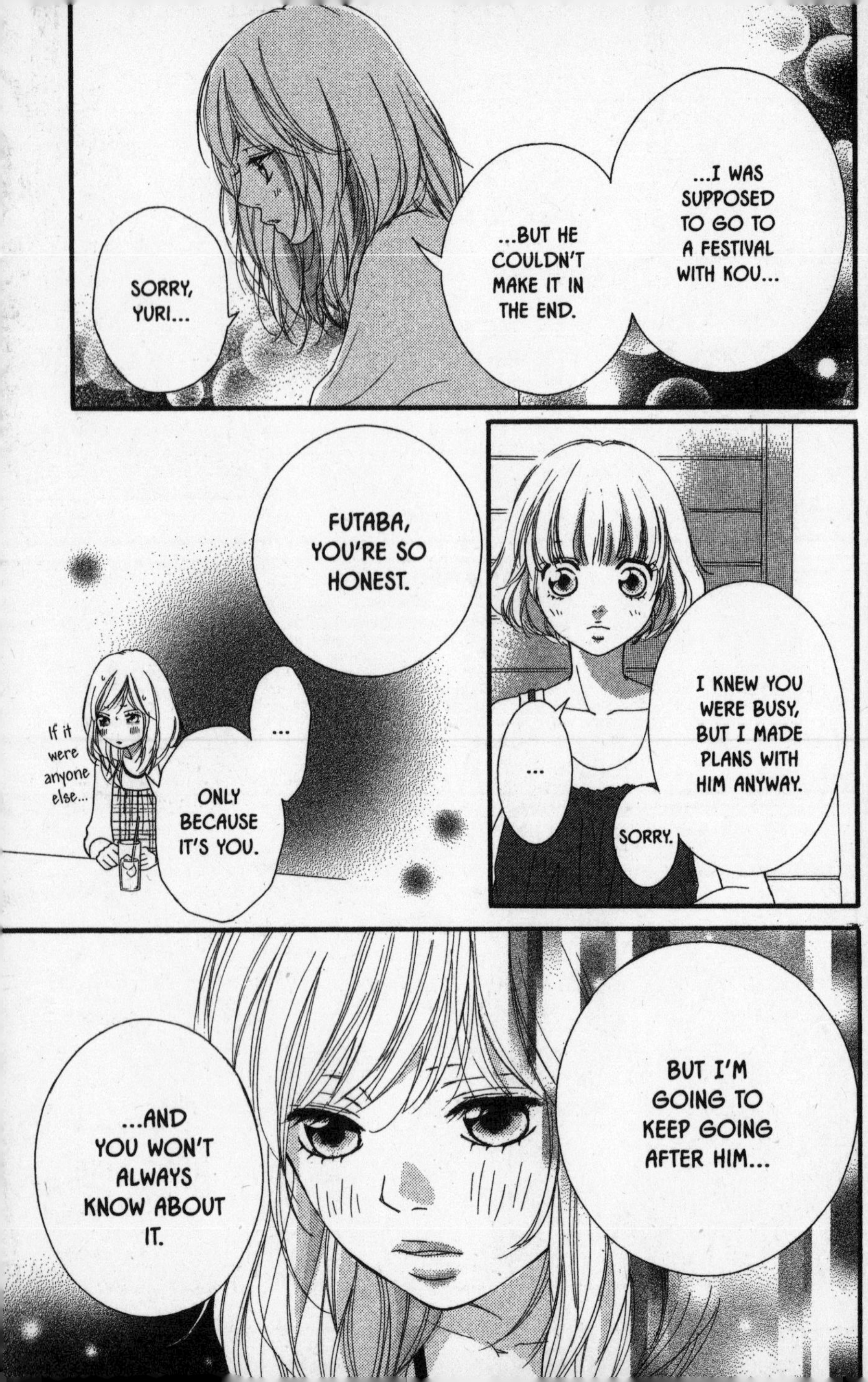
...I WAS SUPPOSED TO GO TO A FESTIVAL WITH KOU...
...BUT HE COULDN'T MAKE IT IN THE END.
SORRY, YURI...
I KNEW YOU WERE BUSY, BUT I MADE PLANS WITH HIM ANYWAY.
SORRY.
...
FUTABA, YOU'RE SO HONEST.
...
ONLY BECAUSE IT'S YOU.
If it were anyone else...
BUT I'M GOING TO KEEP GOING AFTER HIM...
...AND YOU WON'T ALWAYS KNOW ABOUT IT.

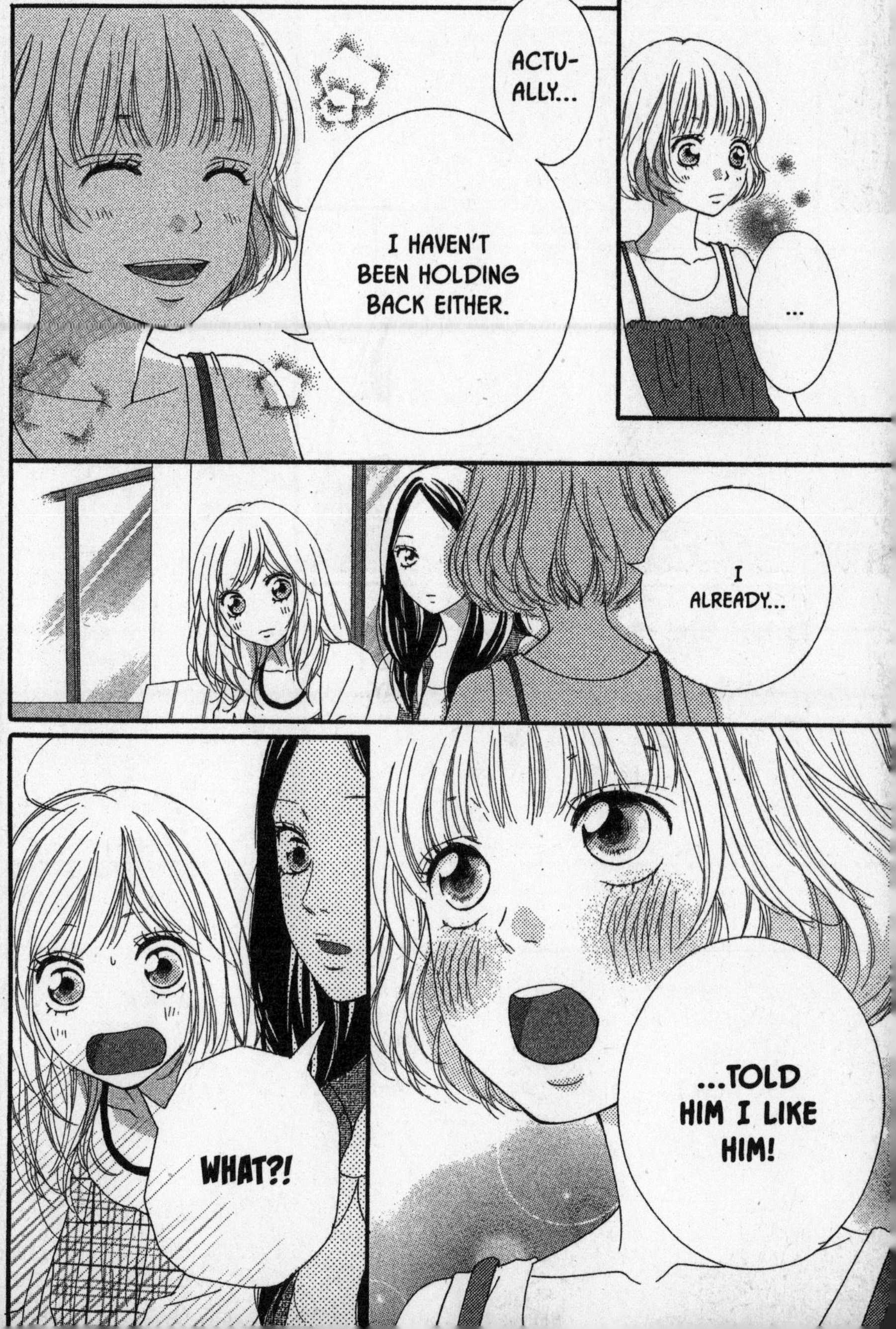
...
ACTU-ALLY...
I HAVEN'T BEEN HOLDING BACK EITHER.
I ALREADY...
...TOLD HIM I LIKE HIM!
WHAT?!

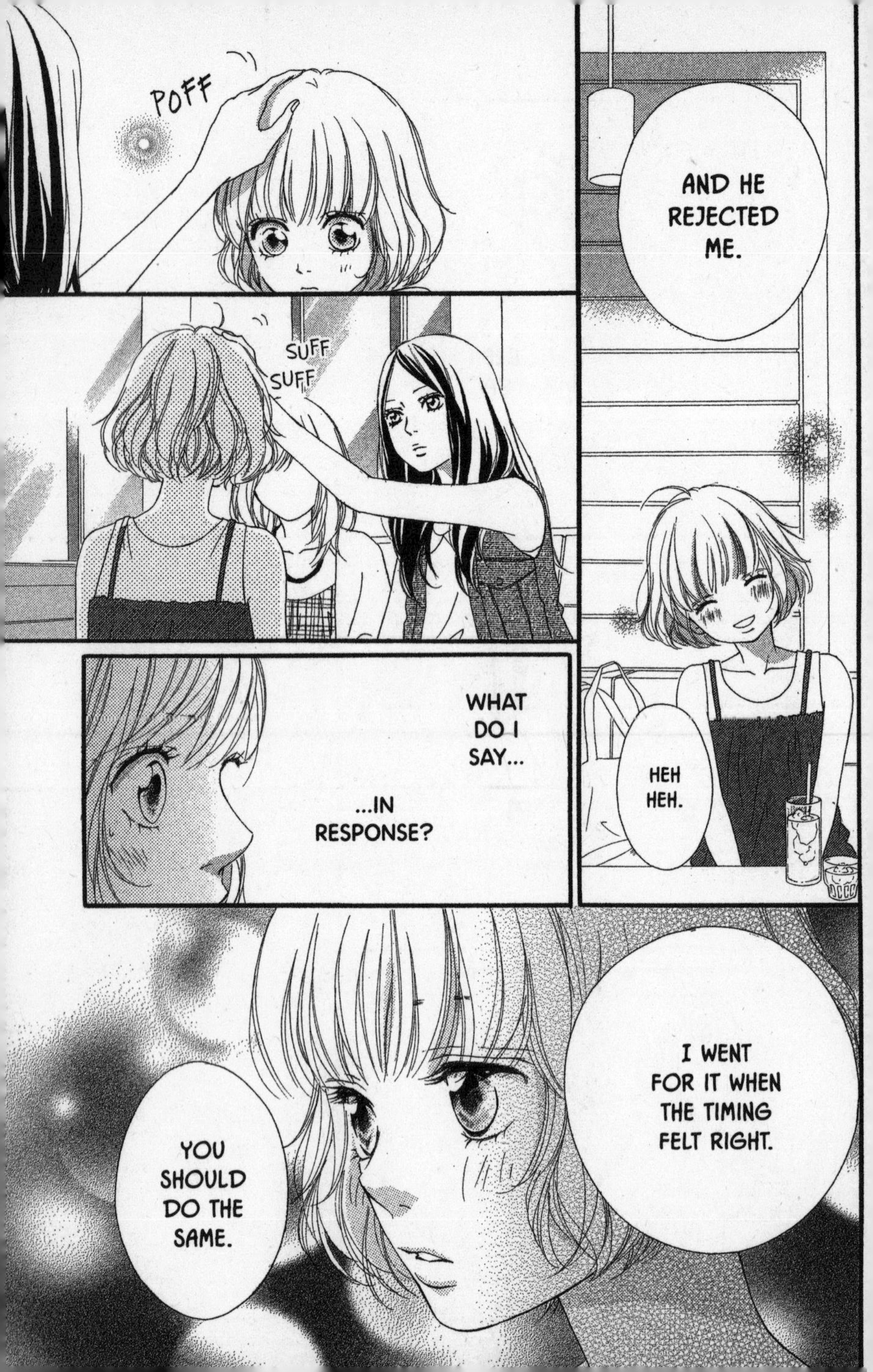
AND HE REJECTED ME.
HEH HEH.
POFF
SUFF SUFF
WHAT DO I SAY...
...IN RESPONSE?
I WENT FOR IT WHEN THE TIMING FELT RIGHT.
YOU SHOULD DO THE SAME.

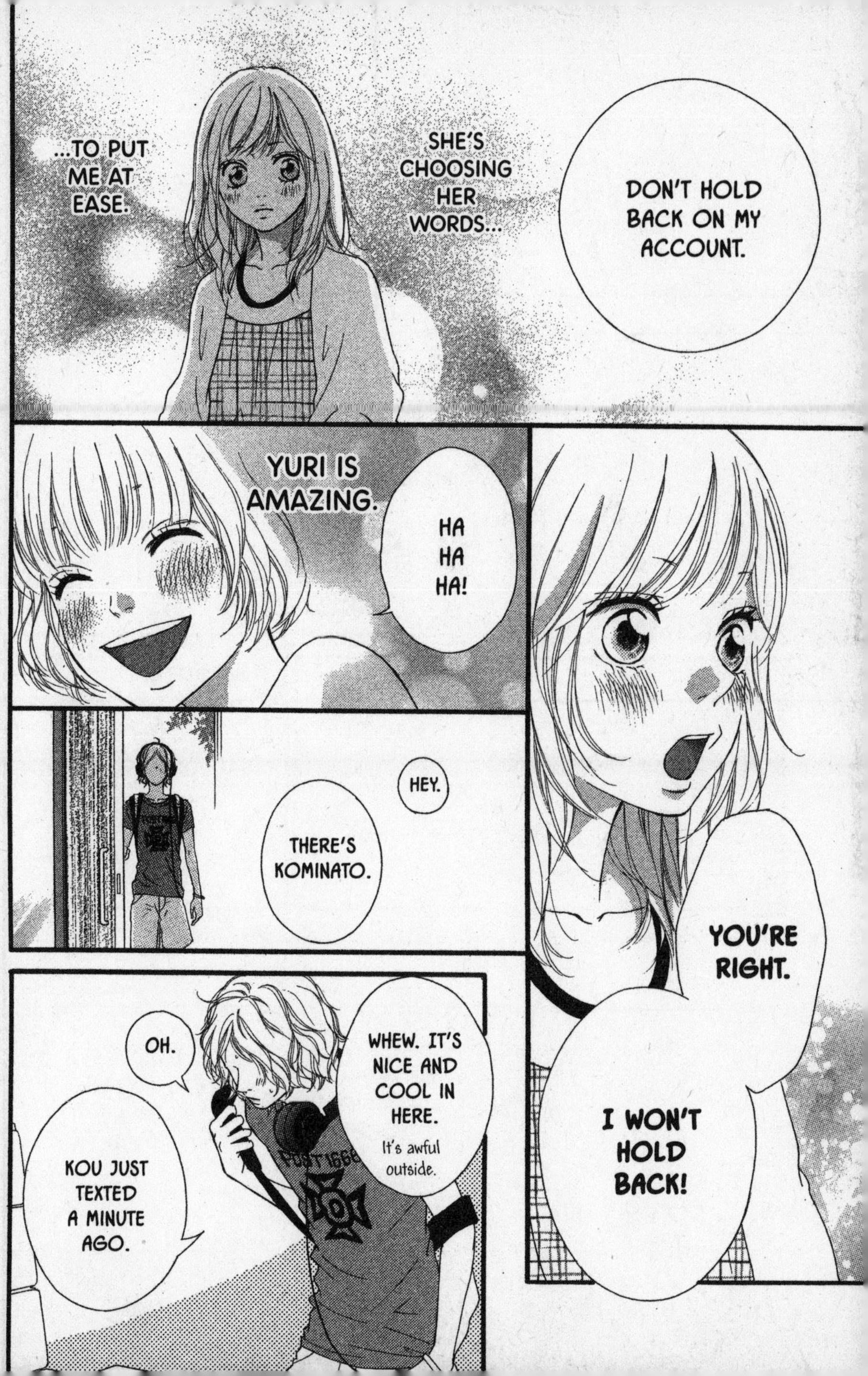
DON'T HOLD BACK ON MY ACCOUNT.
SHE'S CHOOSING HER WORDS...
...TO PUT ME AT EASE.
YOU'RE RIGHT.
I WON'T HOLD BACK!
HA HA HA!
YURI IS AMAZING.
HEY.
THERE'S KOMINATO.
WHEW. IT'S NICE AND COOL IN HERE.
It's awful outside.
OH.
KOU JUST TEXTED A MINUTE AGO.

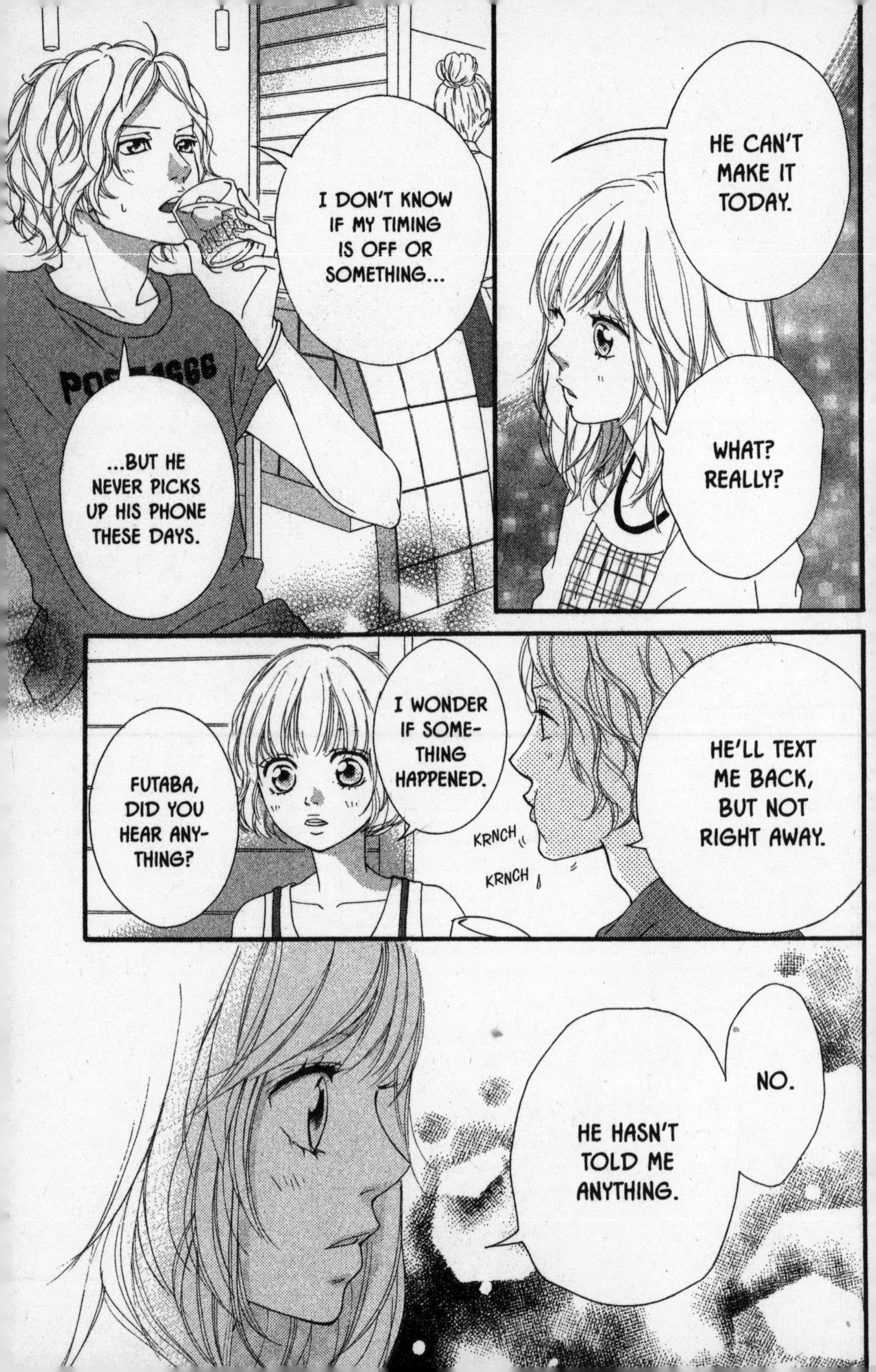
HE CAN'T MAKE IT TODAY.
WHAT? REALLY?
I DON'T KNOW IF MY TIMING IS OFF OR SOMETHING...
...BUT HE NEVER PICKS UP HIS PHONE THESE DAYS.
HE'LL TEXT ME BACK, BUT NOT RIGHT AWAY.
KRNCH
KRNCH
I WONDER IF SOME-THING HAPPENED.
FUTABA, DID YOU HEAR ANY-THING?
NO.
HE HASN'T TOLD ME ANYTHING.

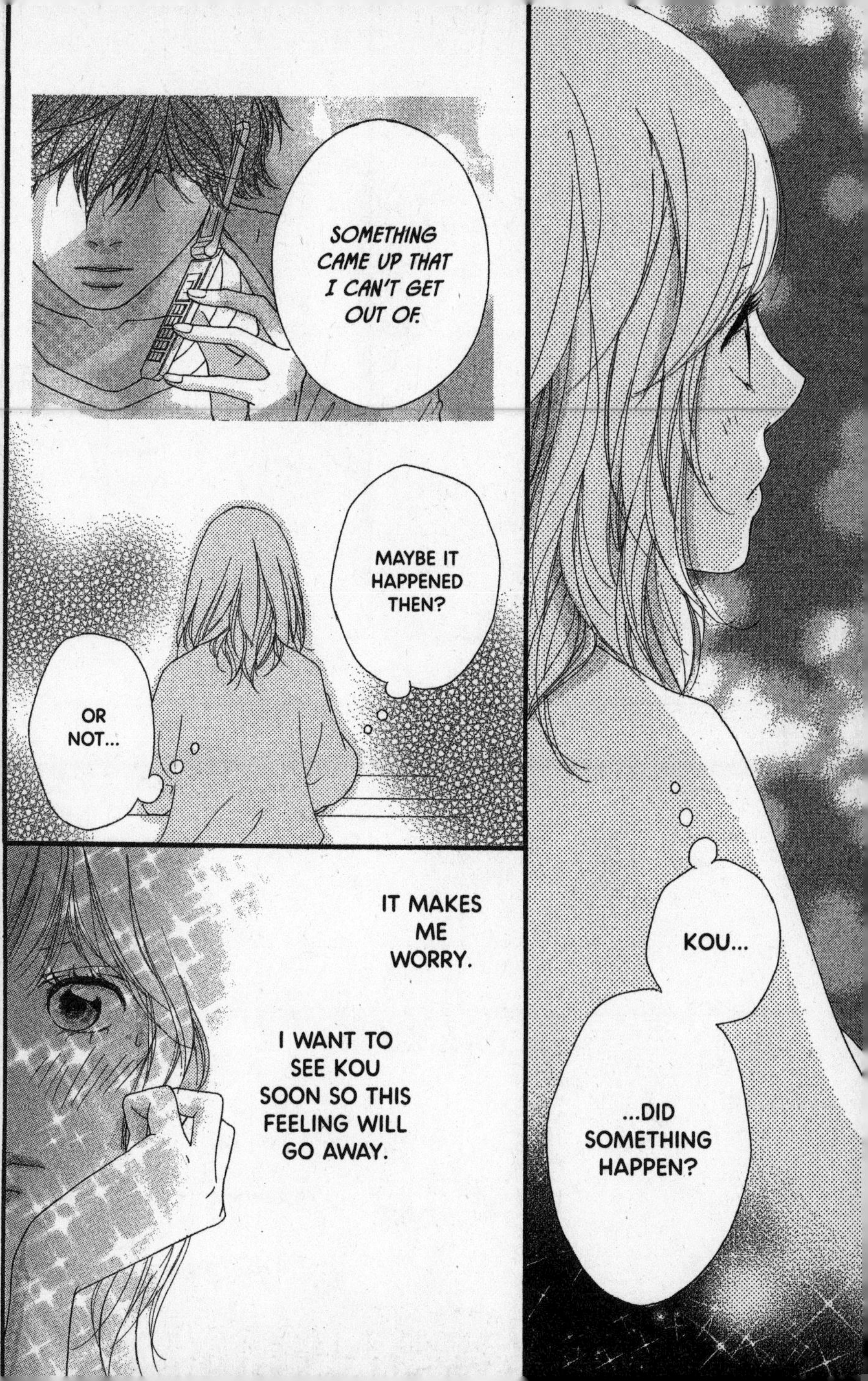
KOU...
...DID SOMETHING HAPPEN?
SOMETHING CAME UP THAT I CAN'T GET OUT OF.
MAYBE IT HAPPENED THEN?
OR NOT...
IT MAKES ME WORRY.
I WANT TO SEE KOU SOON SO THIS FEELING WILL GO AWAY.

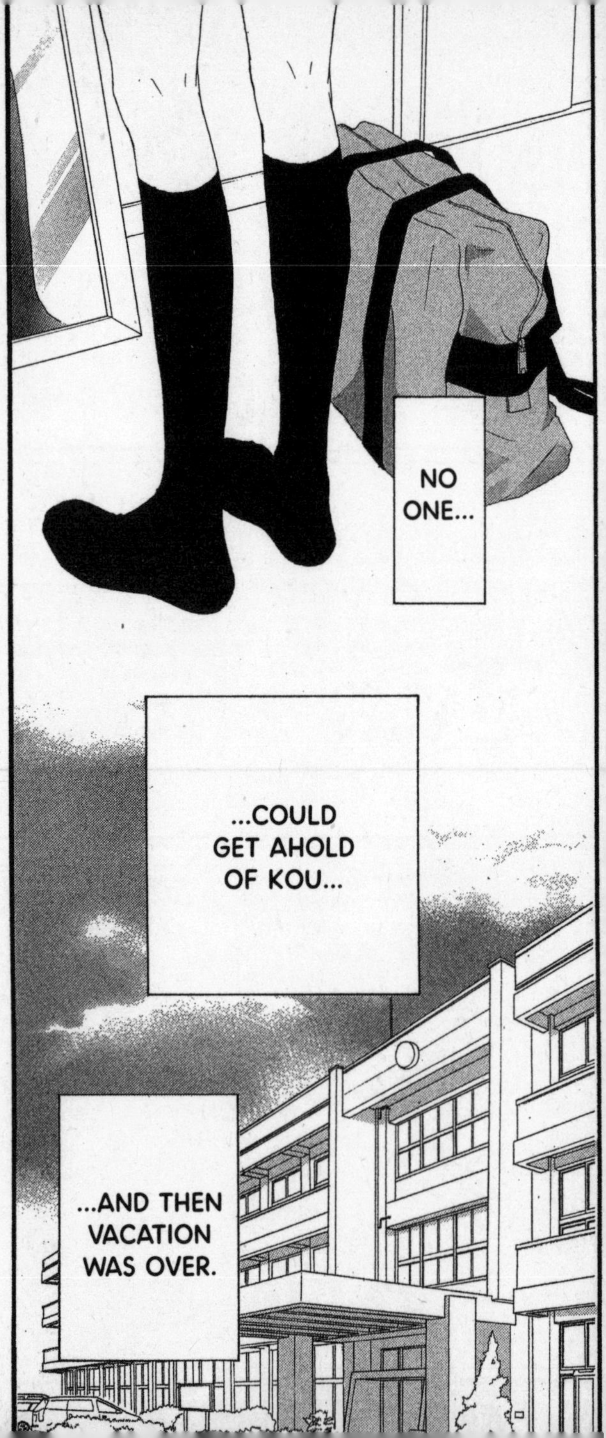
NO ONE...
...COULD GET AHOLD OF KOU...
...AND THEN VACATION WAS OVER.

In my greeting, I wrote that haste makes waste. The other day I experienced this in a big way. Hours before my deadline, I was rushing (of course) to finish my manuscript, and at that moment I spilled correction fluid all over my desk. Thank goodness the manuscript was unharmed, but my pens, rulers and knives were covered in guck. Since I had no time (wah), I had to keep working with the dirty tools, but I couldn't leave the mess as it was, so I wiped and wiped... I was by myself at that time, so there was nobody to laugh with—I faced only silence and sadness. It would have been great to have somebody to turn to and joke about it with. Haste truly does make waste.

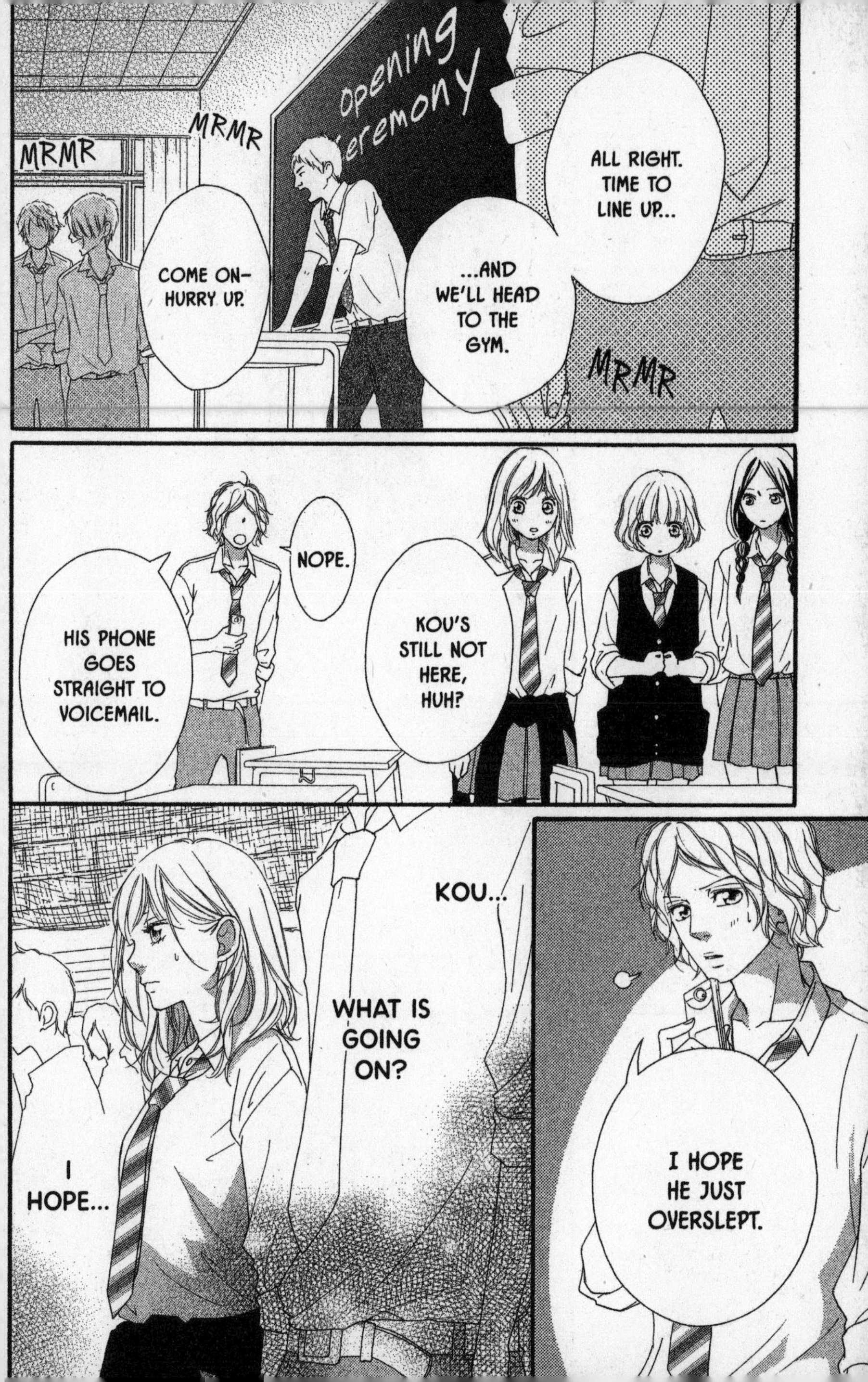
opening ceremony
ALL RIGHT. TIME TO LINE UP...
...AND WE'LL HEAD TO THE GYM.
MRMR
MRMR
COME ON— HURRY UP.
MRMR
KOU'S STILL NOT HERE, HUH?
NOPE.
HIS PHONE GOES STRAIGHT TO VOICEMAIL.
I HOPE HE JUST OVERSLEPT.
KOU...
WHAT IS GOING ON?
I HOPE...

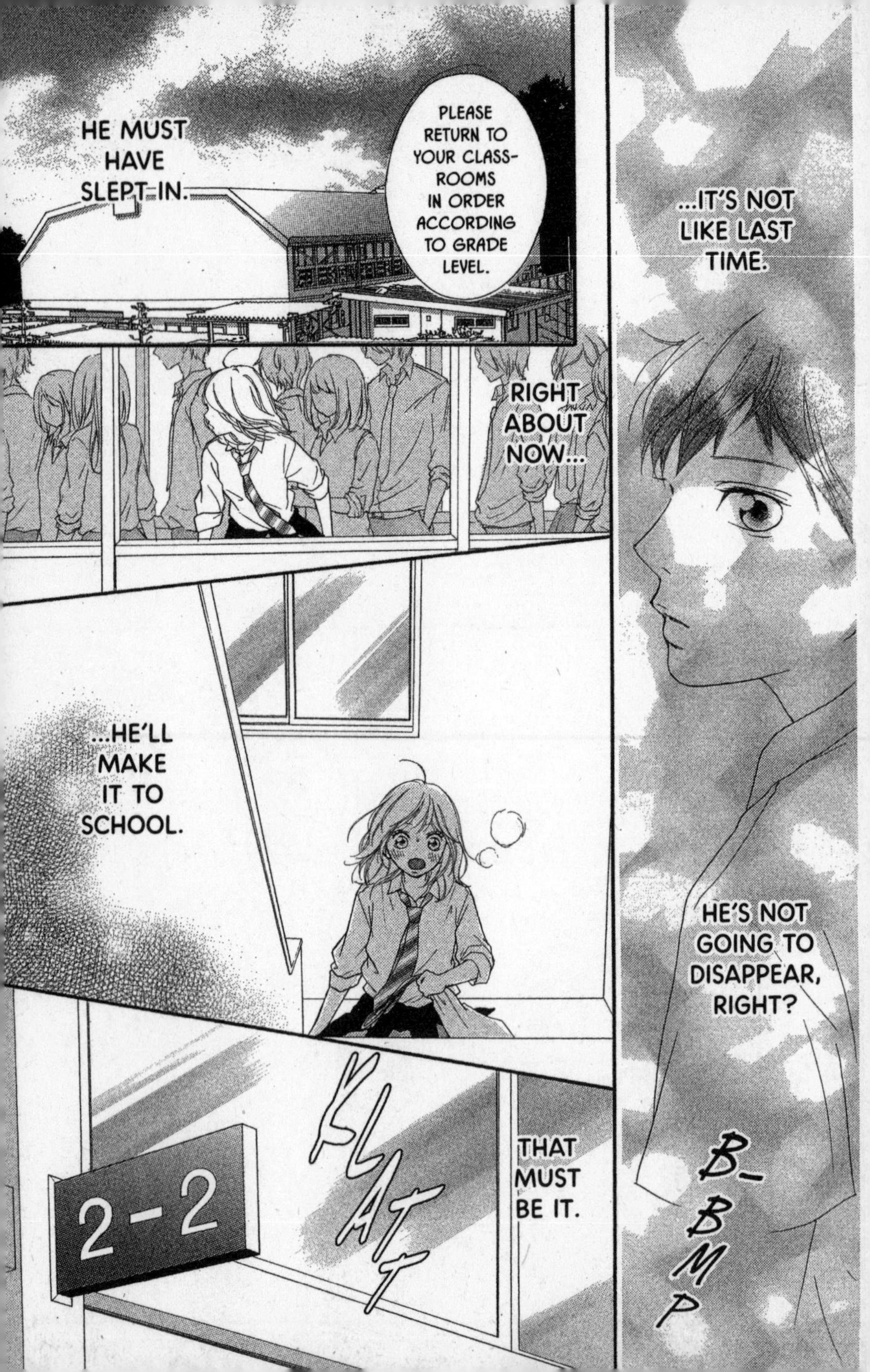

...IT'S NOT LIKE LAST TIME.
HE'S NOT GOING TO DISAPPEAR, RIGHT?
B-BMP
PLEASE RETURN TO YOUR CLASS-ROOMS IN ORDER ACCORDING TO GRADE LEVEL.
HE MUST HAVE SLEPT IN.
RIGHT ABOUT NOW...
...HE'LL MAKE IT TO SCHOOL.
KLAT
THAT MUST BE IT.
2-2

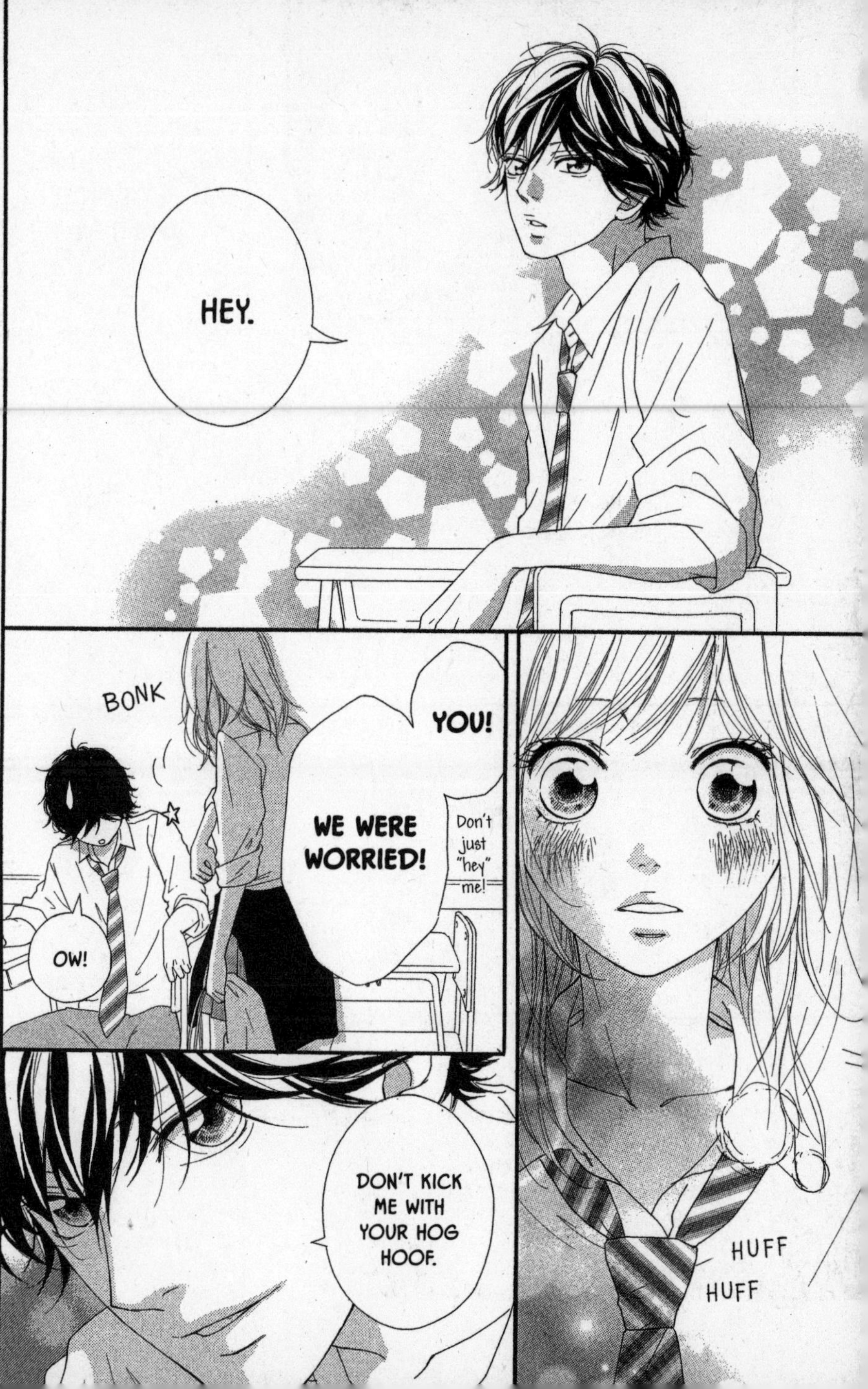
HEY.
HUFF
HUFF
YOU!
WE WERE WORRIED!
Don't just "hey" me!
BONK
OW!
DON'T KICK ME WITH YOUR HOG HOOF.

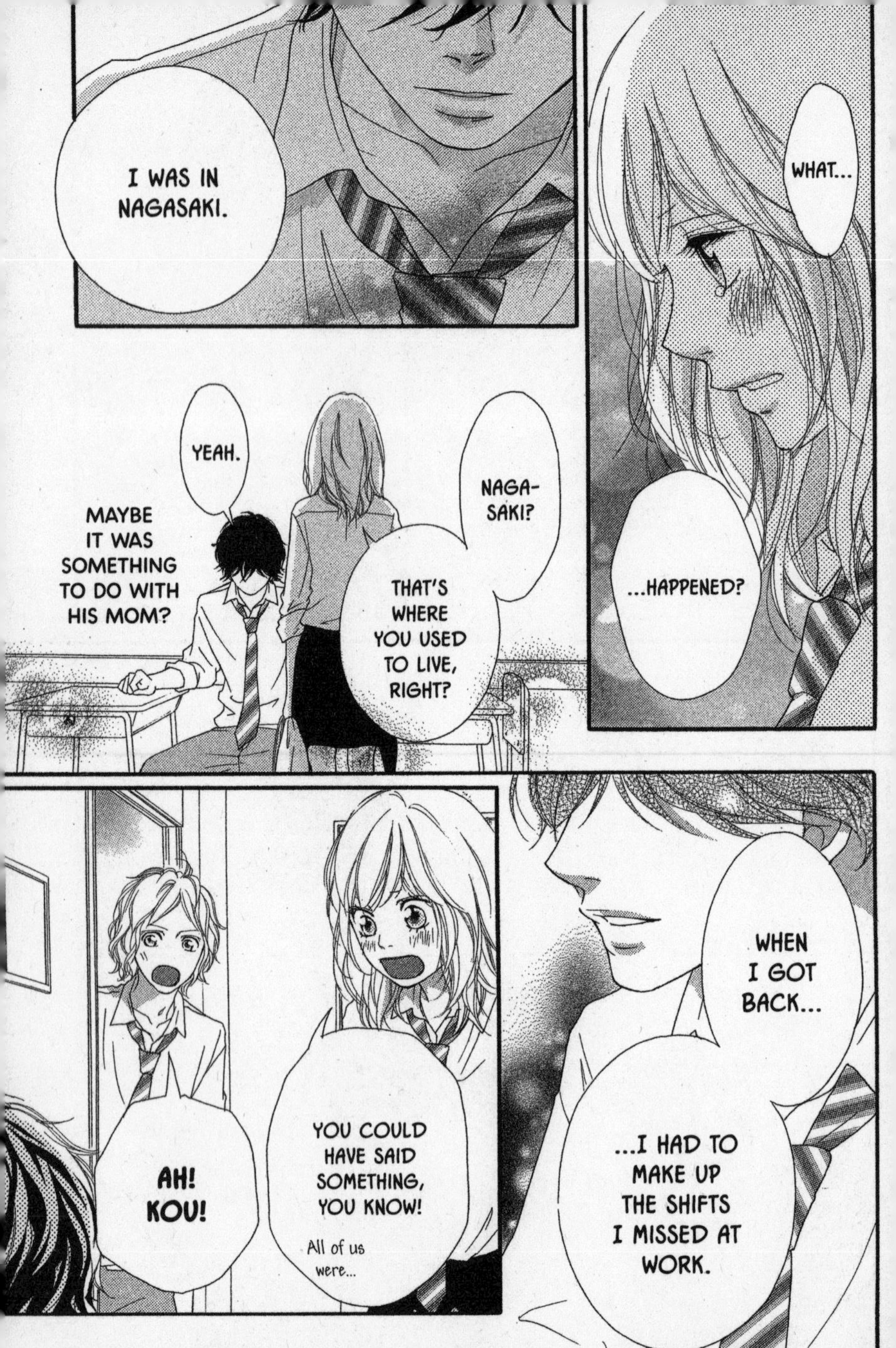
WHAT...
...HAPPENED?
I WAS IN NAGASAKI.
NAGA-SAKI?
THAT'S WHERE YOU USED TO LIVE, RIGHT?
YEAH.
MAYBE IT WAS SOMETHING TO DO WITH HIS MOM?
WHEN I GOT BACK...
...I HAD TO MAKE UP THE SHIFTS I MISSED AT WORK.
YOU COULD HAVE SAID SOMETHING, YOU KNOW!
All of us were...
AH! KOU!

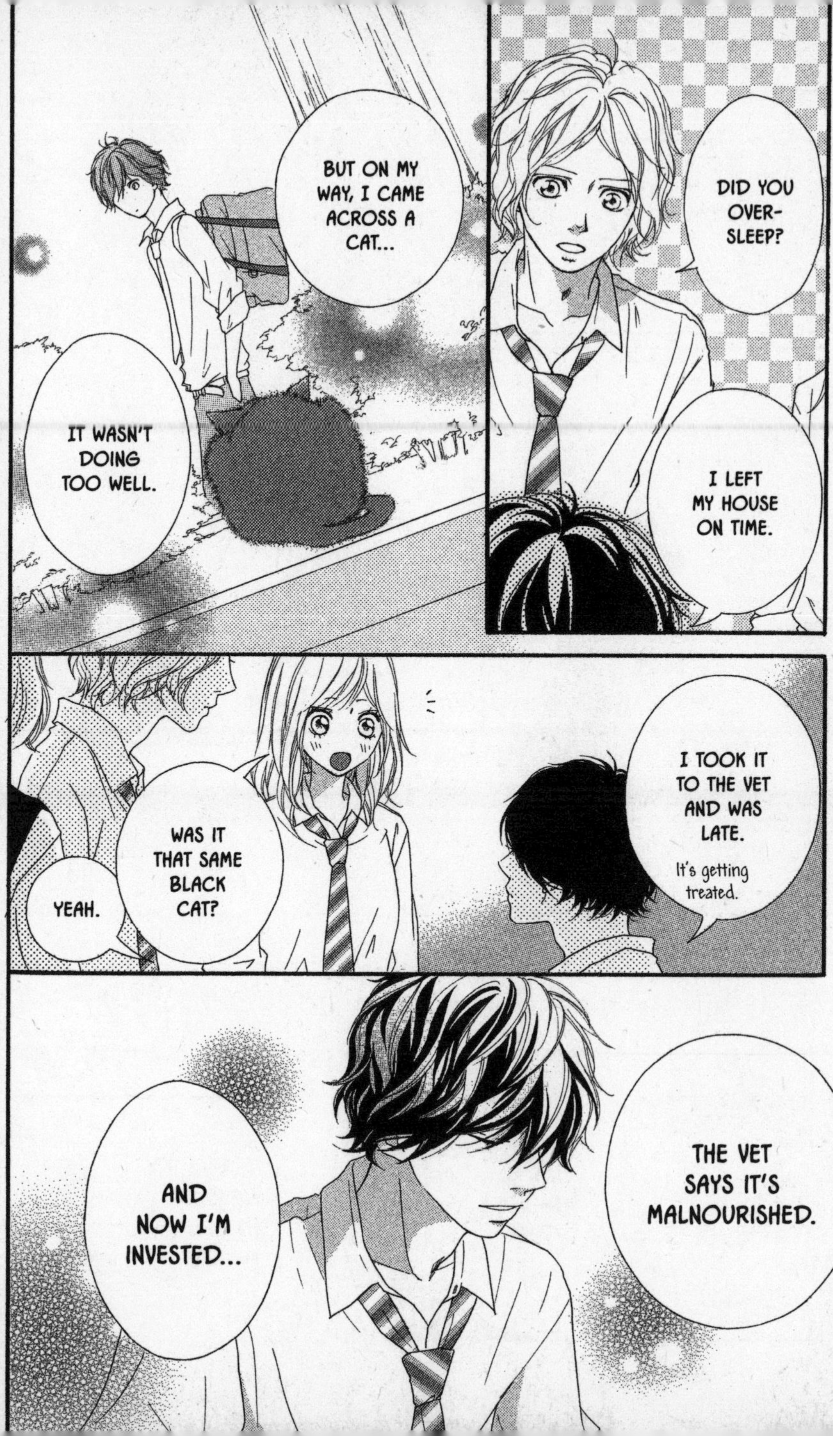
DID YOU OVER-SLEEP?
I LEFT MY HOUSE ON TIME.
BUT ON MY WAY, I CAME ACROSS A CAT...
IT WASN'T DOING TOO WELL.
I TOOK IT TO THE VET AND WAS LATE.
It's getting treated.
WAS IT THAT SAME BLACK CAT?
YEAH.
THE VET SAYS IT'S MALNOURISHED.
AND NOW I'M INVESTED...

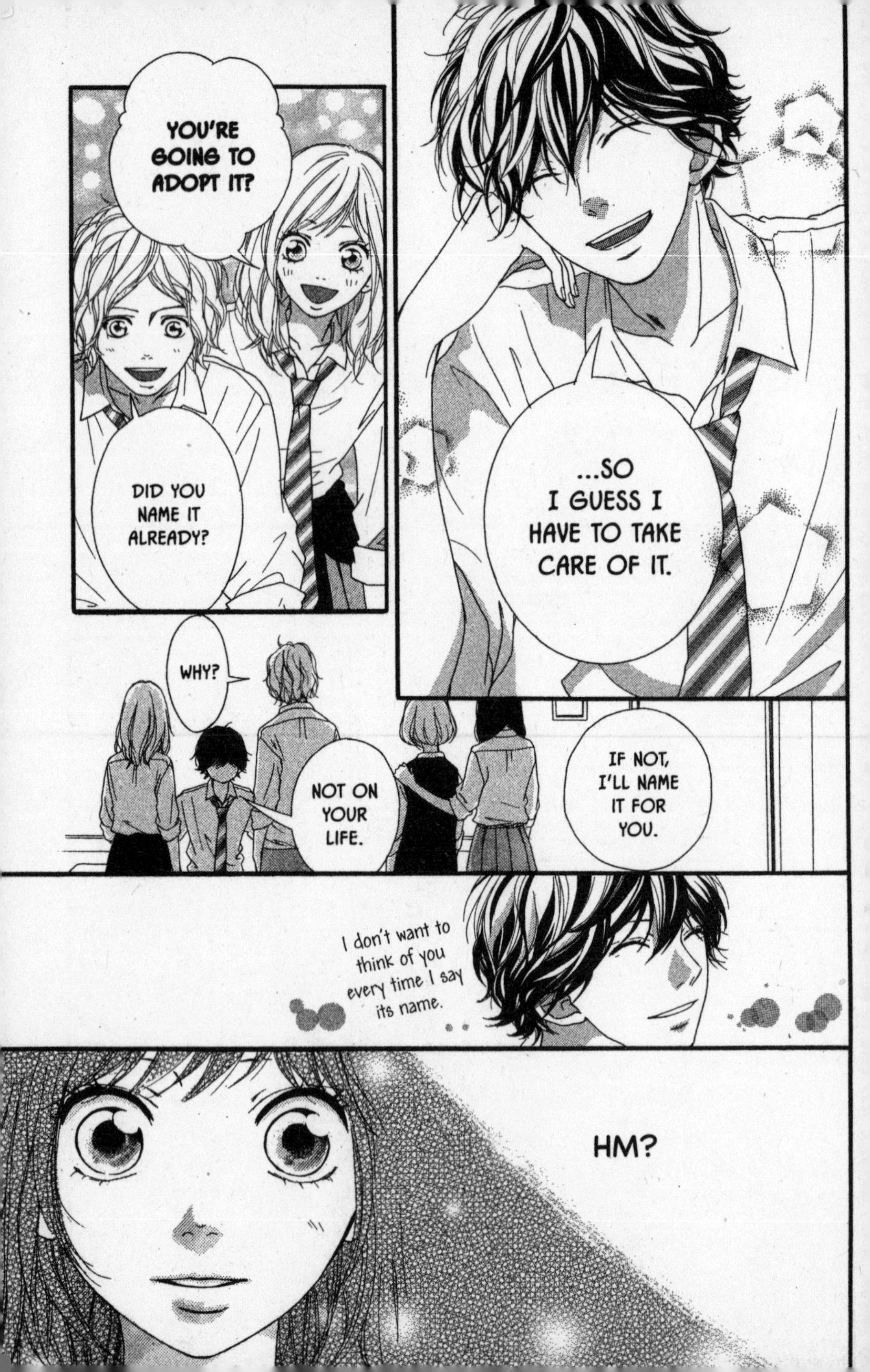
...SO I GUESS I HAVE TO TAKE CARE OF IT.
YOU'RE GOING TO ADOPT IT?
DID YOU NAME IT ALREADY?
IF NOT, I'LL NAME IT FOR YOU.
NOT ON YOUR LIFE.
WHY?
I don't want to think of you every time I say its name.
HM?

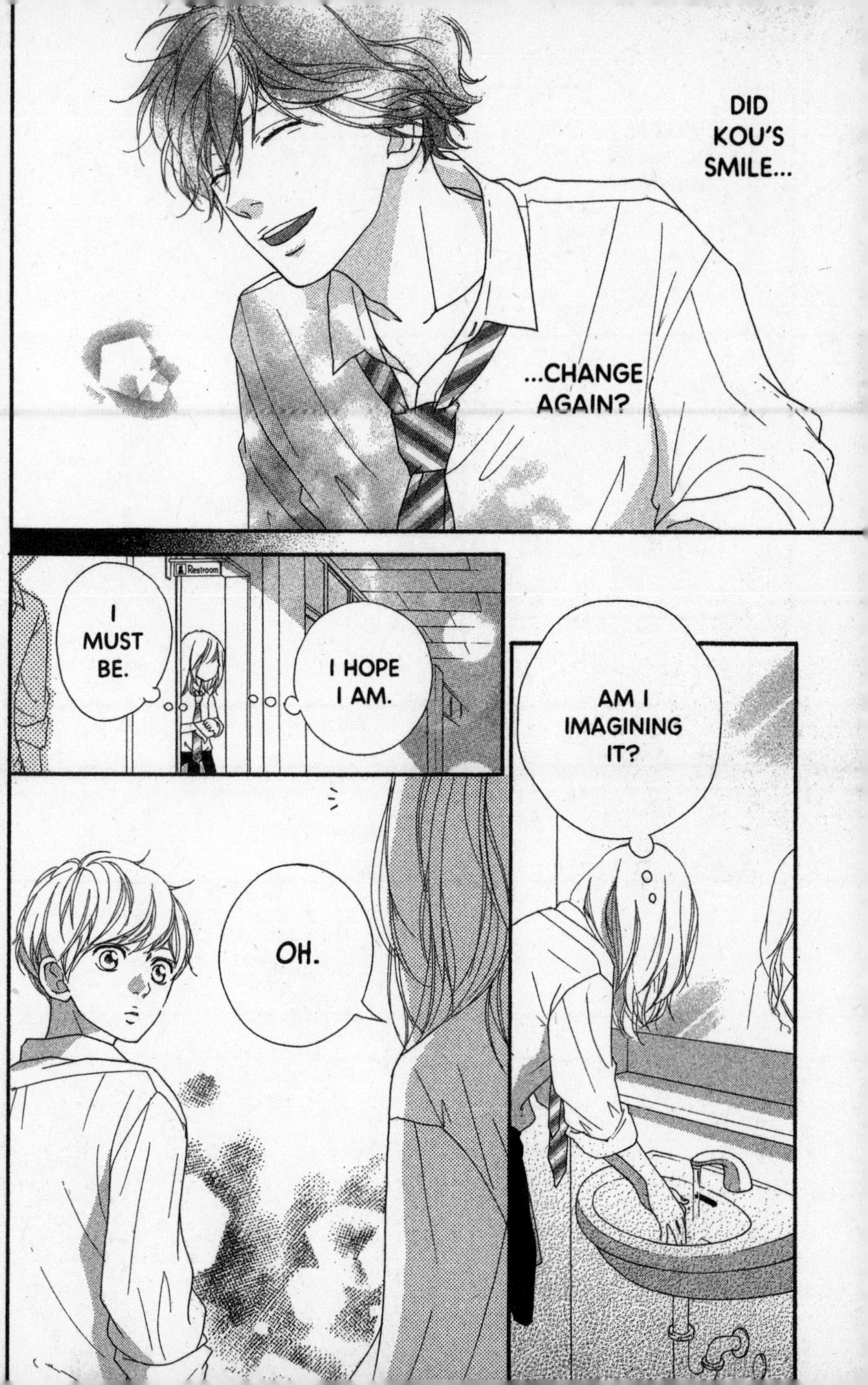
DID KOU'S SMILE...
...CHANGE AGAIN?
AM I IMAGINING IT?
I HOPE I AM.
Restroom
I MUST BE.
OH.

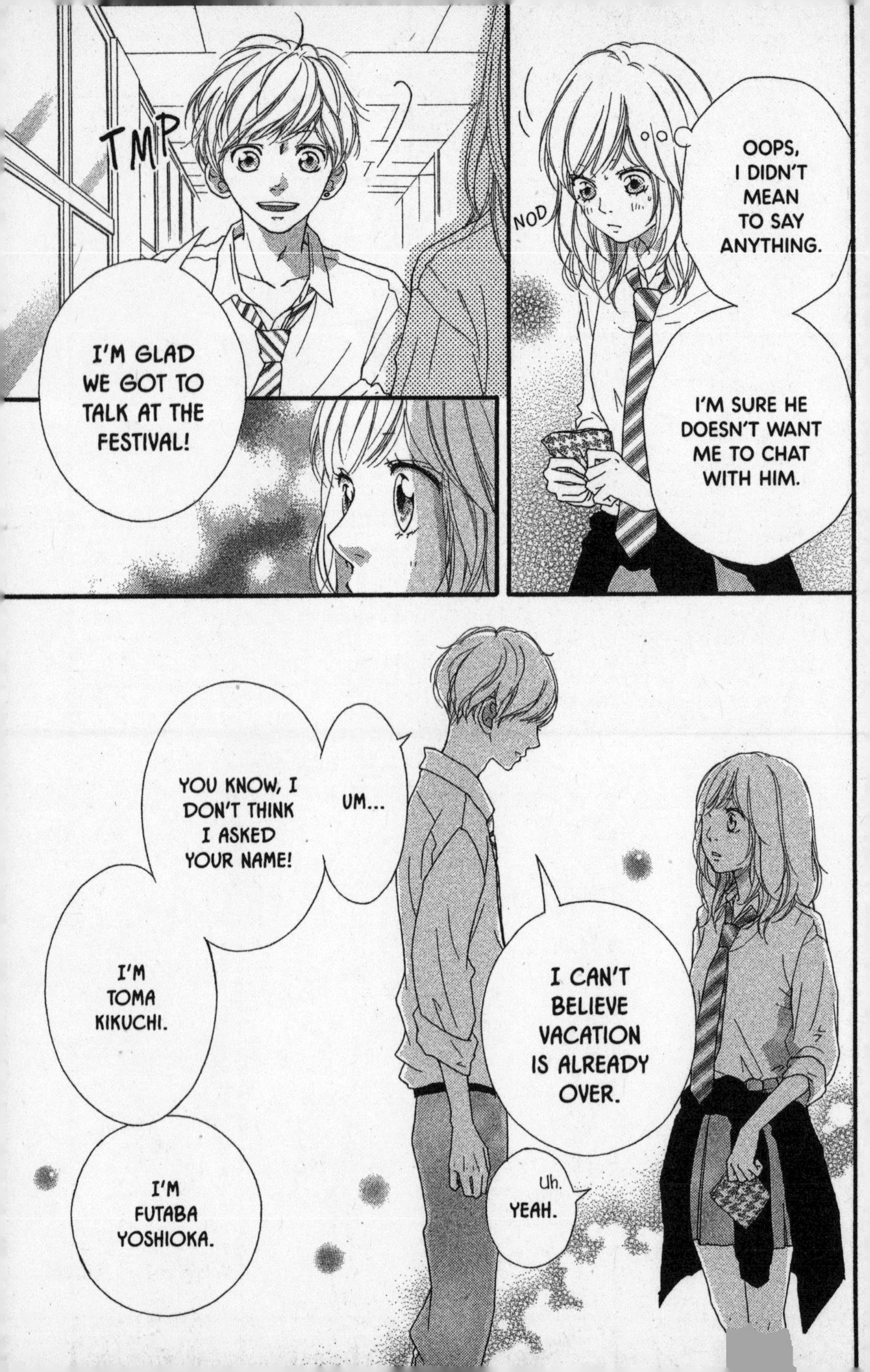
NOD
OOPS, I DIDN'T MEAN TO SAY ANYTHING.
I'M SURE HE DOESN'T WANT ME TO CHAT WITH HIM.
TMP
I'M GLAD WE GOT TO TALK AT THE FESTIVAL!
I CAN'T BELIEVE VACATION IS ALREADY OVER.
Uh. YEAH.
UM...
YOU KNOW, I DON'T THINK I ASKED YOUR NAME!
I'M TOMA KIKUCHI.
I'M FUTABA YOSHIOKA.

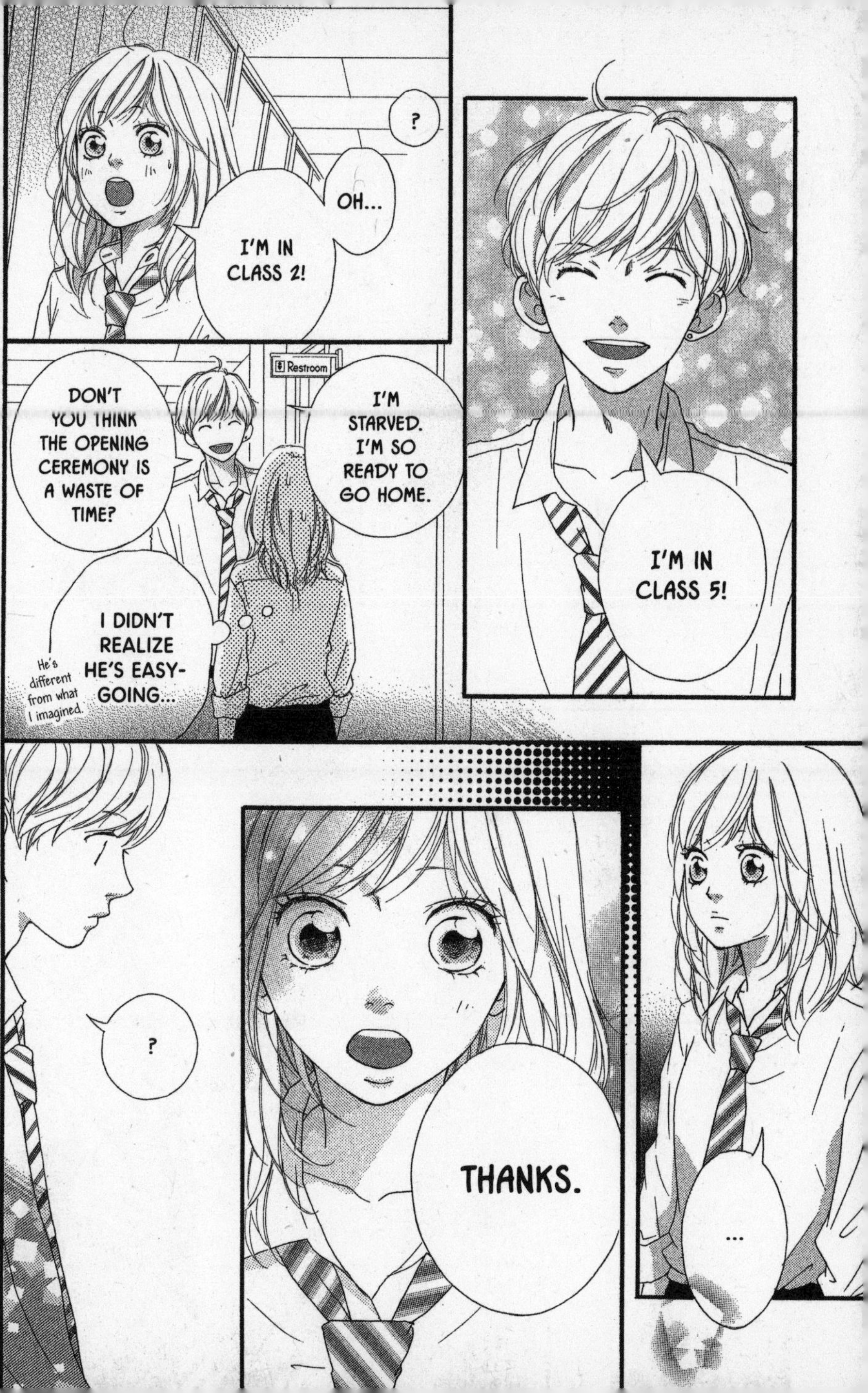
I'M IN CLASS 5!
?
OH...
I'M IN CLASS 2!
I'M STARVED. I'M SO READY TO GO HOME.
DON'T YOU THINK THE OPENING CEREMONY IS A WASTE OF TIME?
Restroom
I DIDN'T REALIZE HE'S EASY-GOING...
He's different from what I imagined.
...
THANKS.
?

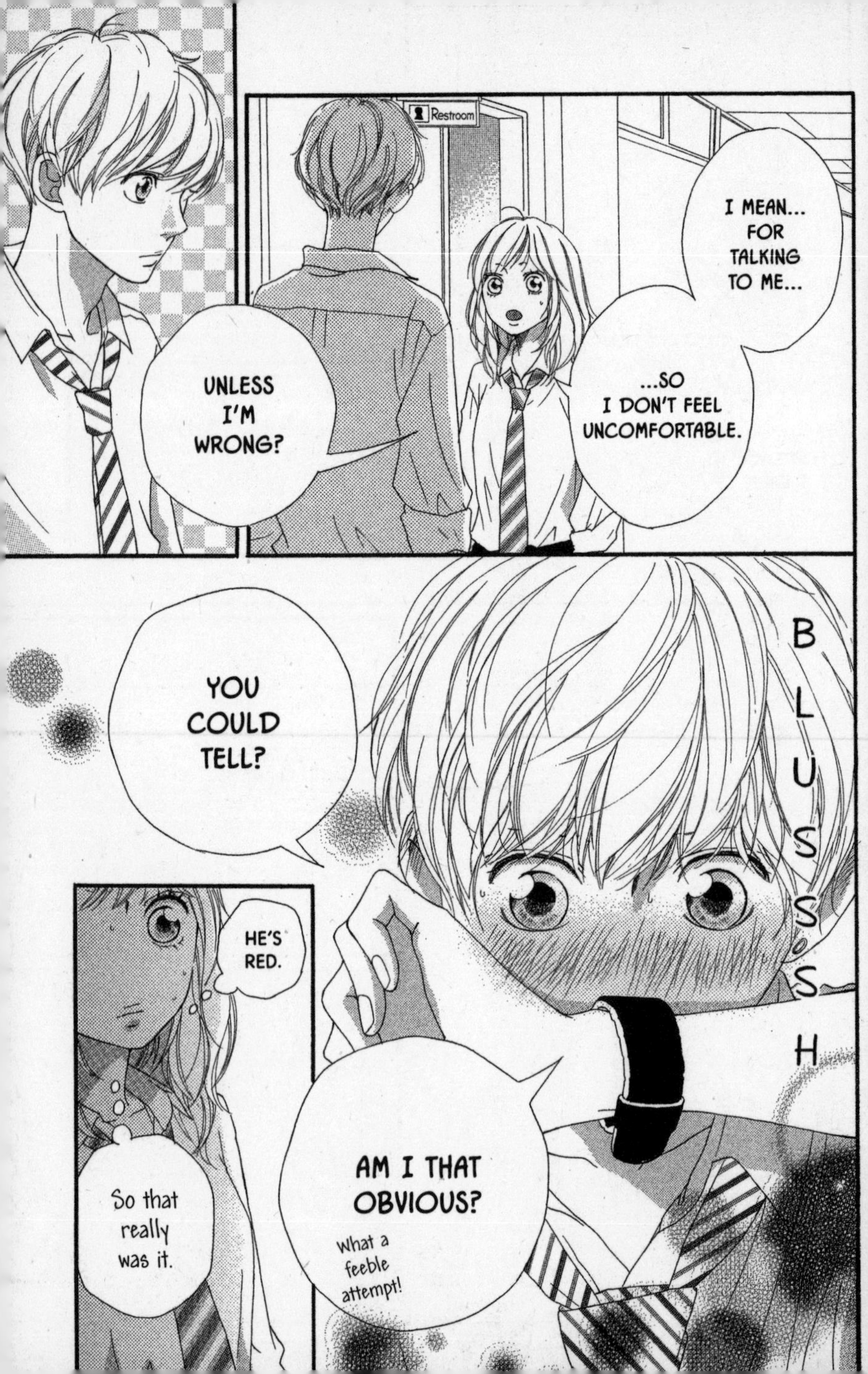
Restroom
I MEAN... FOR TALKING TO ME...
...SO I DON'T FEEL UNCOMFORTABLE.
UNLESS I'M WRONG?
YOU COULD TELL?
BLUSSH
AM I THAT OBVIOUS?
What a feeble attempt!
HE'S RED.
So that really was it.

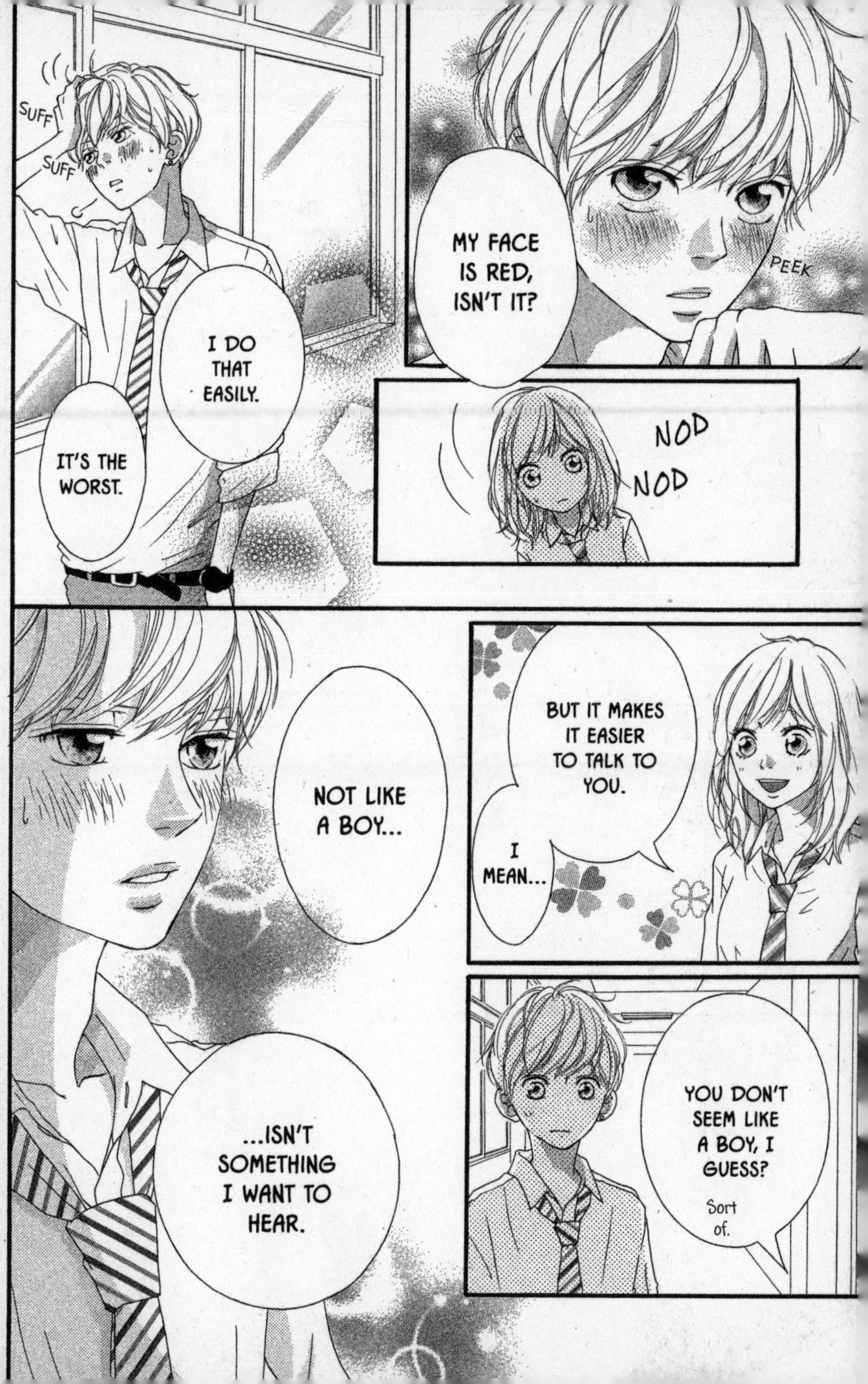
MY FACE IS RED, ISN'T IT?
PEEK
NOD
NOD
SUFF
SUFF
I DO THAT EASILY.
IT'S THE WORST.
BUT IT MAKES IT EASIER TO TALK TO YOU.
I MEAN...
YOU DON'T SEEM LIKE A BOY, I GUESS?
Sort of.
NOT LIKE A BOY...
...ISN'T SOMETHING I WANT TO HEAR.

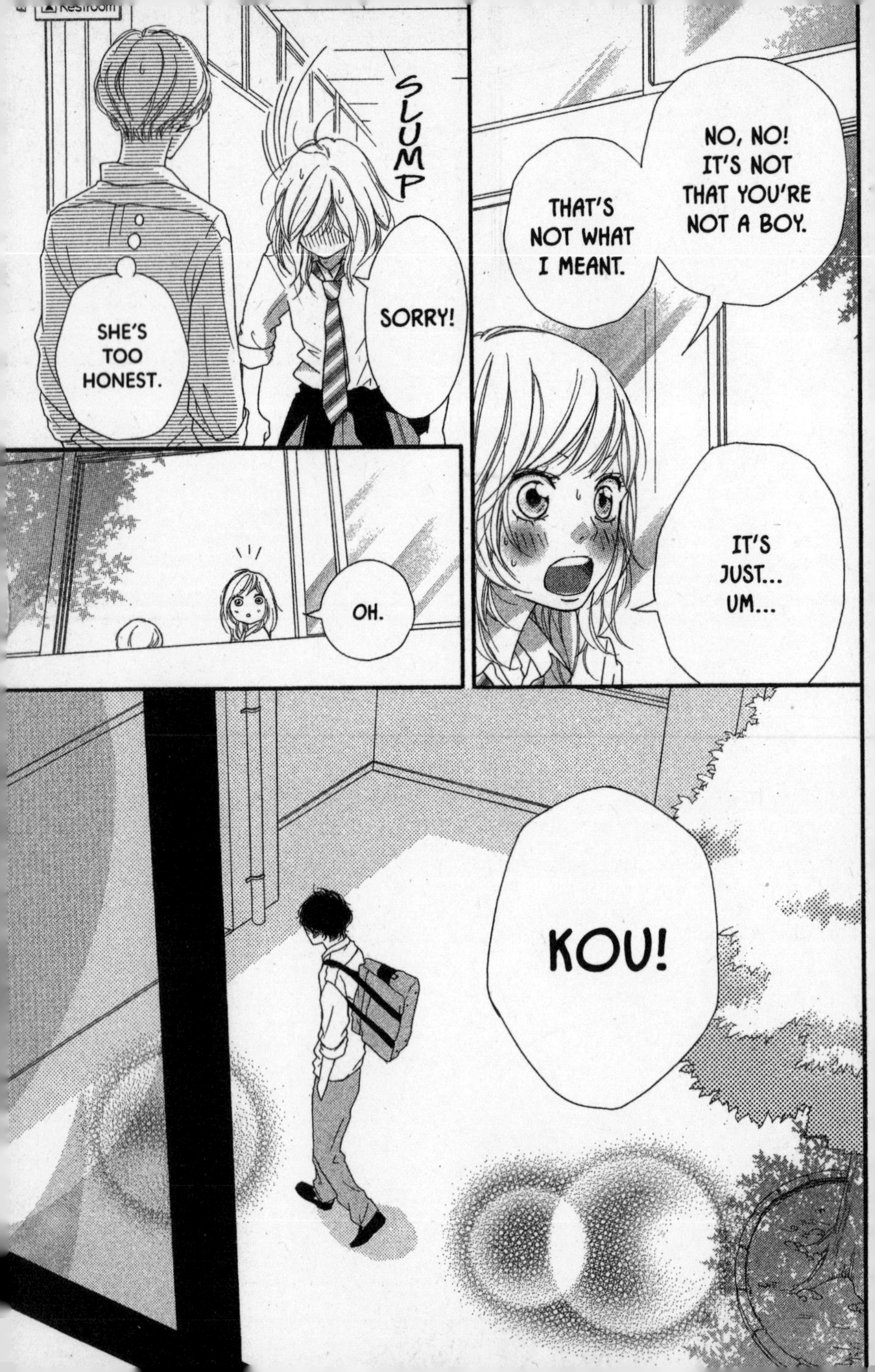
NO, NO! IT'S NOT THAT YOU'RE NOT A BOY.
THAT'S NOT WHAT I MEANT.
IT'S JUST... UM...
Restroom
SLUMP
SORRY!
SHE'S TOO HONEST.
OH.
KOU!

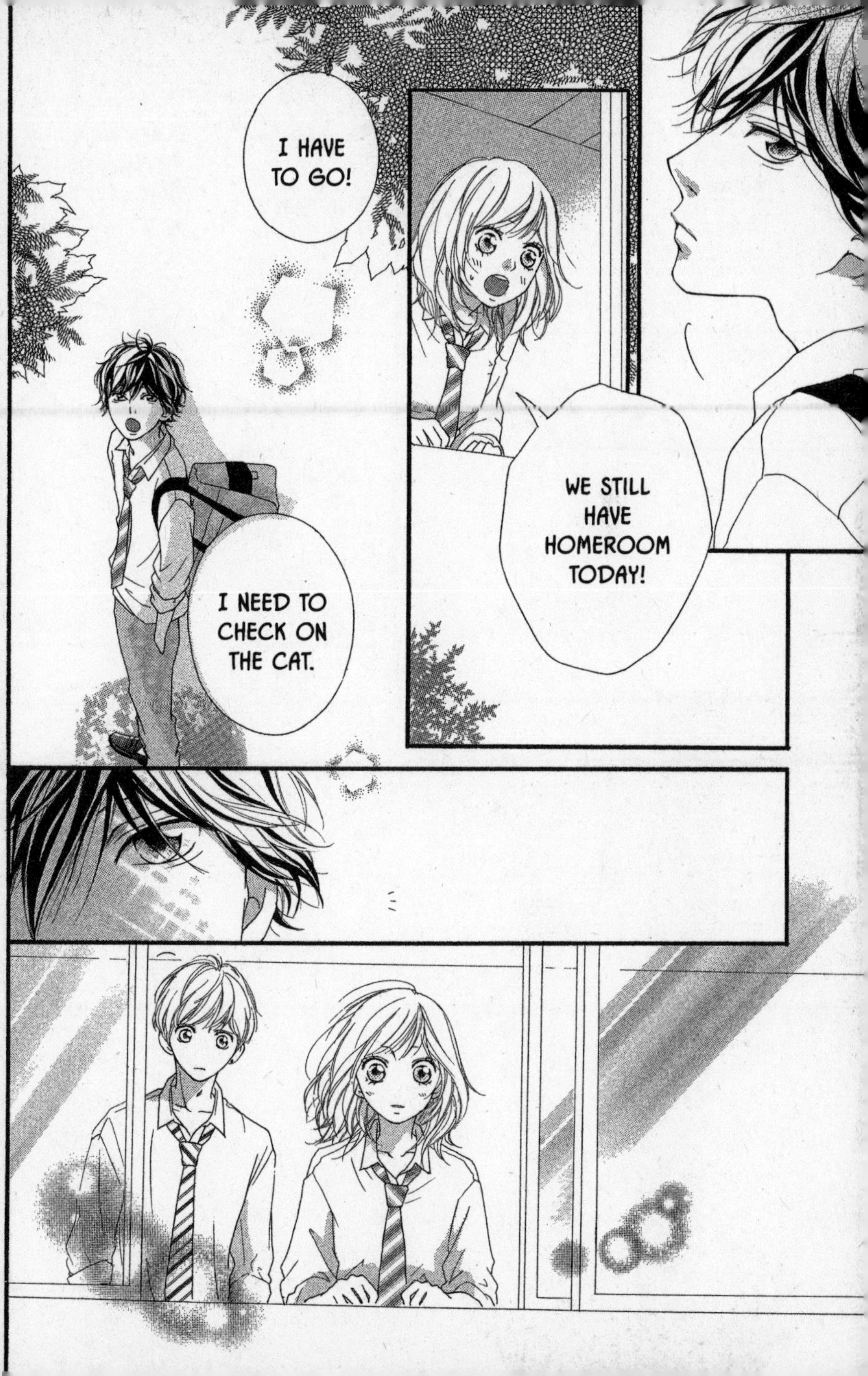
WE STILL HAVE HOMEROOM TODAY!
I HAVE TO GO!
I NEED TO CHECK ON THE CAT.

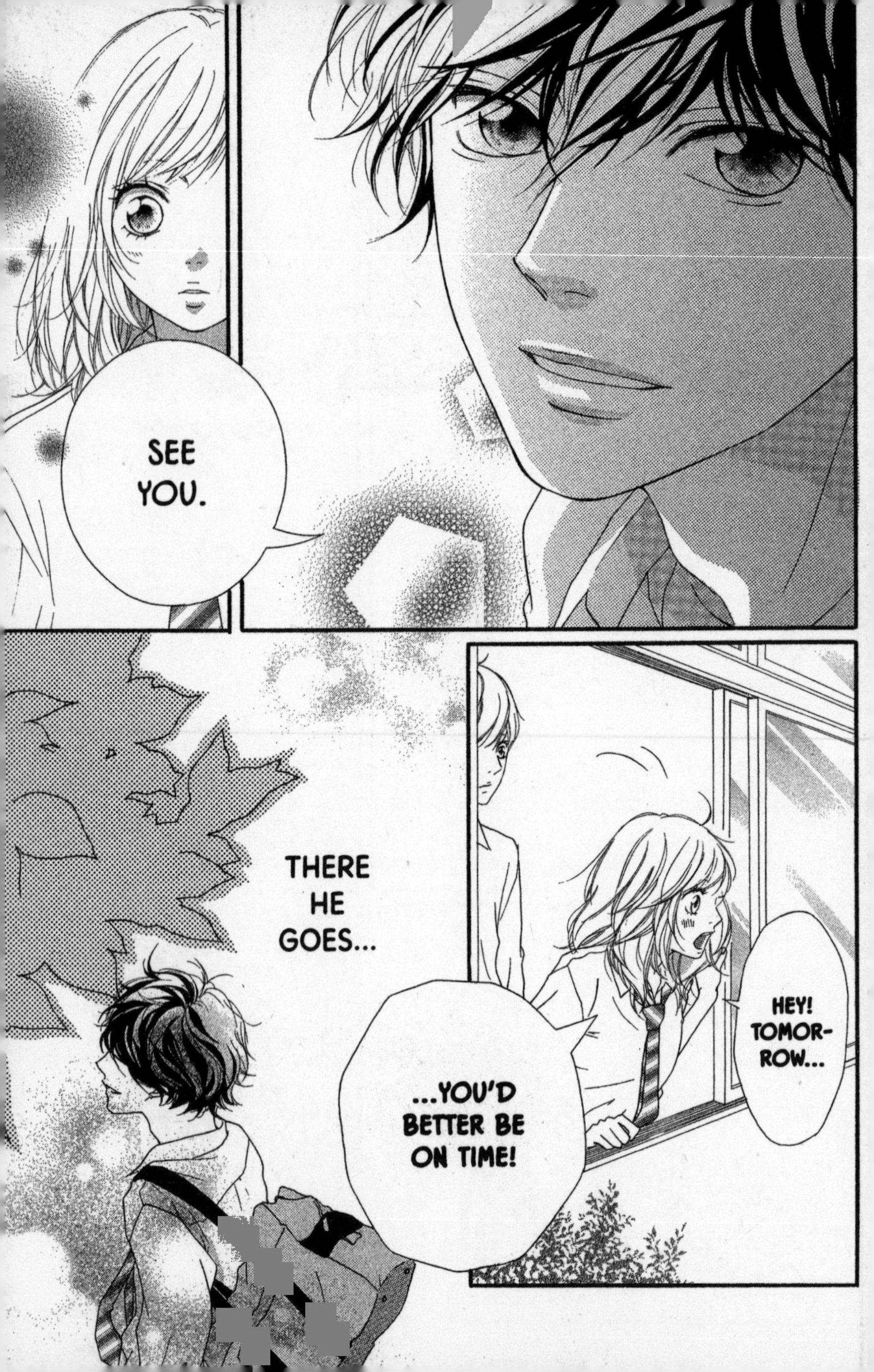
SEE YOU.
HEY! TOMOR-ROW...
...YOU'D BETTER BE ON TIME!
THERE HE GOES...

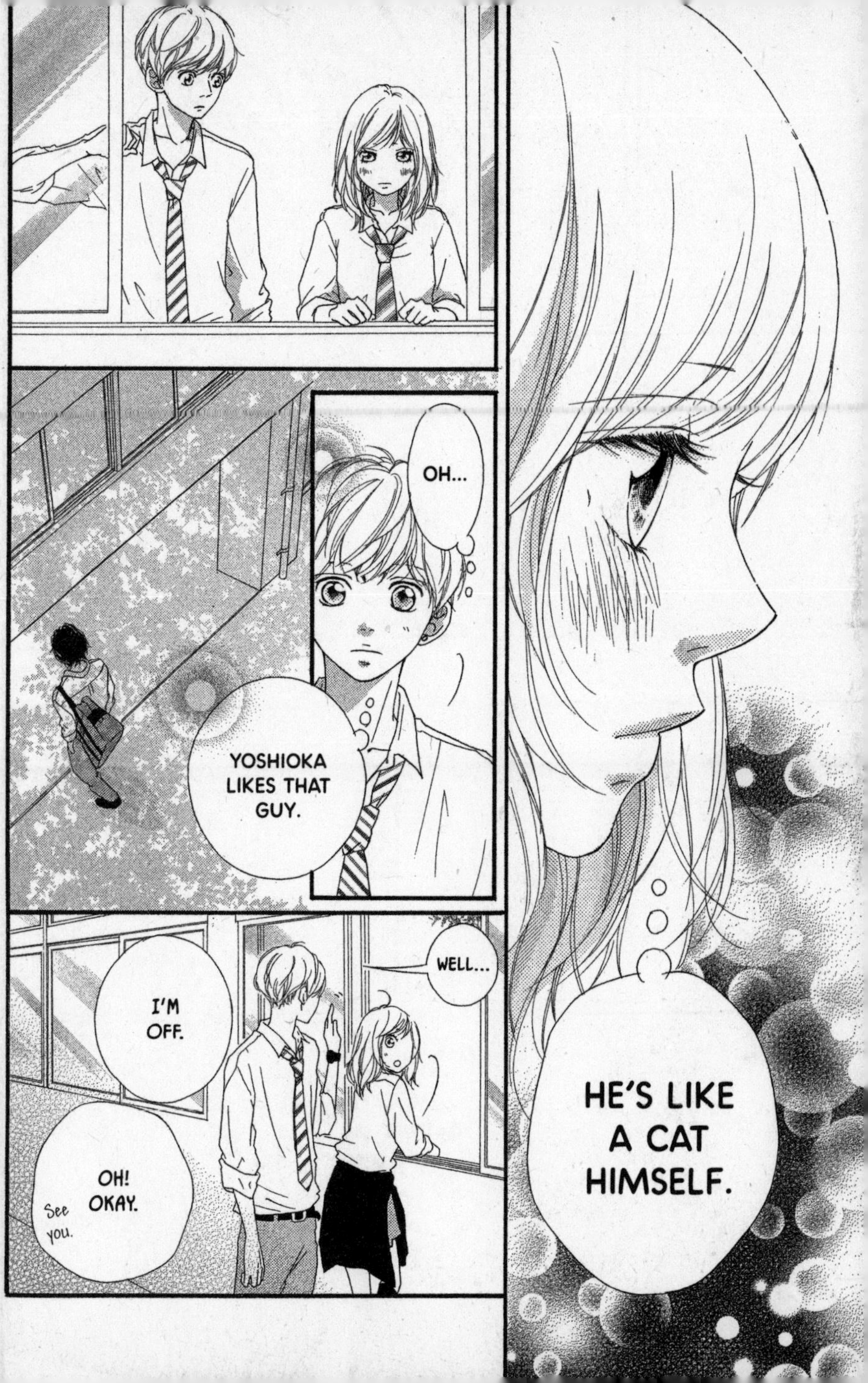
HE'S LIKE A CAT HIMSELF.
OH...
YOSHIOKA LIKES THAT GUY.
WELL...
I'M OFF.
OH! OKAY.
See you.

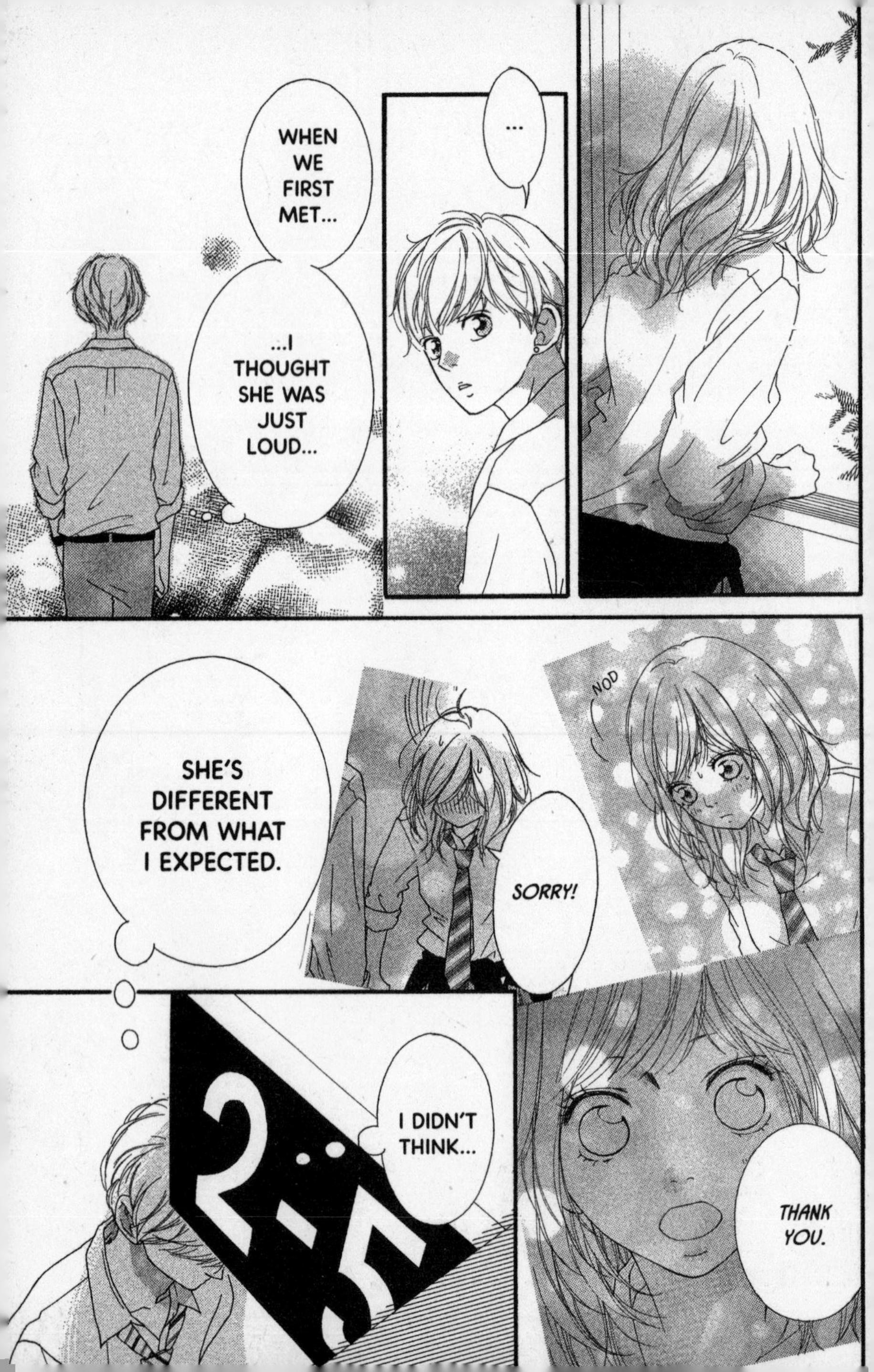
...
WHEN WE FIRST MET...
...I THOUGHT SHE WAS JUST LOUD...
NOD
SORRY!
SHE'S DIFFERENT FROM WHAT I EXPECTED.
THANK YOU.
I DIDN'T THINK...

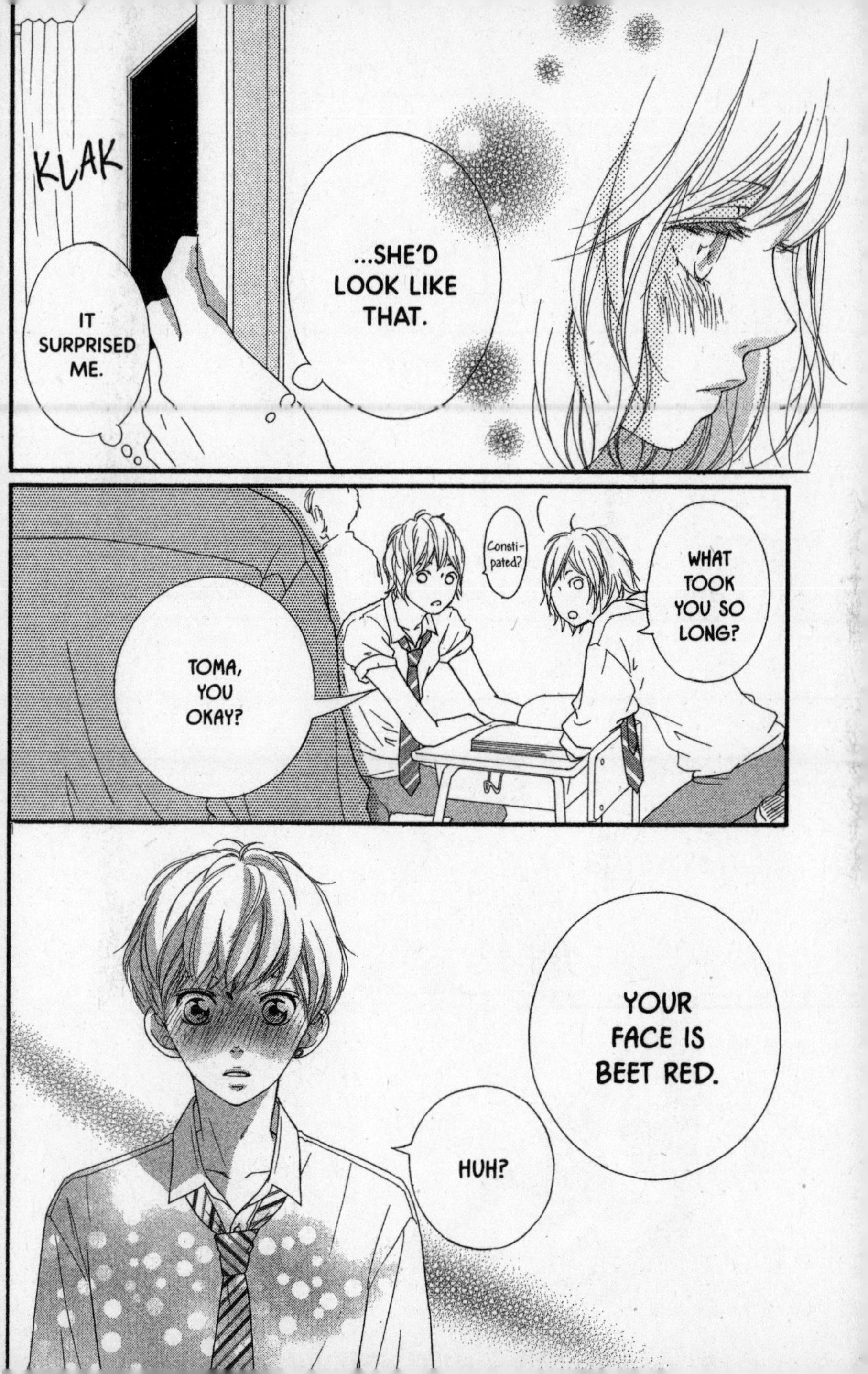
...SHE'D LOOK LIKE THAT.
KLAK
IT SURPRISED ME.
WHAT TOOK YOU SO LONG?
Consti-pated?
TOMA, YOU OKAY?
YOUR FACE IS BEET RED.
HUH?

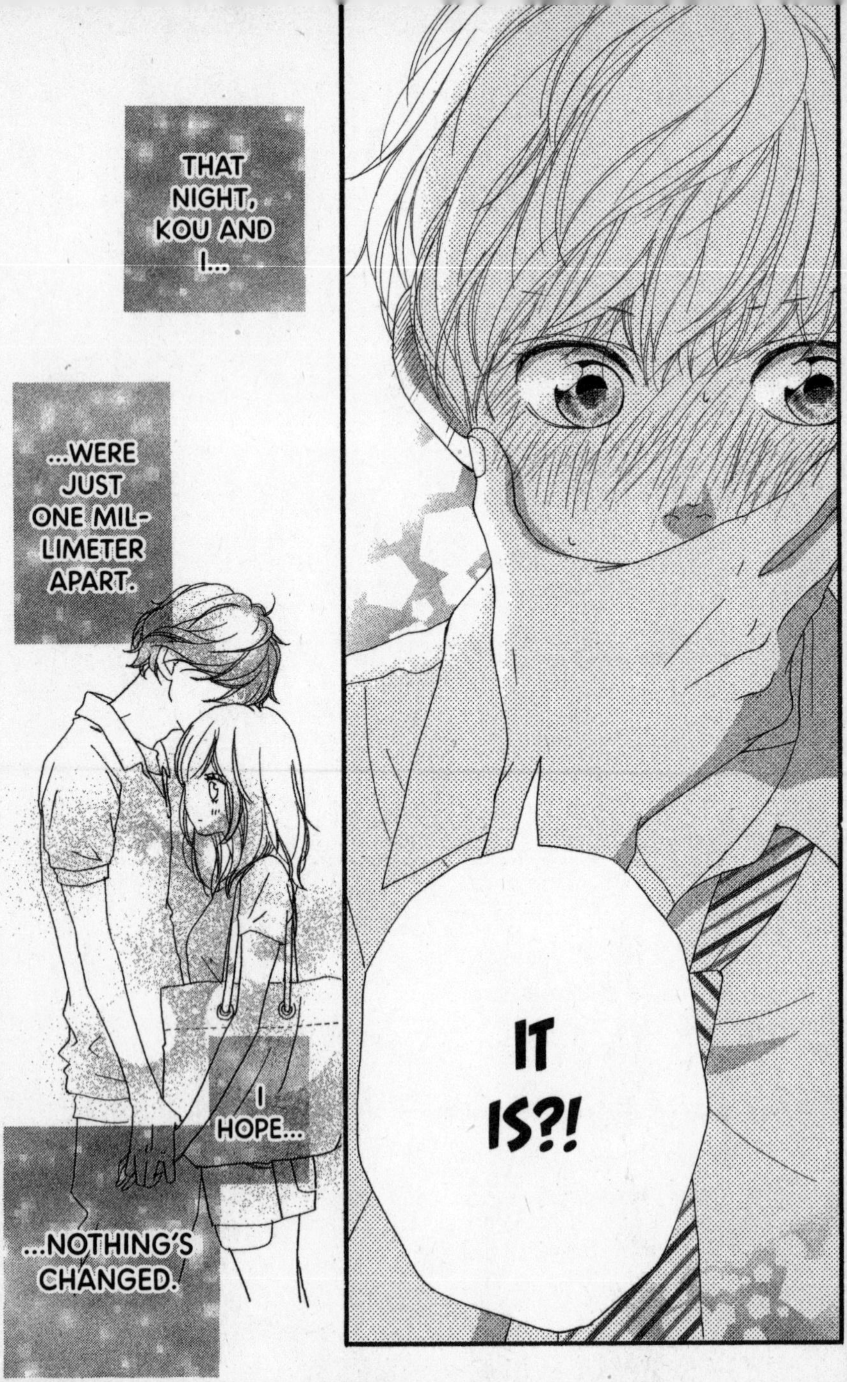
IT IS?!
THAT NIGHT, KOU AND I...
...WERE JUST ONE MIL-LIMETER APART.
I HOPE...
...NOTHING'S CHANGED.

Toma Kikuchi

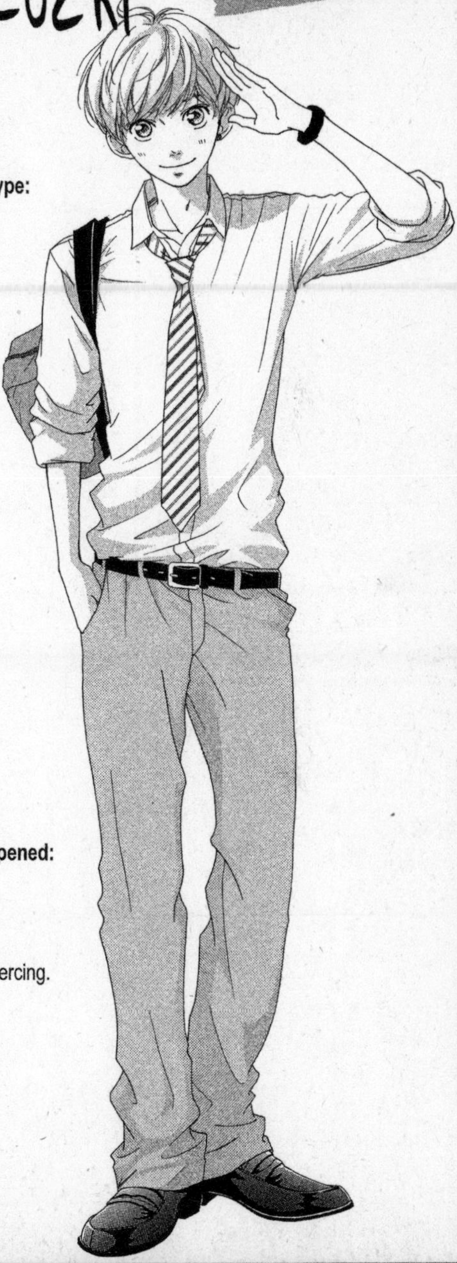

Birthday:
February 1st

Astrological Sign, Blood Type:
Aquarius, type A

Height, Weight:
5'10", 135 lbs.

Favorite Subject:
English

Least Favorite Subject:
Social Studies

Favorite Food:
Ginger pork

Least Favorite Food:
Tomatoes

Favorite Music:
ELLEGARDEN

Siblings:
Two older sisters

Age When First Crush Happened:
Second year of junior high

Fun Fact:
My ear lobe is stretched for piercing.

Favorite Snack:
Fruit gummies (grape)

Favorite Drink:
Pilkul

Favorite Color:
Baby-chick yellow

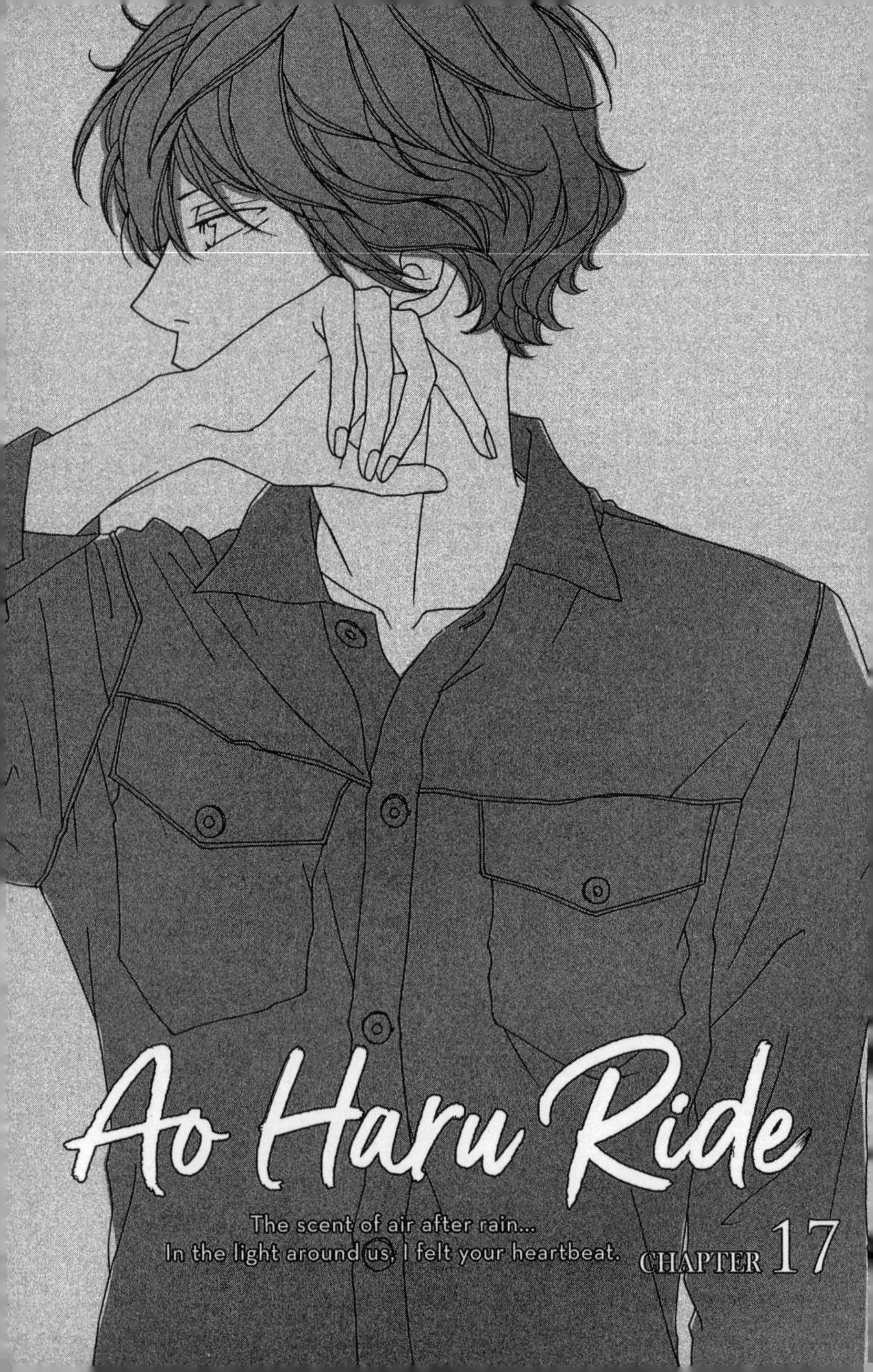
Ao Haru Ride
The scent of air after rain...
In the light around us, I felt your heartbeat.
CHAPTER 17

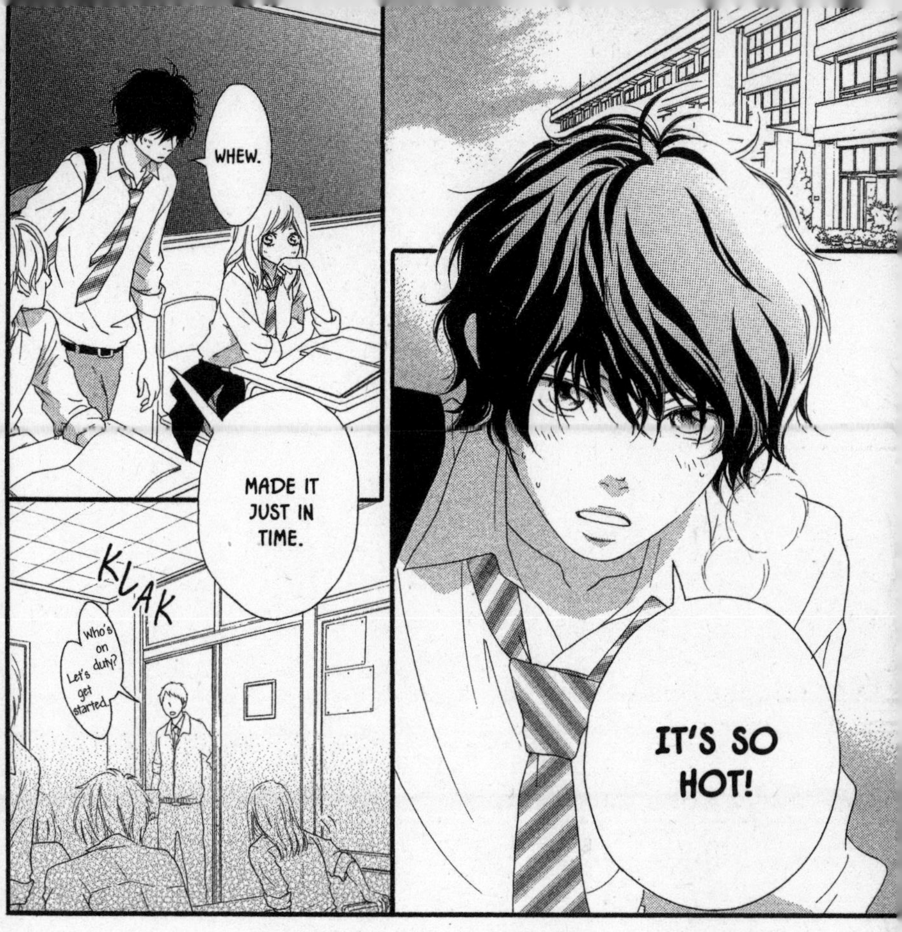
IT'S SO HOT!
WHEW.
MADE IT JUST IN TIME.
KLAK
Who's on duty? Let's get started.

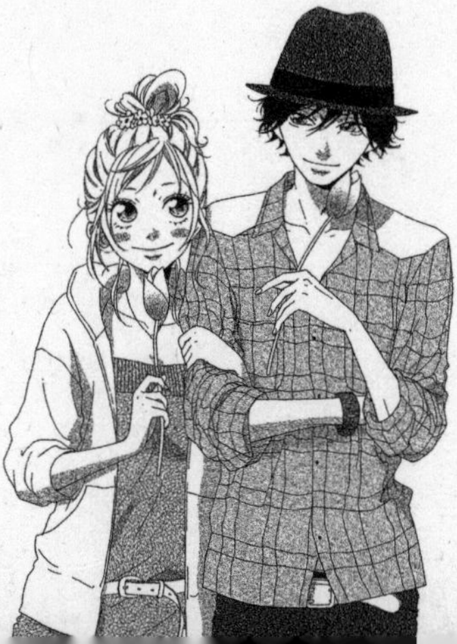

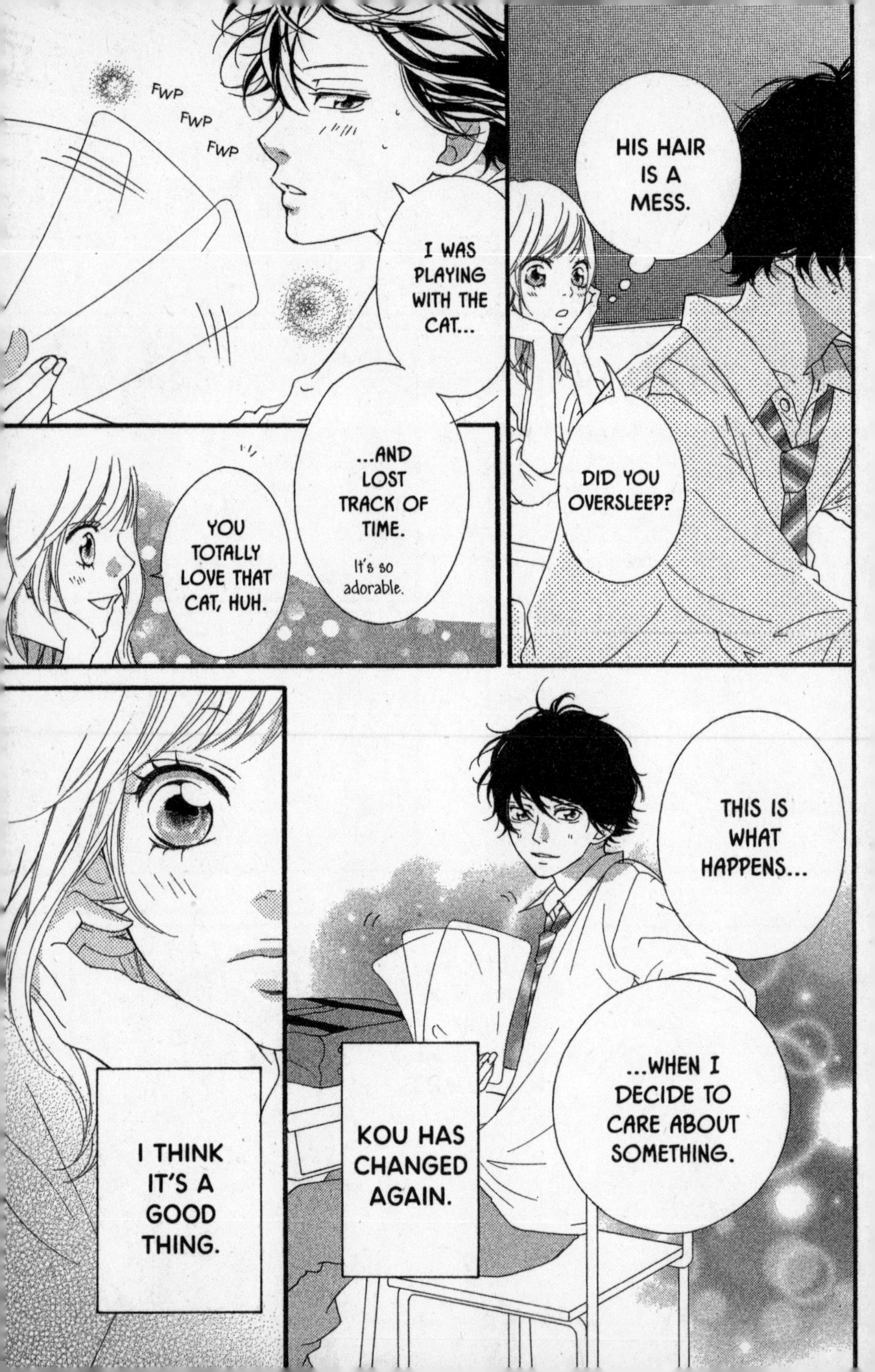
HIS HAIR IS A MESS.
DID YOU OVERSLEEP?
FWP FWP FWP
I WAS PLAYING WITH THE CAT...
...AND LOST TRACK OF TIME.
It's so adorable.
YOU TOTALLY LOVE THAT CAT, HUH.
THIS IS WHAT HAPPENS...
...WHEN I DECIDE TO CARE ABOUT SOMETHING.
KOU HAS CHANGED AGAIN.
I THINK IT'S A GOOD THING.

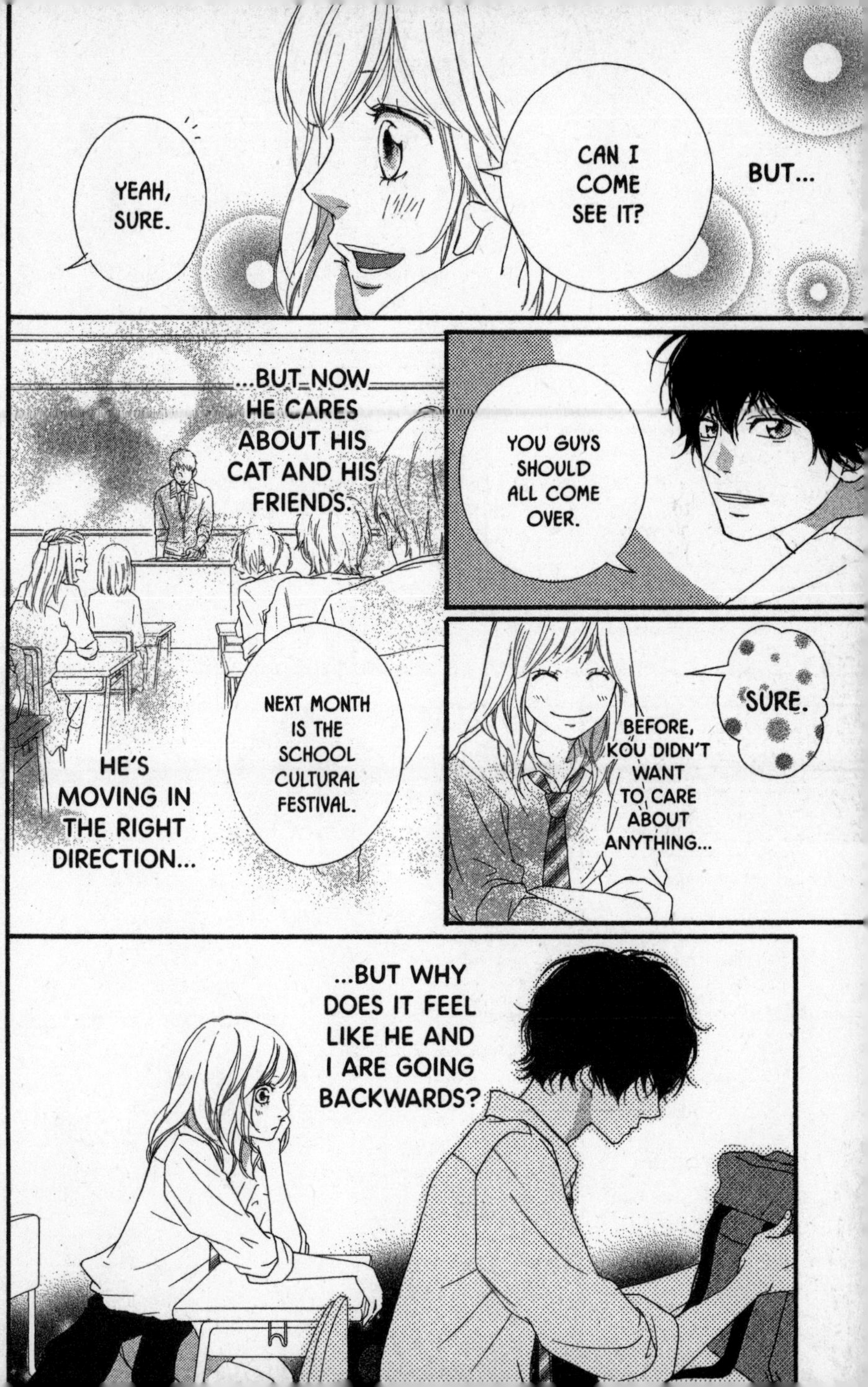
BUT...
CAN I COME SEE IT?
YEAH, SURE.
YOU GUYS SHOULD ALL COME OVER.
SURE.
BEFORE, KOU DIDN'T WANT TO CARE ABOUT ANYTHING...
...BUT NOW HE CARES ABOUT HIS CAT AND HIS FRIENDS.
NEXT MONTH IS THE SCHOOL CULTURAL FESTIVAL.
HE'S MOVING IN THE RIGHT DIRECTION...
...BUT WHY DOES IT FEEL LIKE HE AND I ARE GOING BACKWARDS?

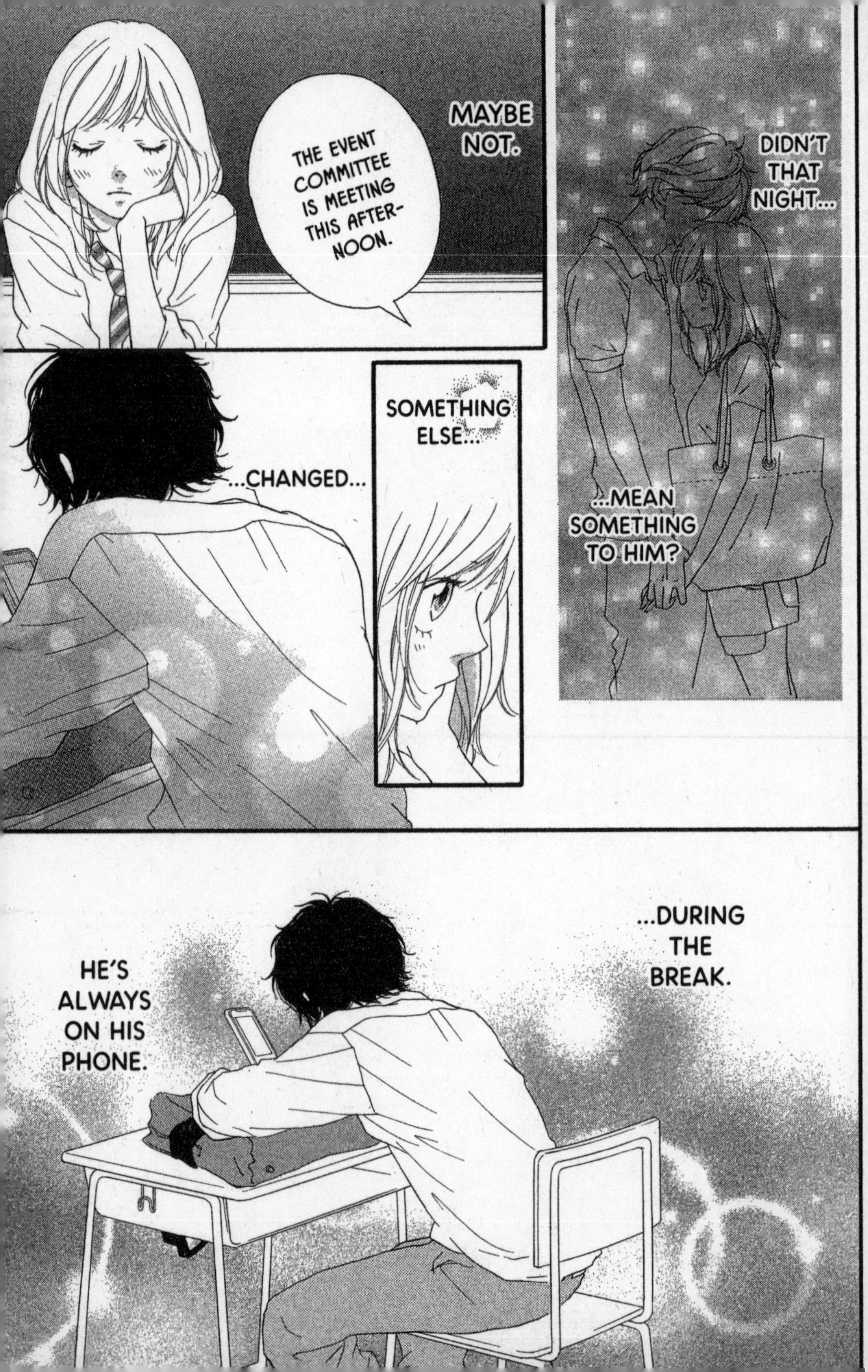
DIDN'T THAT NIGHT...
...MEAN SOMETHING TO HIM?
MAYBE NOT.
THE EVENT COMMITTEE IS MEETING THIS AFTER-NOON.
SOMETHING ELSE...
...CHANGED...
...DURING THE BREAK.
HE'S ALWAYS ON HIS PHONE.

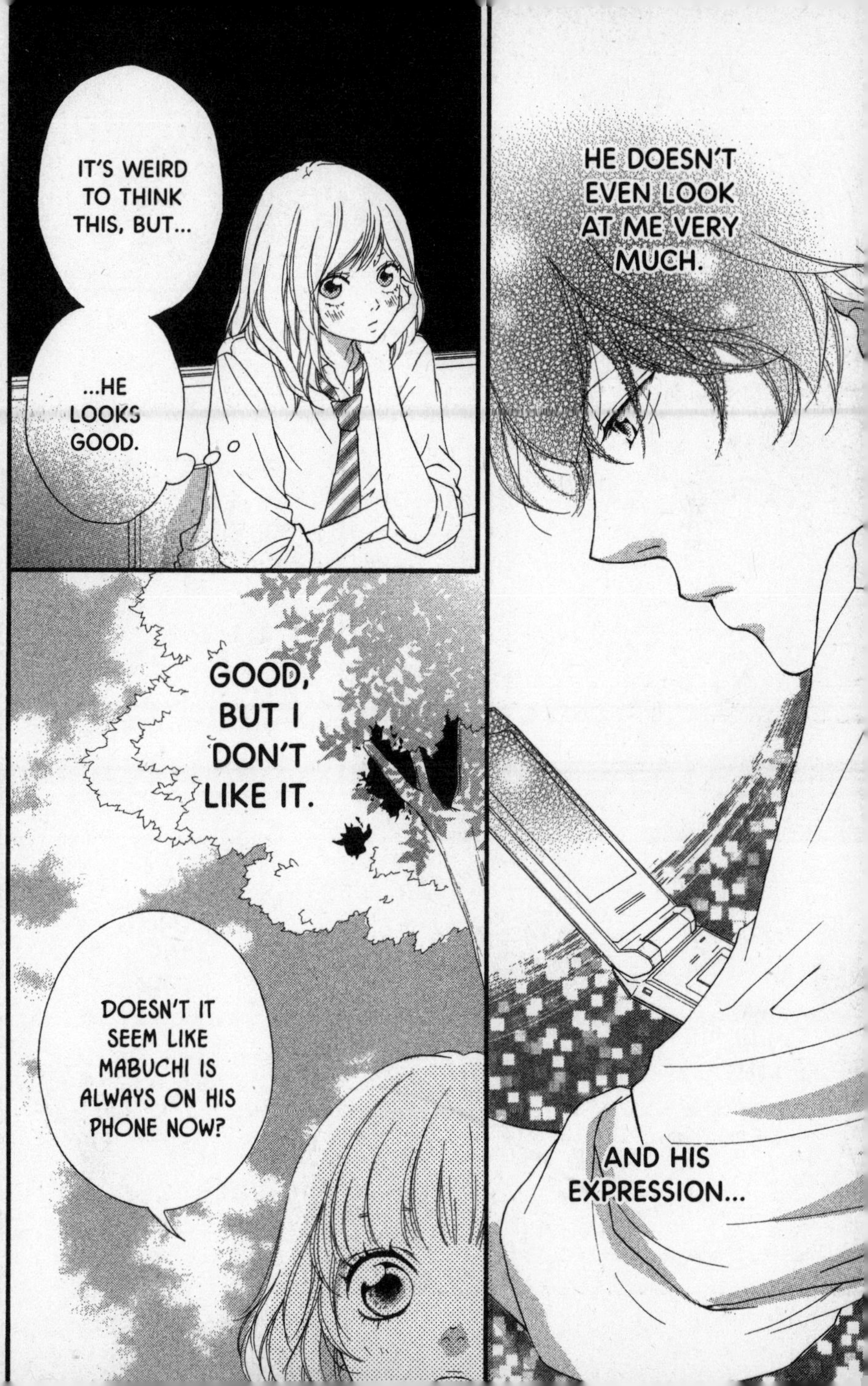
HE DOESN'T EVEN LOOK AT ME VERY MUCH.
AND HIS EXPRESSION...
IT'S WEIRD TO THINK THIS, BUT...
...HE LOOKS GOOD.
GOOD, BUT I DON'T LIKE IT.
DOESN'T IT SEEM LIKE MABUCHI IS ALWAYS ON HIS PHONE NOW?

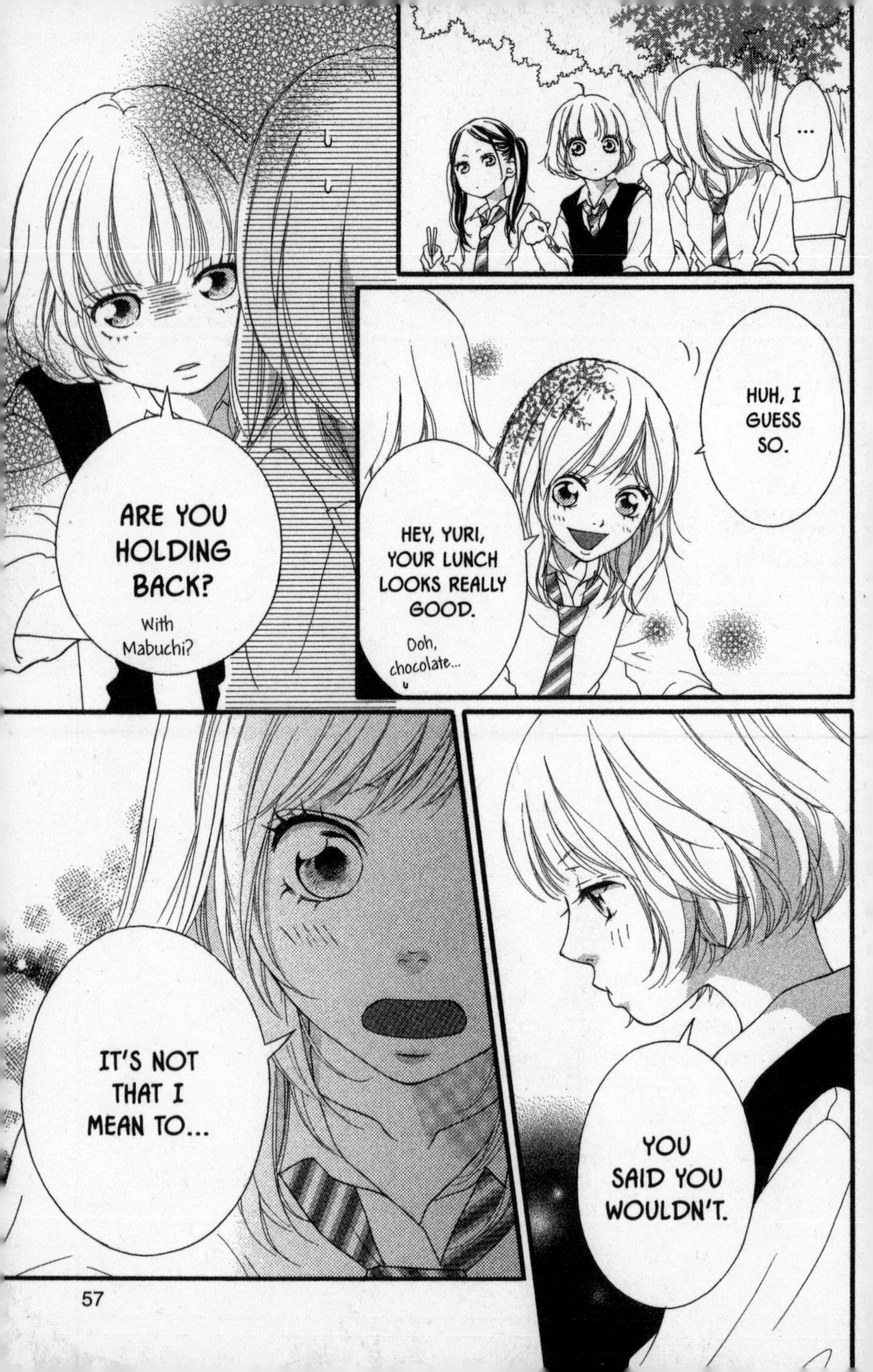

...
HUH, I GUESS SO.
HEY, YURI, YOUR LUNCH LOOKS REALLY GOOD.
Ooh, chocolate...
ARE YOU HOLDING BACK?
With Mabuchi?
YOU SAID YOU WOULDN'T.
IT'S NOT THAT I MEAN TO...

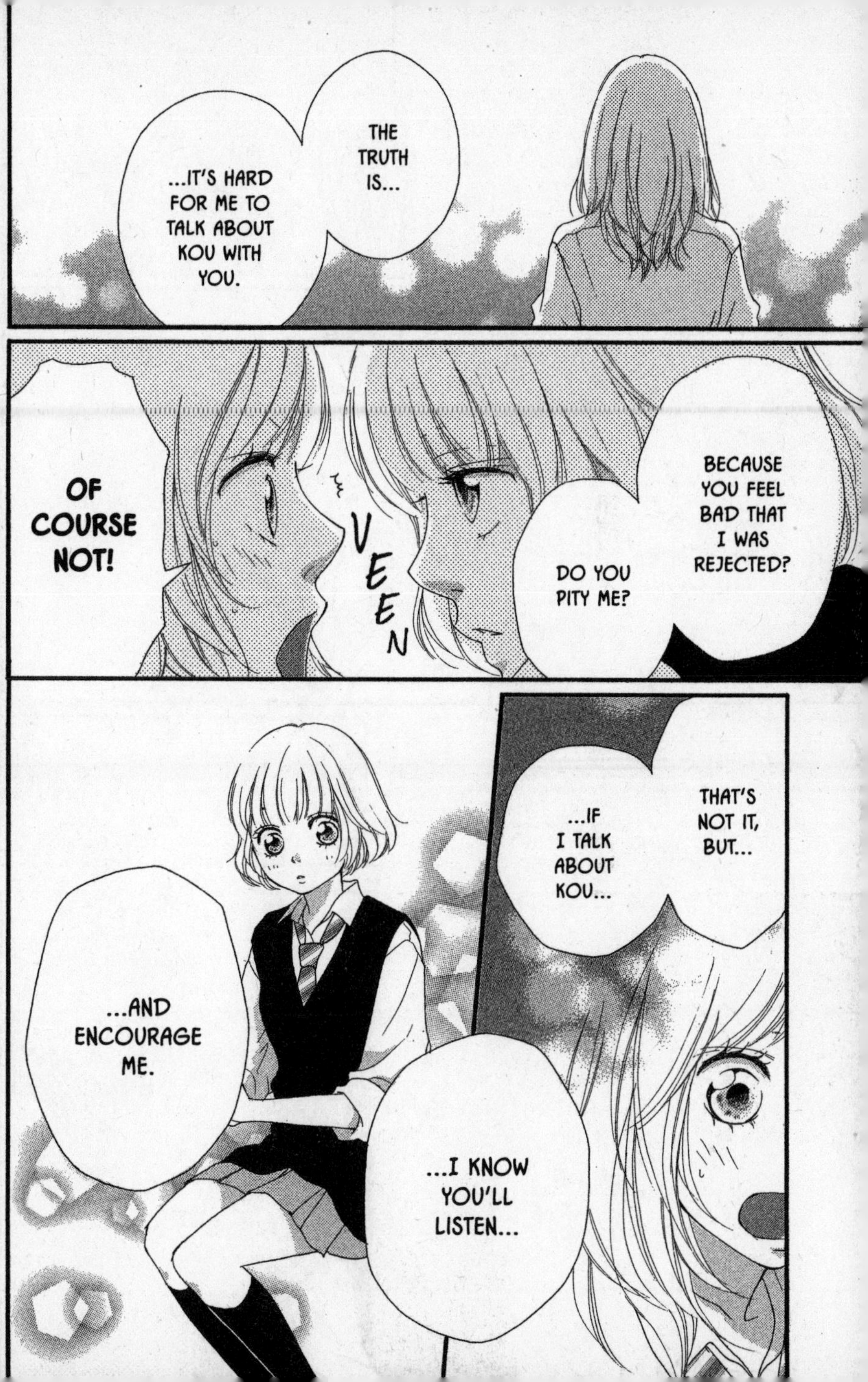
THE TRUTH IS...
...IT'S HARD FOR ME TO TALK ABOUT KOU WITH YOU.
BECAUSE YOU FEEL BAD THAT I WAS REJECTED?
DO YOU PITY ME?
VEEN
OF COURSE NOT!
THAT'S NOT IT, BUT...
...IF I TALK ABOUT KOU...
...I KNOW YOU'LL LISTEN...
...AND ENCOURAGE ME.

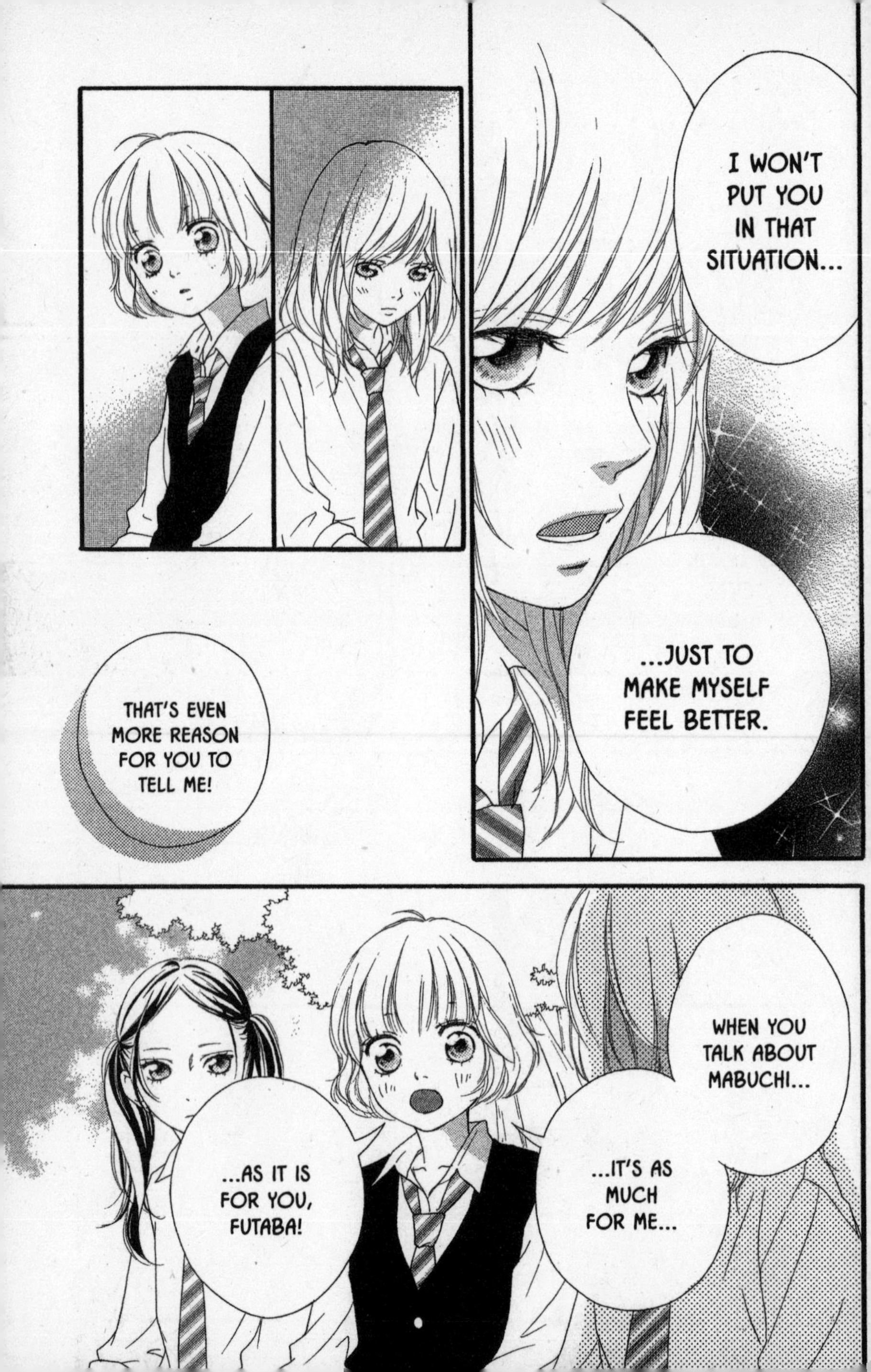
I WON'T PUT YOU IN THAT SITUATION...
...JUST TO MAKE MYSELF FEEL BETTER.
THAT'S EVEN MORE REASON FOR YOU TO TELL ME!
WHEN YOU TALK ABOUT MABUCHI...
...IT'S AS MUCH FOR ME...
...AS IT IS FOR YOU, FUTABA!

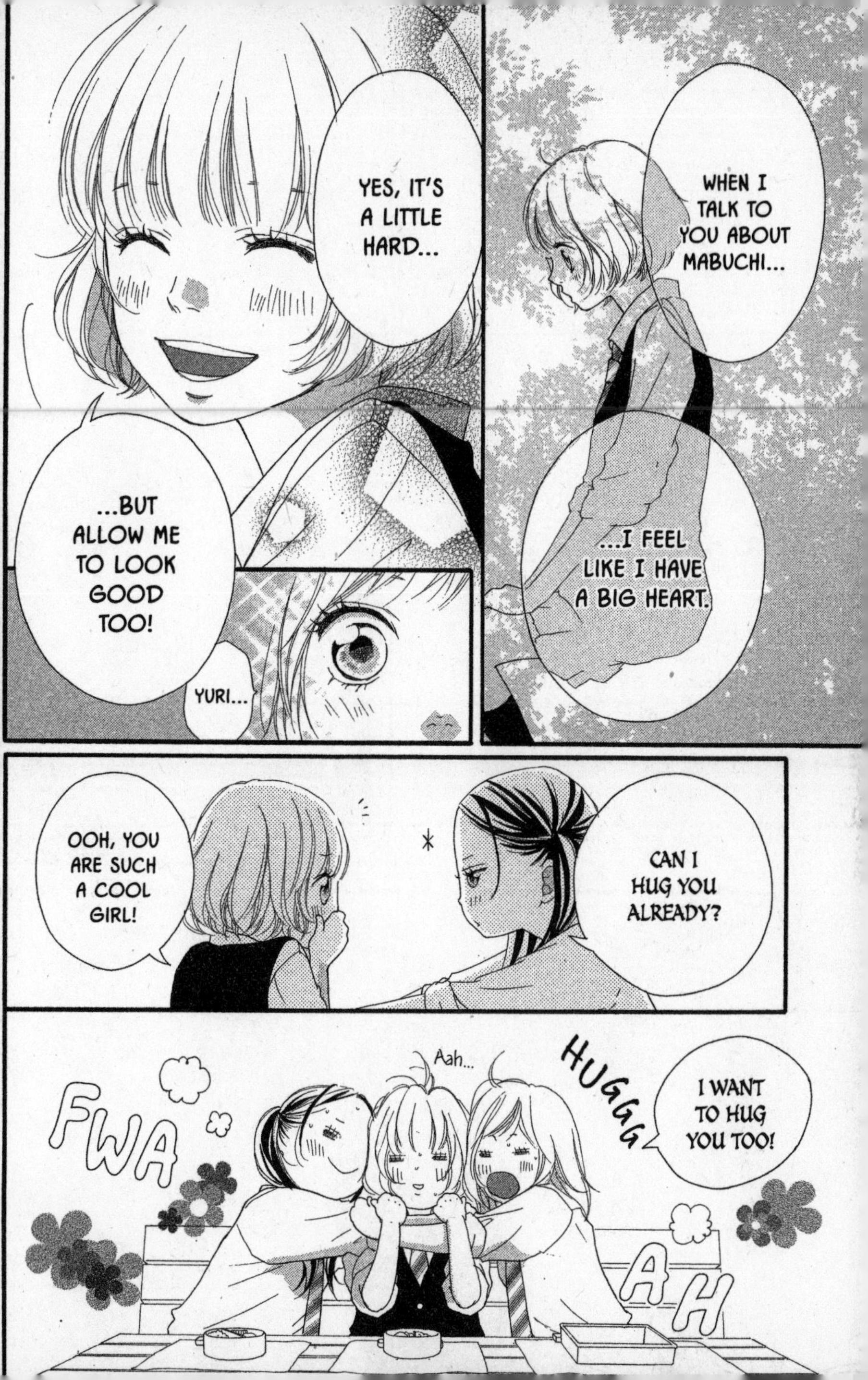
WHEN I TALK TO YOU ABOUT MABUCHI...
...I FEEL LIKE I HAVE A BIG HEART.
YES, IT'S A LITTLE HARD...
...BUT ALLOW ME TO LOOK GOOD TOO!
YURI...
CAN I HUG YOU ALREADY?
OOH, YOU ARE SUCH A COOL GIRL!
I WANT TO HUG YOU TOO!
HUGGG
AH
Aah...
FWA

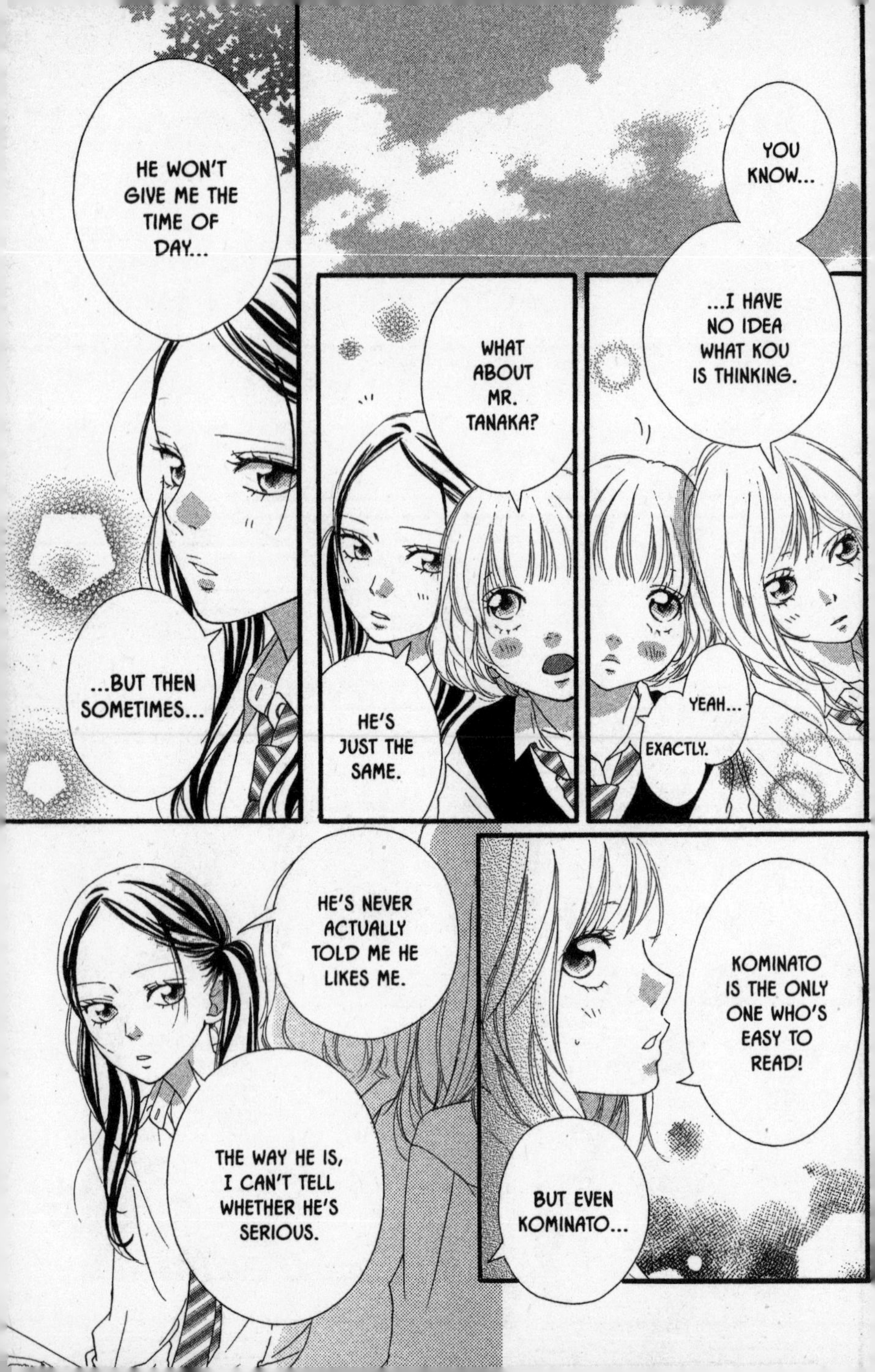
YOU KNOW...
...I HAVE NO IDEA WHAT KOU IS THINKING.
YEAH... EXACTLY.
WHAT ABOUT MR. TANAKA?
HE'S JUST THE SAME.
HE WON'T GIVE ME THE TIME OF DAY...
...BUT THEN SOMETIMES...
KOMINATO IS THE ONLY ONE WHO'S EASY TO READ!
BUT EVEN KOMINATO...
HE'S NEVER ACTUALLY TOLD ME HE LIKES ME.
THE WAY HE IS, I CAN'T TELL WHETHER HE'S SERIOUS.

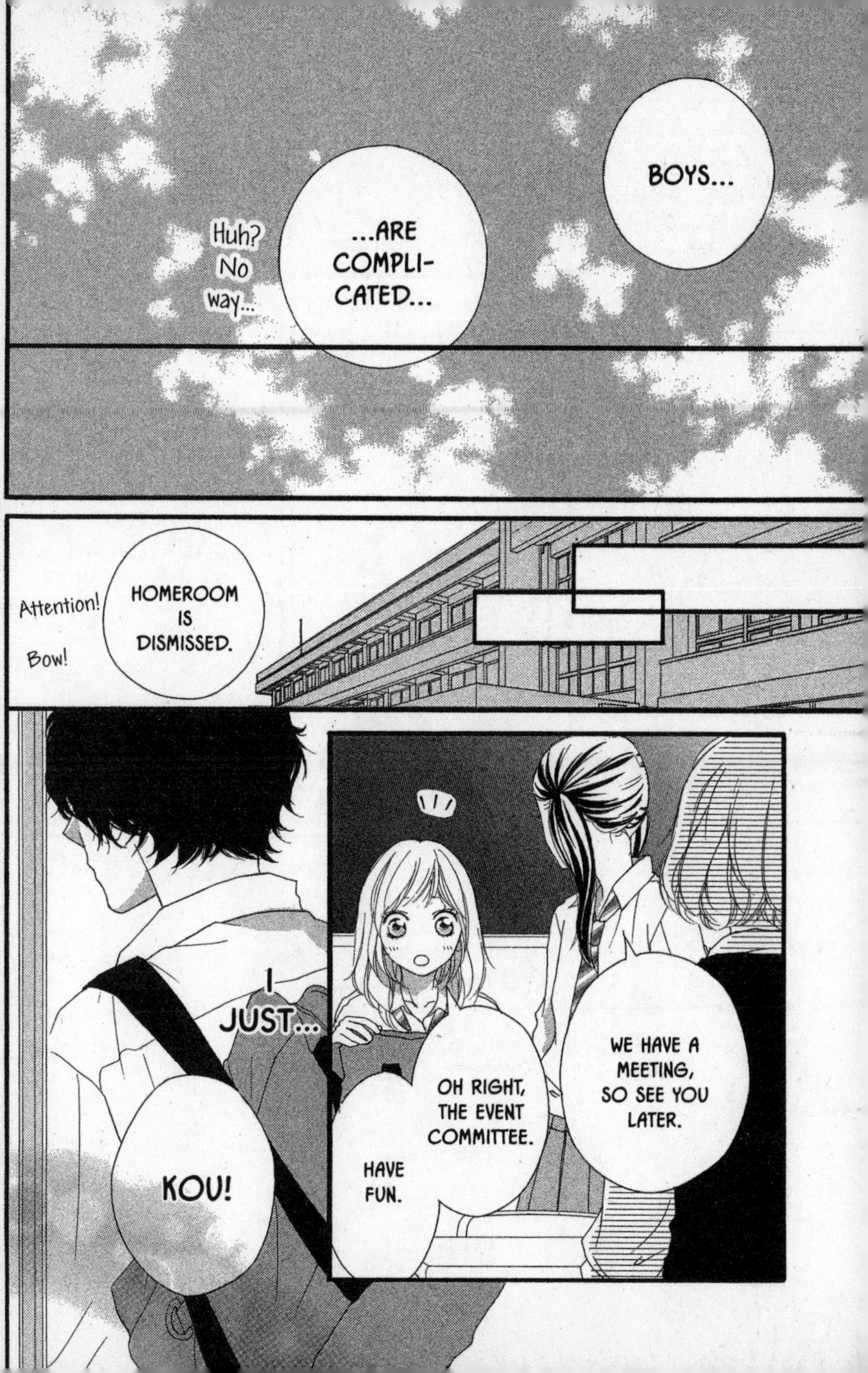
BOYS...
...ARE COMPLI-CATED...
Huh? No way...
HOMEROOM IS DISMISSED.
Attention!
Bow!
WE HAVE A MEETING, SO SEE YOU LATER.
OH RIGHT, THE EVENT COMMITTEE.
HAVE FUN.
I JUST...
KOU!

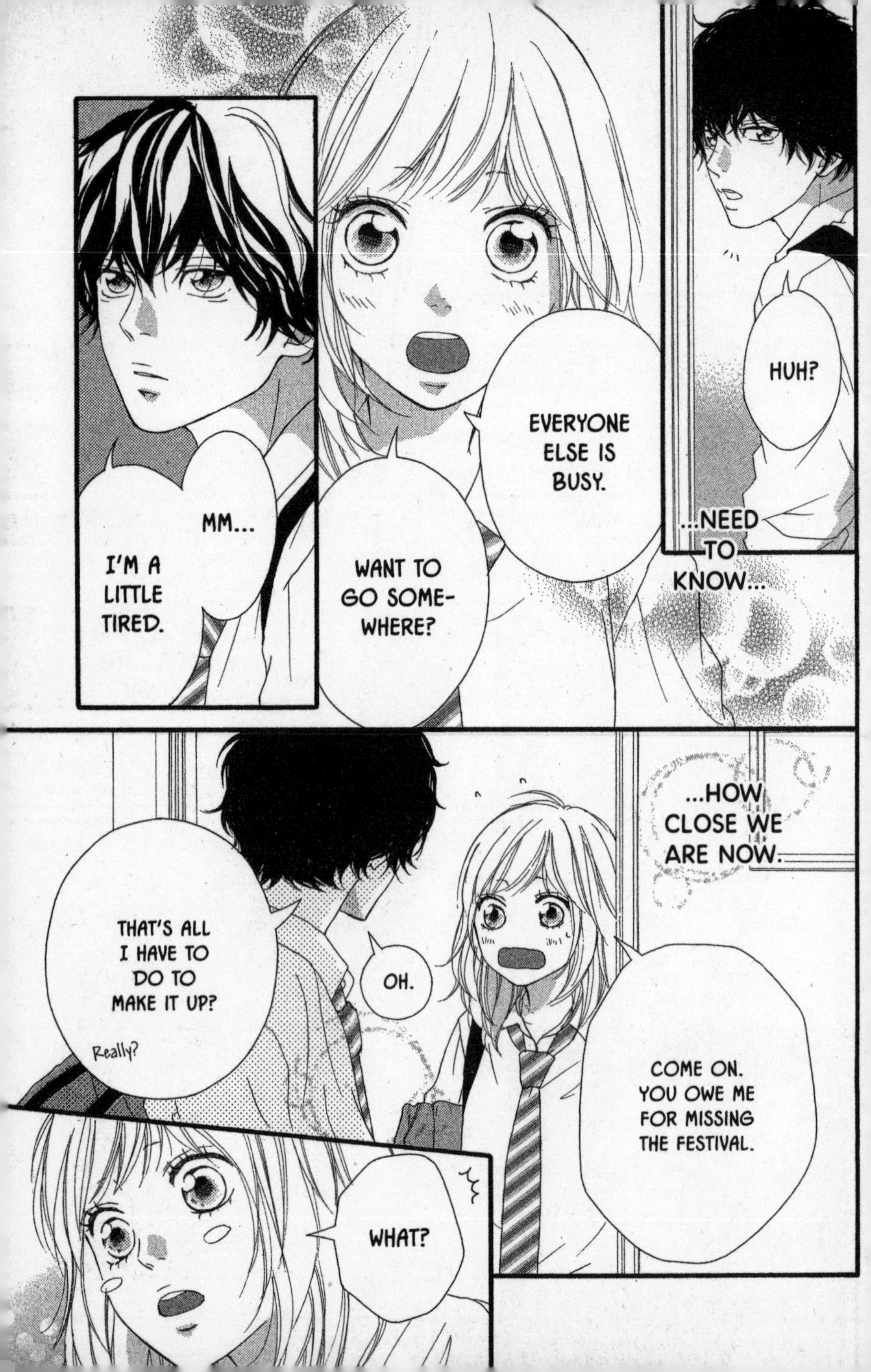
HUH?
...NEED TO KNOW...
EVERYONE ELSE IS BUSY.
WANT TO GO SOME-WHERE?
MM...
I'M A LITTLE TIRED.
...HOW CLOSE WE ARE NOW.
COME ON. YOU OWE ME FOR MISSING THE FESTIVAL.
OH.
THAT'S ALL I HAVE TO DO TO MAKE IT UP?
Really?
WHAT?

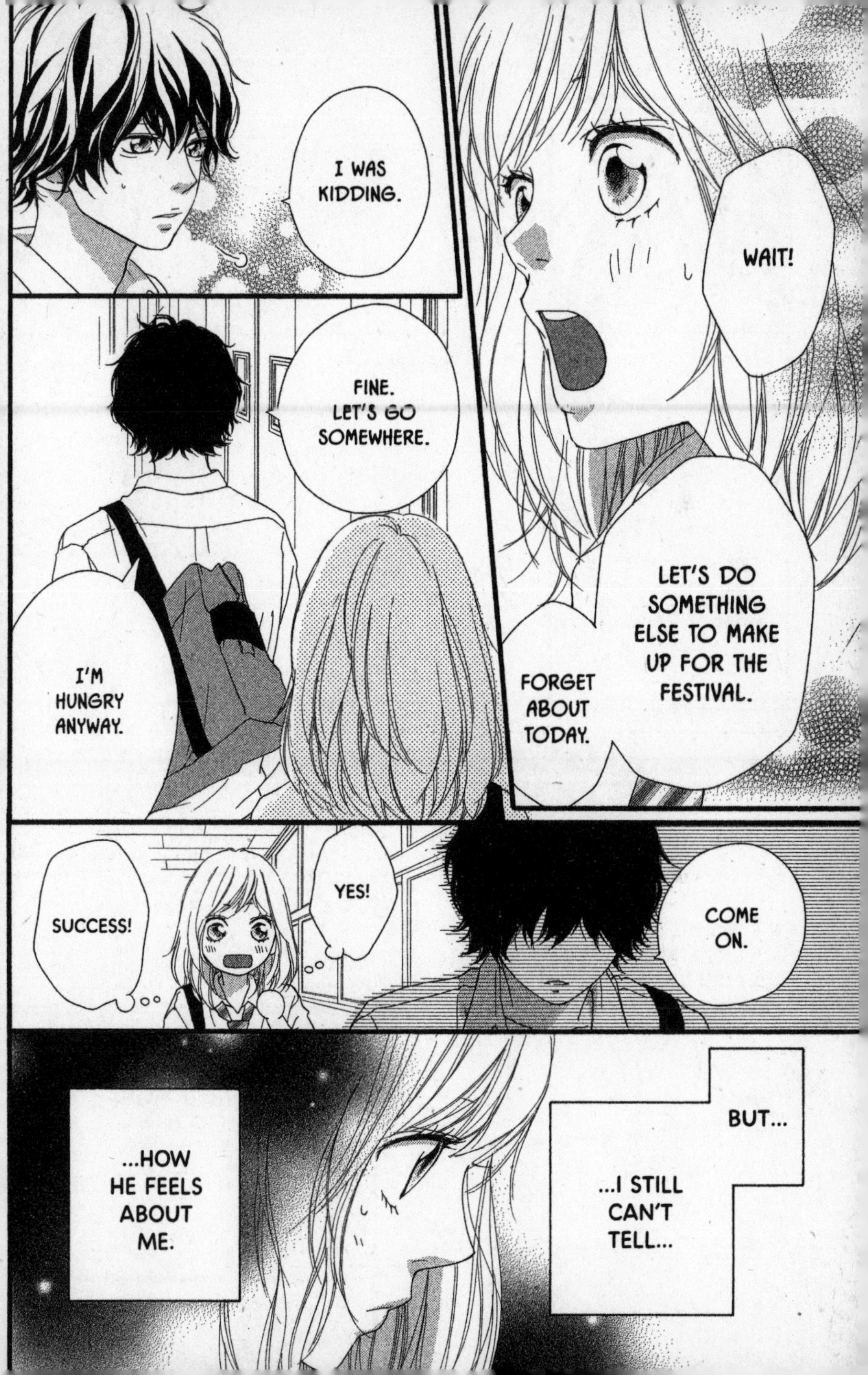
WAIT!
LET'S DO SOMETHING ELSE TO MAKE UP FOR THE FESTIVAL.
FORGET ABOUT TODAY.
I WAS KIDDING.
FINE. LET'S GO SOMEWHERE.
I'M HUNGRY ANYWAY.
COME ON.
YES!
SUCCESS!
BUT...
...I STILL CAN'T TELL...
...HOW HE FEELS ABOUT ME.

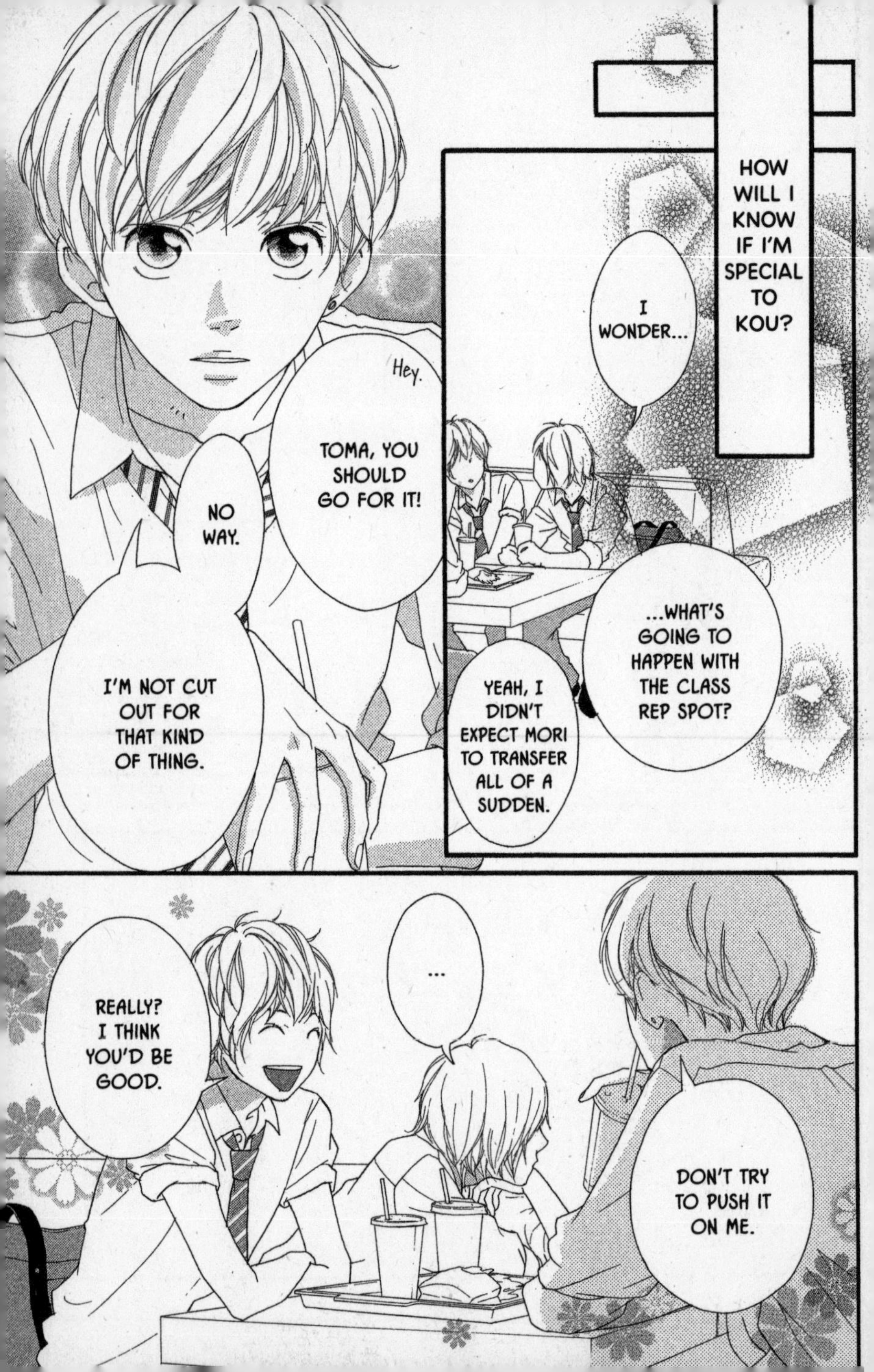
HOW WILL I KNOW IF I'M SPECIAL TO KOU?
I WONDER...
...WHAT'S GOING TO HAPPEN WITH THE CLASS REP SPOT?
YEAH, I DIDN'T EXPECT MORI TO TRANSFER ALL OF A SUDDEN.
Hey.
TOMA, YOU SHOULD GO FOR IT!
NO WAY.
I'M NOT CUT OUT FOR THAT KIND OF THING.
DON'T TRY TO PUSH IT ON ME.
...
REALLY? I THINK YOU'D BE GOOD.

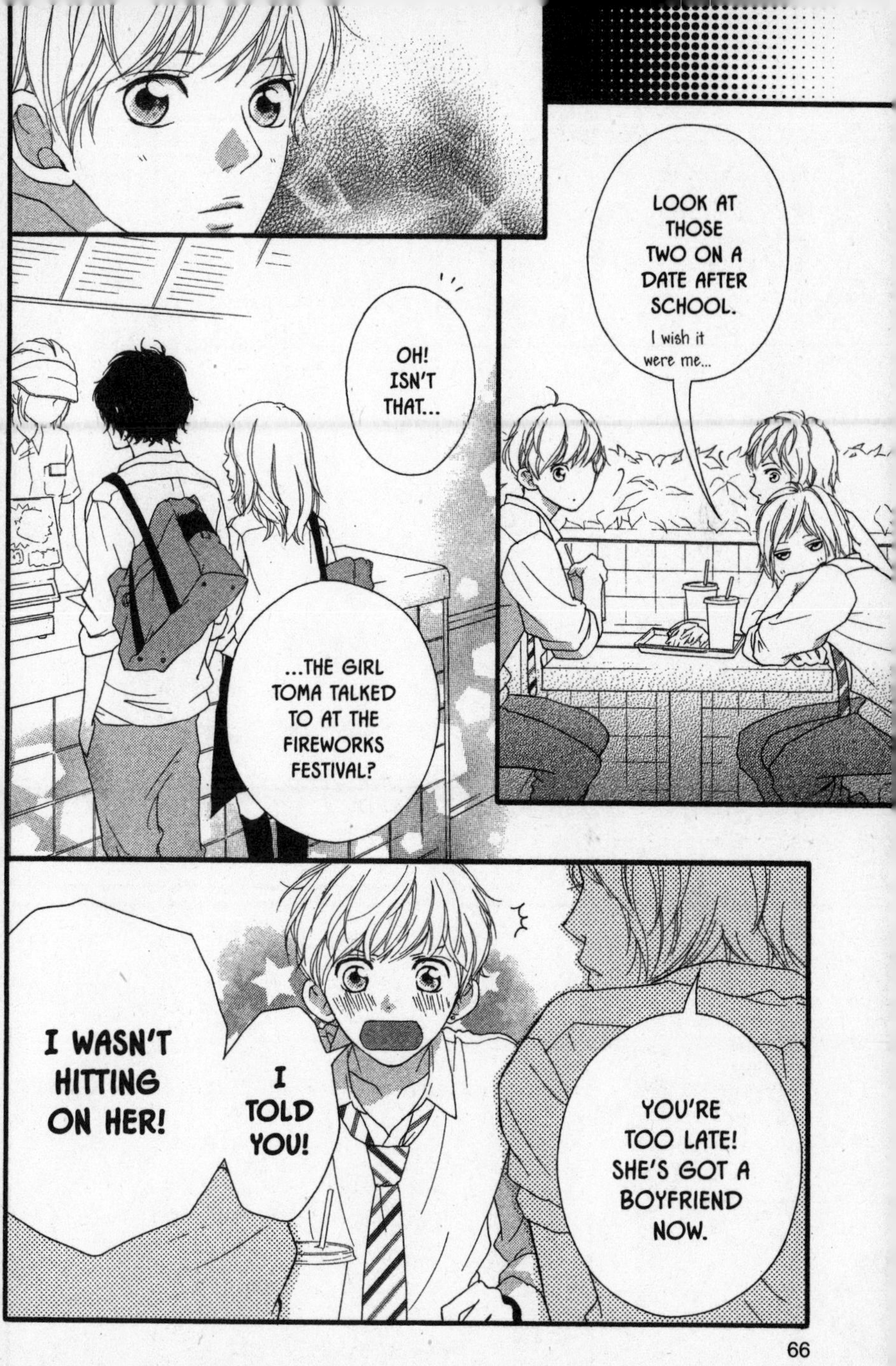
LOOK AT THOSE TWO ON A DATE AFTER SCHOOL.
I wish it were me...
OH! ISN'T THAT...
...THE GIRL TOMA TALKED TO AT THE FIREWORKS FESTIVAL?
YOU'RE TOO LATE! SHE'S GOT A BOYFRIEND NOW.
I TOLD YOU!
I WASN'T HITTING ON HER!

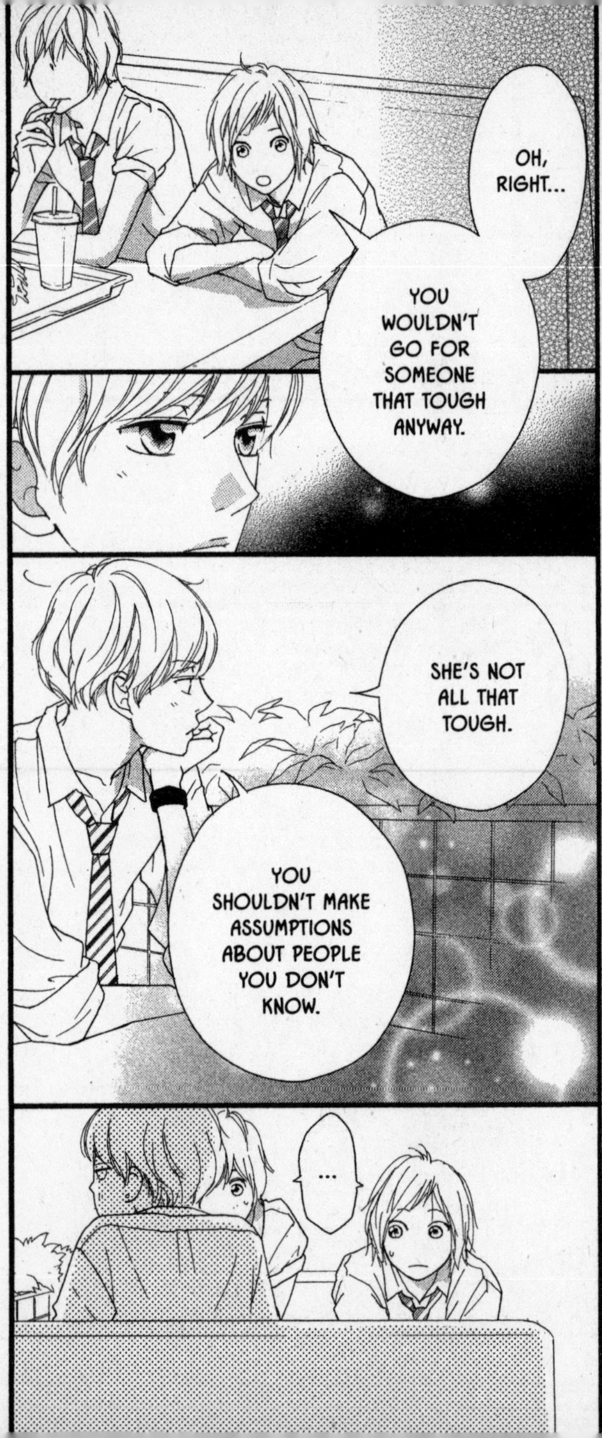
OH, RIGHT...
YOU WOULDN'T GO FOR SOMEONE THAT TOUGH ANYWAY.
SHE'S NOT ALL THAT TOUGH.
YOU SHOULDN'T MAKE ASSUMPTIONS ABOUT PEOPLE YOU DON'T KNOW.
...

Hello to all those in the Towelket Club! And hello to everyone who's not in the Towelket Club! Though I'd always thought of myself as a towelket fanatic, rather than a towel fanatic, it seems that it's not just the towelket that brings me joy—it's also towel fabric. I recently bought new pillows and upgraded the pillowcases to towel fabric. I have to say, having a towel cover on top of a fluffy pillow is absolutely divine. I also acquired a body pillow not long ago and wrapped one of my regular towelkets around it. It is divine. My editor gifted me an eye mask, and the side that touches my eyelids is made of towel material—also divine. It's as if the towel fabric knew all along that it would bring me comfort... I am in love.

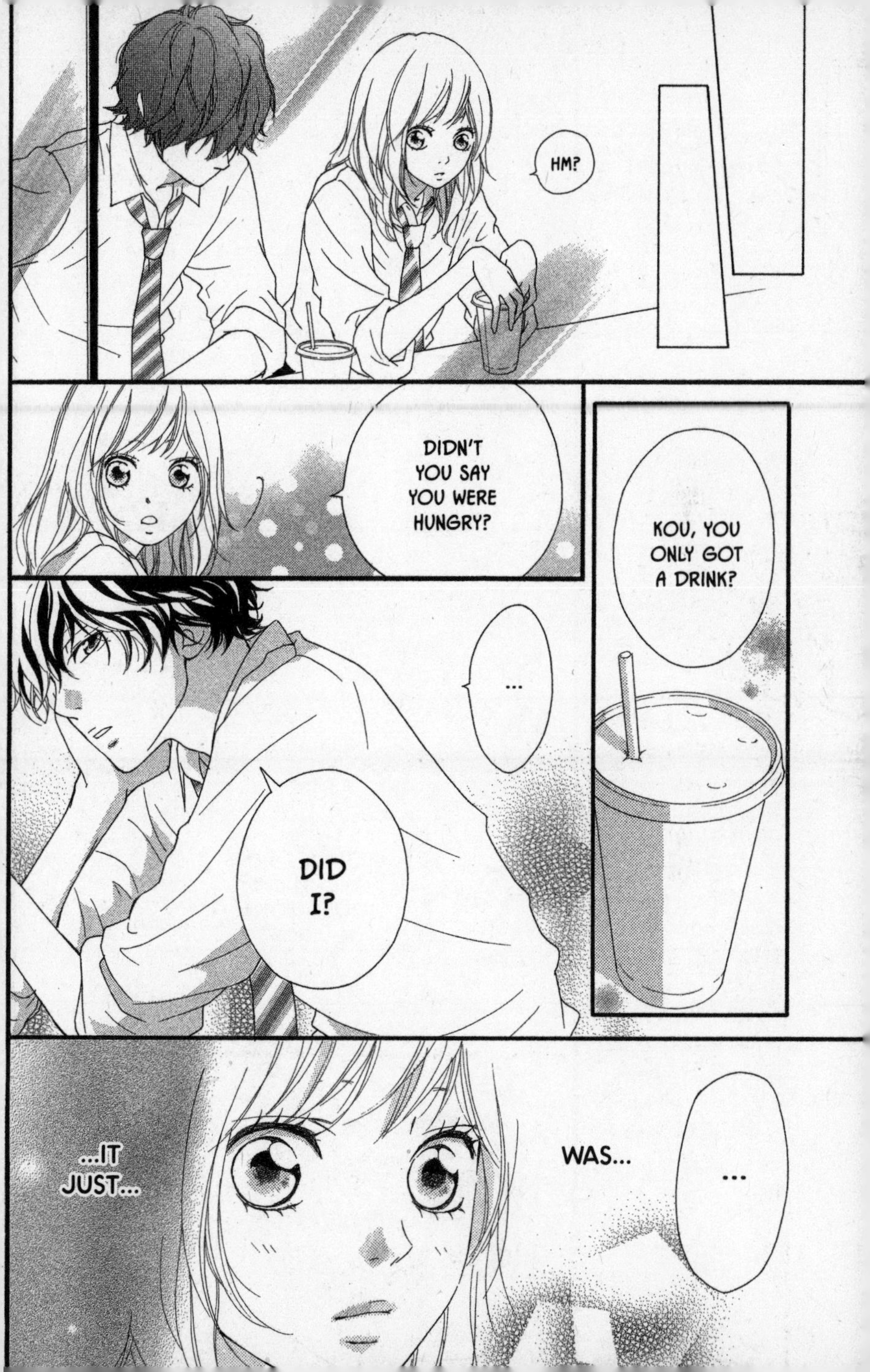
HM?
KOU, YOU ONLY GOT A DRINK?
DIDN'T YOU SAY YOU WERE HUNGRY?
...
DID I?
...
WAS...
...IT JUST...

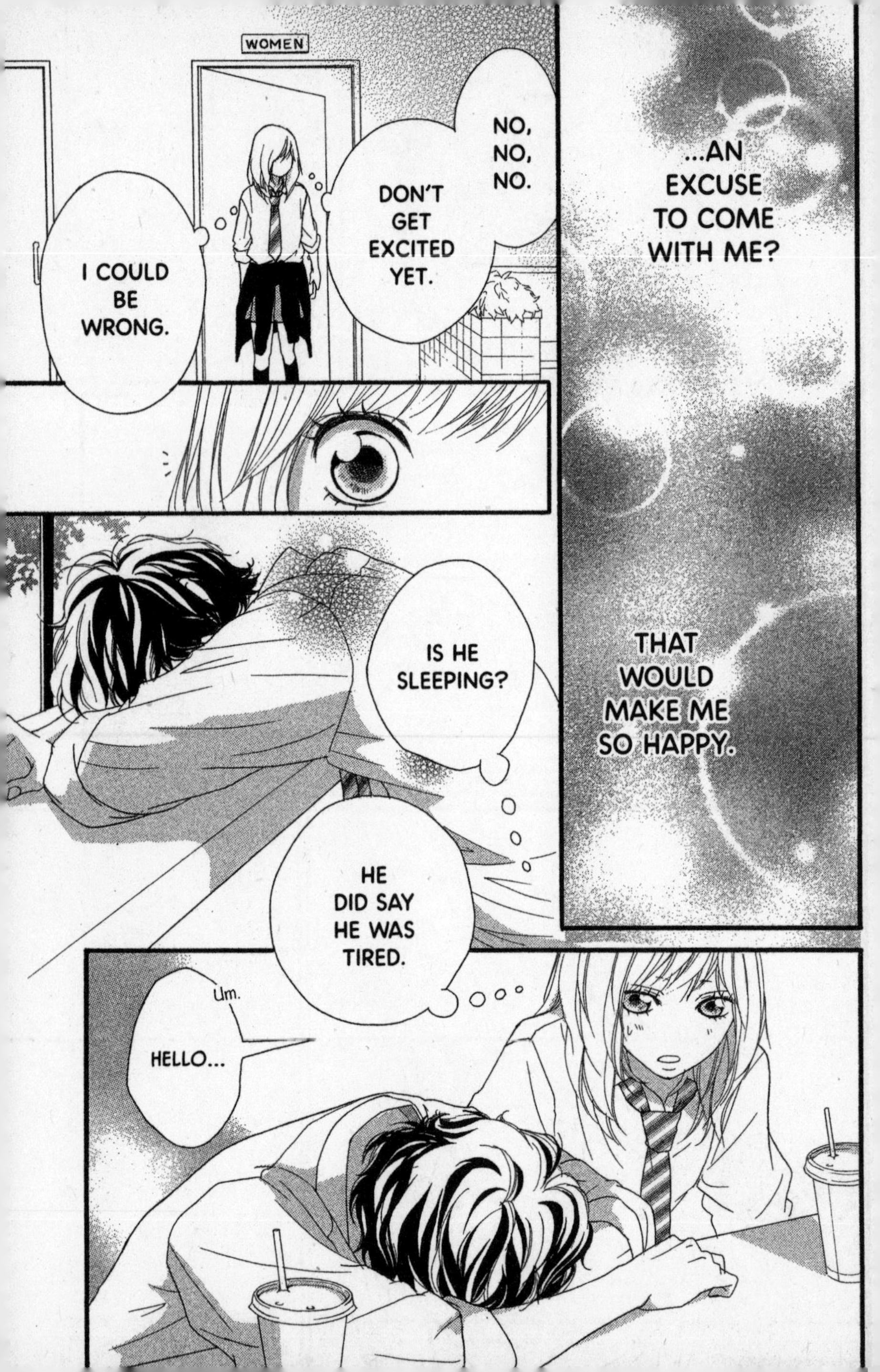
...AN EXCUSE TO COME WITH ME?
THAT WOULD MAKE ME SO HAPPY.
WOMEN
NO, NO, NO.
DON'T GET EXCITED YET.
I COULD BE WRONG.
IS HE SLEEPING?
HE DID SAY HE WAS TIRED.
Um.
HELLO...

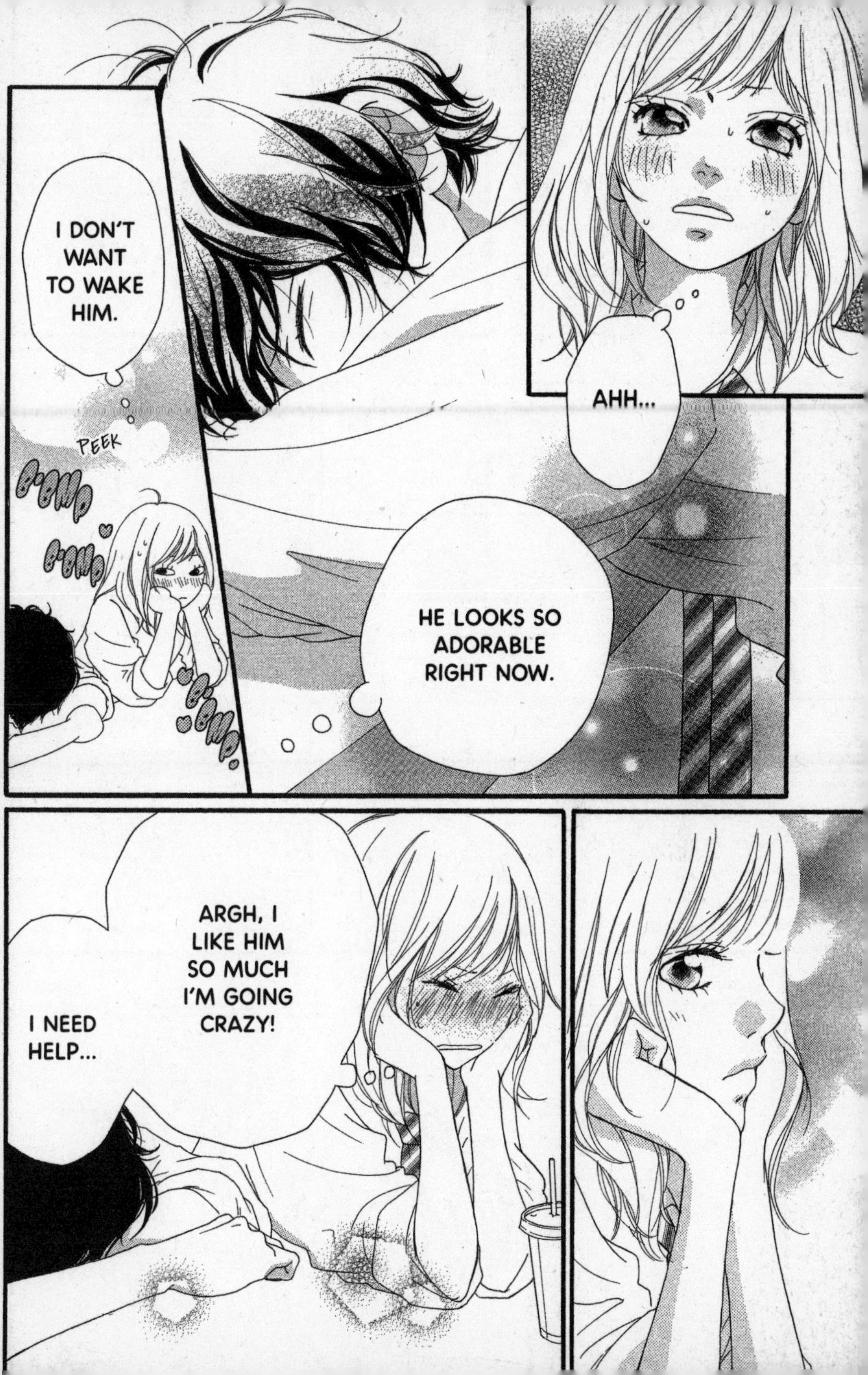
AHH...
HE LOOKS SO ADORABLE RIGHT NOW.
I DON'T WANT TO WAKE HIM.
PEEK
ARGH, I LIKE HIM SO MUCH I'M GOING CRAZY!
I NEED HELP...

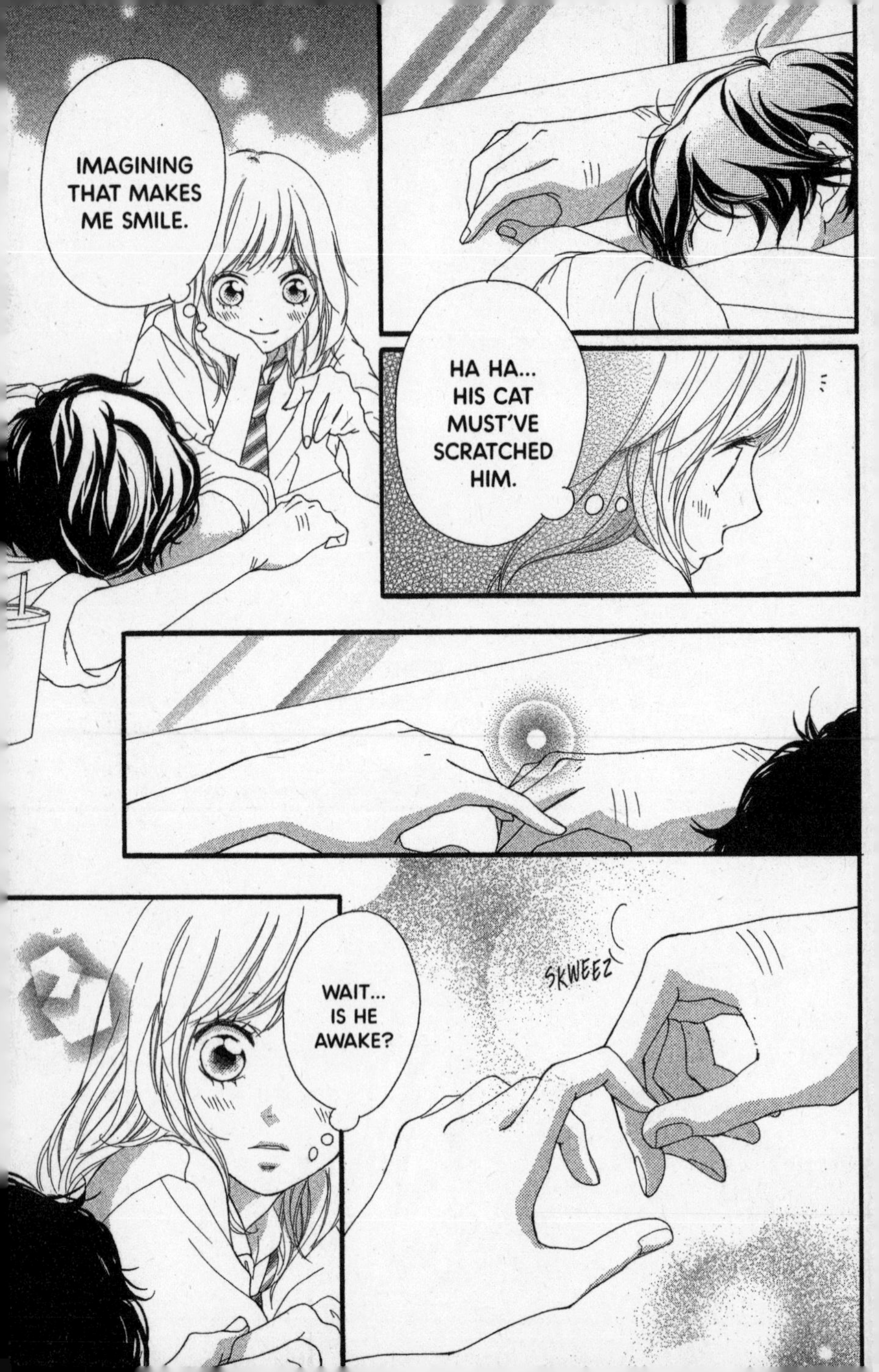
HA HA... HIS CAT MUST'VE SCRATCHED HIM.
IMAGINING THAT MAKES ME SMILE.
SKWEEZ
WAIT... IS HE AWAKE?

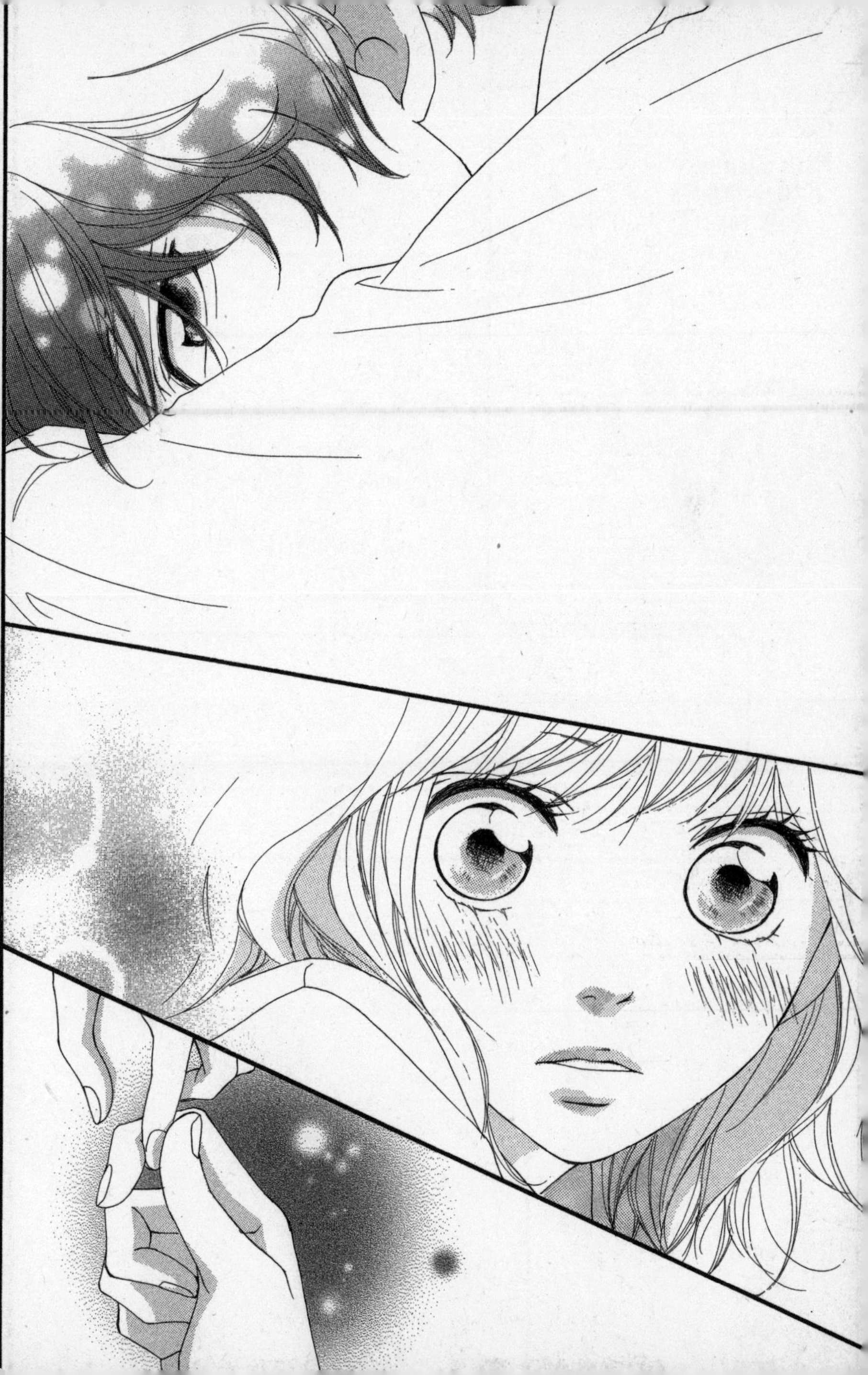

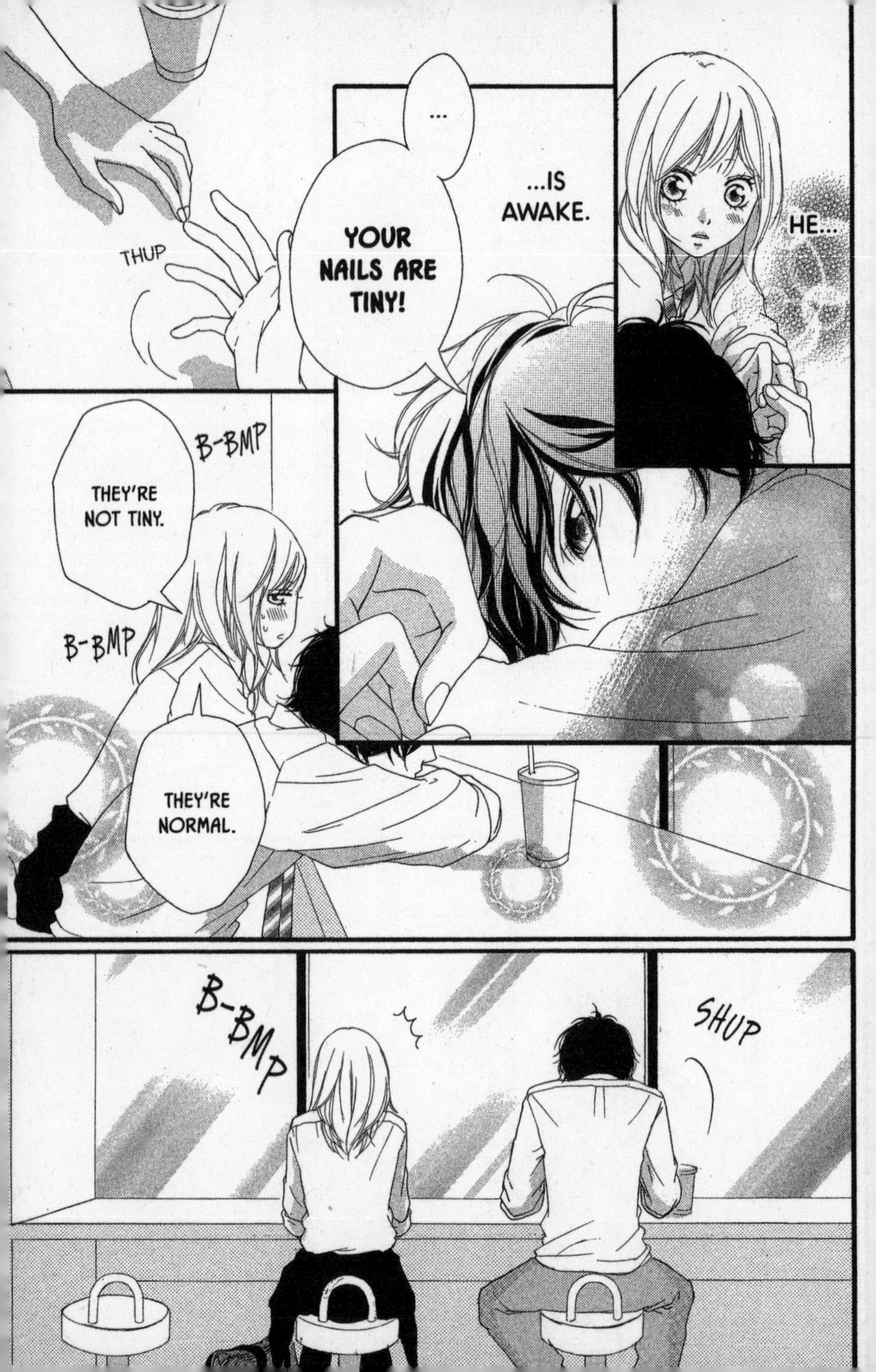
HE...
...IS AWAKE.
...
YOUR NAILS ARE TINY!
THUP
B-BMP
THEY'RE NOT TINY.
B-BMP
THEY'RE NORMAL.
SHUP
B-BMP

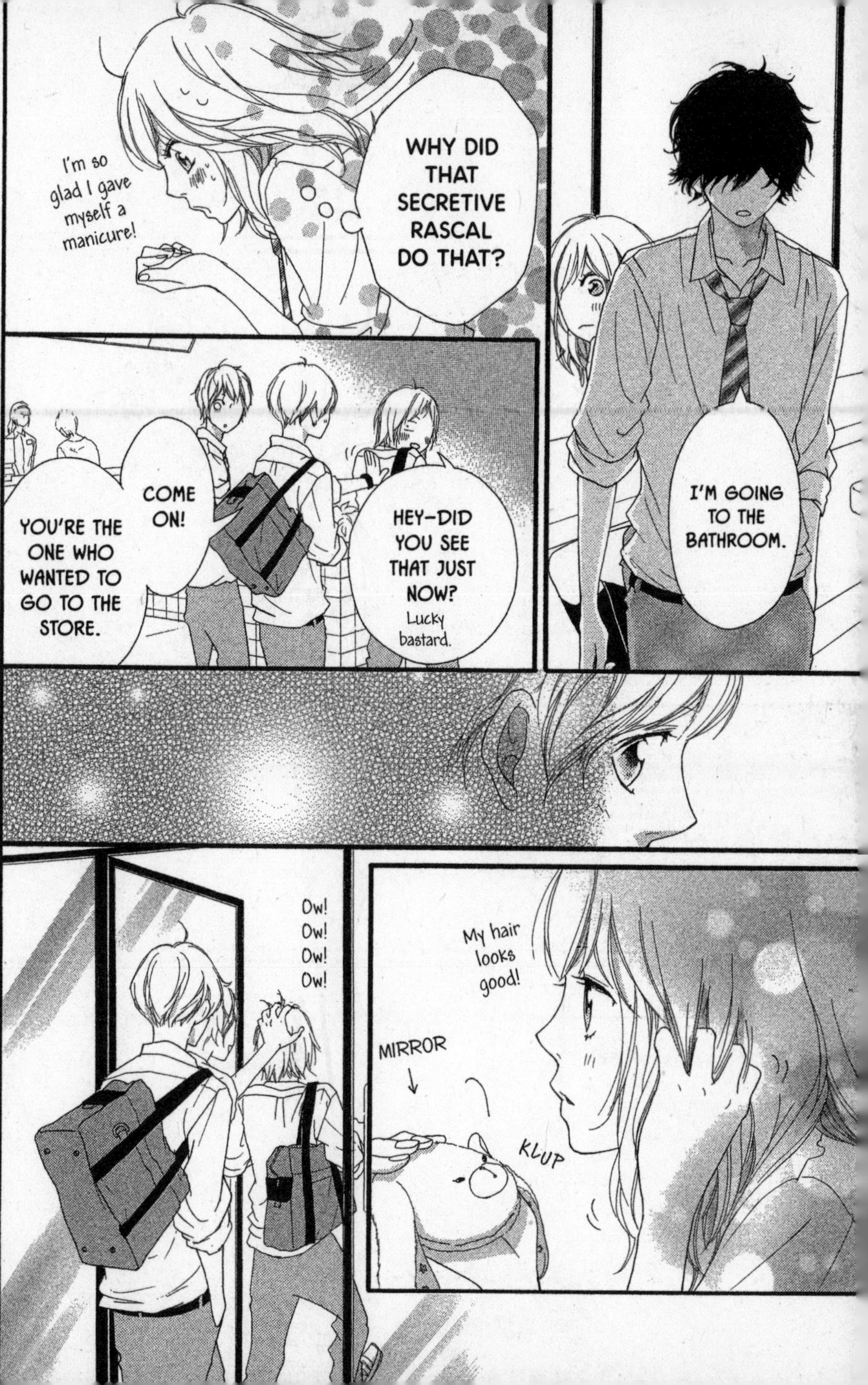
I'M GOING TO THE BATHROOM.
WHY DID THAT SECRETIVE RASCAL DO THAT?
I'm so glad I gave myself a manicure!
HEY-DID YOU SEE THAT JUST NOW?
Lucky bastard.
COME ON!
YOU'RE THE ONE WHO WANTED TO GO TO THE STORE.
My hair looks good!
MIRROR
KLUP
Ow! Ow! Ow! Ow!

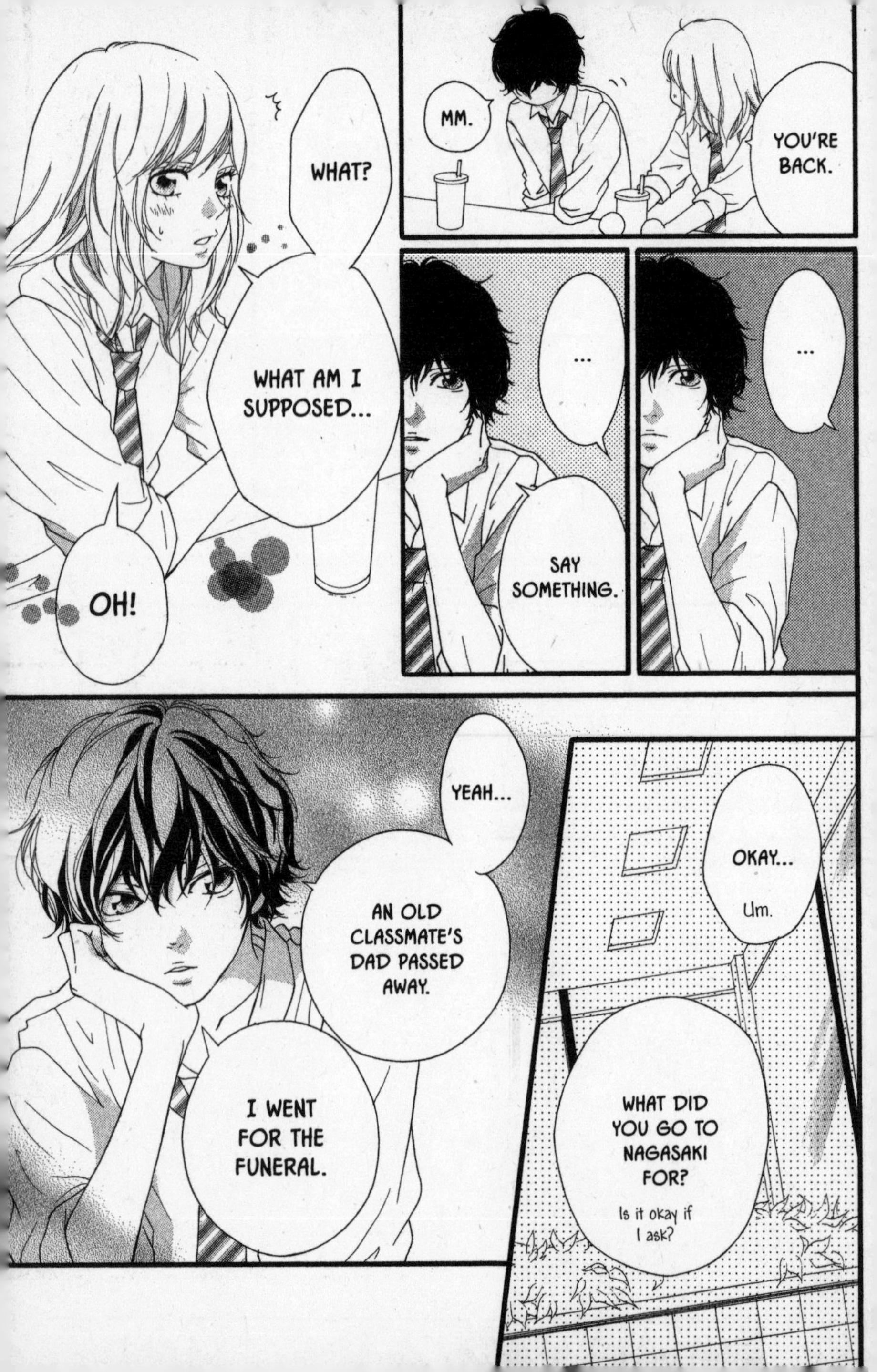
YOU'RE BACK.
MM.
...
...
SAY SOMETHING.
WHAT?
WHAT AM I SUPPOSED...
OH!
OKAY...
Um.
WHAT DID YOU GO TO NAGASAKI FOR?
Is it okay if I ask?
YEAH...
AN OLD CLASSMATE'S DAD PASSED AWAY.
I WENT FOR THE FUNERAL.

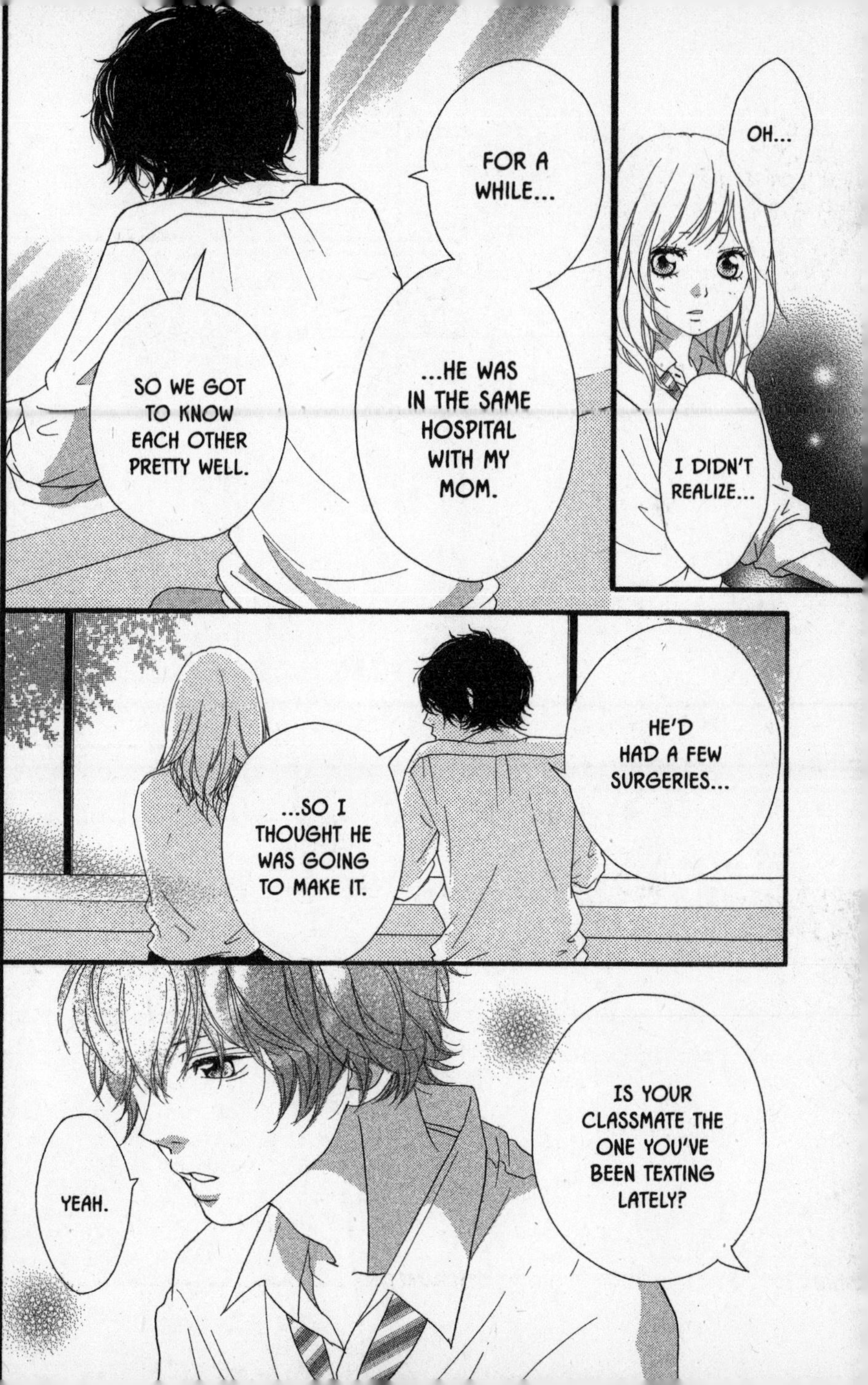
OH...
I DIDN'T REALIZE...
FOR A WHILE...
...HE WAS IN THE SAME HOSPITAL WITH MY MOM.
SO WE GOT TO KNOW EACH OTHER PRETTY WELL.
HE'D HAD A FEW SURGERIES...
...SO I THOUGHT HE WAS GOING TO MAKE IT.
IS YOUR CLASSMATE THE ONE YOU'VE BEEN TEXTING LATELY?
YEAH.

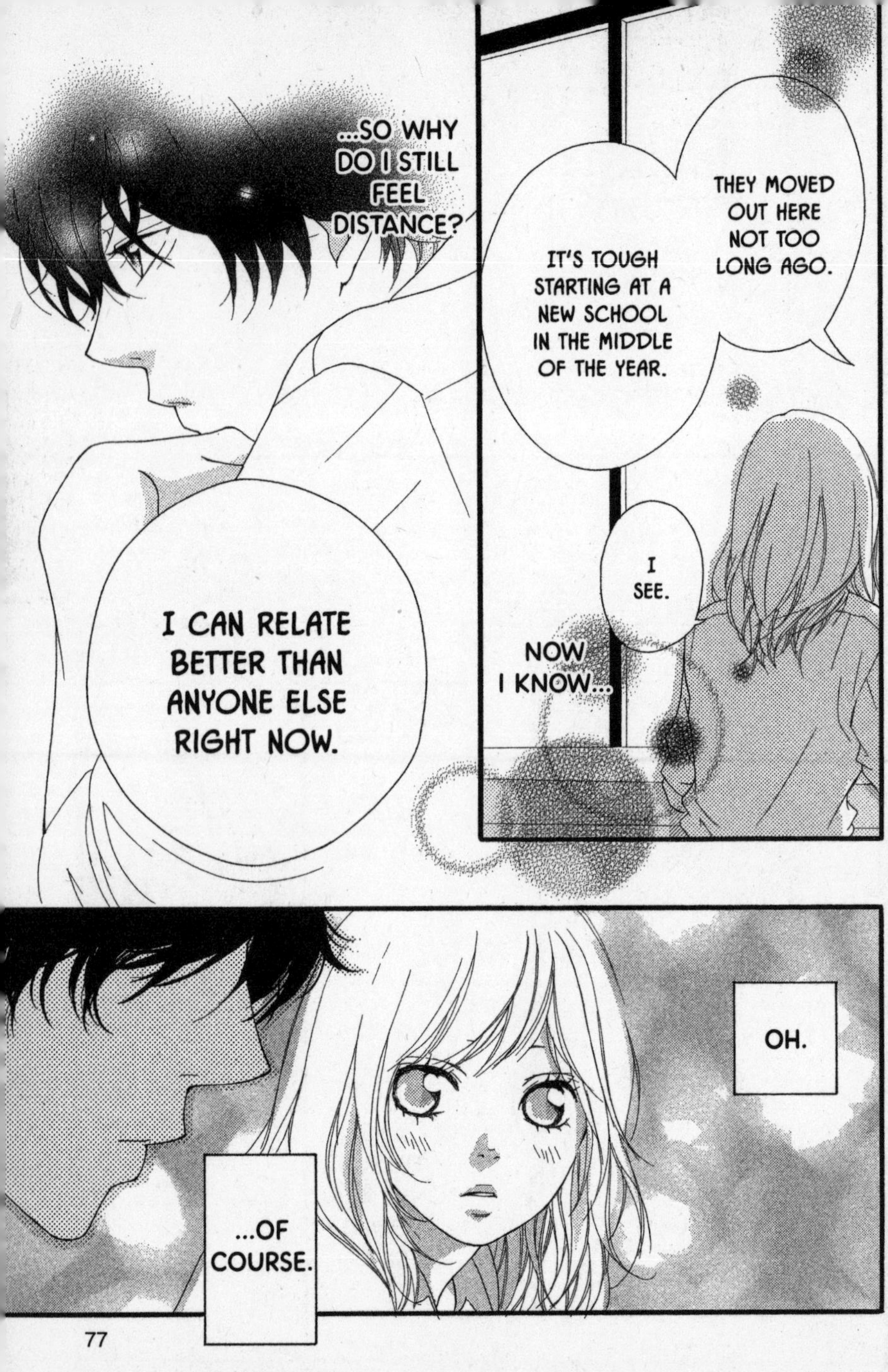
THEY MOVED OUT HERE NOT TOO LONG AGO.
IT'S TOUGH STARTING AT A NEW SCHOOL IN THE MIDDLE OF THE YEAR.
I SEE.
NOW I KNOW...
...SO WHY DO I STILL FEEL DISTANCE?
I CAN RELATE BETTER THAN ANYONE ELSE RIGHT NOW.
OH.
...OF COURSE.

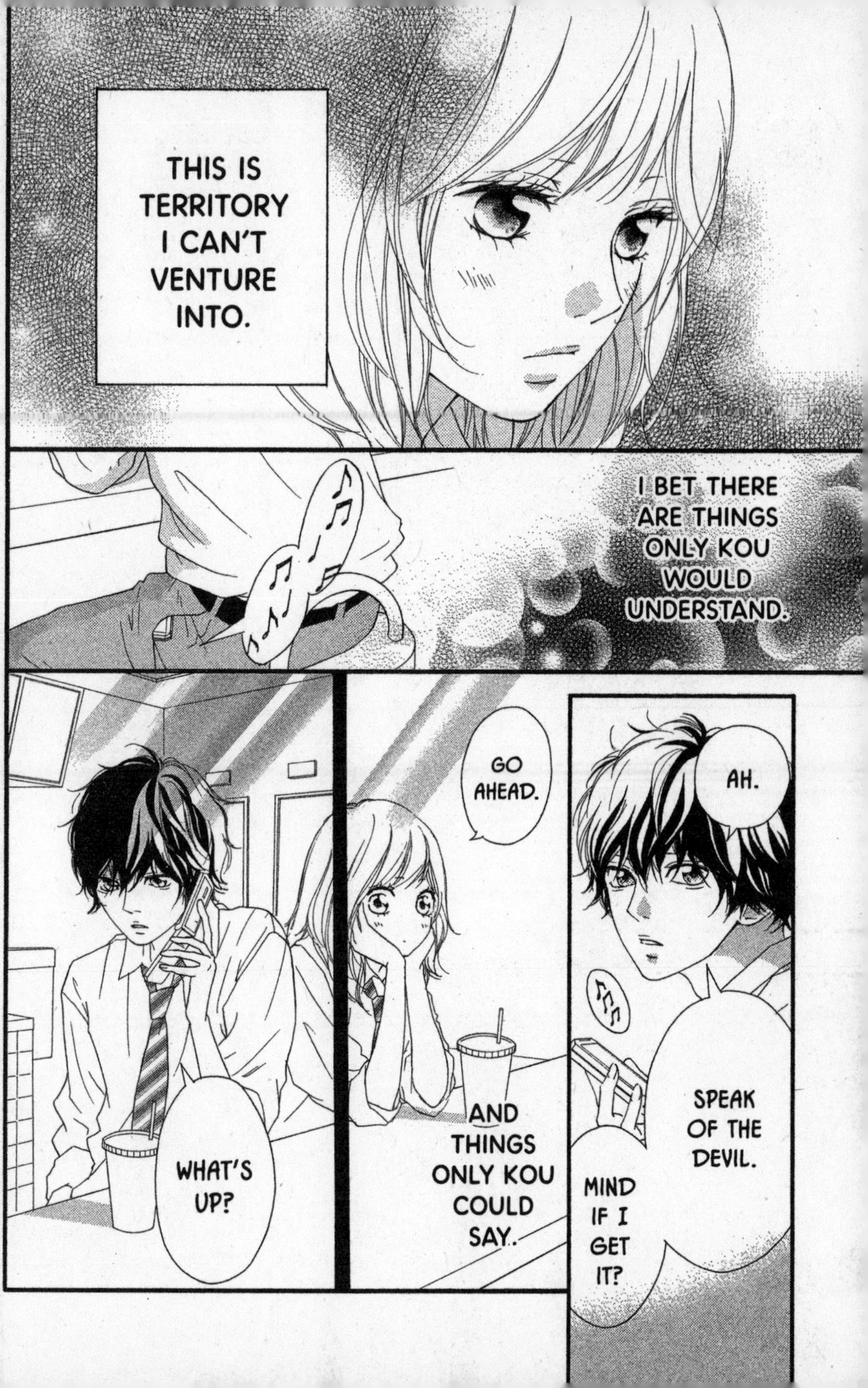
THIS IS TERRITORY I CAN'T VENTURE INTO.
I BET THERE ARE THINGS ONLY KOU WOULD UNDERSTAND.
AH.
SPEAK OF THE DEVIL.
MIND IF I GET IT?
GO AHEAD.
AND THINGS ONLY KOU COULD SAY.
WHAT'S UP?

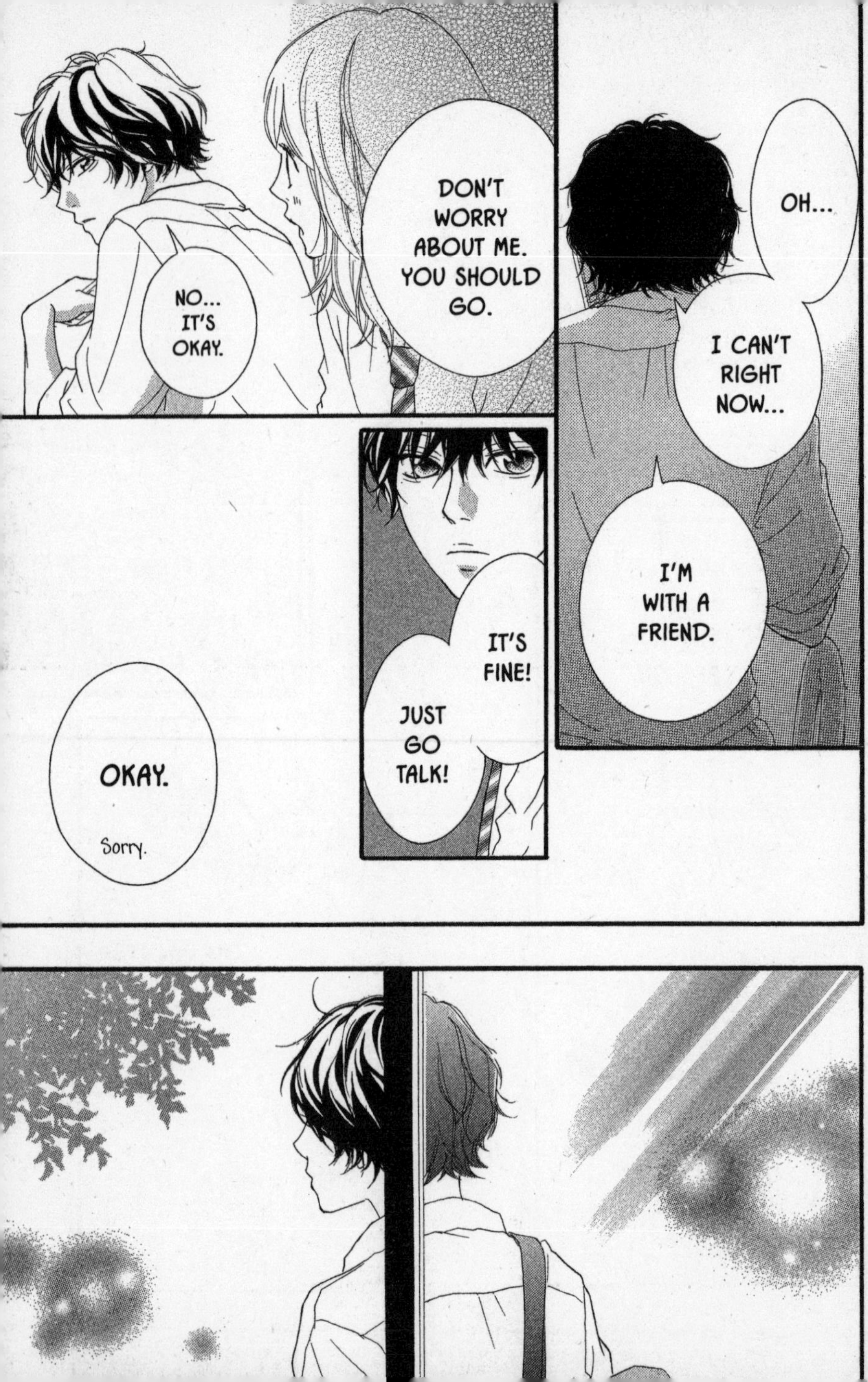
OH...
I CAN'T RIGHT NOW...
I'M WITH A FRIEND.
DON'T WORRY ABOUT ME. YOU SHOULD GO.
NO... IT'S OKAY.
IT'S FINE!
JUST GO TALK!
OKAY.
Sorry.

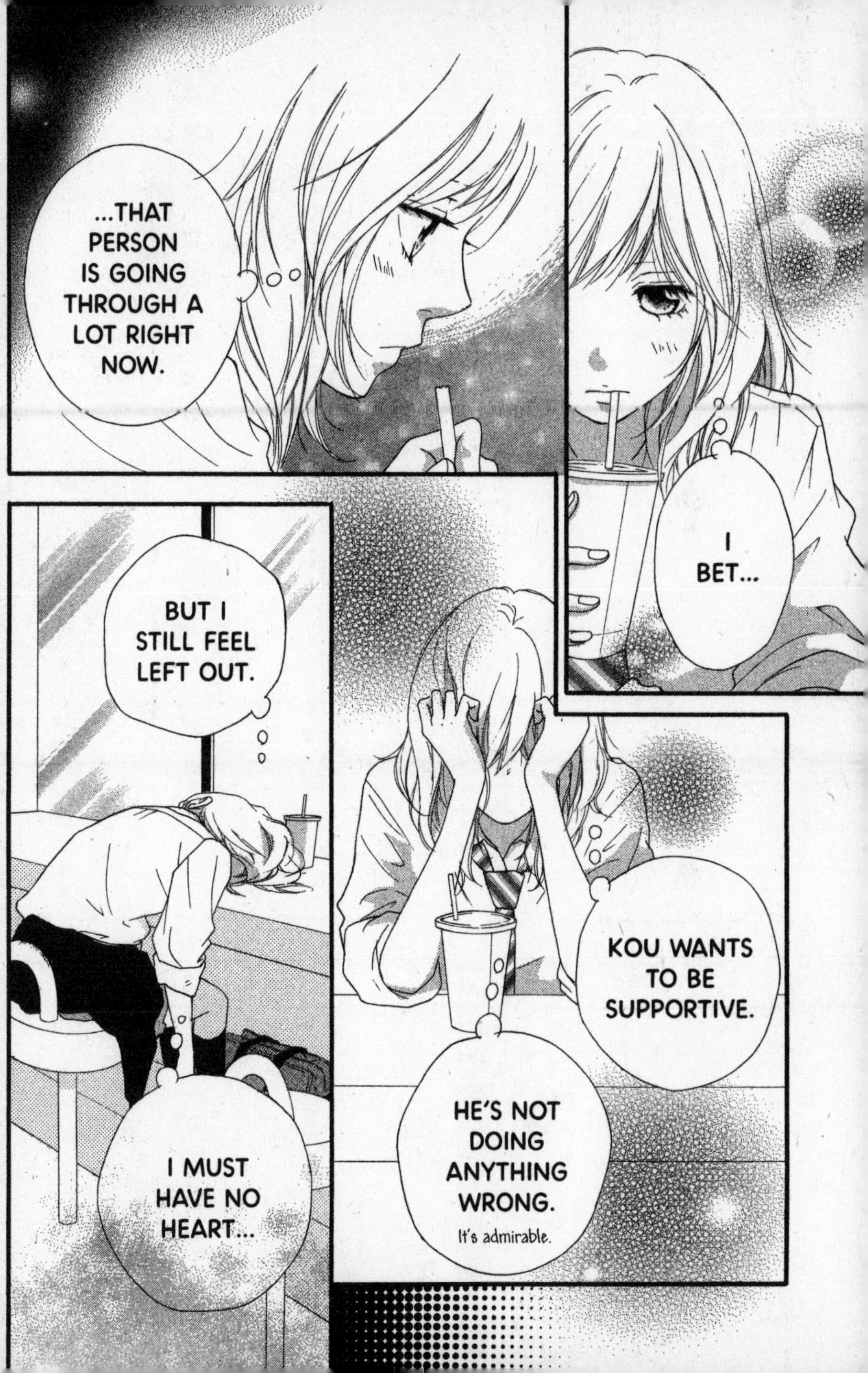
...THAT PERSON IS GOING THROUGH A LOT RIGHT NOW.
I BET...
KOU WANTS TO BE SUPPORTIVE.
HE'S NOT DOING ANYTHING WRONG.
It's admirable.
BUT I STILL FEEL LEFT OUT.
I MUST HAVE NO HEART...

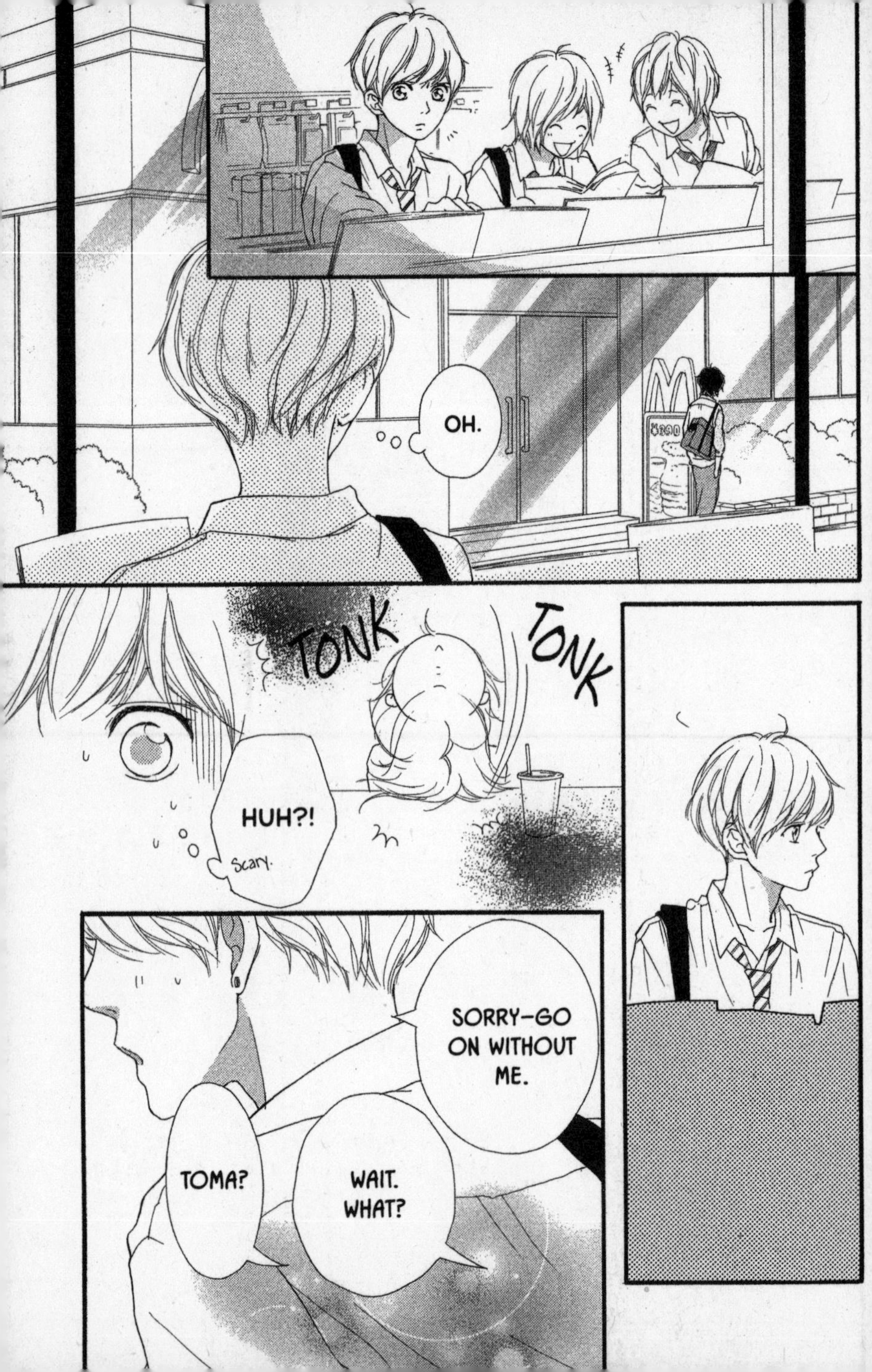
OH.
TONK
TONK
HUH?!
Scary.
SORRY—GO ON WITHOUT ME.
WAIT. WHAT?
TOMA?

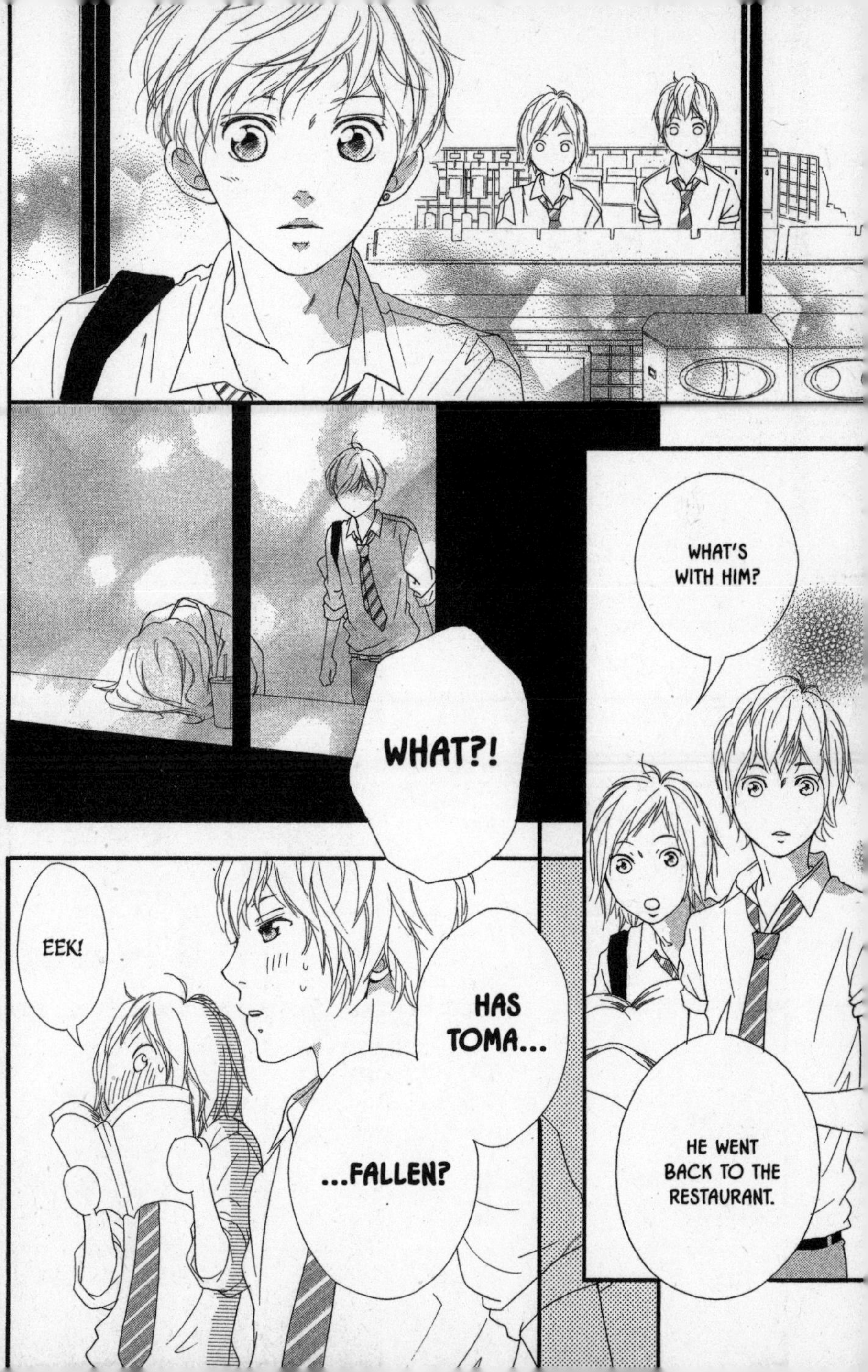
WHAT'S WITH HIM?
HE WENT BACK TO THE RESTAURANT.
WHAT?!
HAS TOMA...
...FALLEN?
EEK!

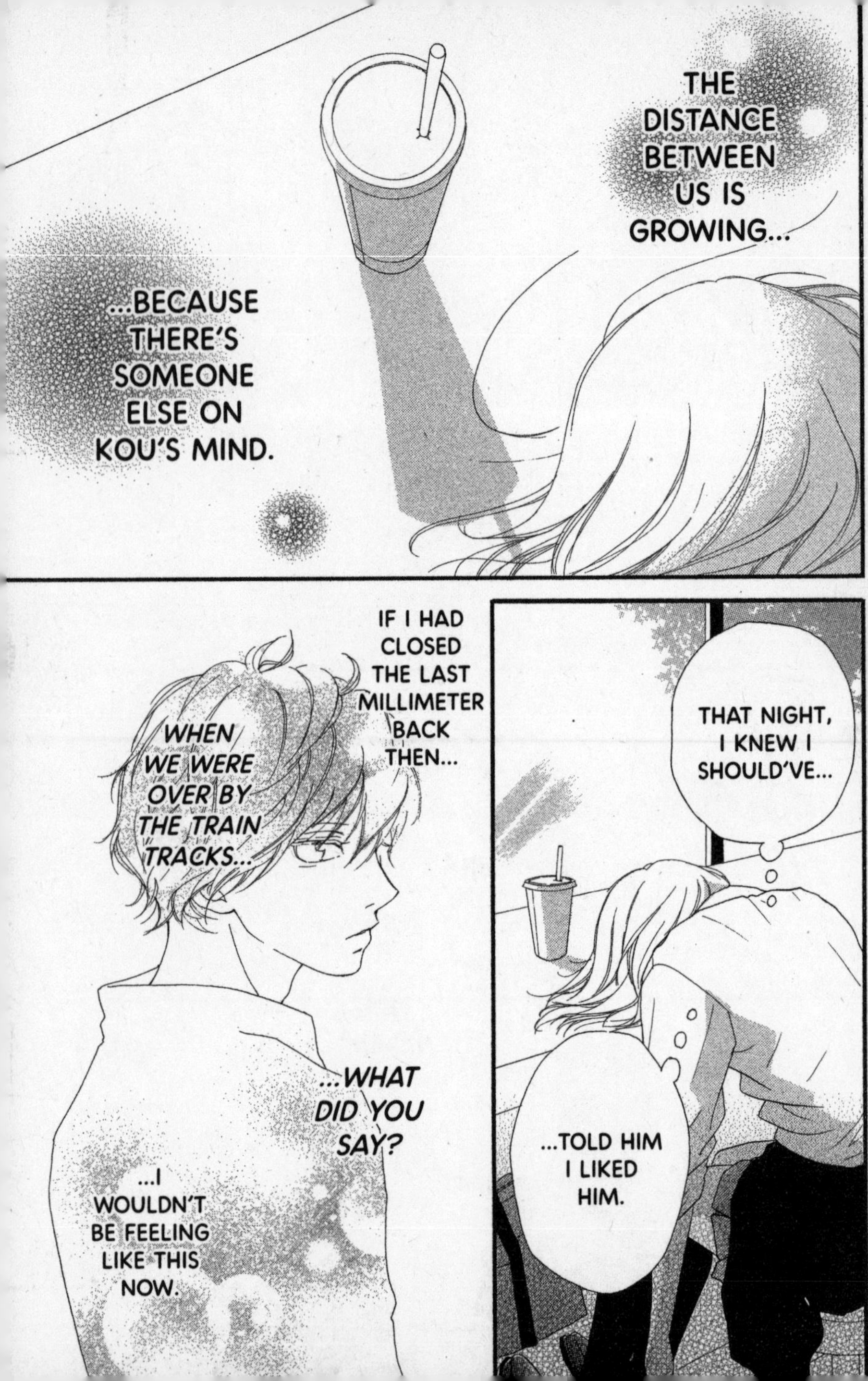
THE DISTANCE BETWEEN US IS GROWING...
...BECAUSE THERE'S SOMEONE ELSE ON KOU'S MIND.
THAT NIGHT, I KNEW I SHOULD'VE...
...TOLD HIM I LIKED HIM.
IF I HAD CLOSED THE LAST MILLIMETER BACK THEN...
WHEN WE WERE OVER BY THE TRAIN TRACKS...
...WHAT DID YOU SAY?
...I WOULDN'T BE FEELING LIKE THIS NOW.

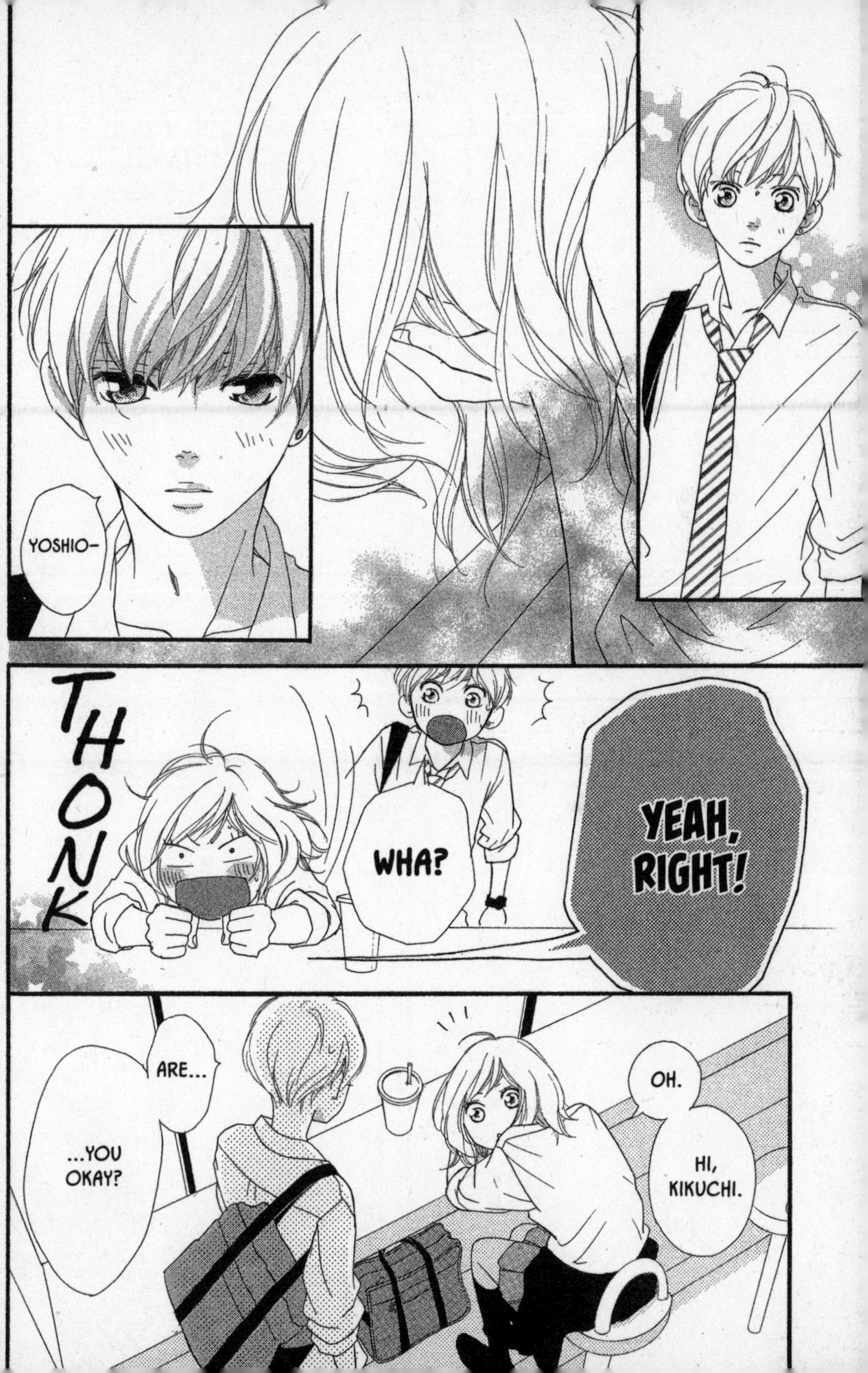
YOSHIO–
YEAH, RIGHT!
WHA?
THONK
OH.
HI, KIKUCHI.
ARE...
...YOU OKAY?

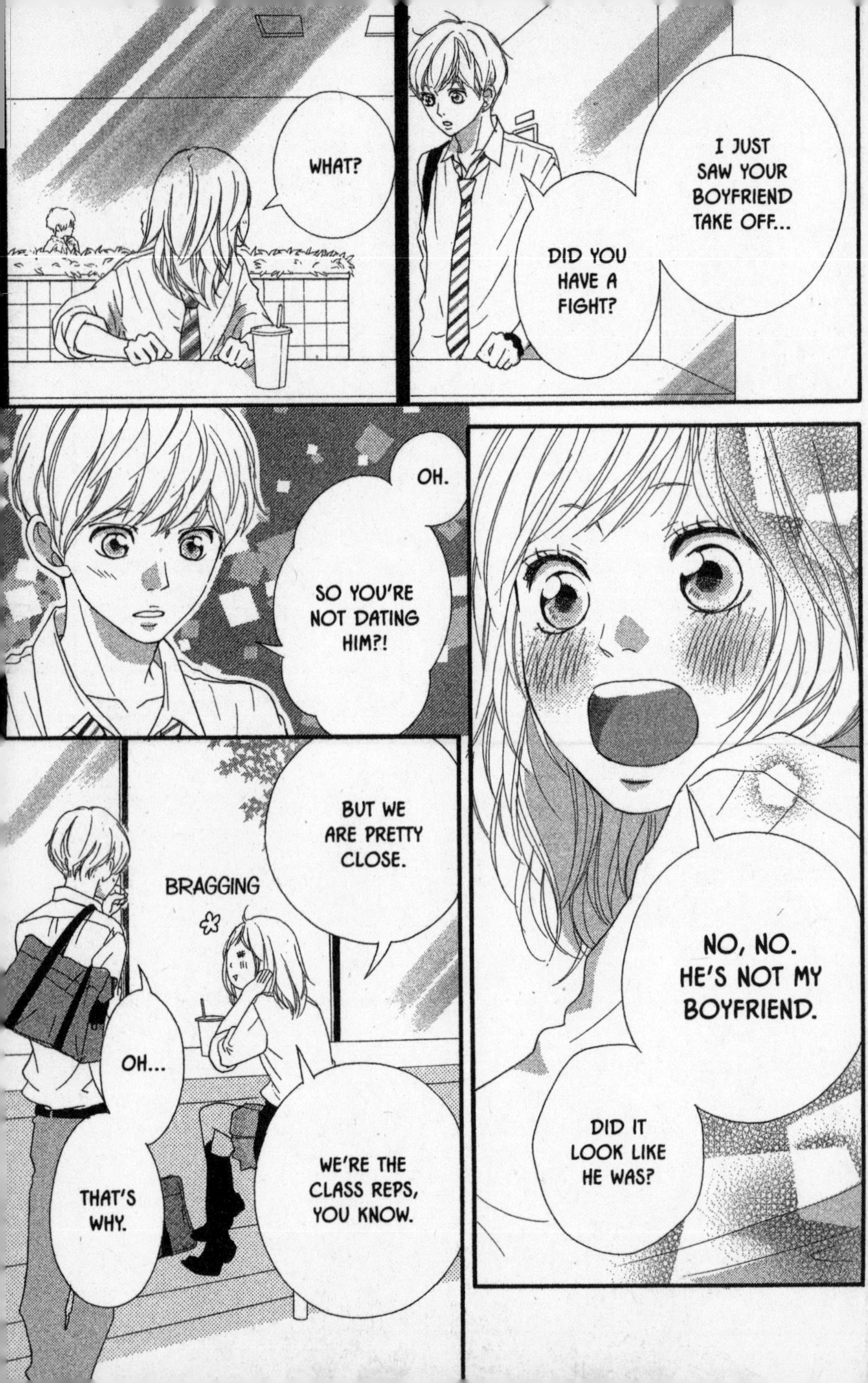
I JUST SAW YOUR BOYFRIEND TAKE OFF...
DID YOU HAVE A FIGHT?
WHAT?
NO, NO. HE'S NOT MY BOYFRIEND.
DID IT LOOK LIKE HE WAS?
OH.
SO YOU'RE NOT DATING HIM?!
BUT WE ARE PRETTY CLOSE.
BRAGGING
WE'RE THE CLASS REPS, YOU KNOW.
OH...
THAT'S WHY.

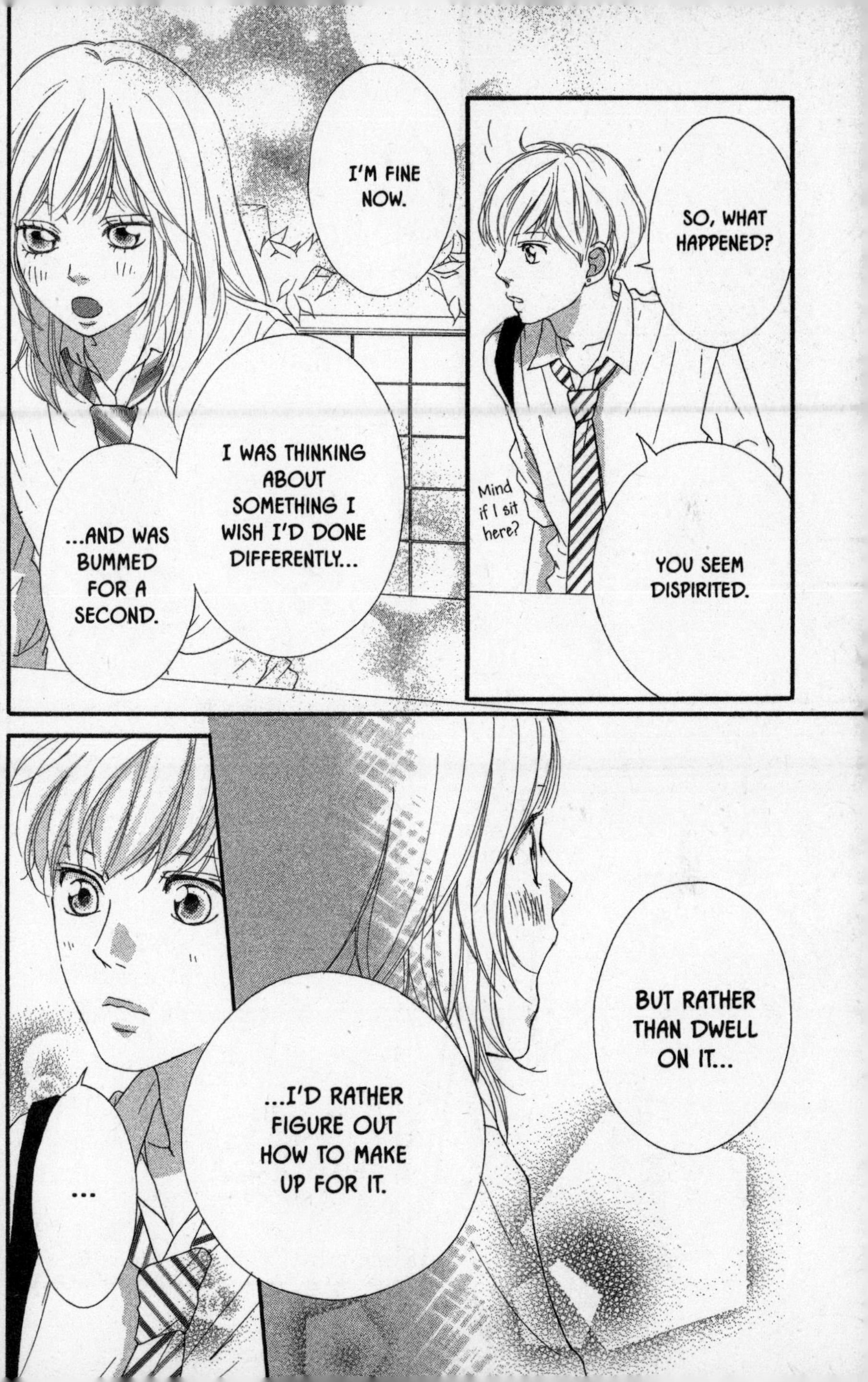
SO, WHAT HAPPENED?
Mind if I sit here?
YOU SEEM DISPIRITED.
I'M FINE NOW.
I WAS THINKING ABOUT SOMETHING I WISH I'D DONE DIFFERENTLY...
...AND WAS BUMMED FOR A SECOND.
BUT RATHER THAN DWELL ON IT...
...I'D RATHER FIGURE OUT HOW TO MAKE UP FOR IT.
...

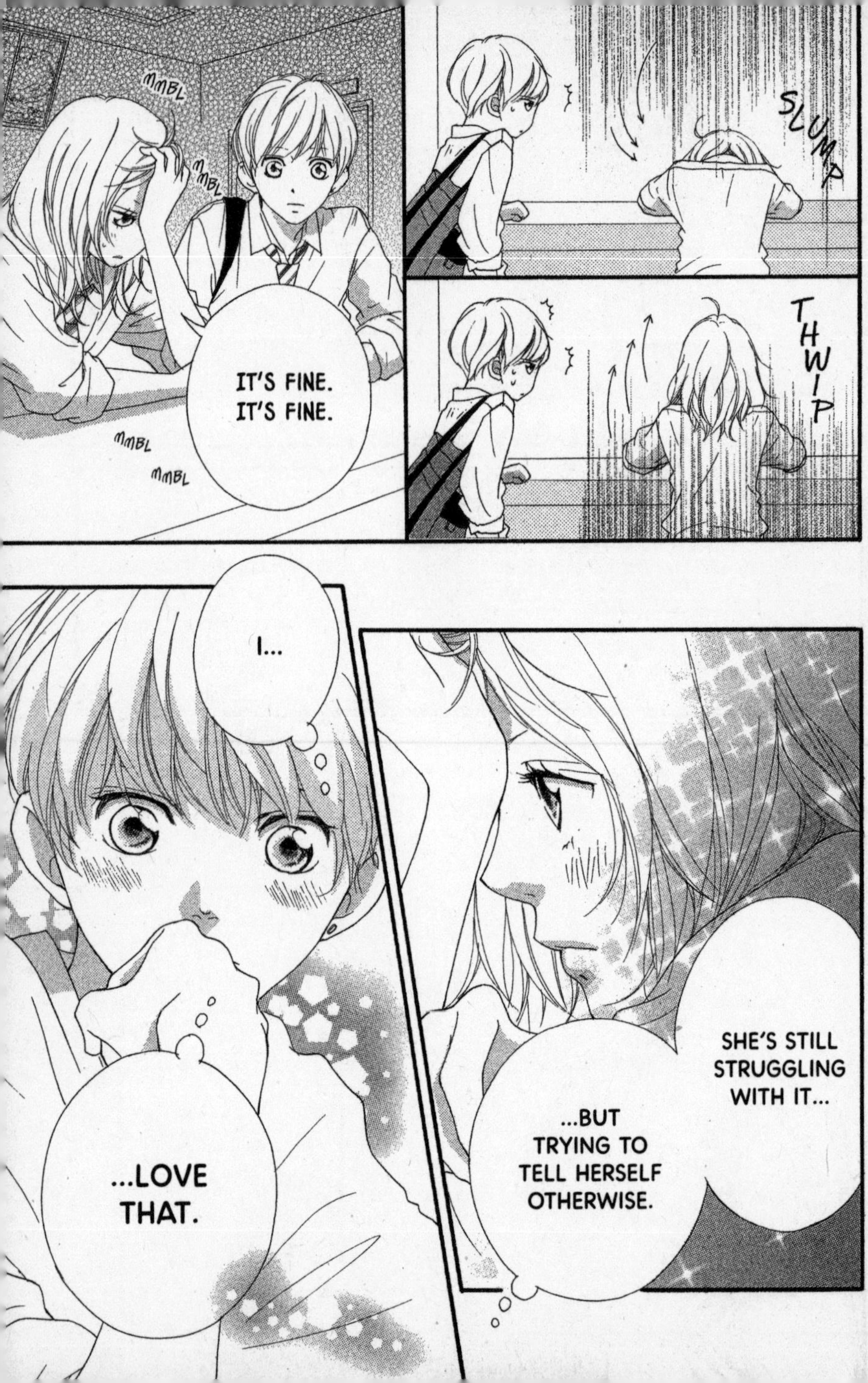
SLUMP
THWIP
MMBL
MMBL
IT'S FINE. IT'S FINE.
MMBL
MMBL
SHE'S STILL STRUGGLING WITH IT...
...BUT TRYING TO TELL HERSELF OTHERWISE.
I...
...LOVE THAT.

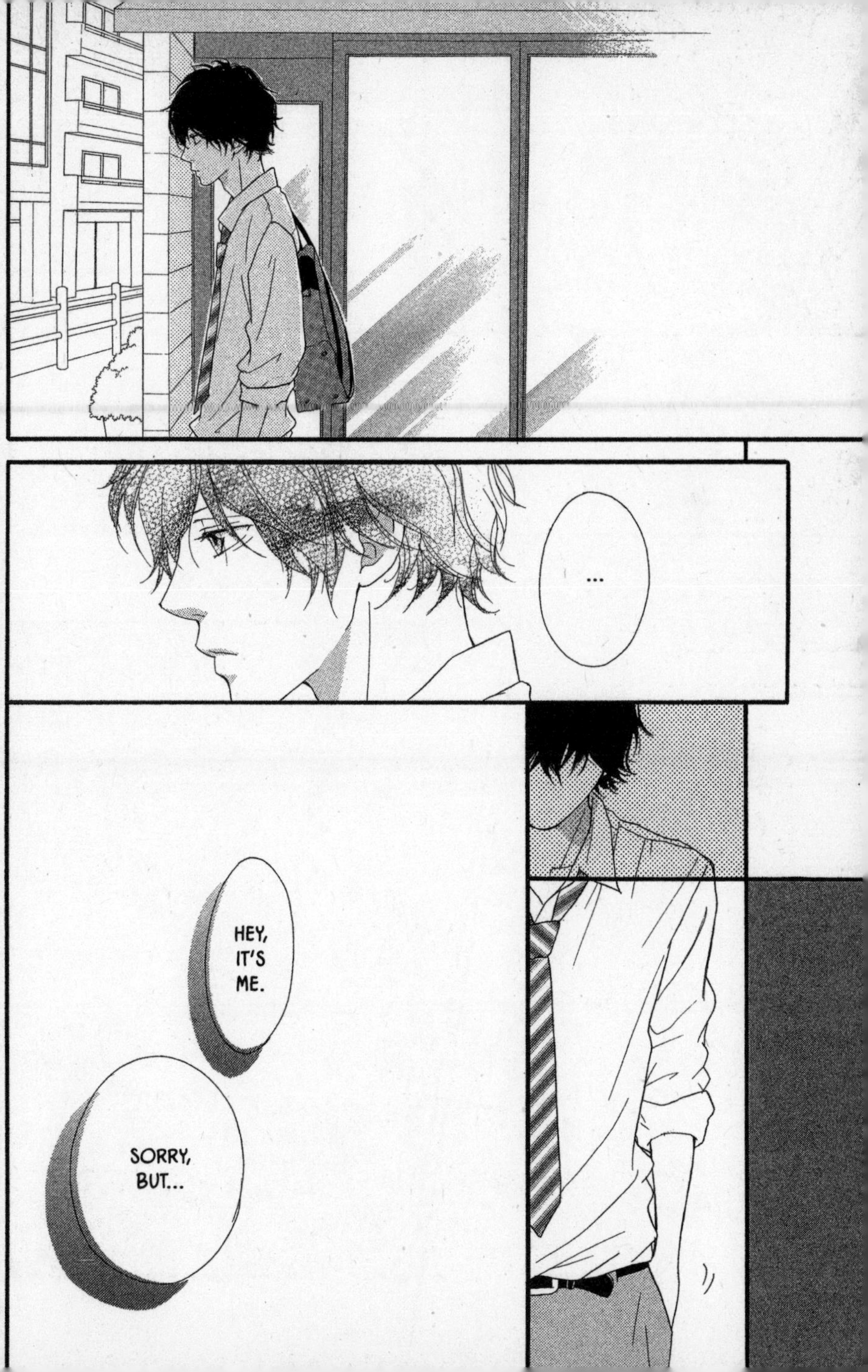
...
HEY, IT'S ME.
SORRY, BUT...

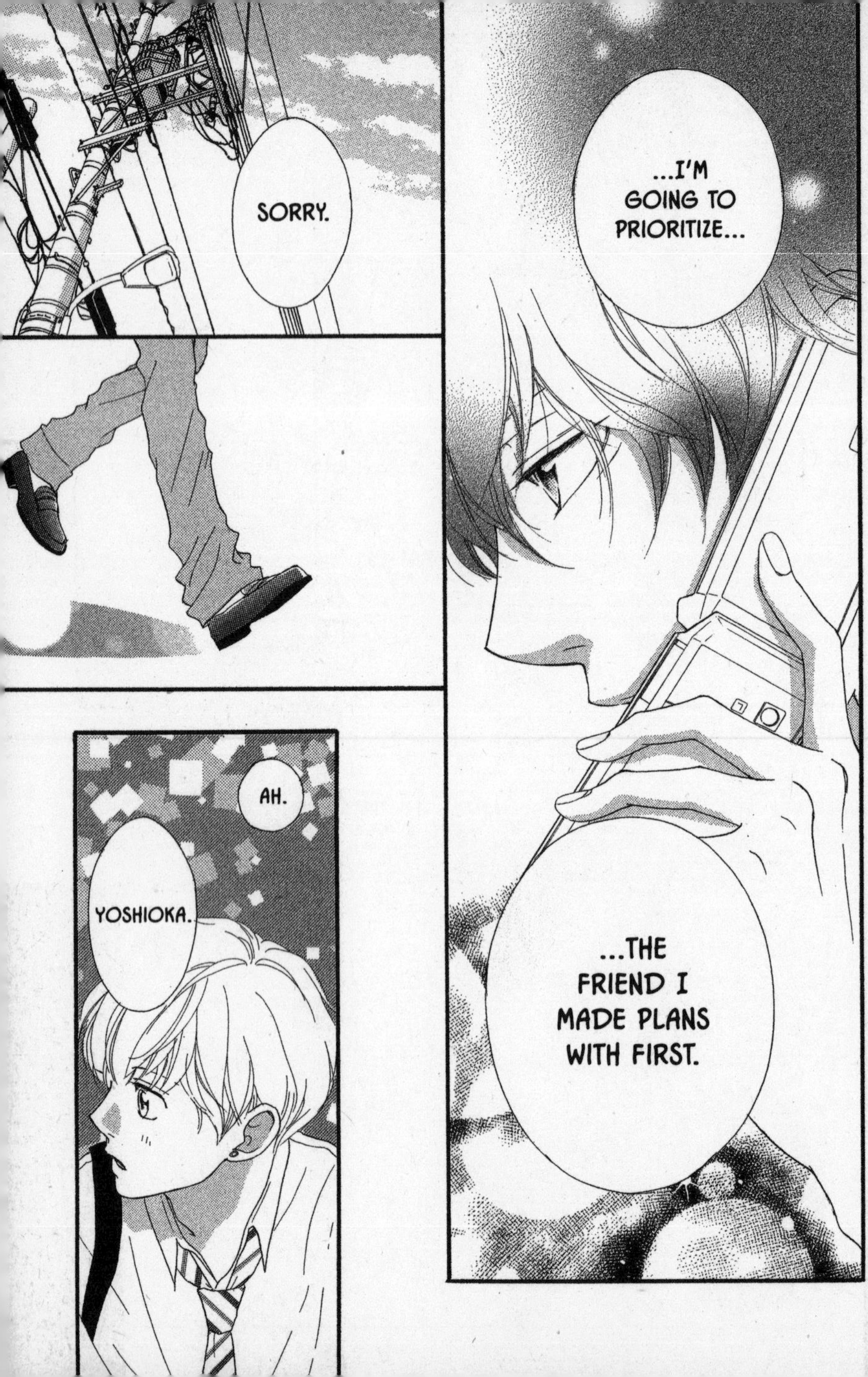
...I'M GOING TO PRIORITIZE...
...THE FRIEND I MADE PLANS WITH FIRST.
SORRY.
AH.
YOSHIOKA.

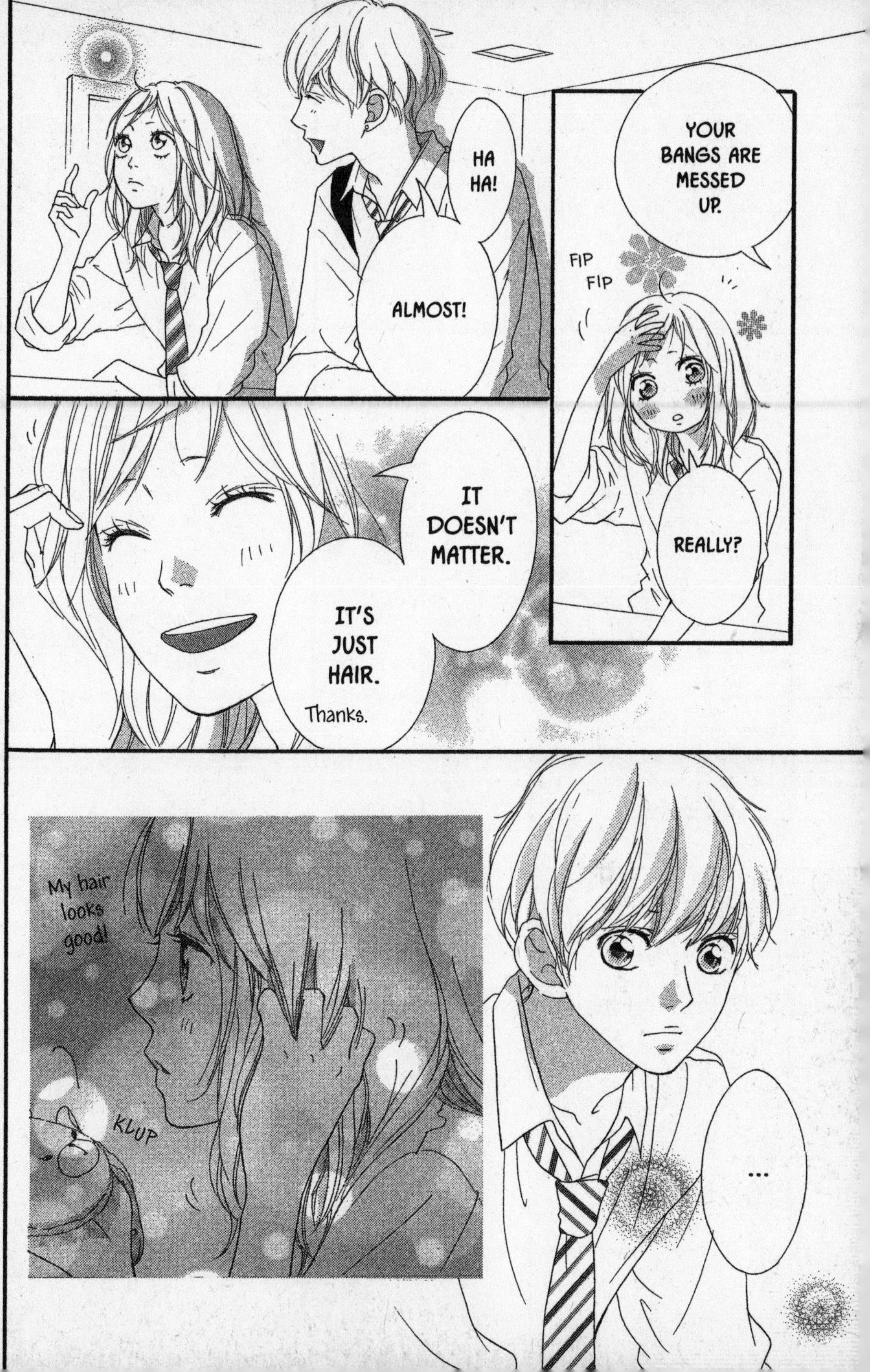
YOUR BANGS ARE MESSED UP.
FIP FIP
REALLY?
HA HA!
ALMOST!
IT DOESN'T MATTER.
IT'S JUST HAIR.
Thanks.
...
My hair looks good!
KLUP

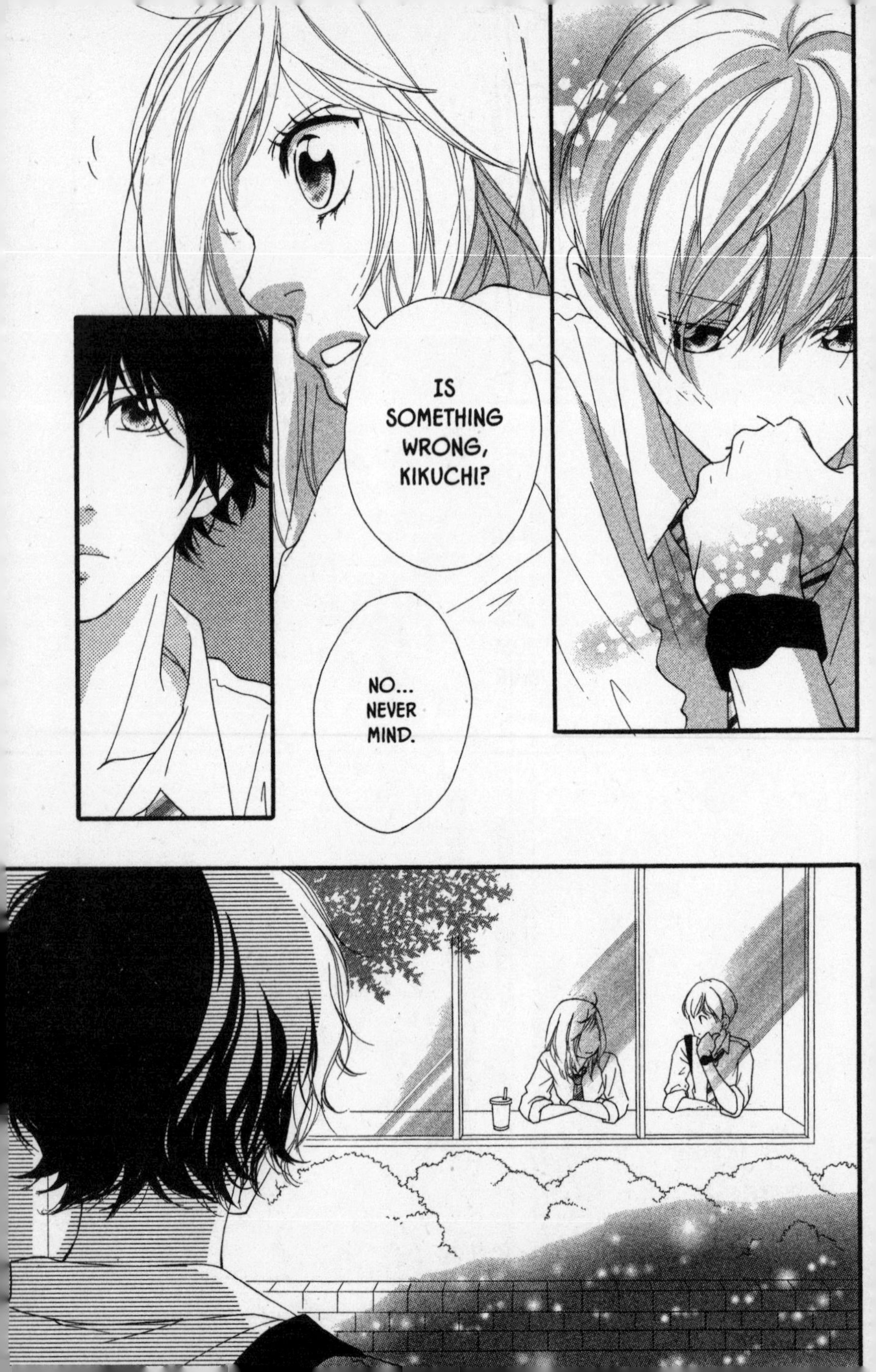
IS SOMETHING WRONG, KIKUCHI?
NO... NEVER MIND.

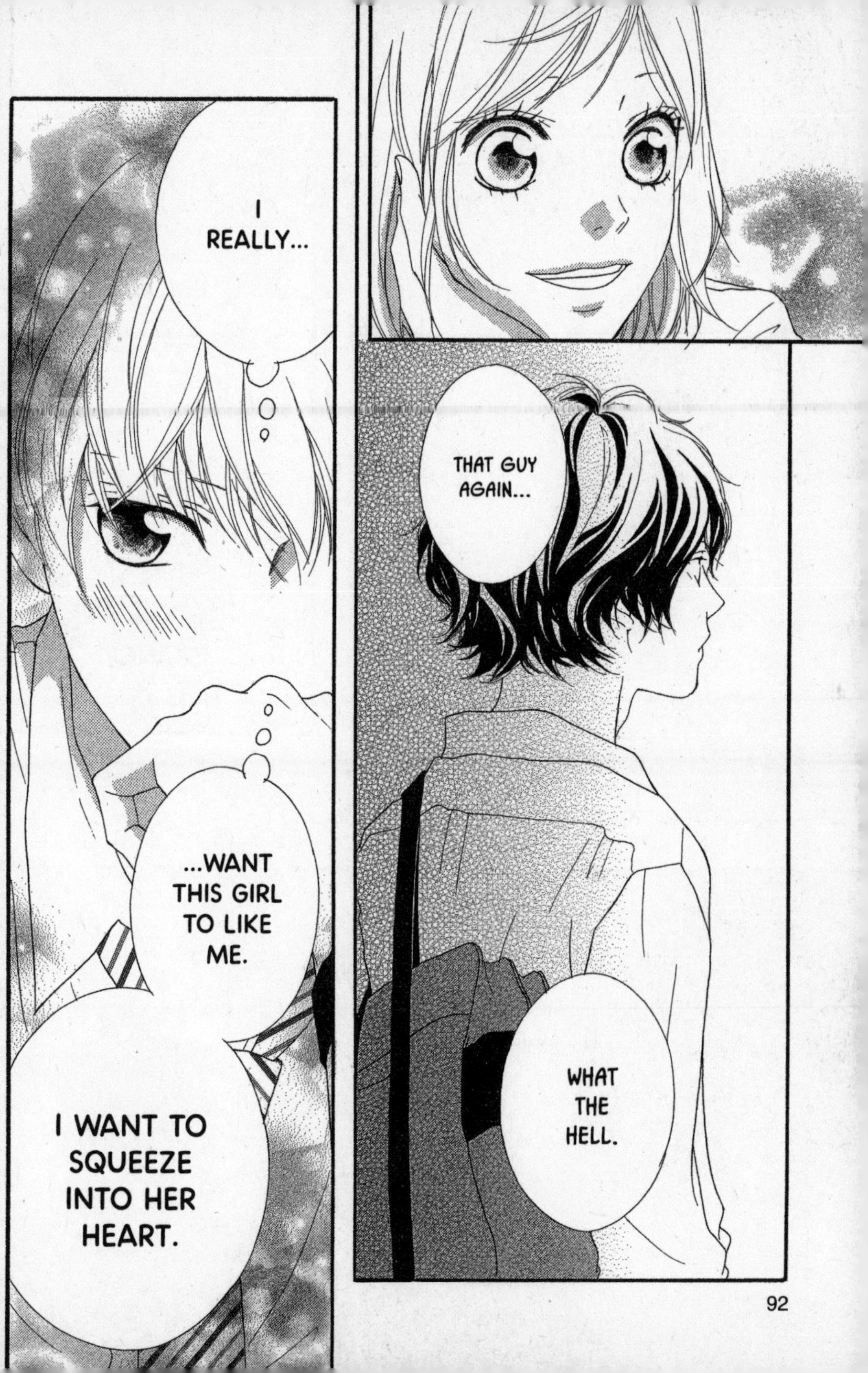
THAT GUY AGAIN...
WHAT THE HELL.
I REALLY...
...WANT THIS GIRL TO LIKE ME.
I WANT TO SQUEEZE INTO HER HEART.

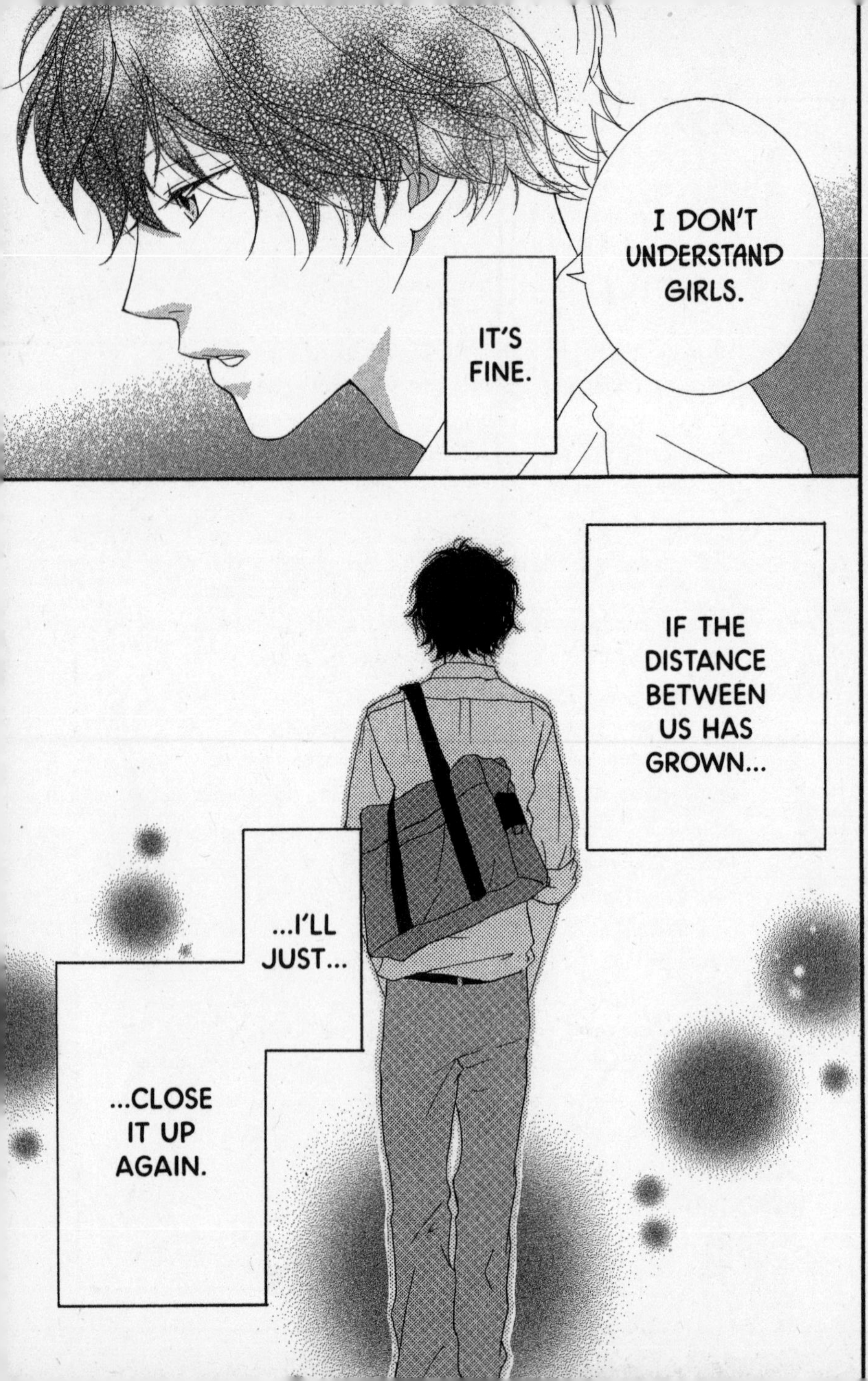
I DON'T UNDERSTAND GIRLS.
IT'S FINE.
IF THE DISTANCE BETWEEN US HAS GROWN...
...I'LL JUST...
...CLOSE IT UP AGAIN.

During the spring of 2012, I went to Taiwan with the young mangaka who help me with my manuscripts. And I just want to say that the people of Taiwan were so kind to us!

When we couldn't find the store we were looking for, we asked a clerk at a convenience store—but he didn't know either, so he went out of his way to call the store to find out. And once he realized it was nearby, he tore off his apron and took us there himself! Such an angel!

When we didn't know how to pay our respects at a temple and were stuck staring at our guidebooks, the people around kindly showed us how and pointed where to go. Such angels! U-mi was so touched by their kindness that she cried.

The weather wasn't very good for sightseeing, but we still went to Jiufen and the night market. We became experts at the subway and hung out at cafés. One time, we ordered a bunch of different kinds of tea at a café and did a blind taste test! It wasn't easy, but I got them all correct and was feeling pretty smug. But then Y-ko, who we all know has an unrefined palate, also got everything right. I was not pleased, and to be honest, I was ready to pick a fight. Yarrgh! (*laugh*)

The food was good, and the people were kind. It was a really great trip. People of Taiwan, thank you! I love you!

I hope we can all go somewhere together again. ✿ Let's make it happen. ✿

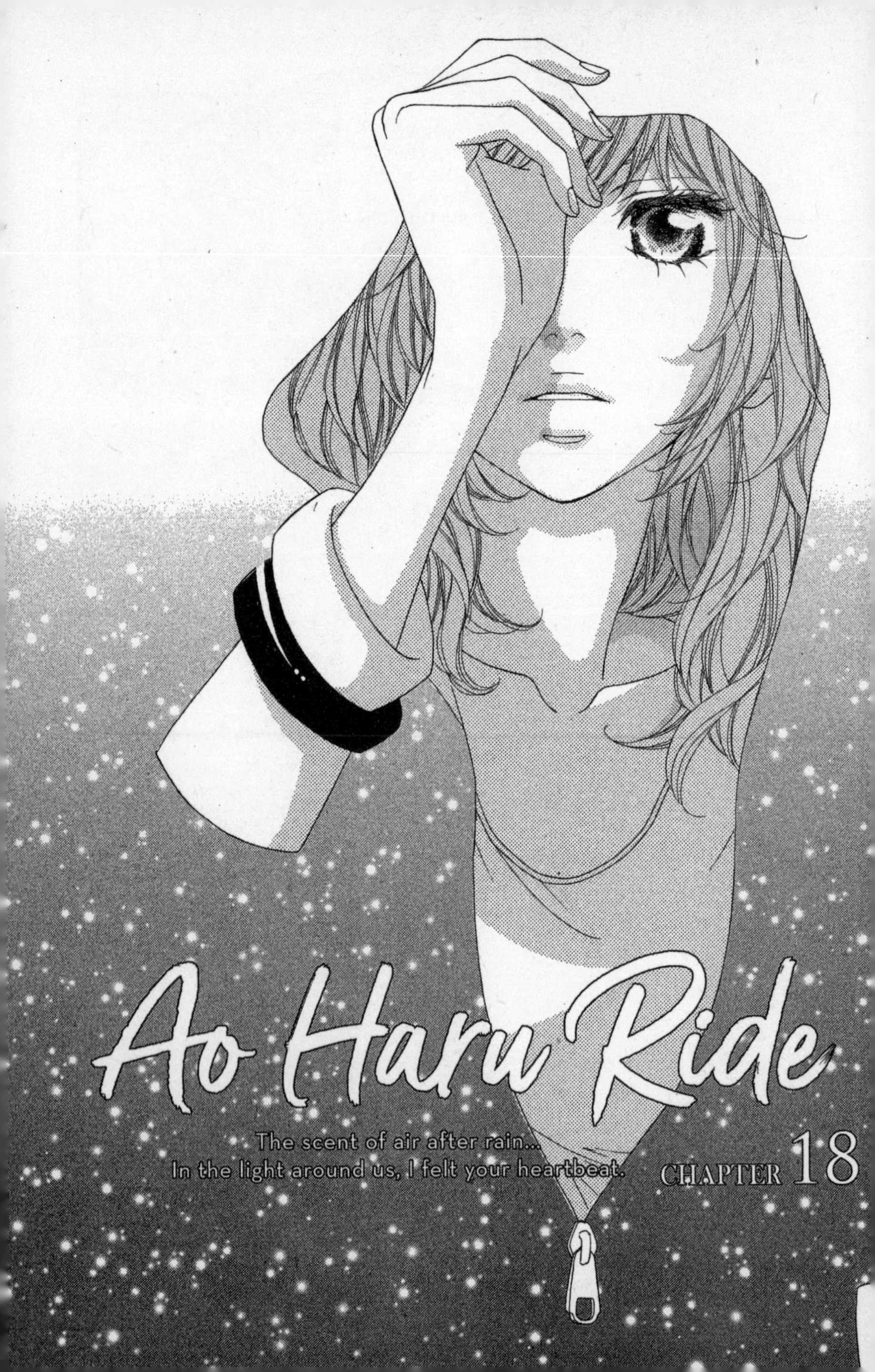
Ao Haru Ride
The scent of air after rain...
In the light around us, I felt your heartbeat.
CHAPTER 18

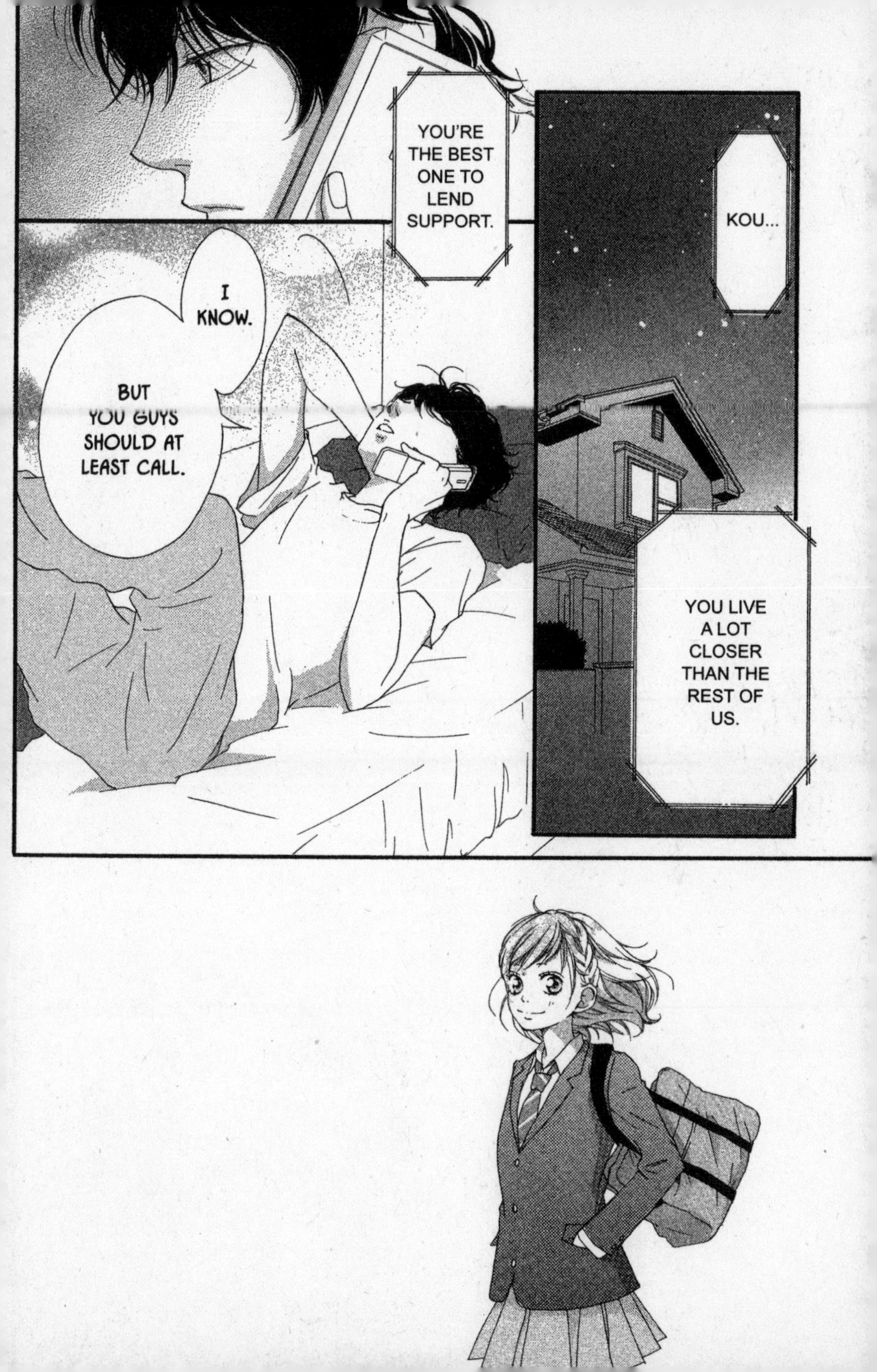
KOU...
YOU LIVE A LOT CLOSER THAN THE REST OF US.
YOU'RE THE BEST ONE TO LEND SUPPORT.
I KNOW.
BUT YOU GUYS SHOULD AT LEAST CALL.

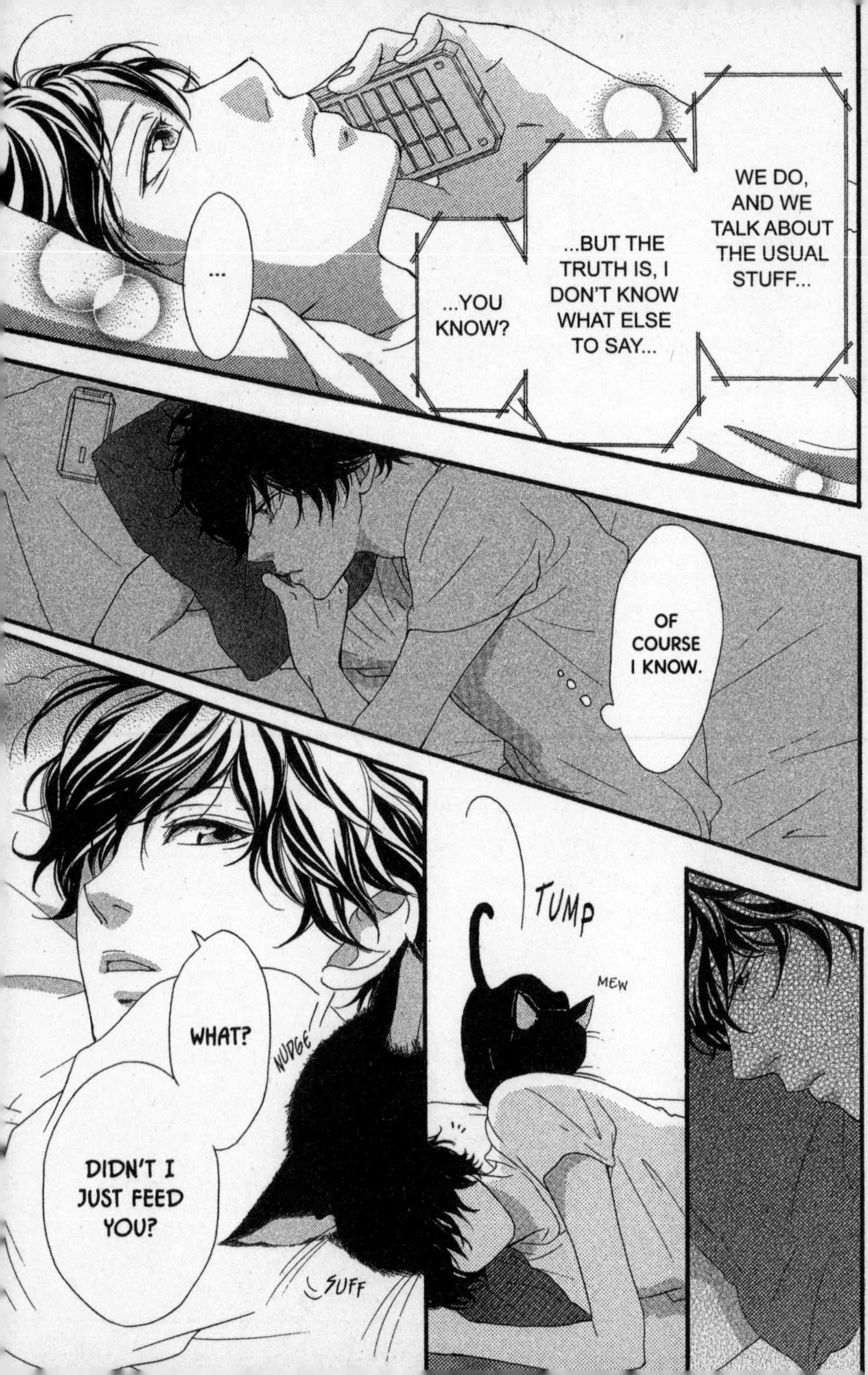
WE DO, AND WE TALK ABOUT THE USUAL STUFF...
...BUT THE TRUTH IS, I DON'T KNOW WHAT ELSE TO SAY...
...YOU KNOW?
...
OF COURSE I KNOW.
TUMP
MEW
WHAT?
NUDGE
DIDN'T I JUST FEED YOU?
SUFF

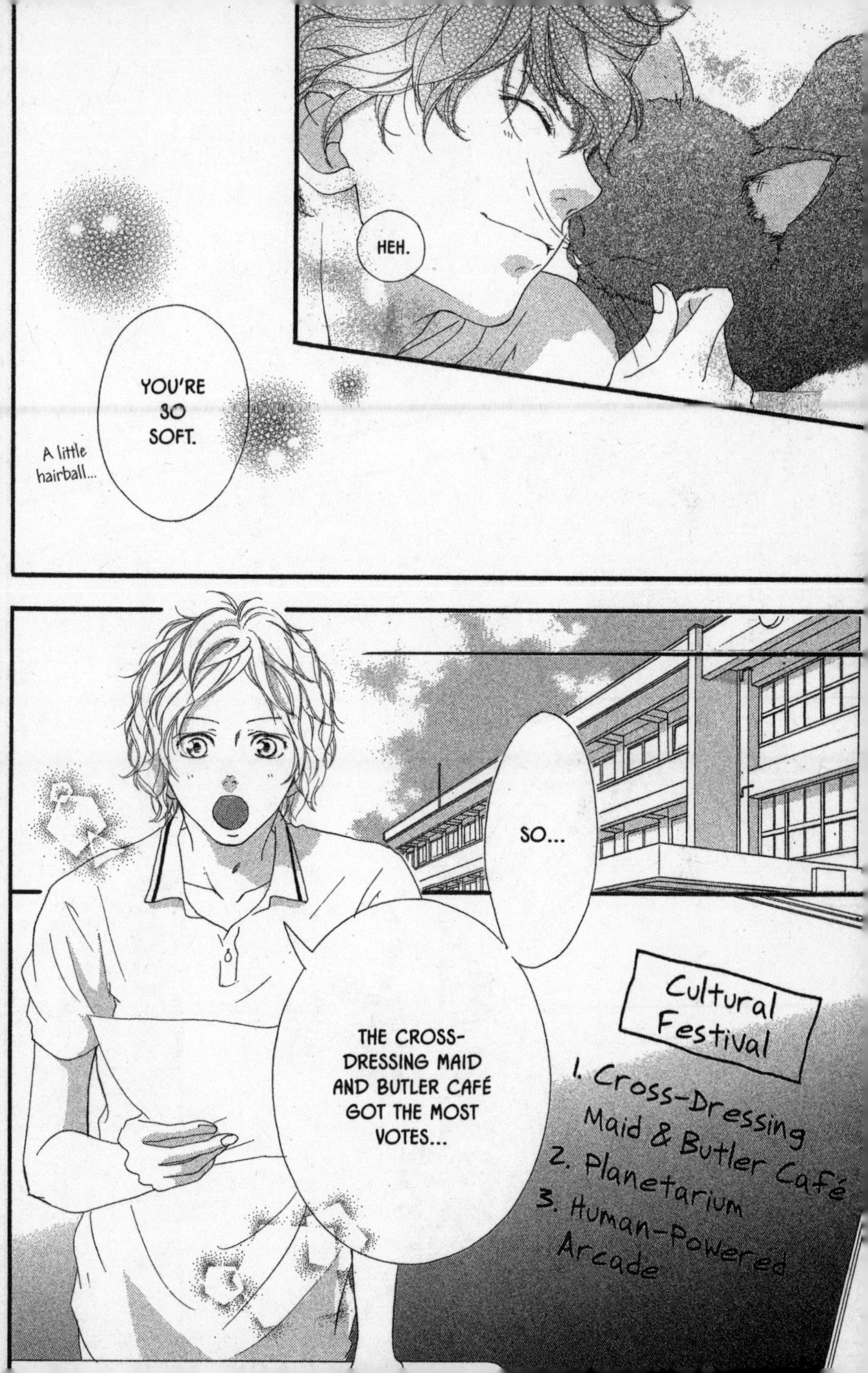
HEH.
YOU'RE SO SOFT.
A little hairball...
SO...
THE CROSS-DRESSING MAID AND BUTLER CAFÉ GOT THE MOST VOTES...
Cultural Festival
1. Cross-Dressing Maid & Butler Café
2. Planetarium
3. Human-Powered Arcade

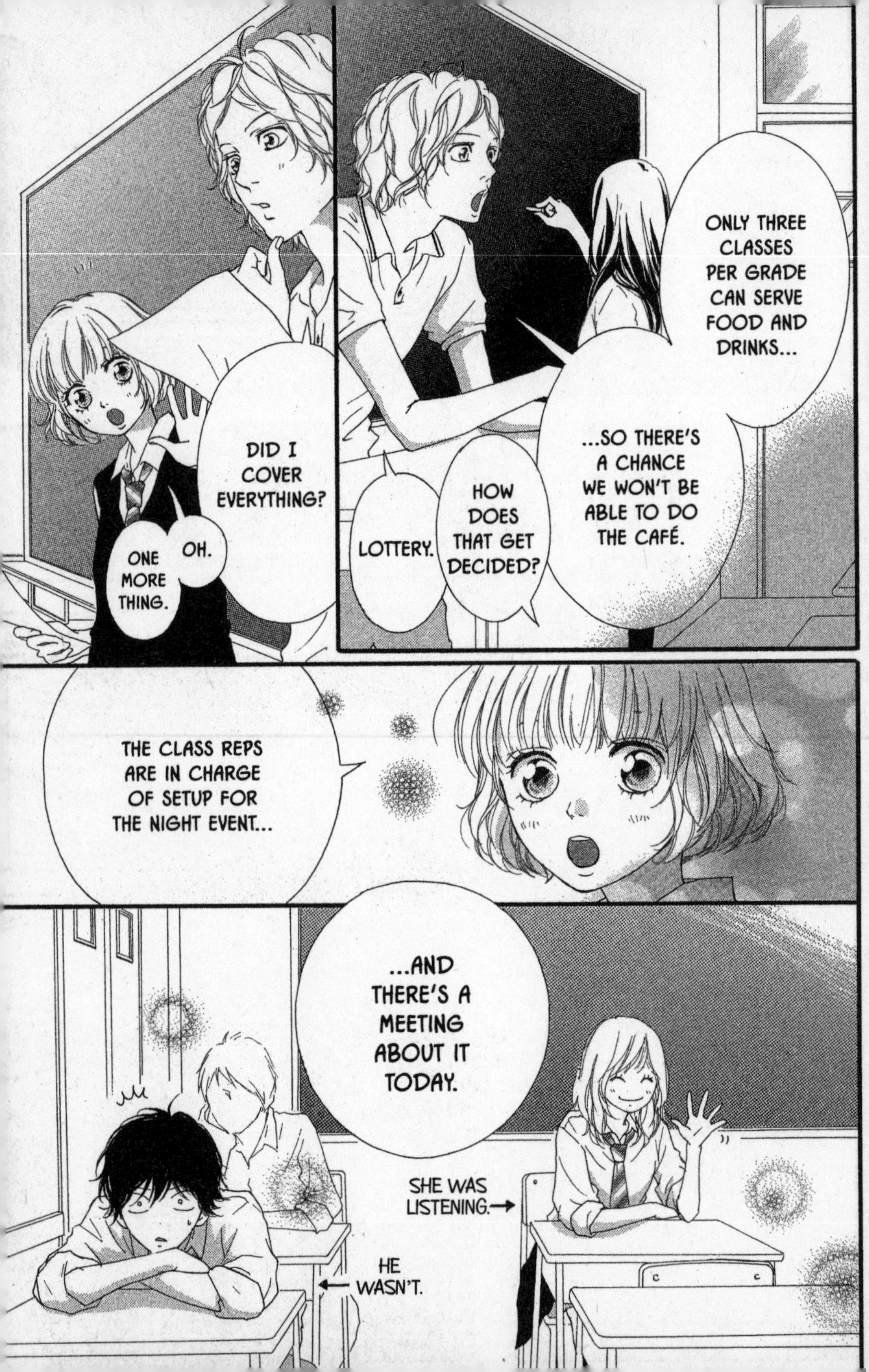
ONLY THREE CLASSES PER GRADE CAN SERVE FOOD AND DRINKS...
...SO THERE'S A CHANCE WE WON'T BE ABLE TO DO THE CAFÉ.
HOW DOES THAT GET DECIDED?
LOTTERY.
DID I COVER EVERYTHING?
OH.
ONE MORE THING.
THE CLASS REPS ARE IN CHARGE OF SETUP FOR THE NIGHT EVENT...
...AND THERE'S A MEETING ABOUT IT TODAY.
SHE WAS LISTENING.
HE WASN'T.

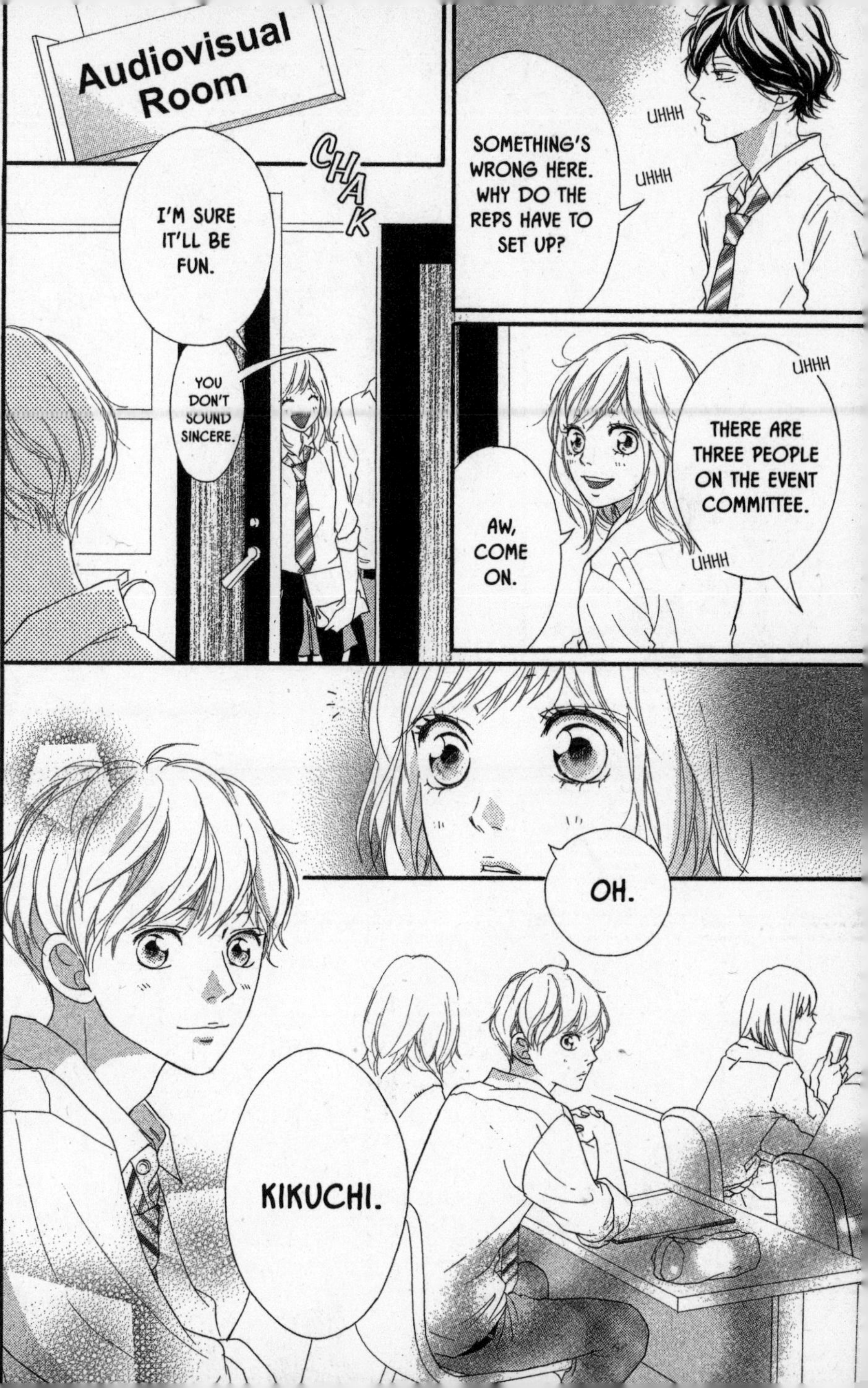
UHHH
UHHH
SOMETHING'S WRONG HERE. WHY DO THE REPS HAVE TO SET UP?
UHHH
THERE ARE THREE PEOPLE ON THE EVENT COMMITTEE.
UHHH
AW, COME ON.
Audiovisual Room
CHAK
I'M SURE IT'LL BE FUN.
YOU DON'T SOUND SINCERE.
OH.
KIKUCHI.

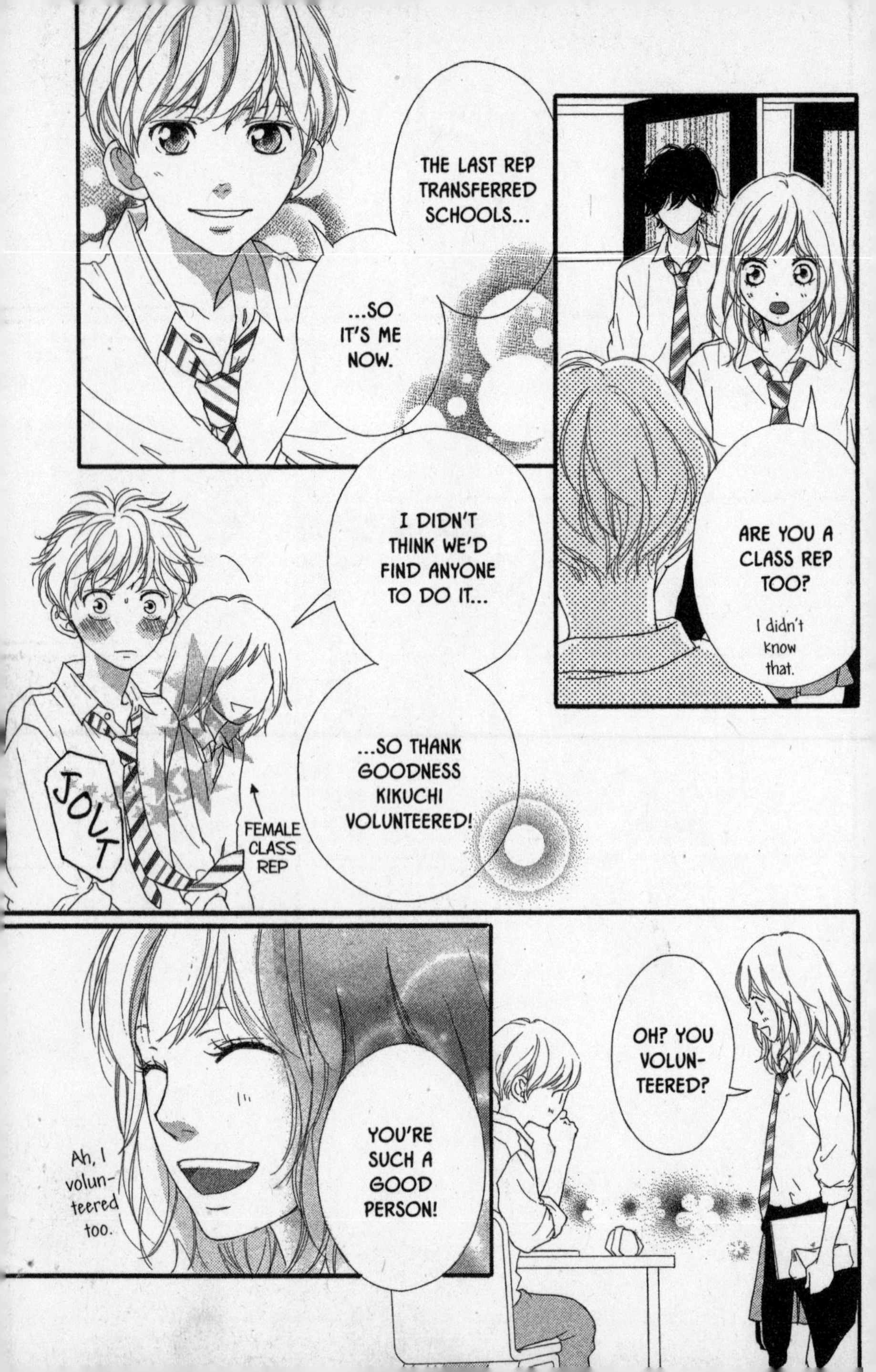
ARE YOU A CLASS REP TOO?
I didn't know that.
THE LAST REP TRANSFERRED SCHOOLS...
...SO IT'S ME NOW.
I DIDN'T THINK WE'D FIND ANYONE TO DO IT...
...SO THANK GOODNESS KIKUCHI VOLUNTEERED!
JOLT
FEMALE CLASS REP
OH? YOU VOLUN-TEERED?
YOU'RE SUCH A GOOD PERSON!
Ah, I volun-teered too.

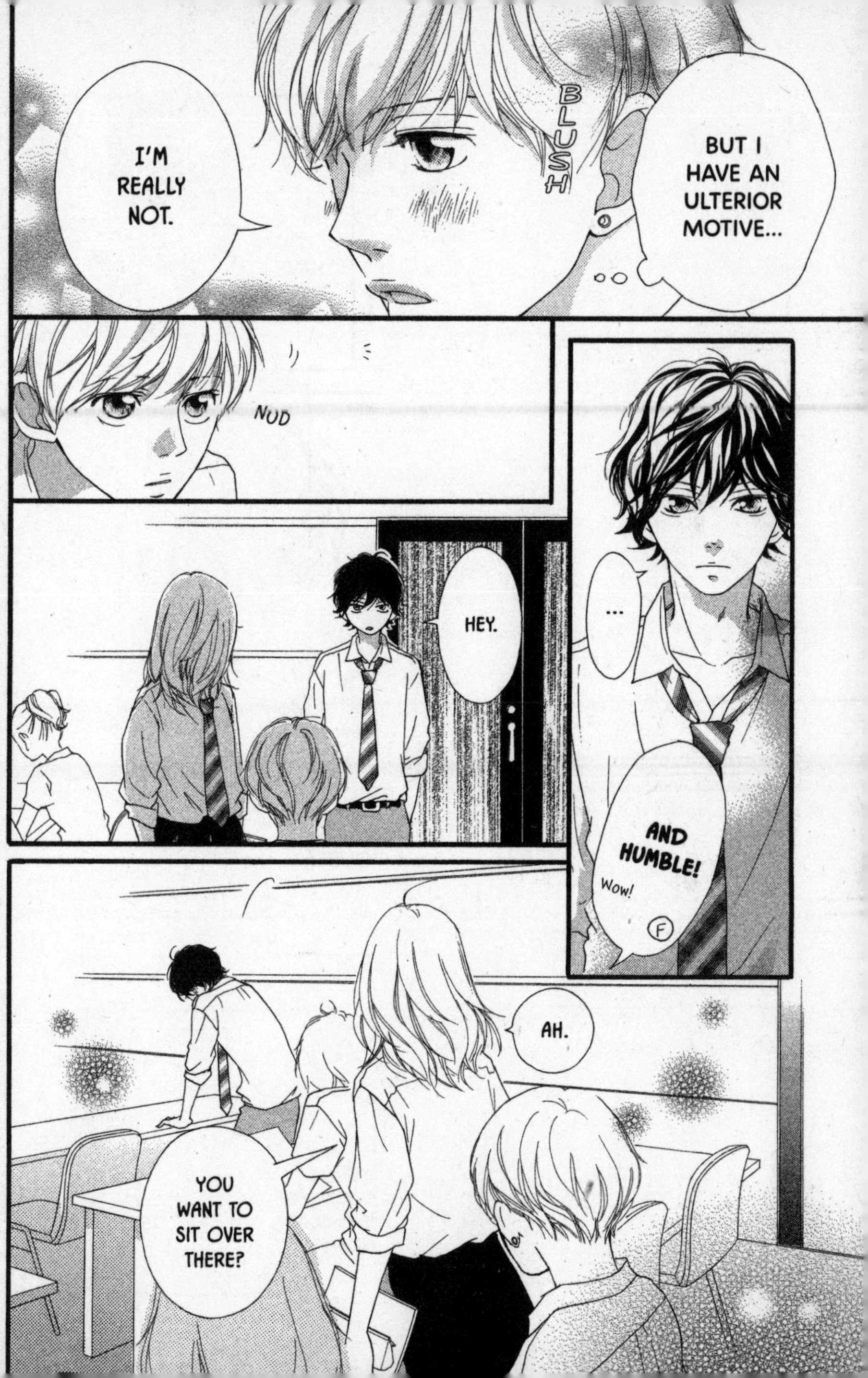
BLUSH
I'M REALLY NOT.
BUT I HAVE AN ULTERIOR MOTIVE...
...
AND HUMBLE!
WOW!
NOD
HEY.
AH.
YOU WANT TO SIT OVER THERE?

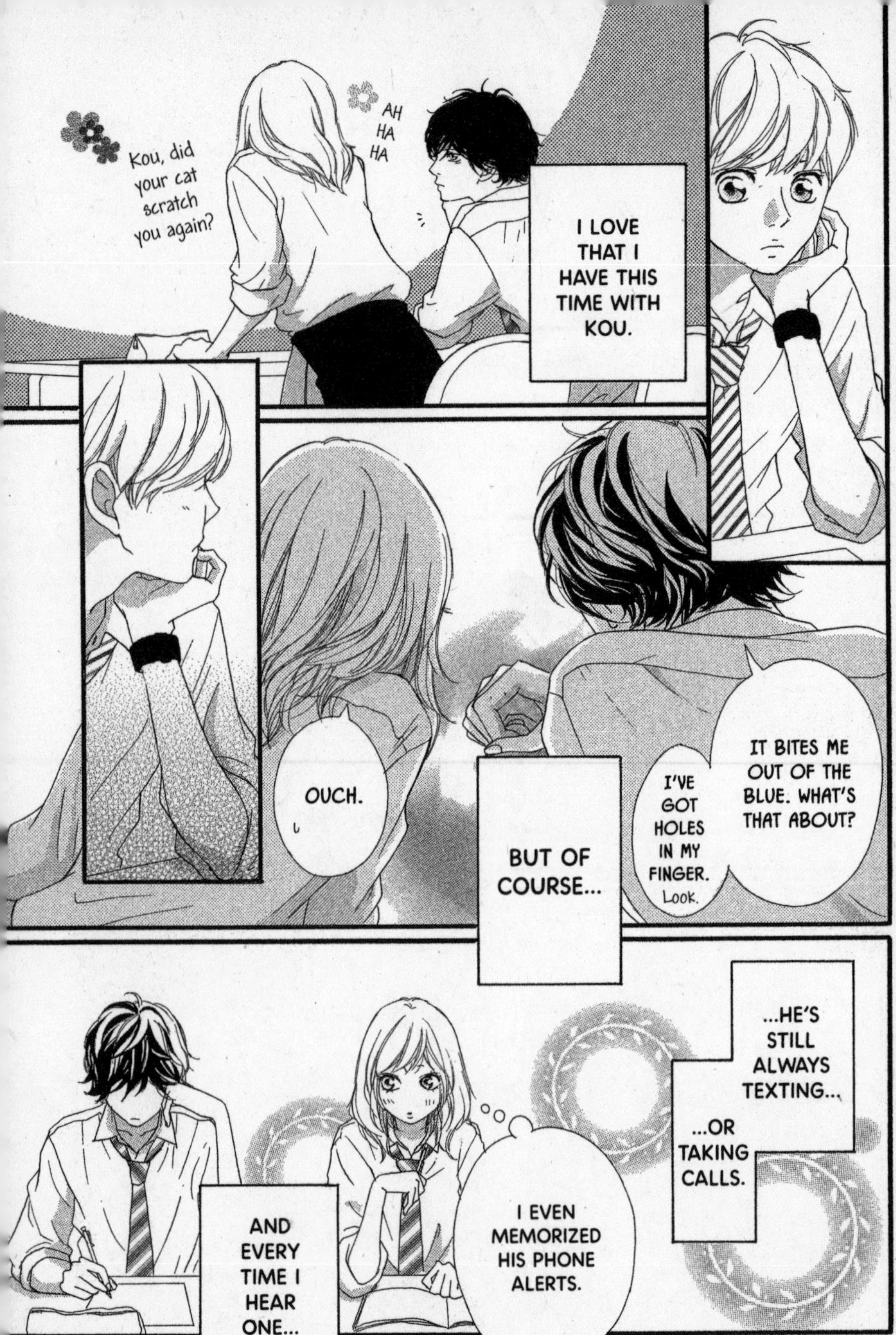
I LOVE THAT I HAVE THIS TIME WITH KOU.
AH HA HA
Kou, did your cat scratch you again?
IT BITES ME OUT OF THE BLUE. WHAT'S THAT ABOUT?
I'VE GOT HOLES IN MY FINGER. Look.
BUT OF COURSE...
OUCH.
...HE'S STILL ALWAYS TEXTING...
...OR TAKING CALLS.
I EVEN MEMORIZED HIS PHONE ALERTS.
AND EVERY TIME I HEAR ONE...

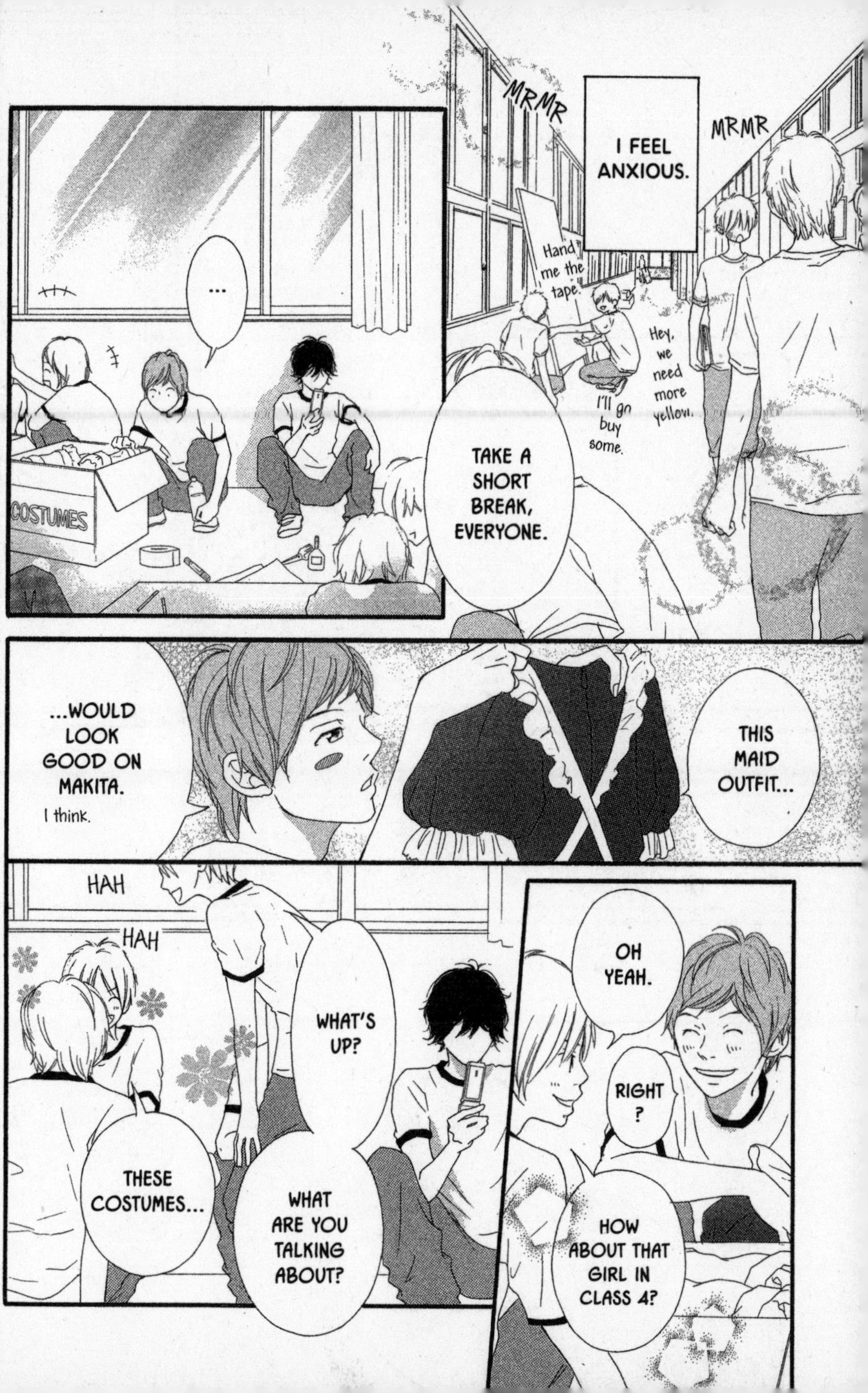
MRMR
I FEEL ANXIOUS.
MRMR
Hey, we need more yellow.
I'll go buy some.
Hand me the tape.
TAKE A SHORT BREAK, EVERYONE.
...
COSTUMES
THIS MAID OUTFIT...
...WOULD LOOK GOOD ON MAKITA.
I think.
OH YEAH.
RIGHT?
HOW ABOUT THAT GIRL IN CLASS 4?
HAH
HAH
WHAT'S UP?
WHAT ARE YOU TALKING ABOUT?
THESE COSTUMES...

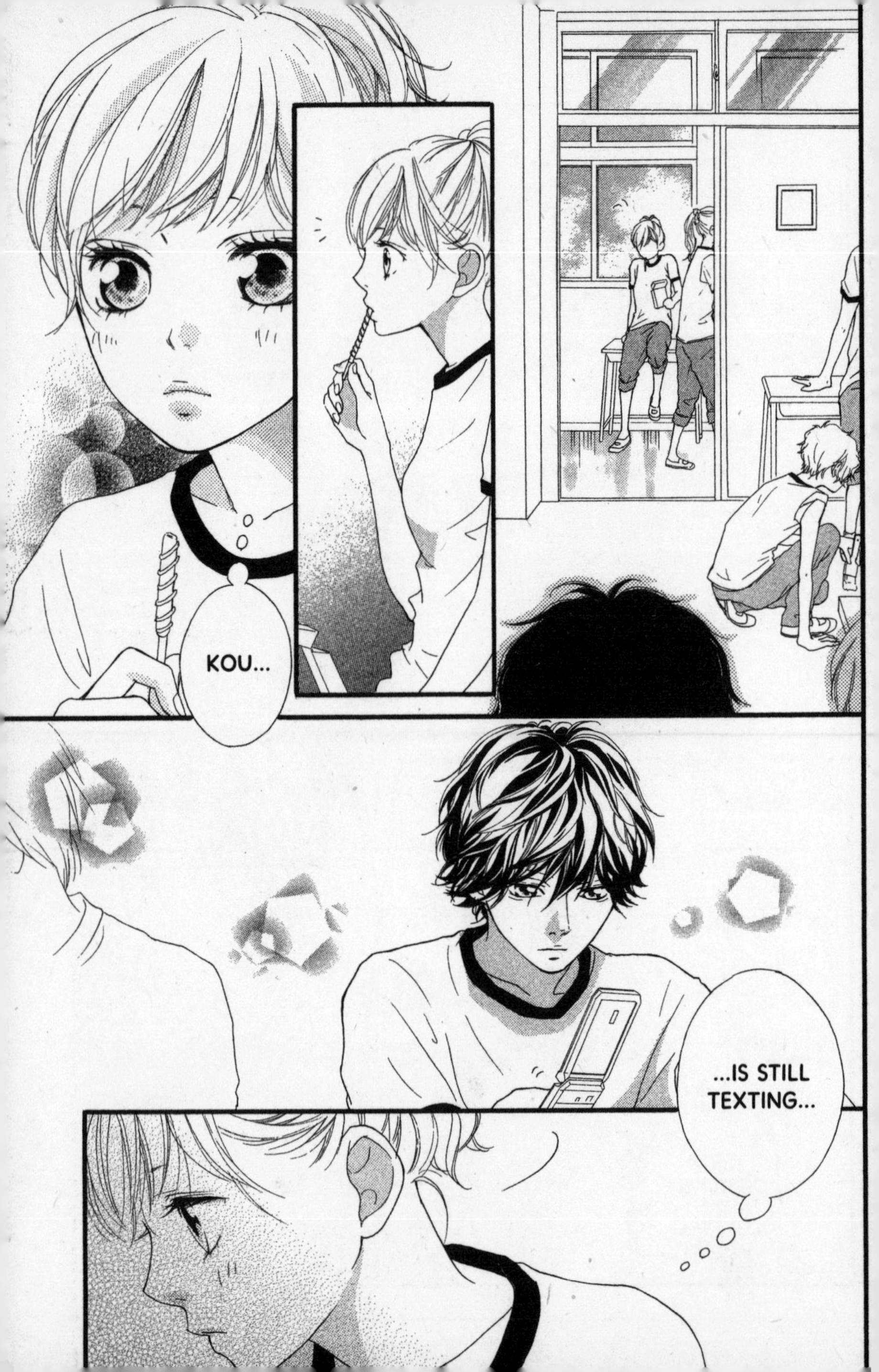
KOU...
...IS STILL TEXTING...

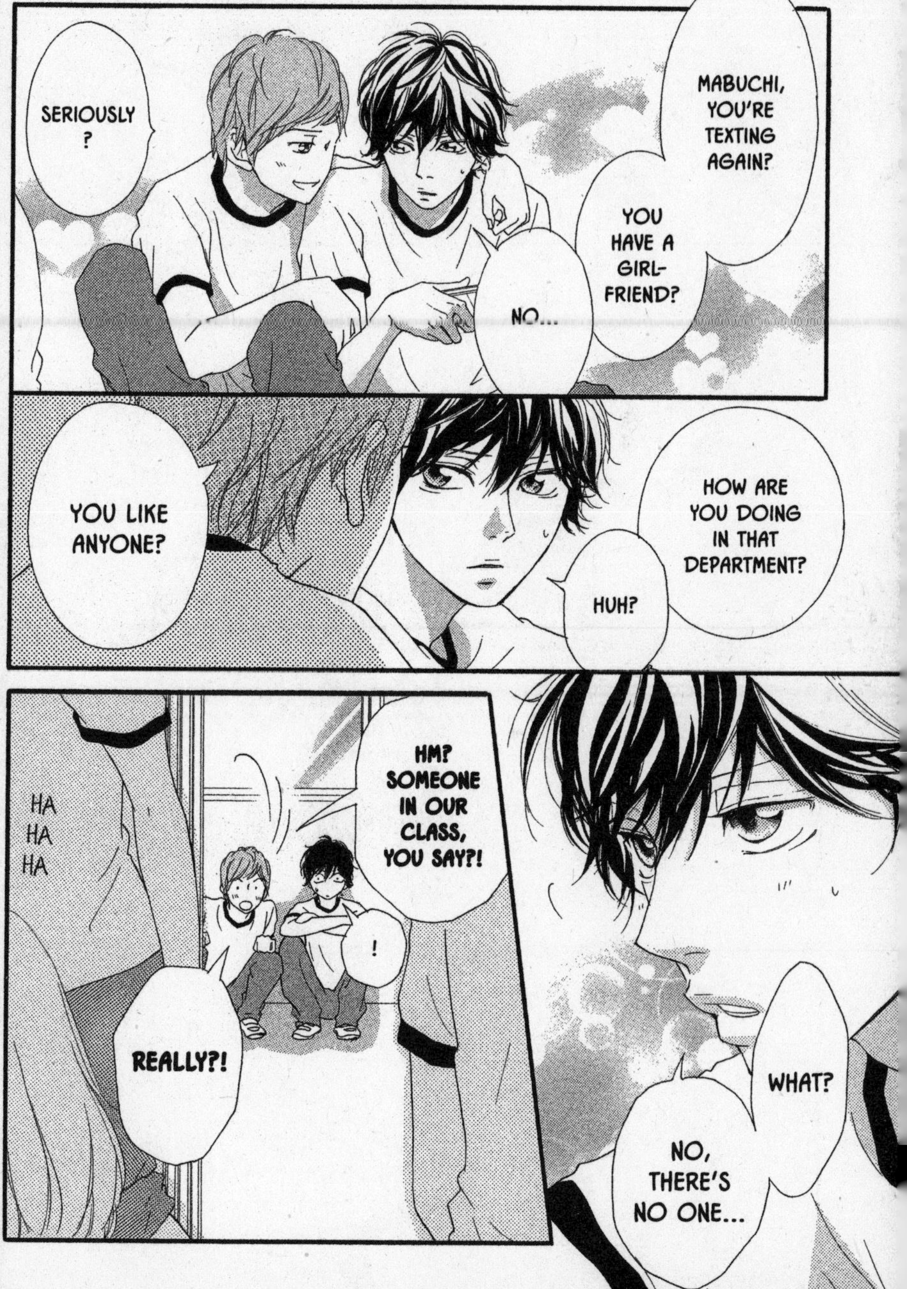
MABUCHI, YOU'RE TEXTING AGAIN?
YOU HAVE A GIRL-FRIEND?
NO...
SERIOUSLY?
HOW ARE YOU DOING IN THAT DEPARTMENT?
HUH?
YOU LIKE ANYONE?
WHAT?
NO, THERE'S NO ONE...
HM? SOMEONE IN OUR CLASS, YOU SAY?!
!
REALLY?!
HA HA HA

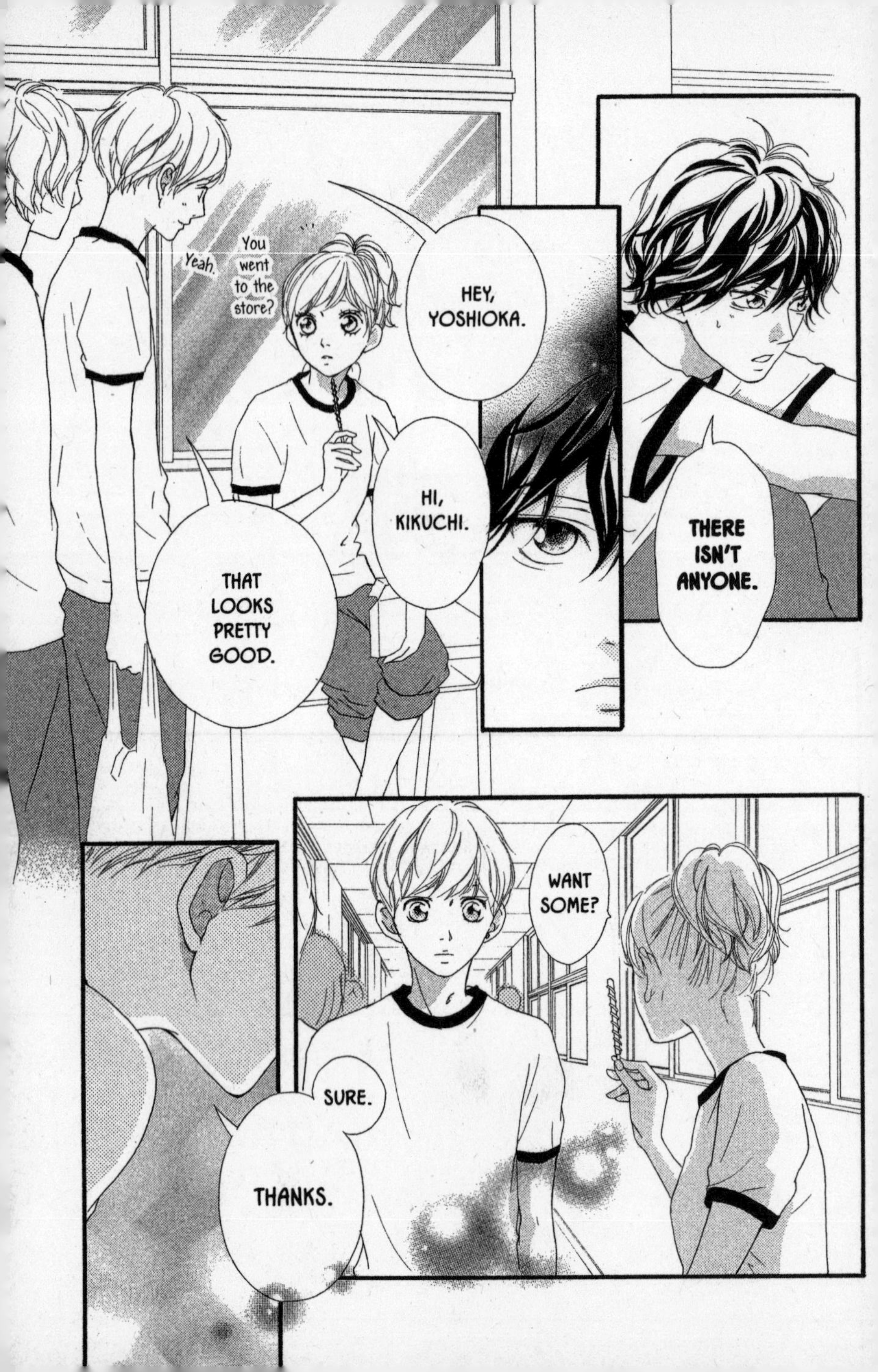

THERE ISN'T ANYONE.
HEY, YOSHIOKA.
You went to the store?
Yeah.
HI, KIKUCHI.
THAT LOOKS PRETTY GOOD.
WANT SOME?
SURE.
THANKS.

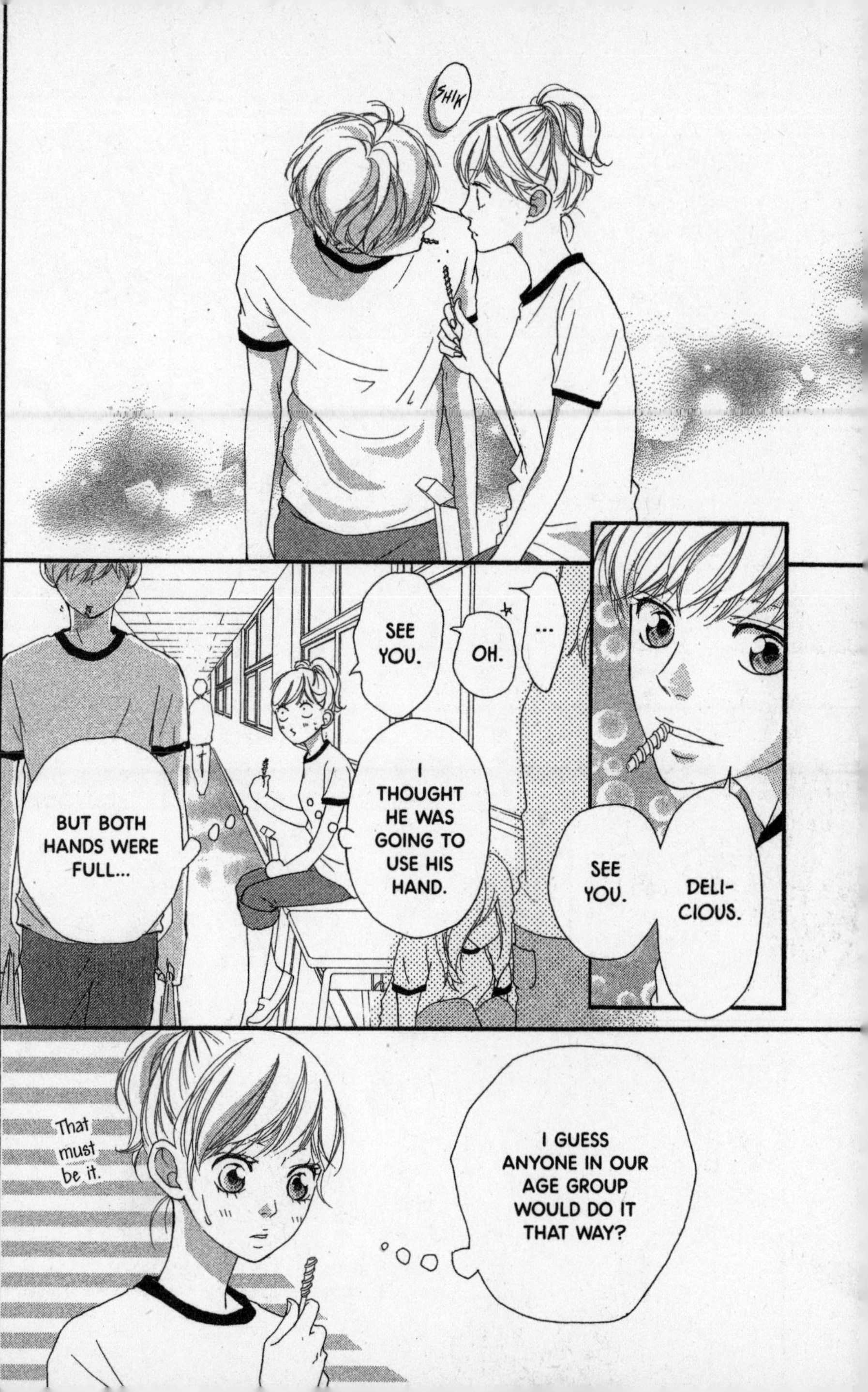
SHIK
DELI-CIOUS.
SEE YOU.
...
OH.
SEE YOU.
I THOUGHT HE WAS GOING TO USE HIS HAND.
BUT BOTH HANDS WERE FULL...
I GUESS ANYONE IN OUR AGE GROUP WOULD DO IT THAT WAY?
That must be it.

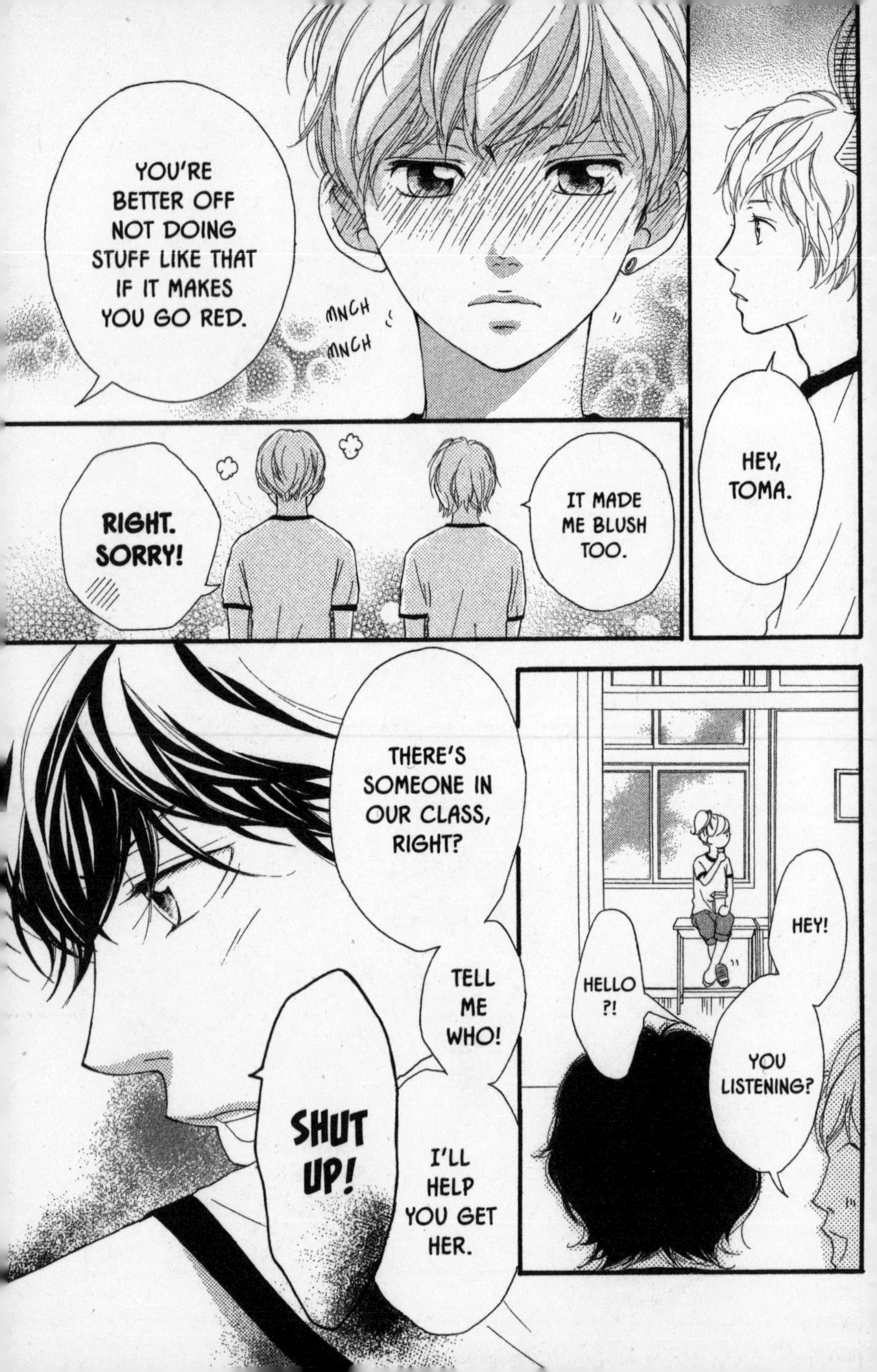
HEY, TOMA.
YOU'RE BETTER OFF NOT DOING STUFF LIKE THAT IF IT MAKES YOU GO RED.
MNCH MNCH
IT MADE ME BLUSH TOO.
RIGHT. SORRY!
HEY!
YOU LISTENING?
HELLO ?!
THERE'S SOMEONE IN OUR CLASS, RIGHT?
TELL ME WHO!
I'LL HELP YOU GET HER.
SHUT UP!

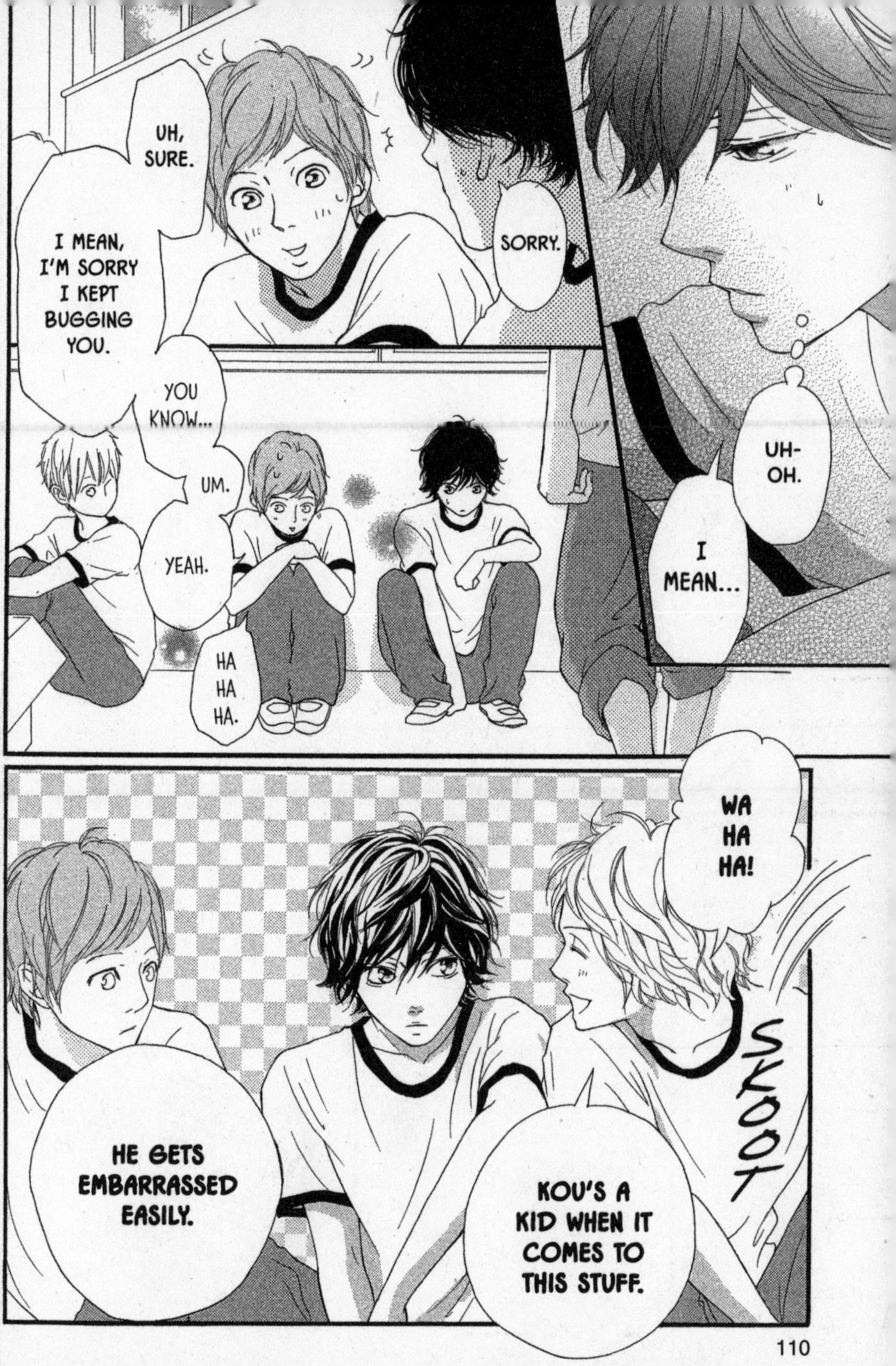
UH-OH.
I MEAN...
SORRY.
UH, SURE.
I MEAN, I'M SORRY I KEPT BUGGING YOU.
YOU KNOW...
UM.
YEAH.
HA HA HA.
WA HA HA!
SKOOT
KOU'S A KID WHEN IT COMES TO THIS STUFF.
HE GETS EMBARRASSED EASILY.

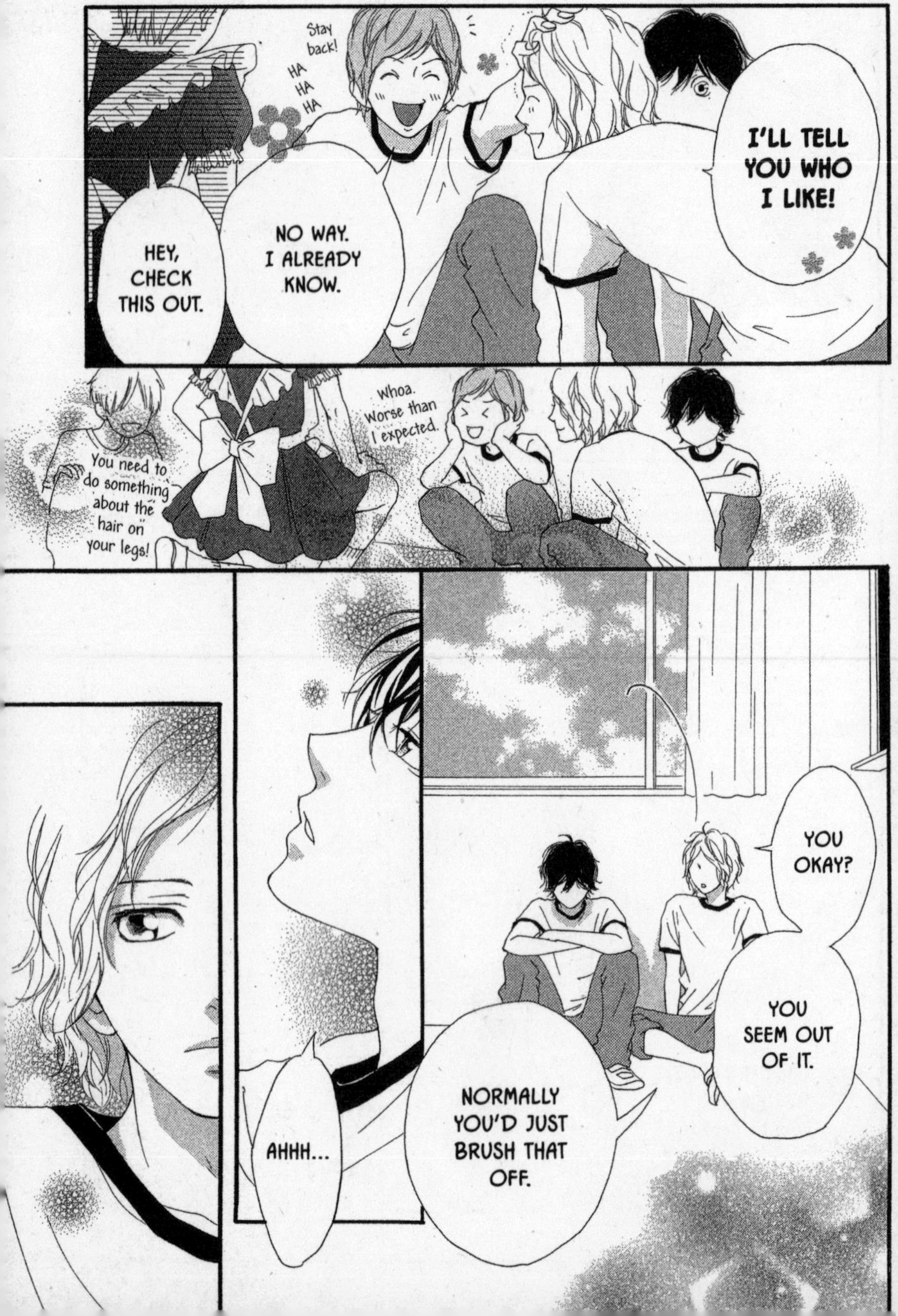
I'LL TELL YOU WHO I LIKE!
Stay back!
HA HA HA
NO WAY. I ALREADY KNOW.
HEY, CHECK THIS OUT.
Whoa. Worse than I expected.
You need to do something about the hair on your legs!
YOU OKAY?
YOU SEEM OUT OF IT.
NORMALLY YOU'D JUST BRUSH THAT OFF.
AHHH...

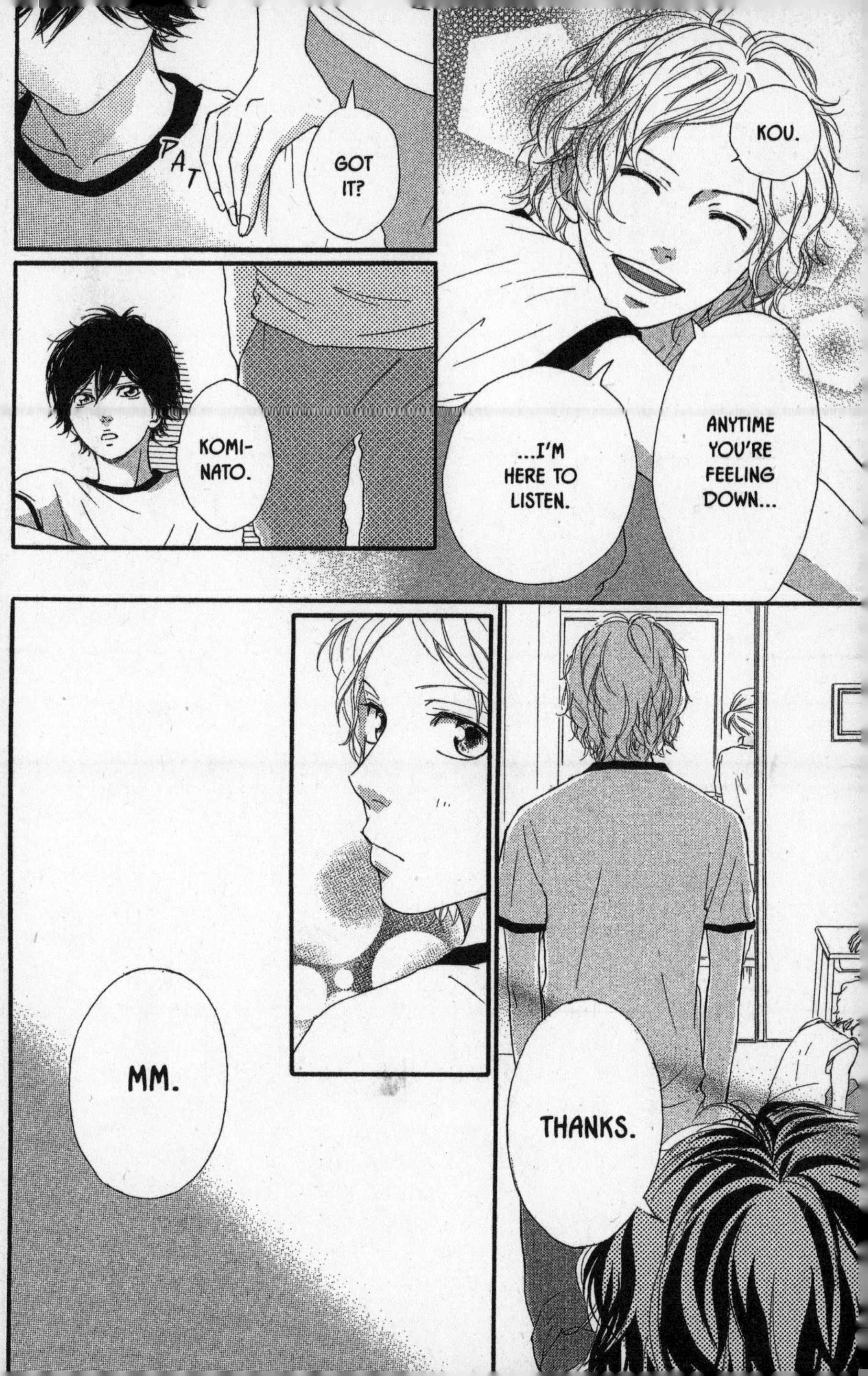
KOU.
ANYTIME YOU'RE FEELING DOWN...
...I'M HERE TO LISTEN.
GOT IT?
PAT
KOMI-NATO.
THANKS.
MM.

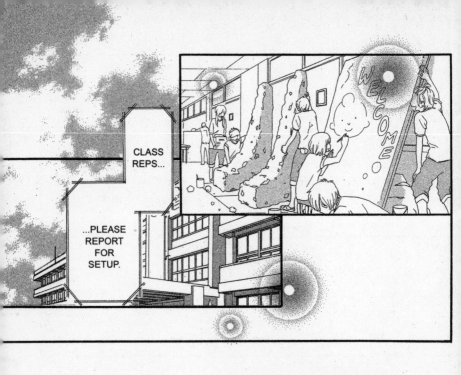

CLASS REPS...

...PLEASE REPORT FOR SETUP.

...

I THINK THAT'S GOOD FOR TONIGHT.

THANKS, EVERYONE!

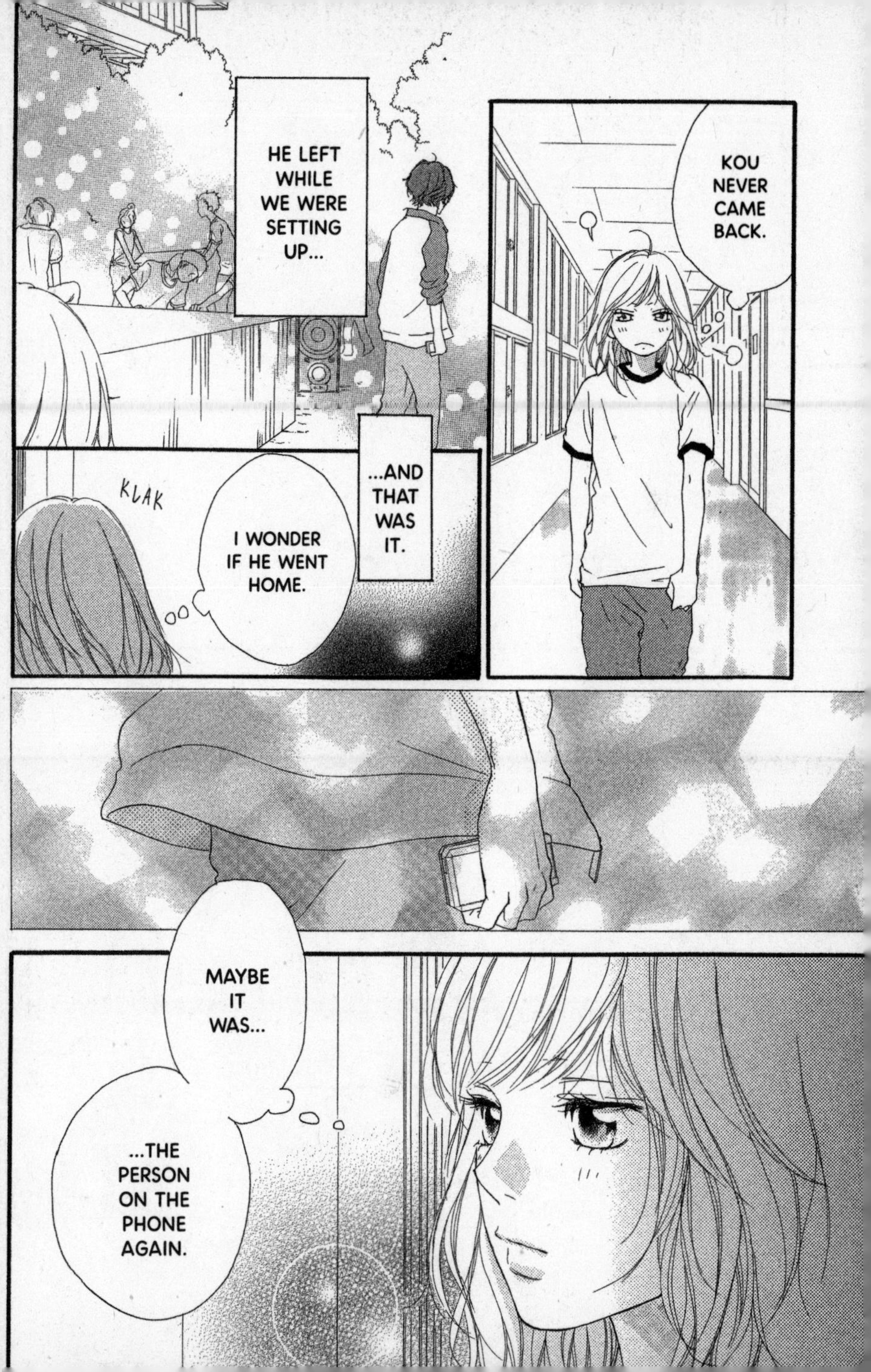
KOU NEVER CAME BACK.
HE LEFT WHILE WE WERE SETTING UP...
...AND THAT WAS IT.
KLAK
I WONDER IF HE WENT HOME.
MAYBE IT WAS...
...THE PERSON ON THE PHONE AGAIN.

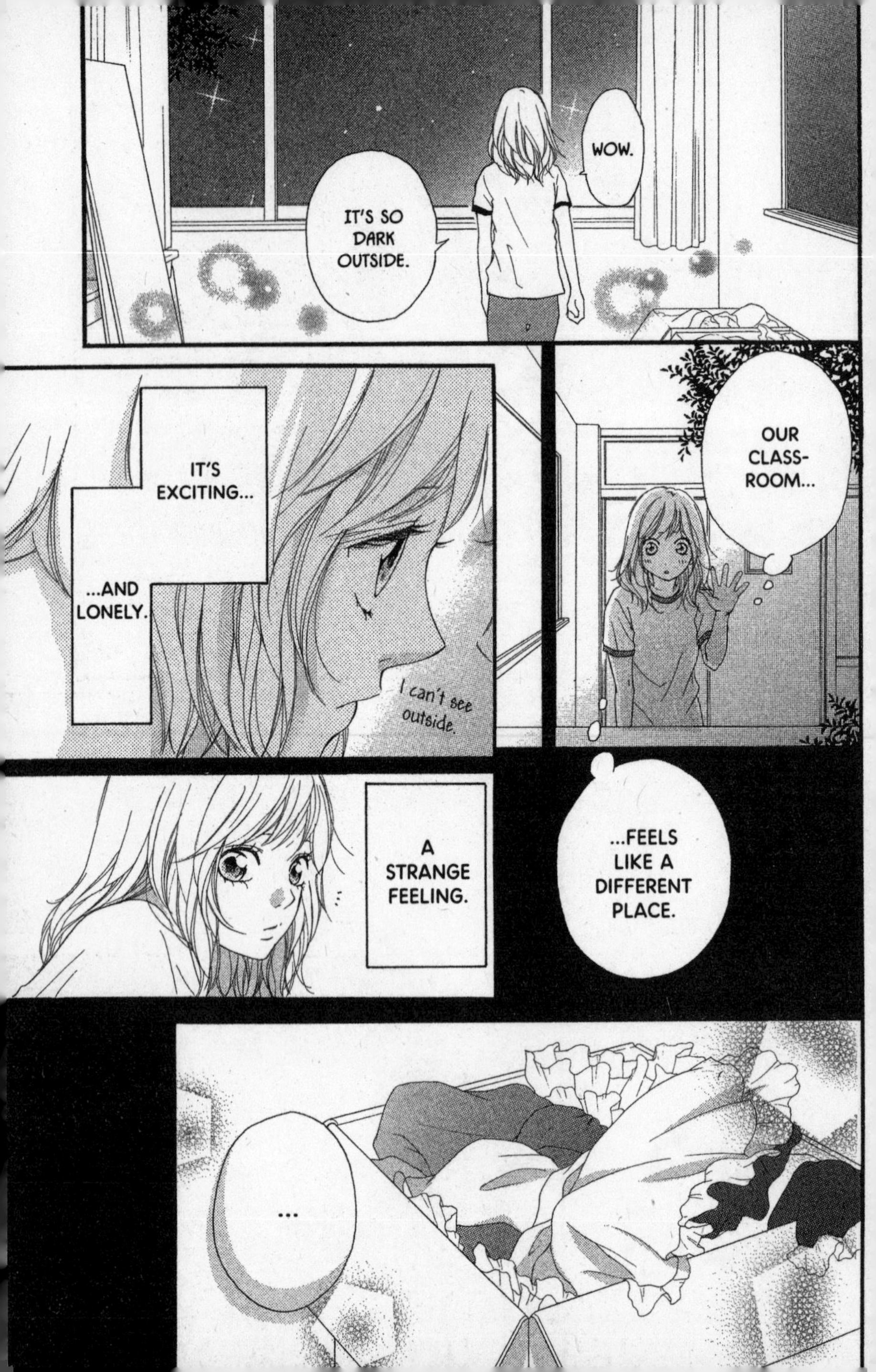
WOW.
IT'S SO DARK OUTSIDE.
OUR CLASS-ROOM...
IT'S EXCITING...
...AND LONELY.
I can't see outside.
...FEELS LIKE A DIFFERENT PLACE.
A STRANGE FEELING.
...

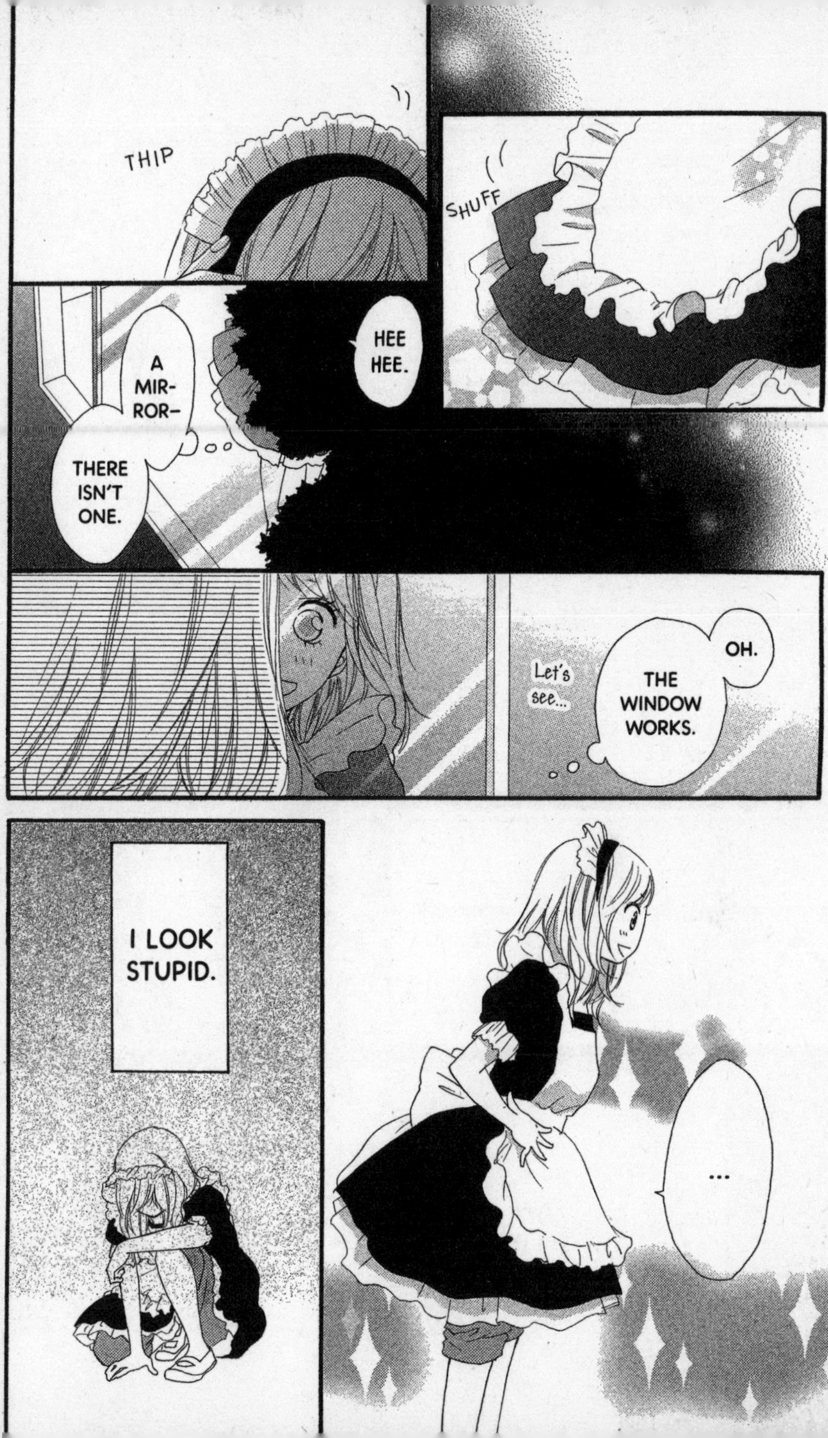
SHUFF
THIP
HEE HEE.
A MIRROR— THERE ISN'T ONE.
OH. THE WINDOW WORKS.
Let's see...
...
I LOOK STUPID.

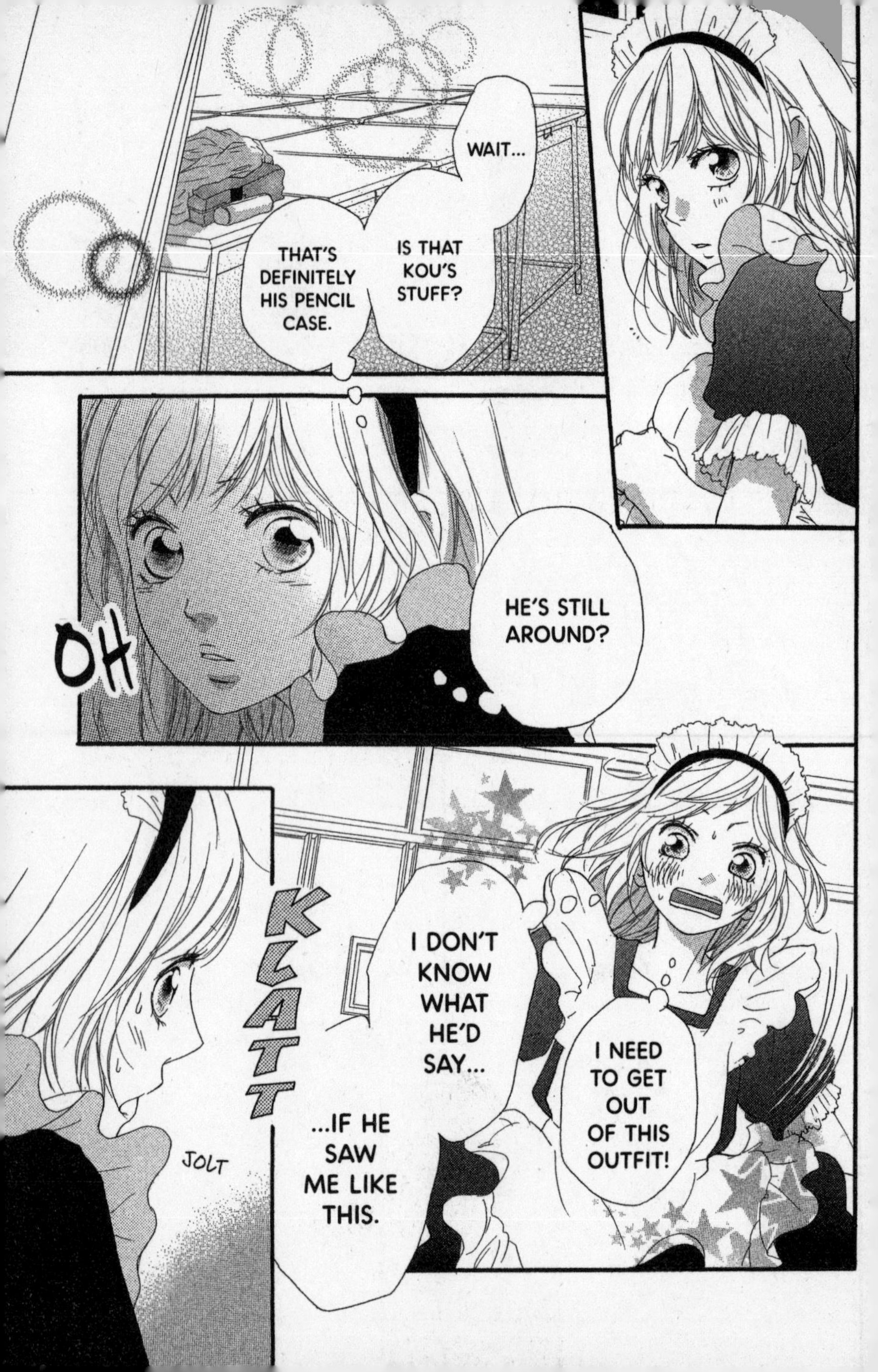
WAIT...
IS THAT KOU'S STUFF?
THAT'S DEFINITELY HIS PENCIL CASE.
HE'S STILL AROUND?
OH
I NEED TO GET OUT OF THIS OUTFIT!
I DON'T KNOW WHAT HE'D SAY...
...IF HE SAW ME LIKE THIS.
KLATT
JOLT

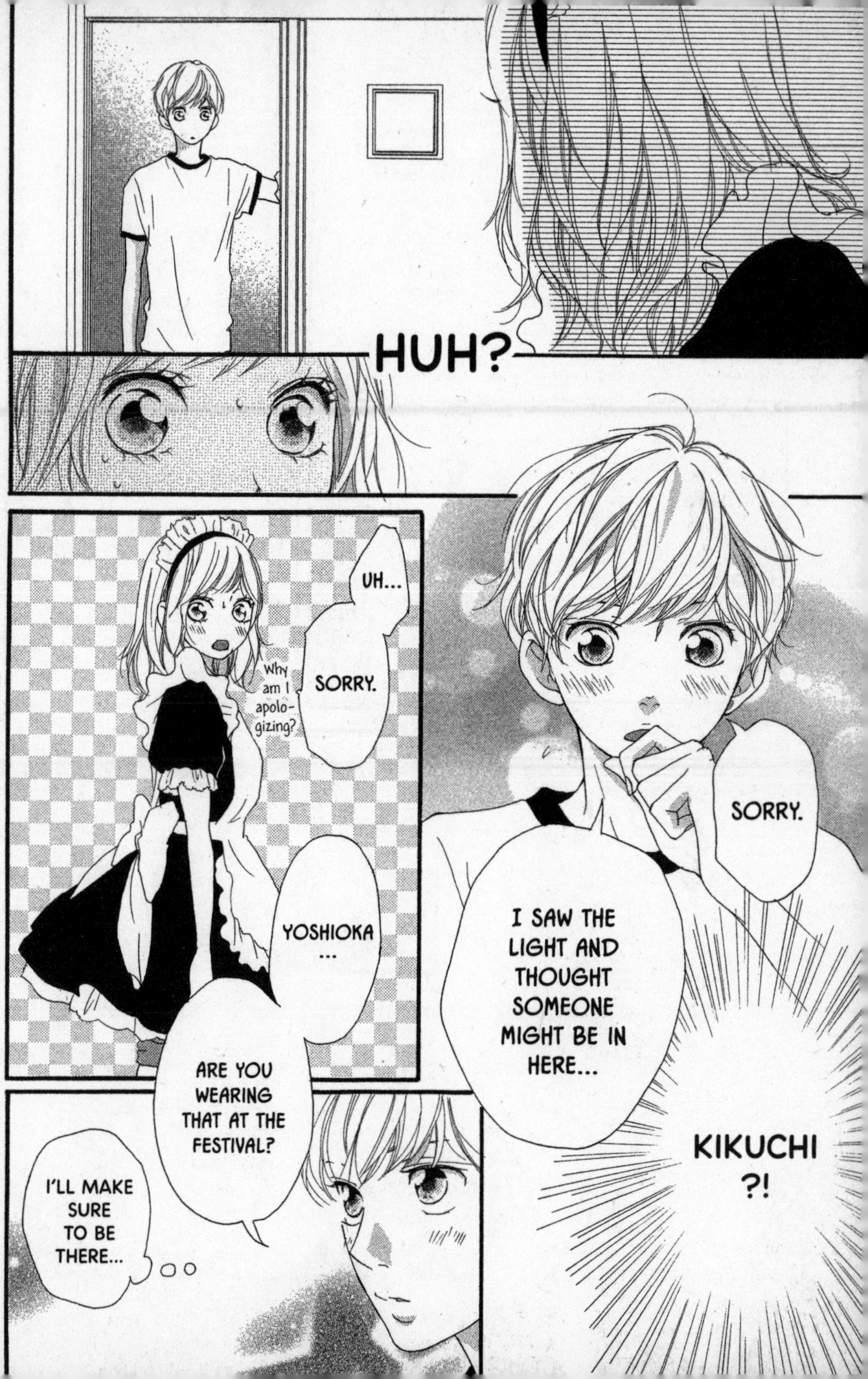
HUH?
KIKUCHI ?!
SORRY.
I SAW THE LIGHT AND THOUGHT SOMEONE MIGHT BE IN HERE...
UH... SORRY.
Why am I apologizing?
YOSHIOKA...
ARE YOU WEARING THAT AT THE FESTIVAL?
I'LL MAKE SURE TO BE THERE...

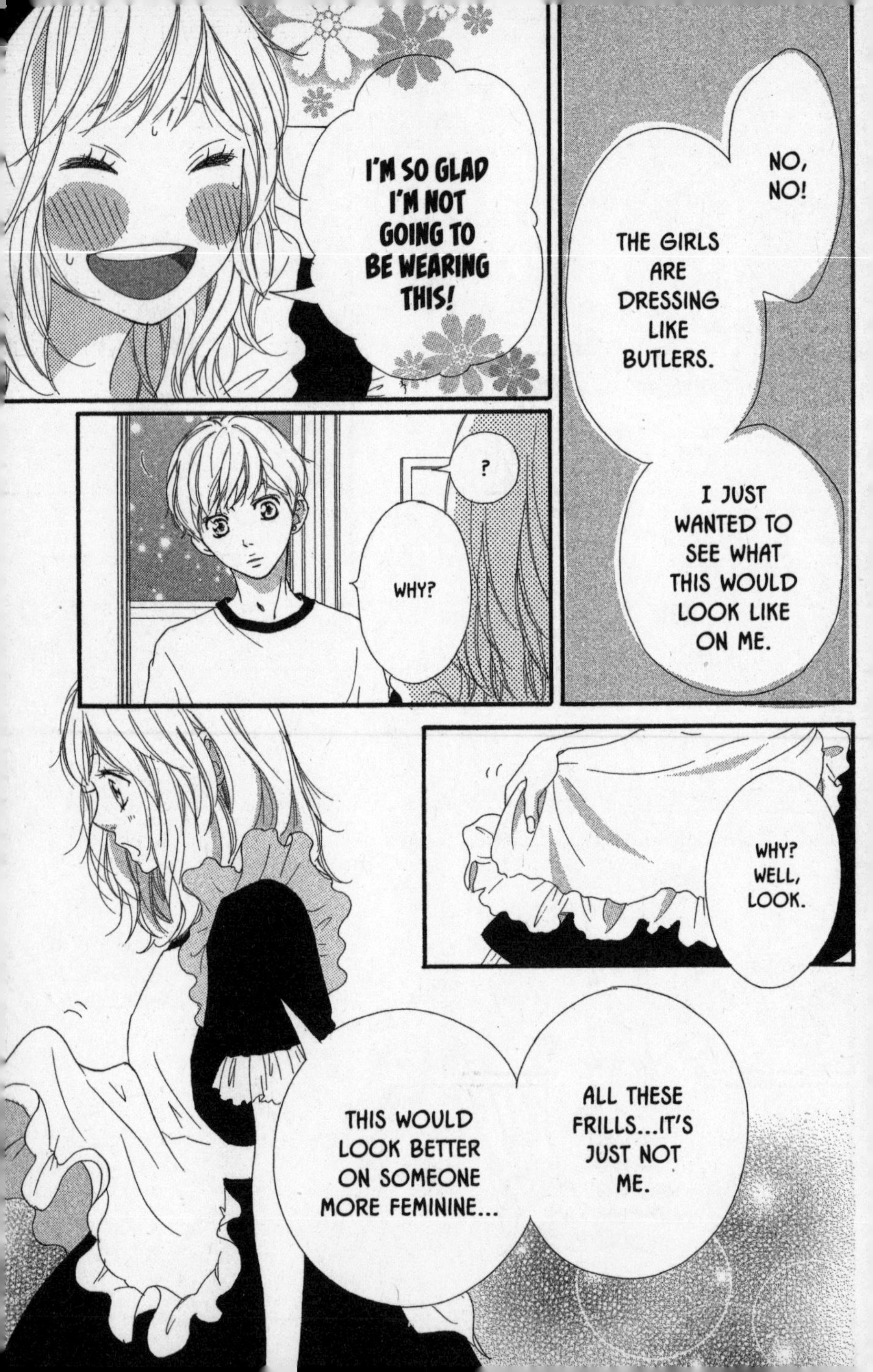
NO, NO!
THE GIRLS ARE DRESSING LIKE BUTLERS.
I JUST WANTED TO SEE WHAT THIS WOULD LOOK LIKE ON ME.
I'M SO GLAD I'M NOT GOING TO BE WEARING THIS!
?
WHY?
WHY? WELL, LOOK.
ALL THESE FRILLS...IT'S JUST NOT ME.
THIS WOULD LOOK BETTER ON SOMEONE MORE FEMININE...

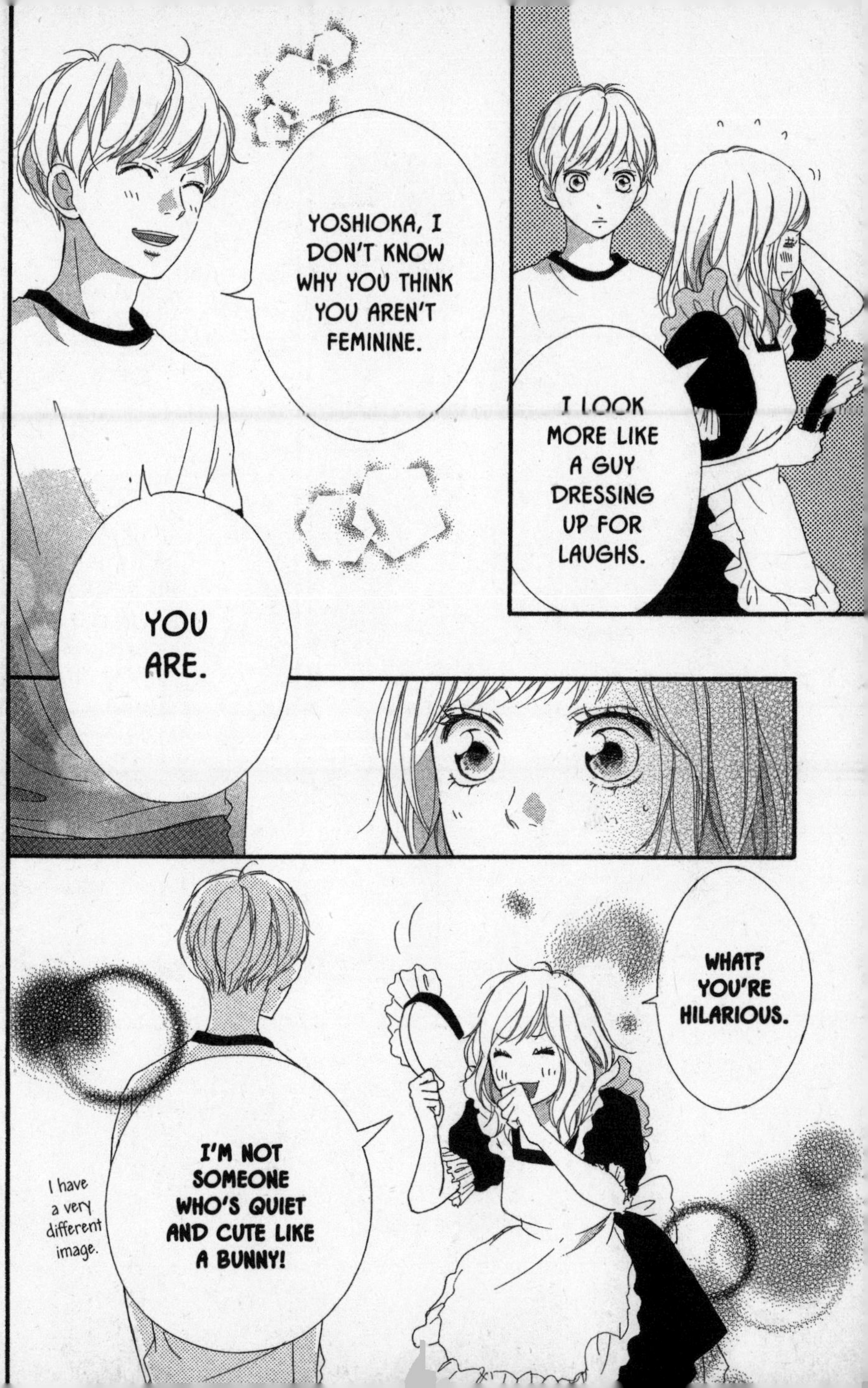
I LOOK MORE LIKE A GUY DRESSING UP FOR LAUGHS.
YOSHIOKA, I DON'T KNOW WHY YOU THINK YOU AREN'T FEMININE.
YOU ARE.
WHAT? YOU'RE HILARIOUS.
I'M NOT SOMEONE WHO'S QUIET AND CUTE LIKE A BUNNY!
I have a very different image.

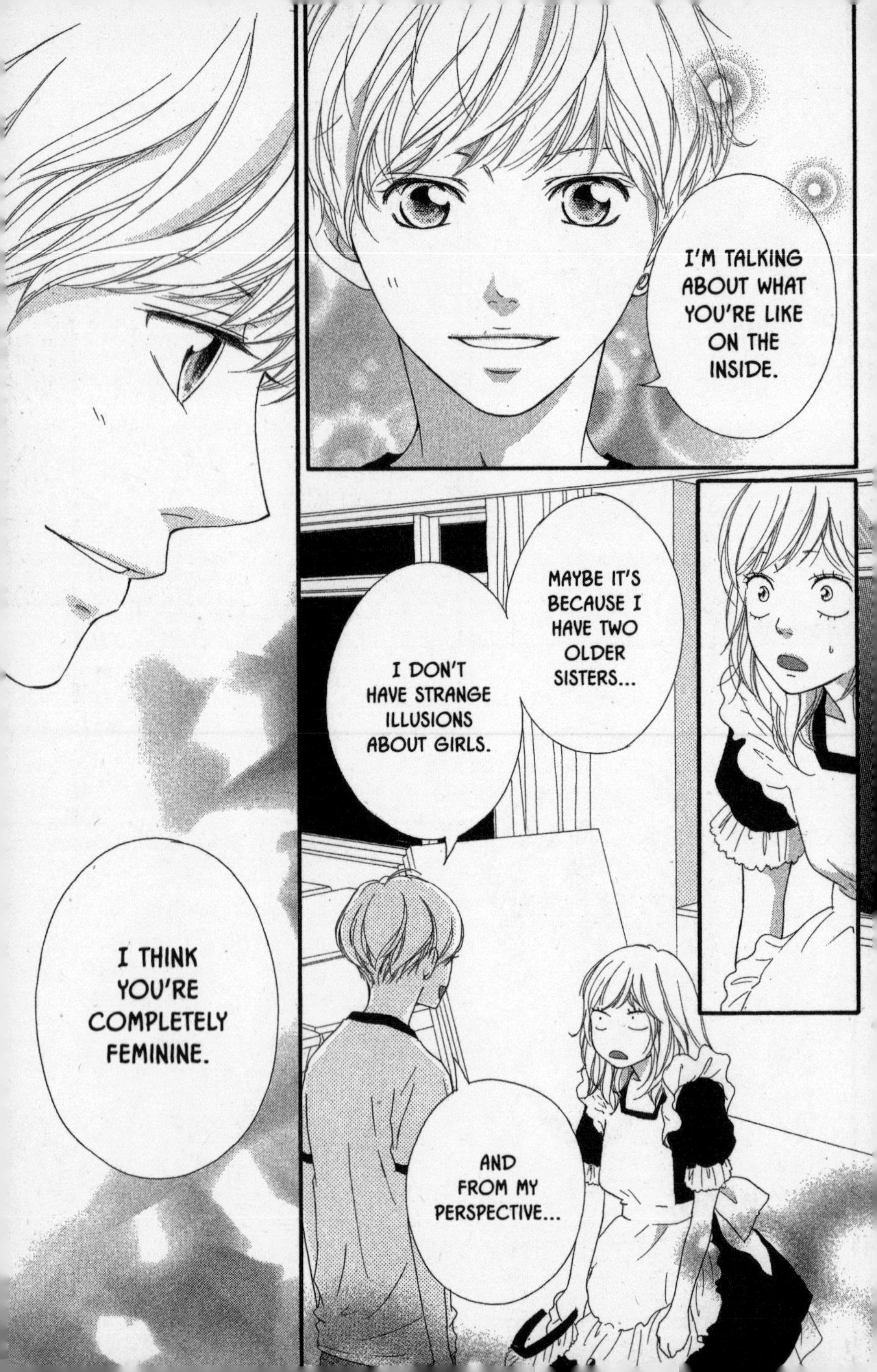
I'M TALKING ABOUT WHAT YOU'RE LIKE ON THE INSIDE.
MAYBE IT'S BECAUSE I HAVE TWO OLDER SISTERS...
I DON'T HAVE STRANGE ILLUSIONS ABOUT GIRLS.
AND FROM MY PERSPECTIVE...
I THINK YOU'RE COMPLETELY FEMININE.

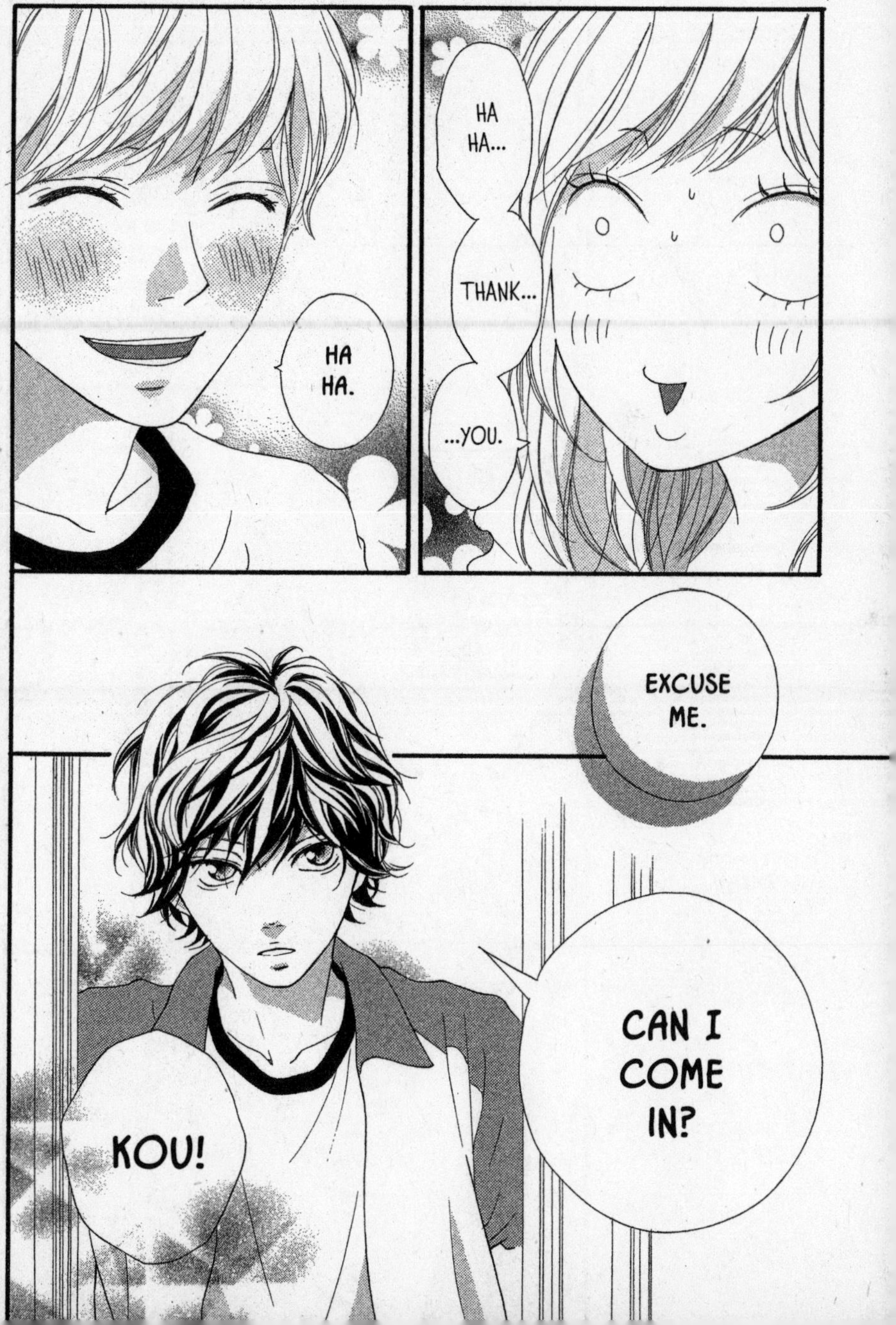
HA HA...
THANK...
...YOU.
HA HA.
EXCUSE ME.
CAN I COME IN?
KOU!

Whenever I vacuum, I think about how vacuums purposely go after your pinky toes. Mine is so good at it that I swear it's like a sniper! When the vacuum gets stuck in the corner and starts giving me trouble, I'll yank the cord back, and it will lunge at me! I really wish it would stop. When my pinky toe gets slammed, I suffer an angry and breath-stopping pain that I can't project anywhere. It really gets me down. Sometimes my vacuum ups its technique and comes after my ankle as well. Where does it learn this stuff? I'm wondering if there are any vacuums out there that don't hurt. Do your pinky toes get attacked too? I've no interest in making up with my vacuum at this point. We don't mesh well!

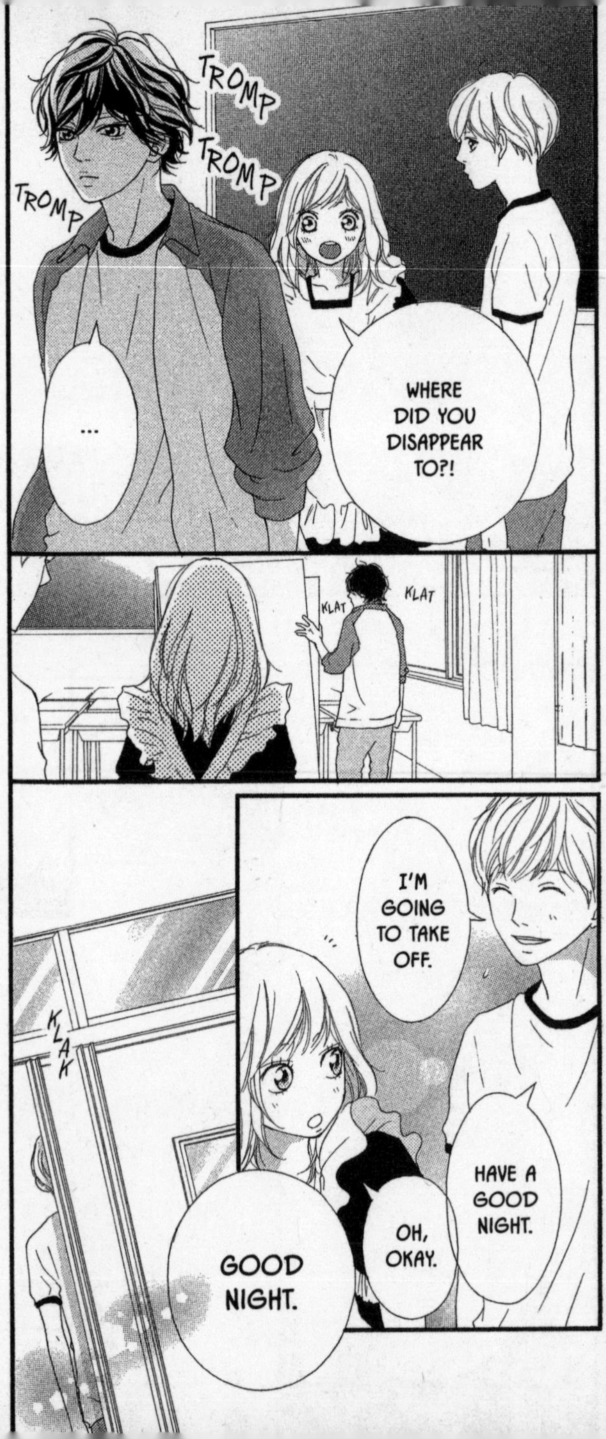
TROMP
TROMP
TROMP
WHERE DID YOU DISAPPEAR TO?!
...
KLAT
KLAT
I'M GOING TO TAKE OFF.
HAVE A GOOD NIGHT.
OH, OKAY.
GOOD NIGHT.
KLAK

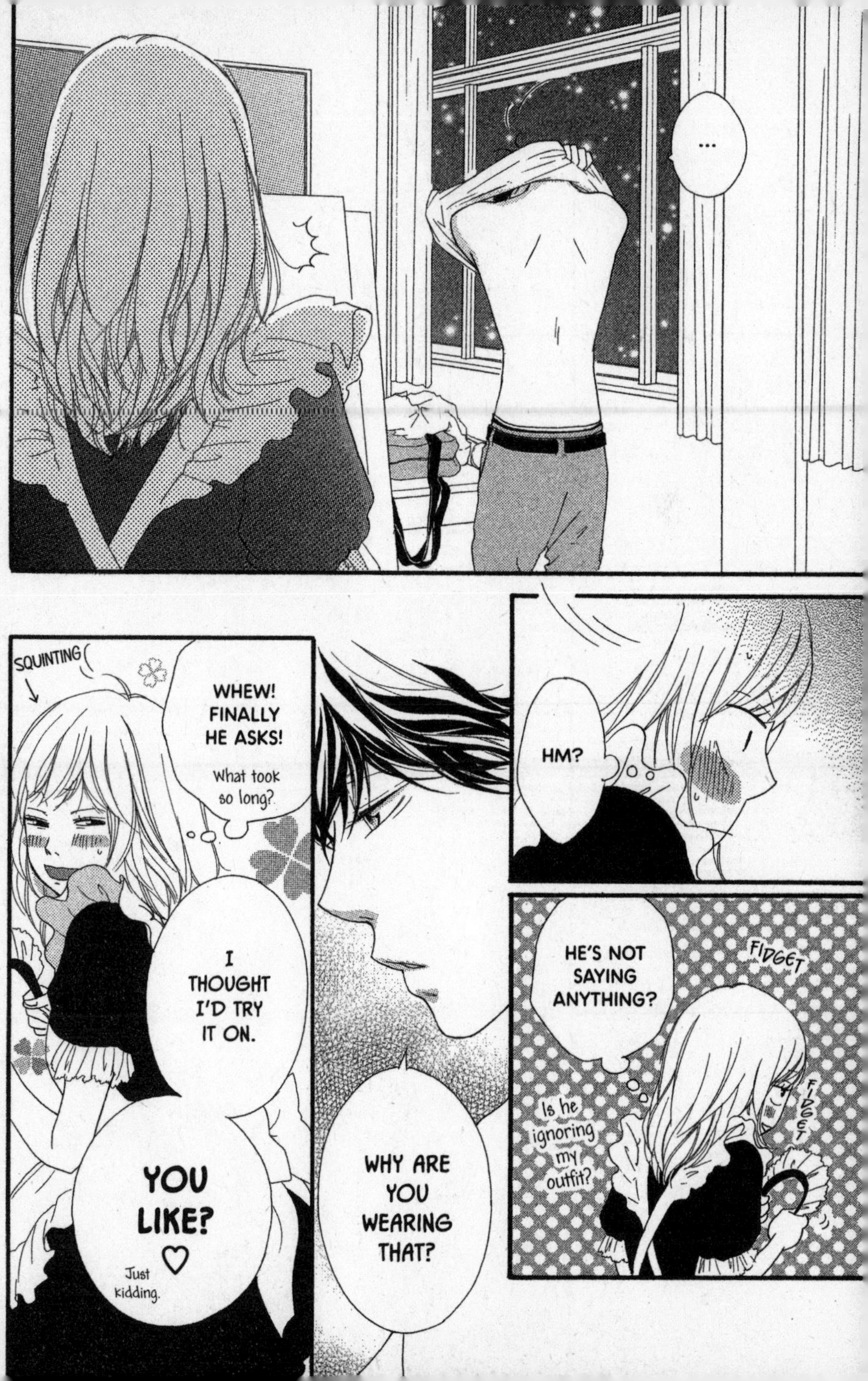
...
HM?
HE'S NOT SAYING ANYTHING?
FIDGET
FIDGET
Is he ignoring my outfit?
WHY ARE YOU WEARING THAT?
SQUINTING
WHEW! FINALLY HE ASKS!
What took so long?
I THOUGHT I'D TRY IT ON.
YOU LIKE? ♡
Just kidding.

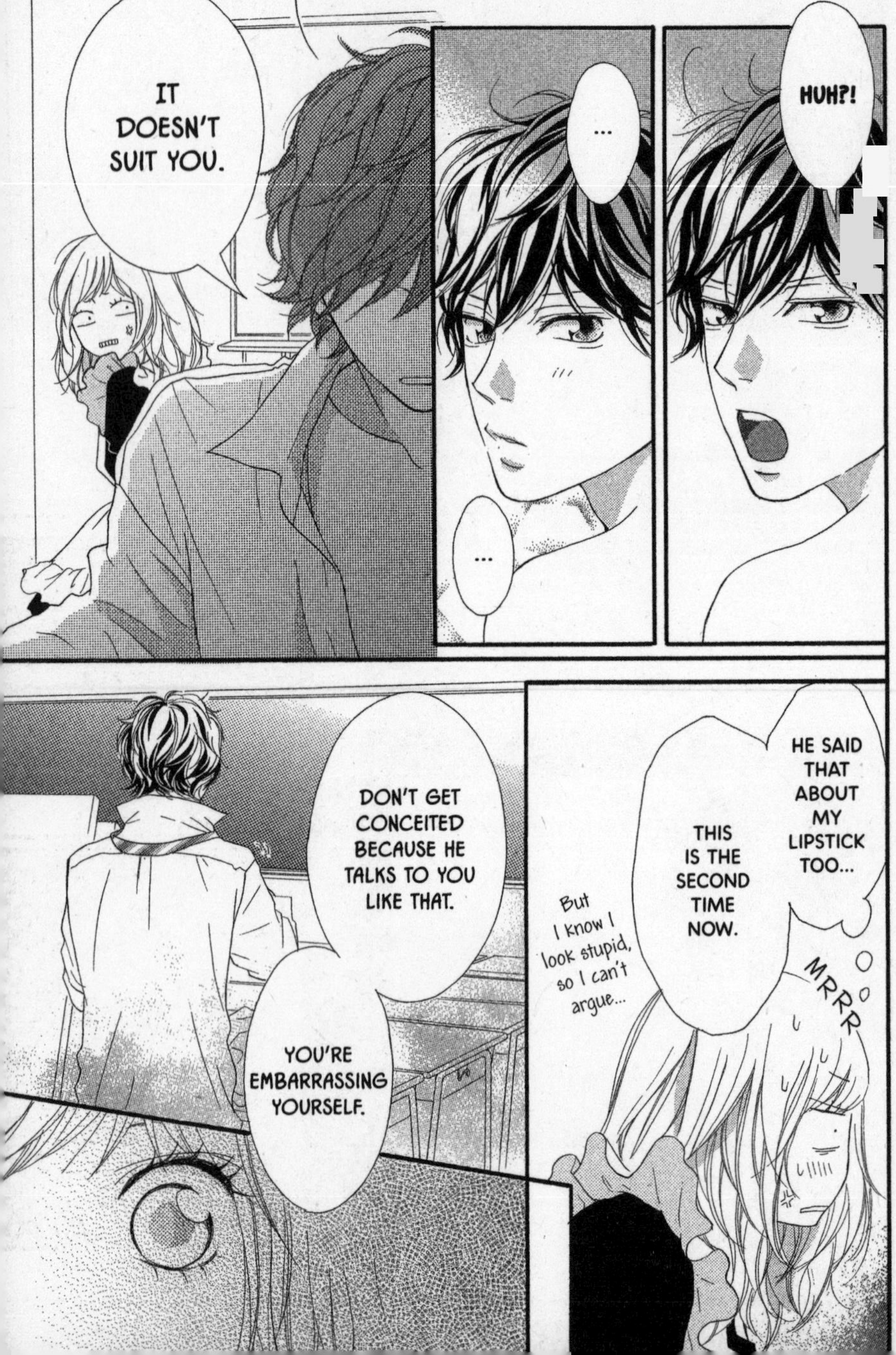
HUH?!
...
...
IT DOESN'T SUIT YOU.
HE SAID THAT ABOUT MY LIPSTICK TOO...
THIS IS THE SECOND TIME NOW.
MRRR
But I know I look stupid, so I can't argue...
DON'T GET CONCEITED BECAUSE HE TALKS TO YOU LIKE THAT.
YOU'RE EMBARRASSING YOURSELF.

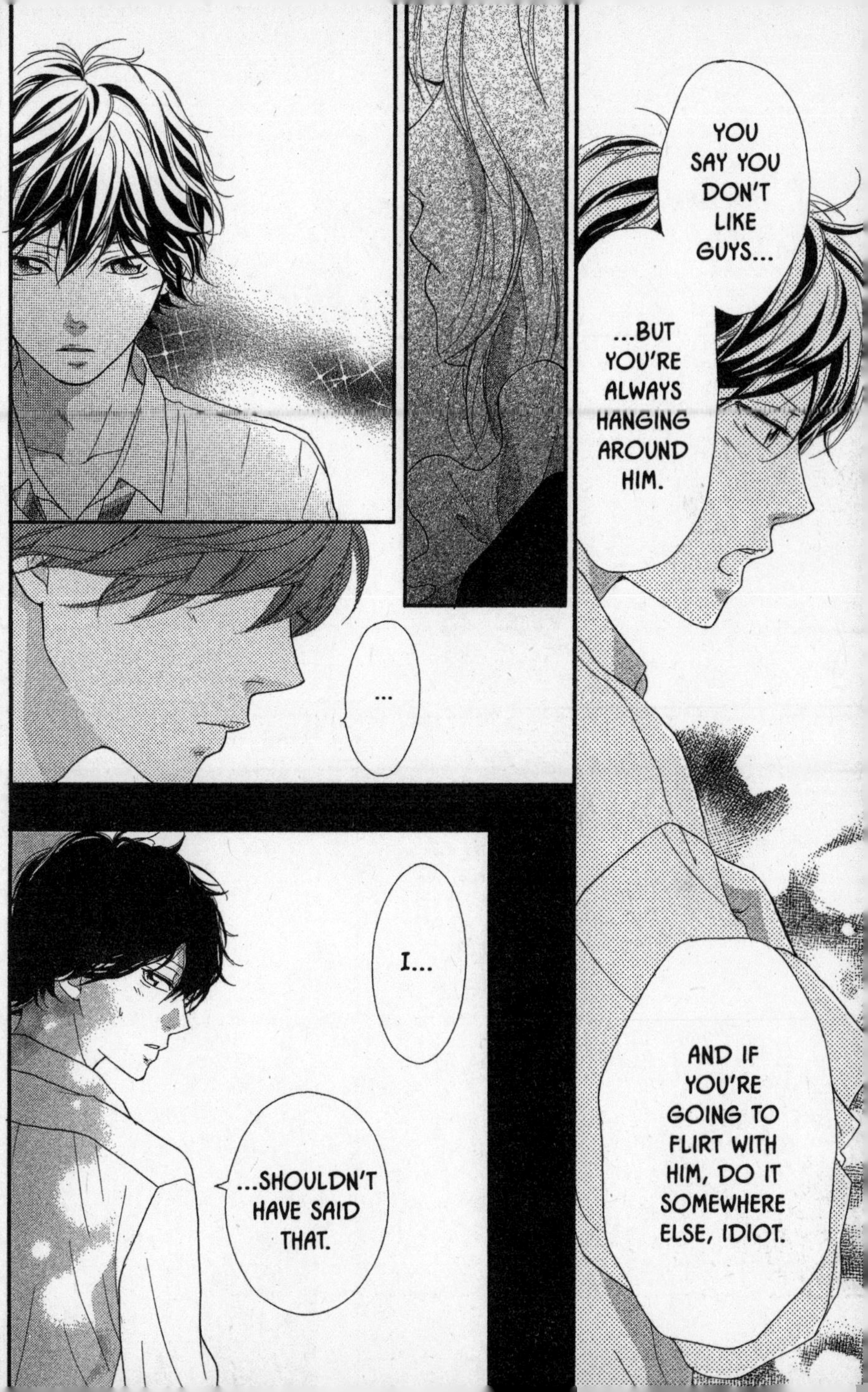
YOU SAY YOU DON'T LIKE GUYS...
...BUT YOU'RE ALWAYS HANGING AROUND HIM.
AND IF YOU'RE GOING TO FLIRT WITH HIM, DO IT SOMEWHERE ELSE, IDIOT.
...
I...
...SHOULDN'T HAVE SAID THAT.

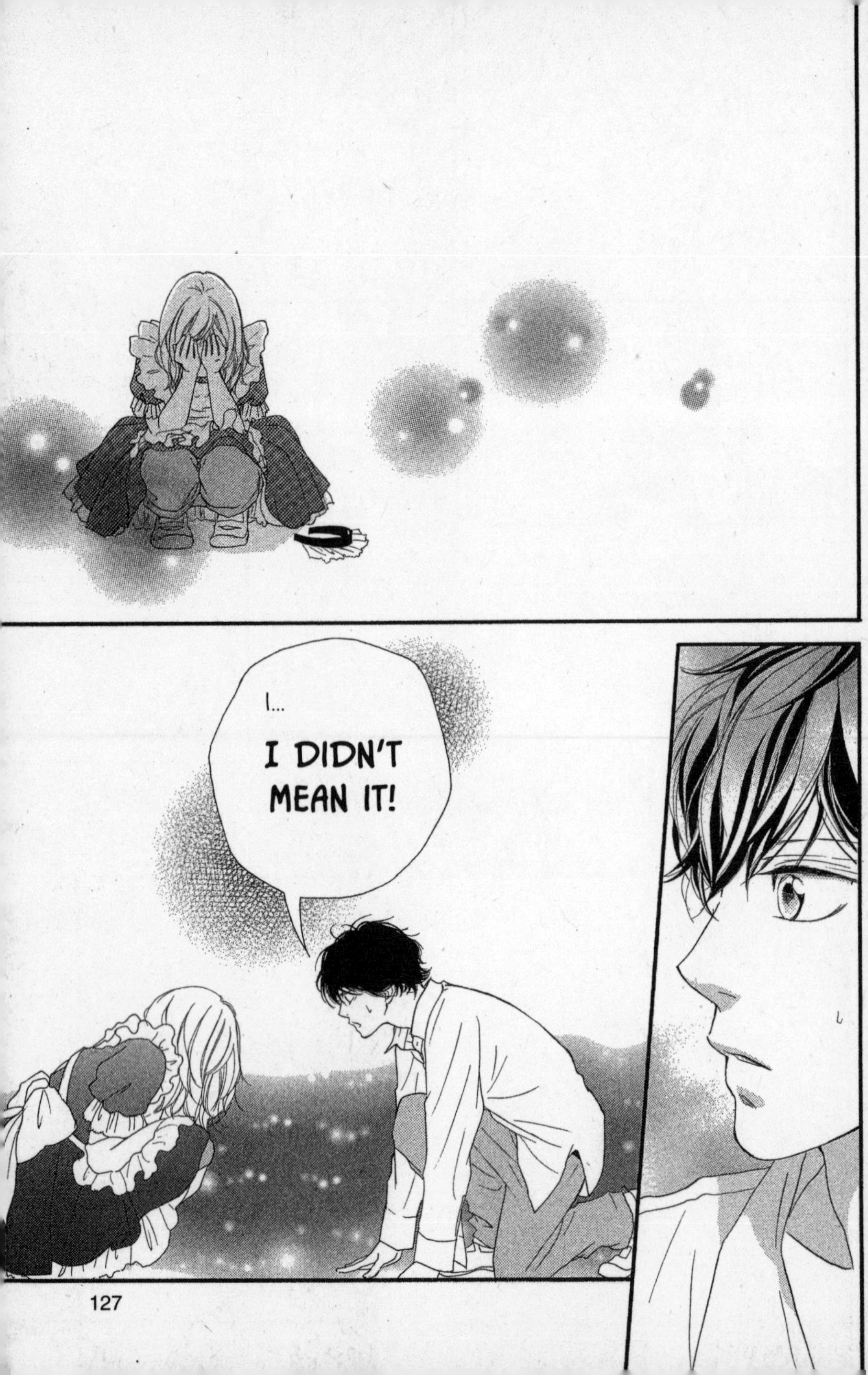
I...
I DIDN'T MEAN IT!

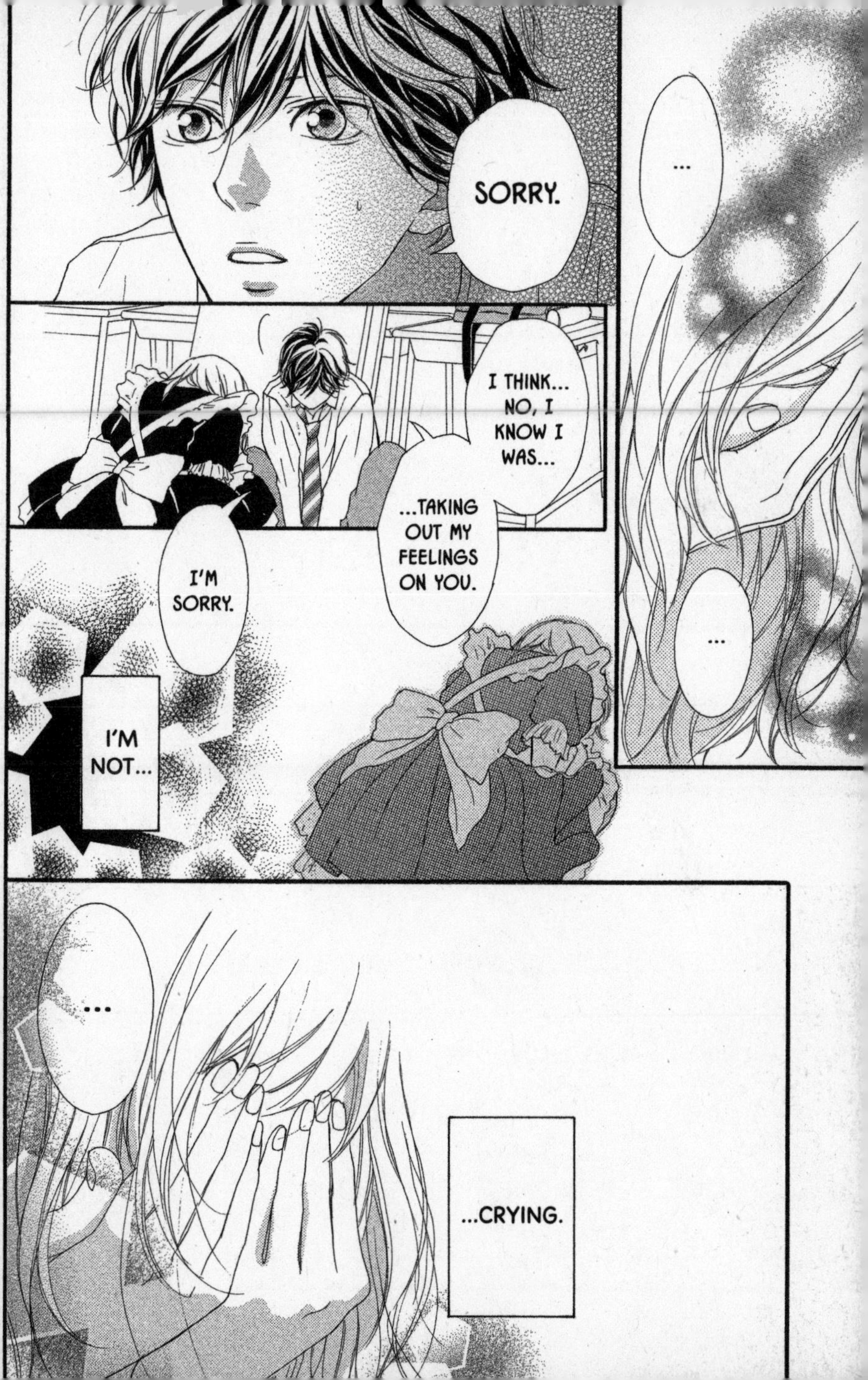
...
...
SORRY.
I THINK... NO, I KNOW I WAS...
...TAKING OUT MY FEELINGS ON YOU.
I'M SORRY.
I'M NOT...
...
...CRYING.

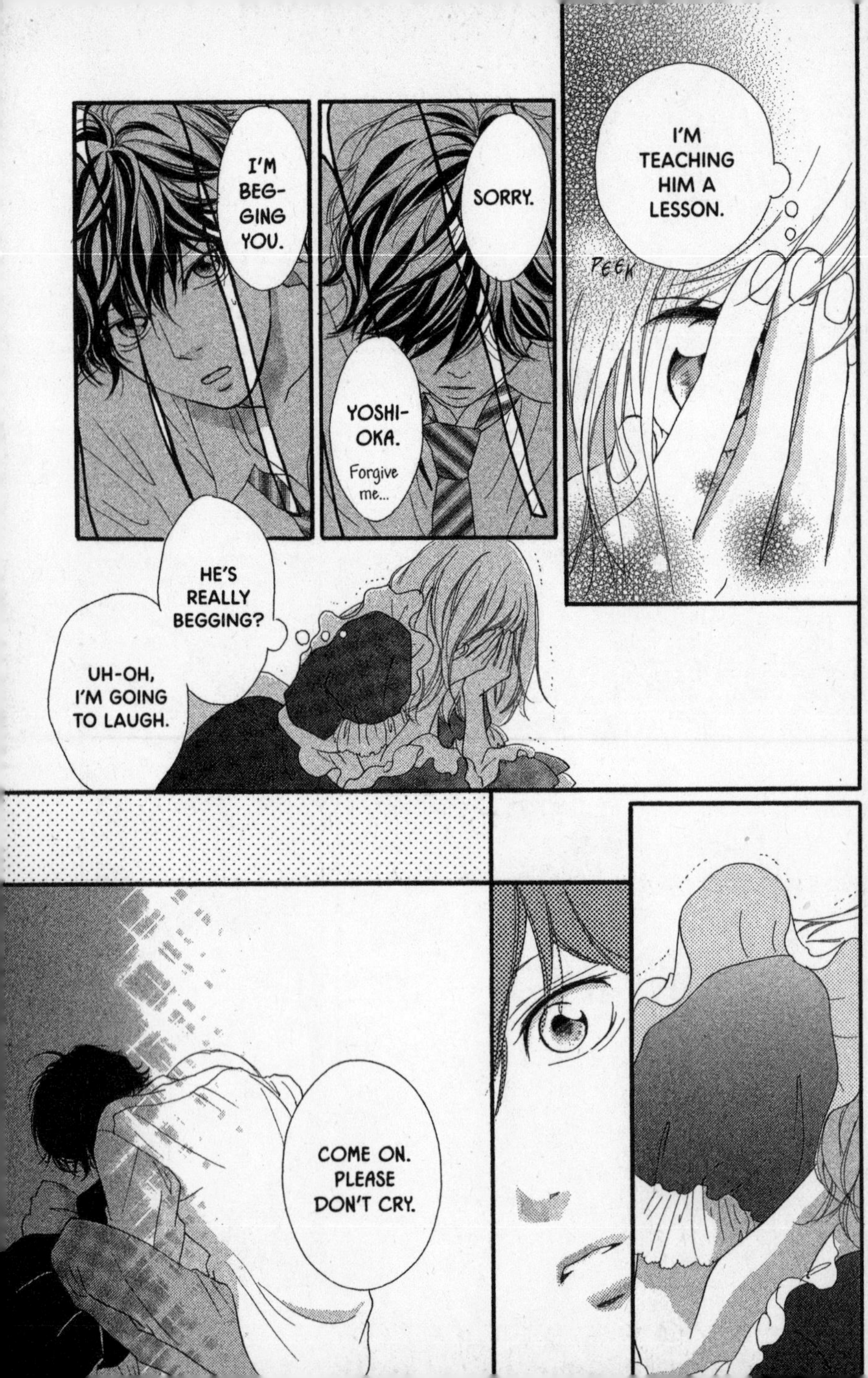
I'M TEACHING HIM A LESSON.
PEEK
SORRY.
YOSHI-OKA.
Forgive me...
I'M BEG-GING YOU.
HE'S REALLY BEGGING?
UH-OH, I'M GOING TO LAUGH.
COME ON. PLEASE DON'T CRY.

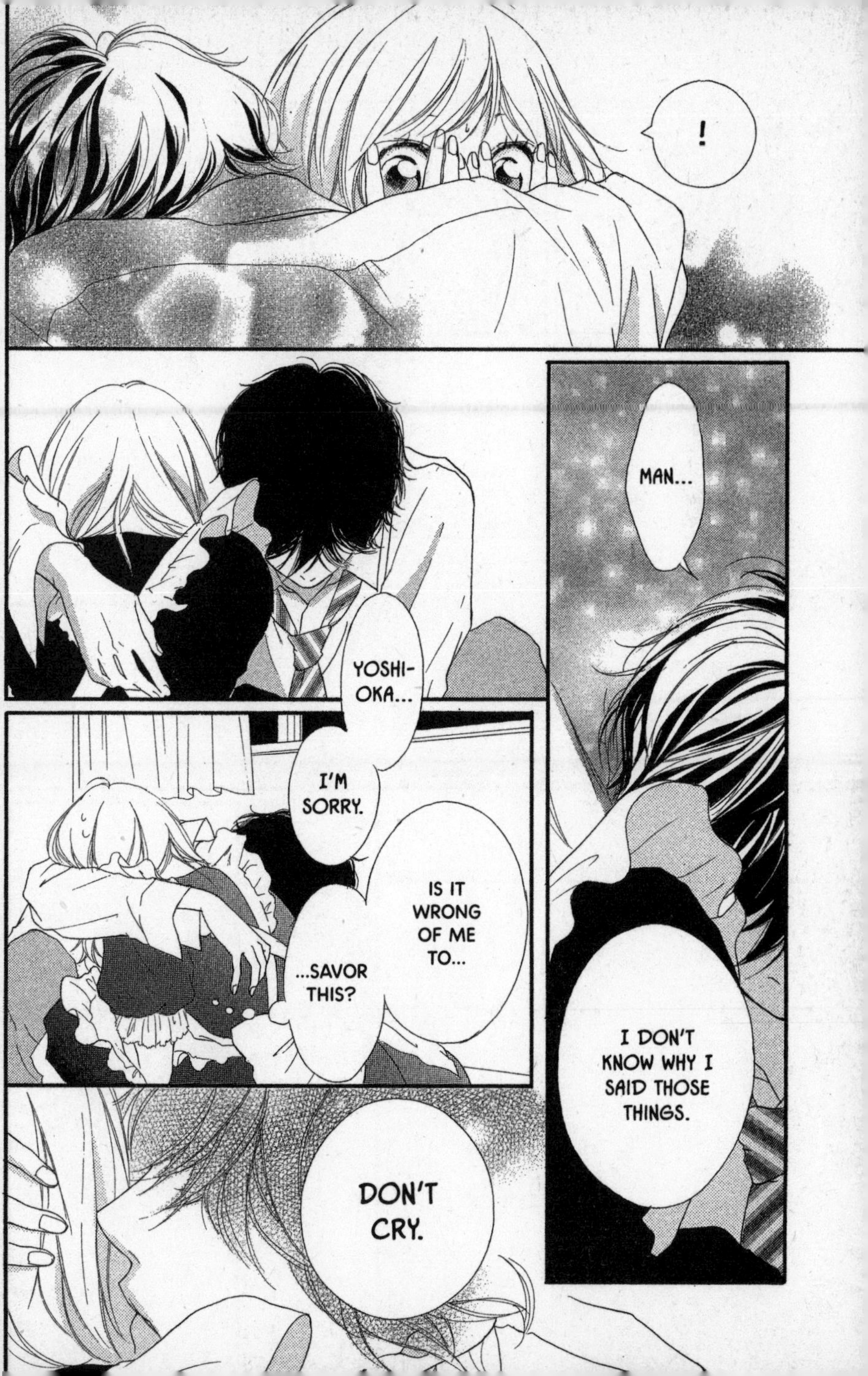
!
MAN...
I DON'T KNOW WHY I SAID THOSE THINGS.
YOSHI-OKA...
I'M SORRY.
IS IT WRONG OF ME TO...
...SAVOR THIS?
DON'T CRY.

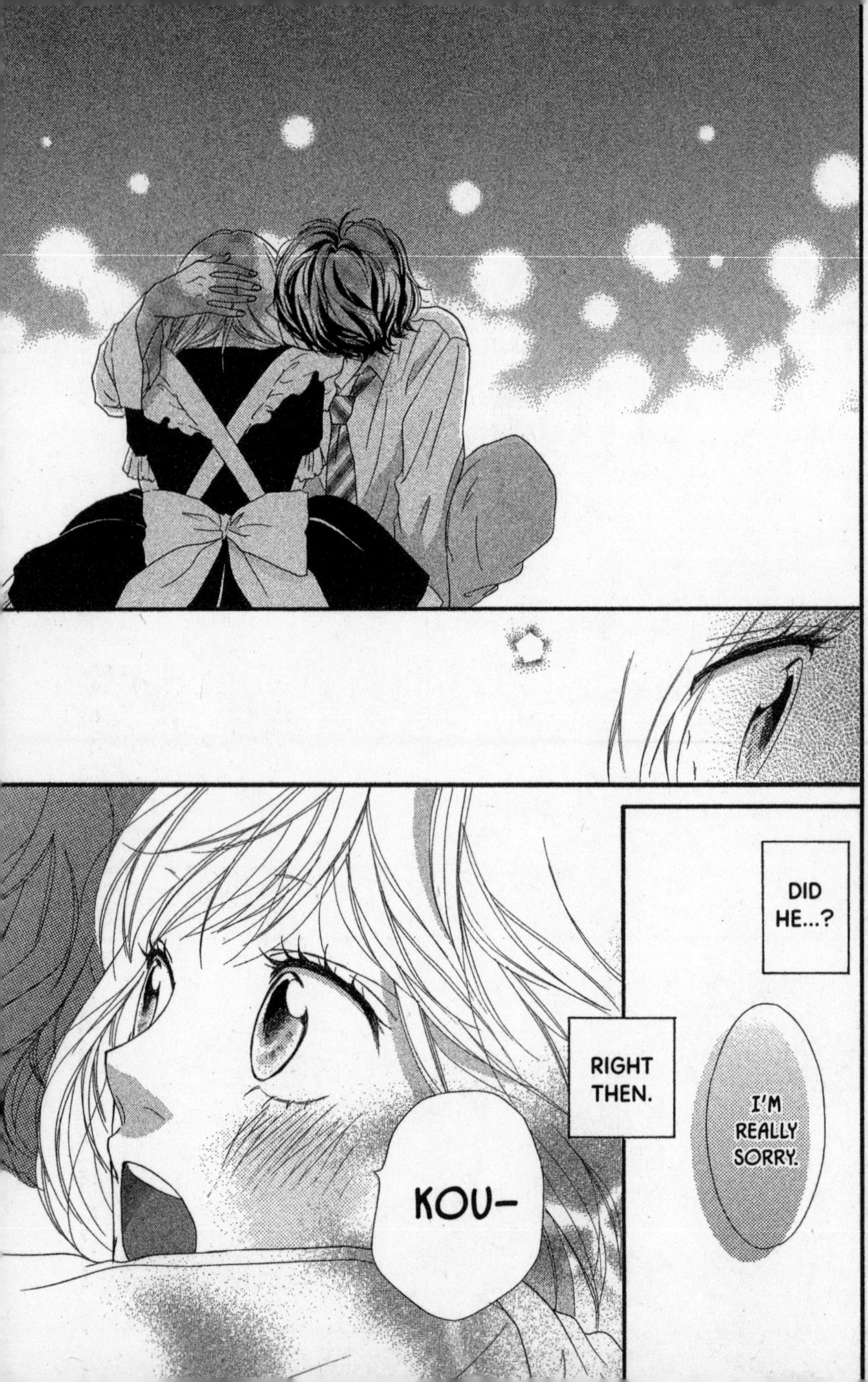
DID HE...?
I'M REALLY SORRY.
RIGHT THEN.
KOU-

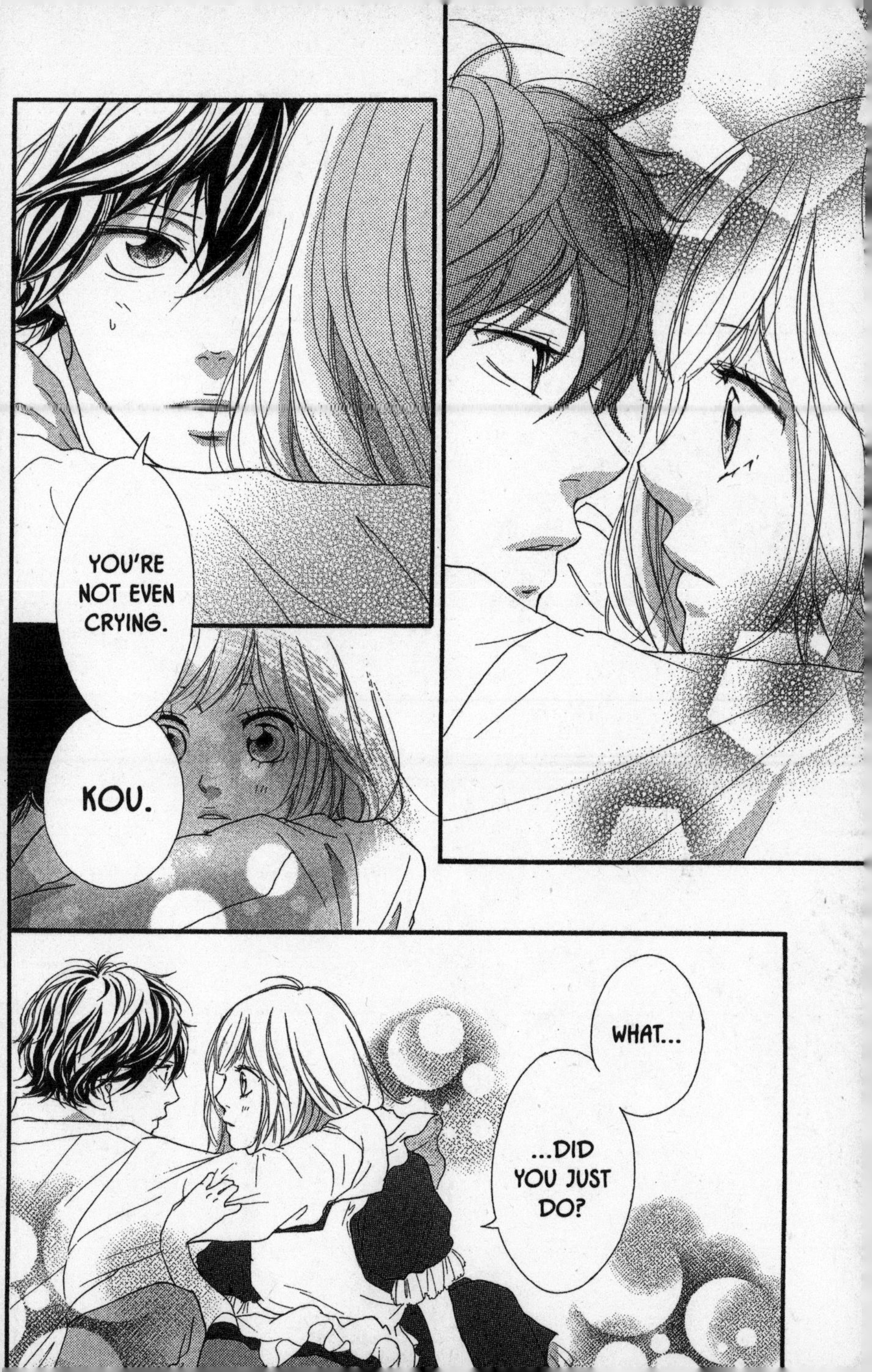
YOU'RE NOT EVEN CRYING.
KOU.
WHAT...
...DID YOU JUST DO?

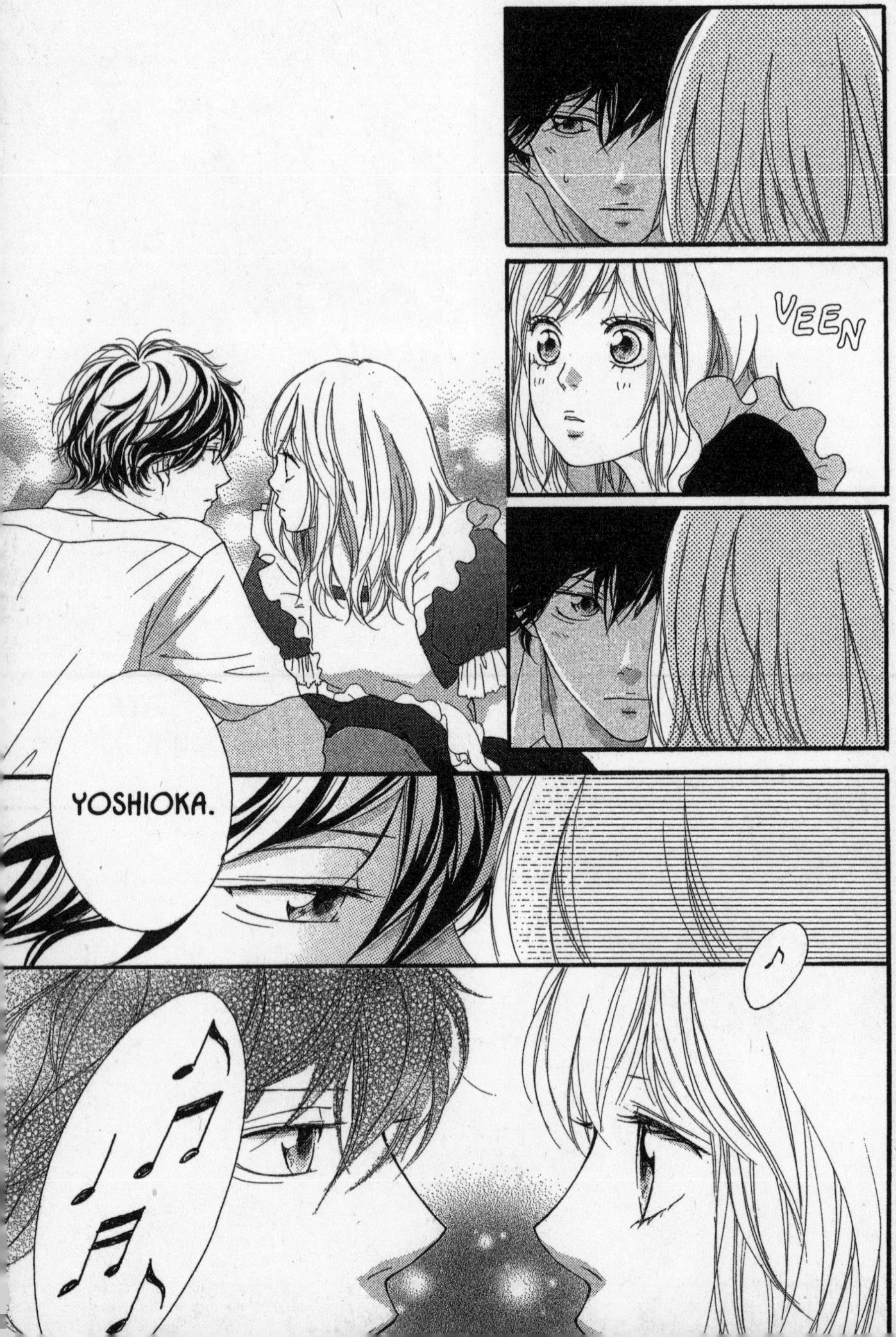
VEEN
YOSHIOKA.
♪
♪

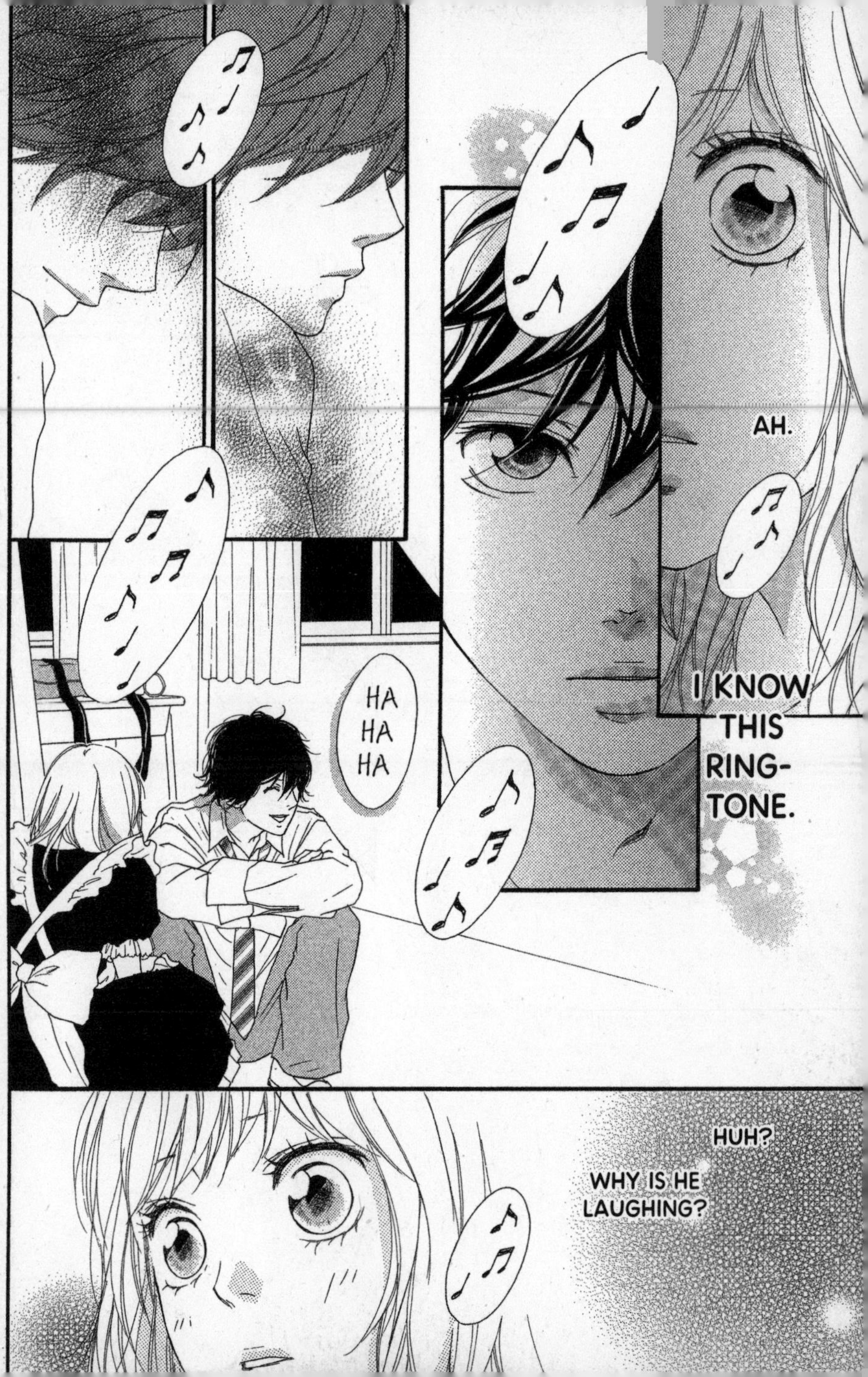
AH.
I KNOW THIS RING-TONE.
HA HA HA
HUH?
WHY IS HE LAUGHING?

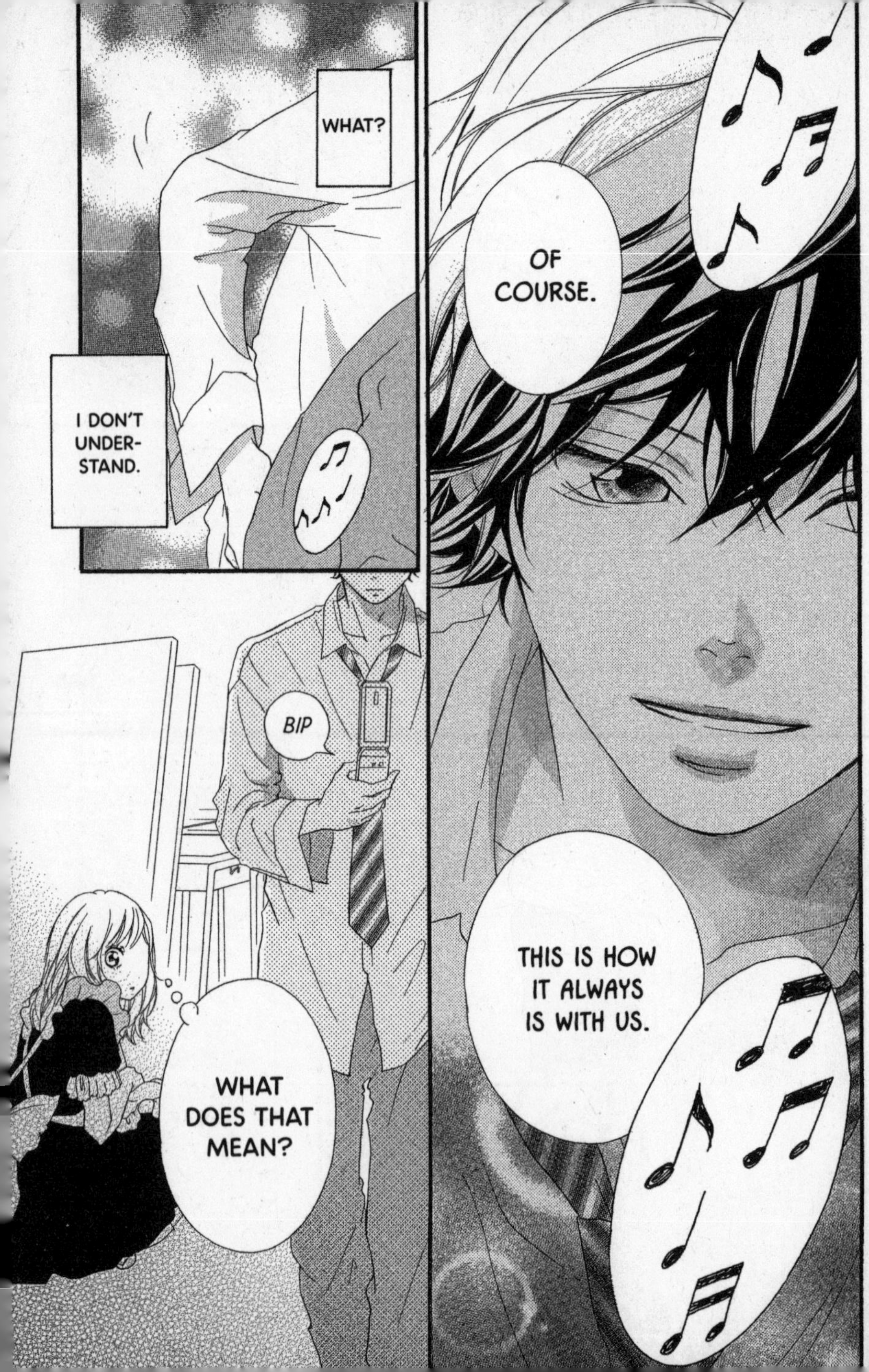
OF COURSE.
THIS IS HOW IT ALWAYS IS WITH US.
WHAT?
I DON'T UNDER-STAND.
BIP
WHAT DOES THAT MEAN?

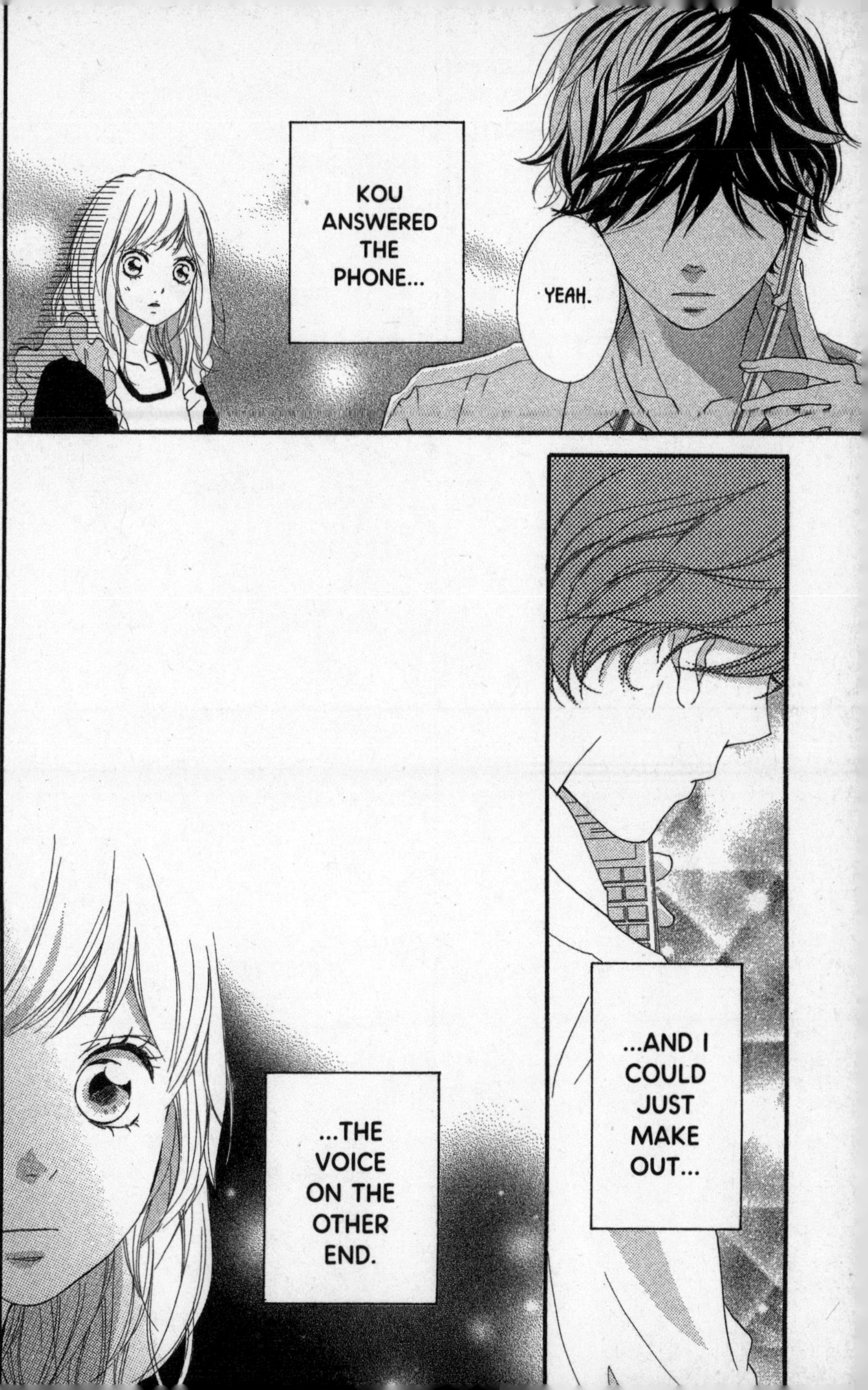
KOU ANSWERED THE PHONE...
YEAH.
...AND I COULD JUST MAKE OUT...
...THE VOICE ON THE OTHER END.

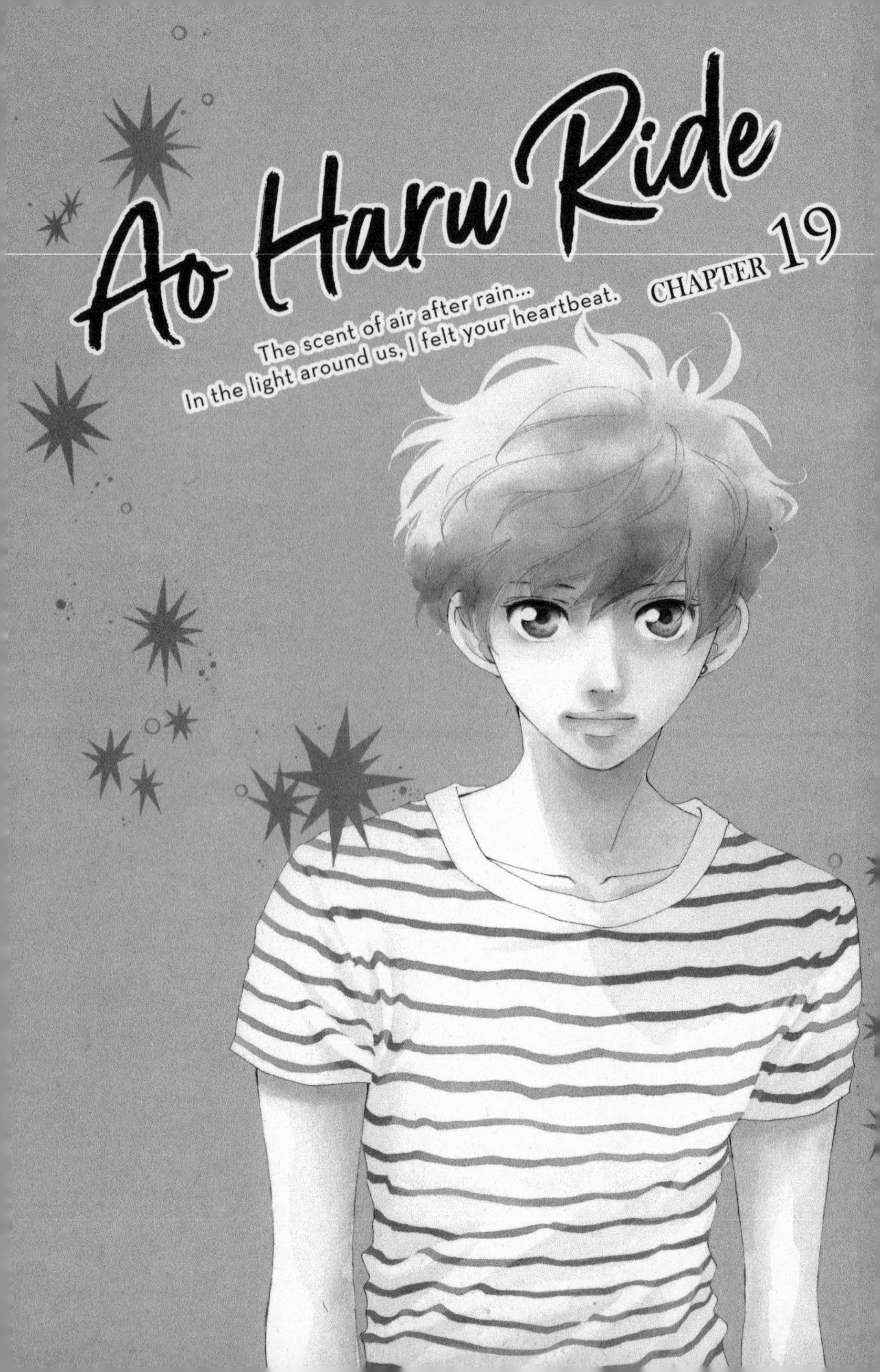
Ao Haru Ride
CHAPTER 19
The scent of air after rain...
In the light around us, I felt your heartbeat.

The room that I work in is tiny. It's overflowing with reference books and toys that keep piling up. I can't take it any longer, so I'm trading my room for the one next door that is slightly larger. Because of my production schedule, I need to move everything over quickly, but I can't move my desk...because I'm using it right now! The truth is, I was supposed to be done with everything already, but of course I'm not. Ha ha ha... At one point, I had wanted to get a new desk, shelf and other things, but that's no longer in the picture, let alone the schedule. Now that I've eliminated any element of fun, I'm just moving things from one room to another, which is a serious pain. Oh, but I am getting new chairs! I love my chair, but after a decade of regular use, my seat cushion is torn and the spongy part is spilling out (I've been covering it up with a towel). It's time to say goodbye. Thank you, Chair! Thank you for many years of support! My assistant's chair squeaks, so I think I'm going to change both out. Also I'm moving my copy machine from my living room to the new room, which is sort of exciting. I wonder if I'll be settled and working out of my new space by the time this book comes out?

☆ Saki ☆

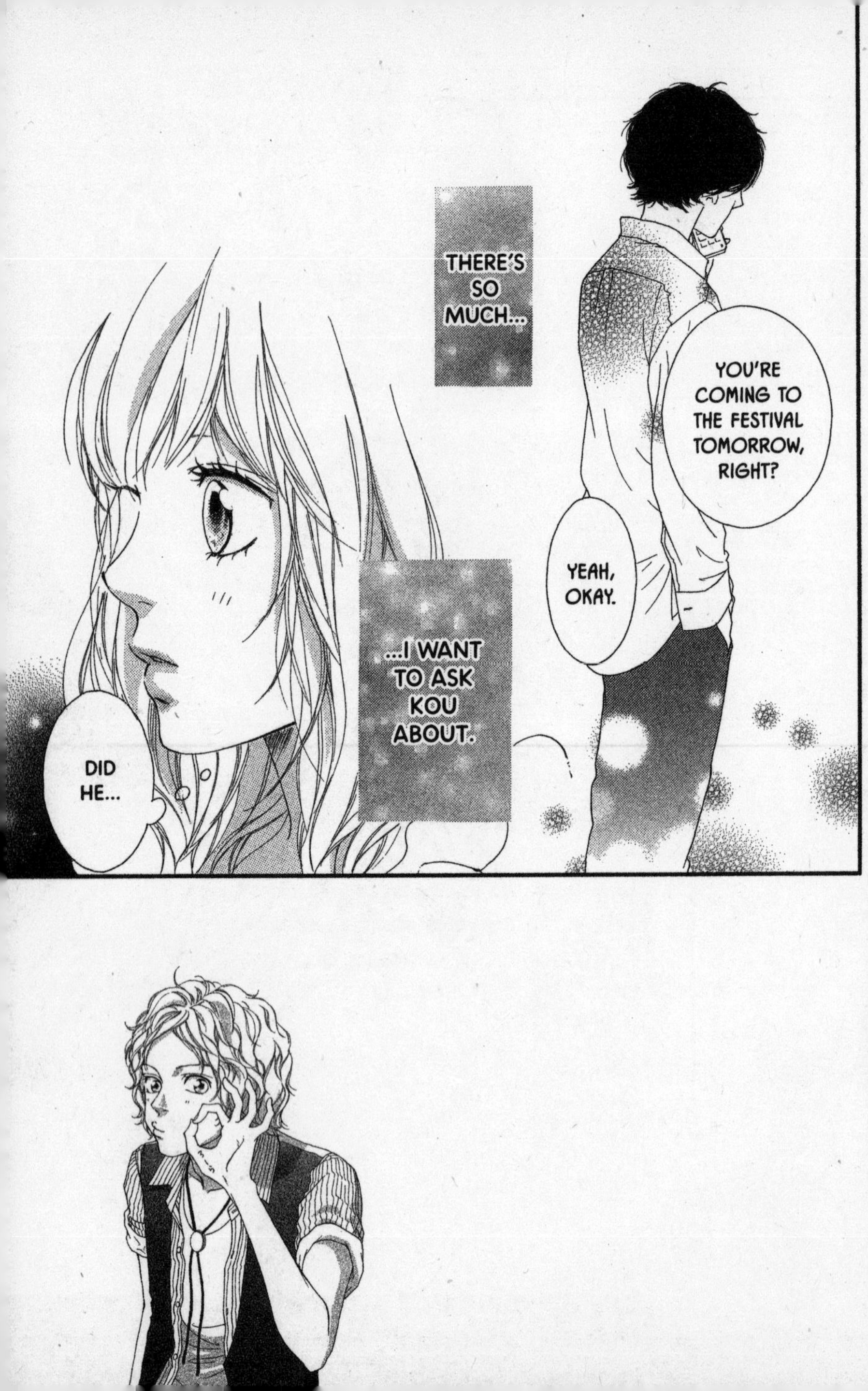
YOU'RE COMING TO THE FESTIVAL TOMORROW, RIGHT?
YEAH, OKAY.
THERE'S SO MUCH...
...I WANT TO ASK KOU ABOUT.
DID HE...

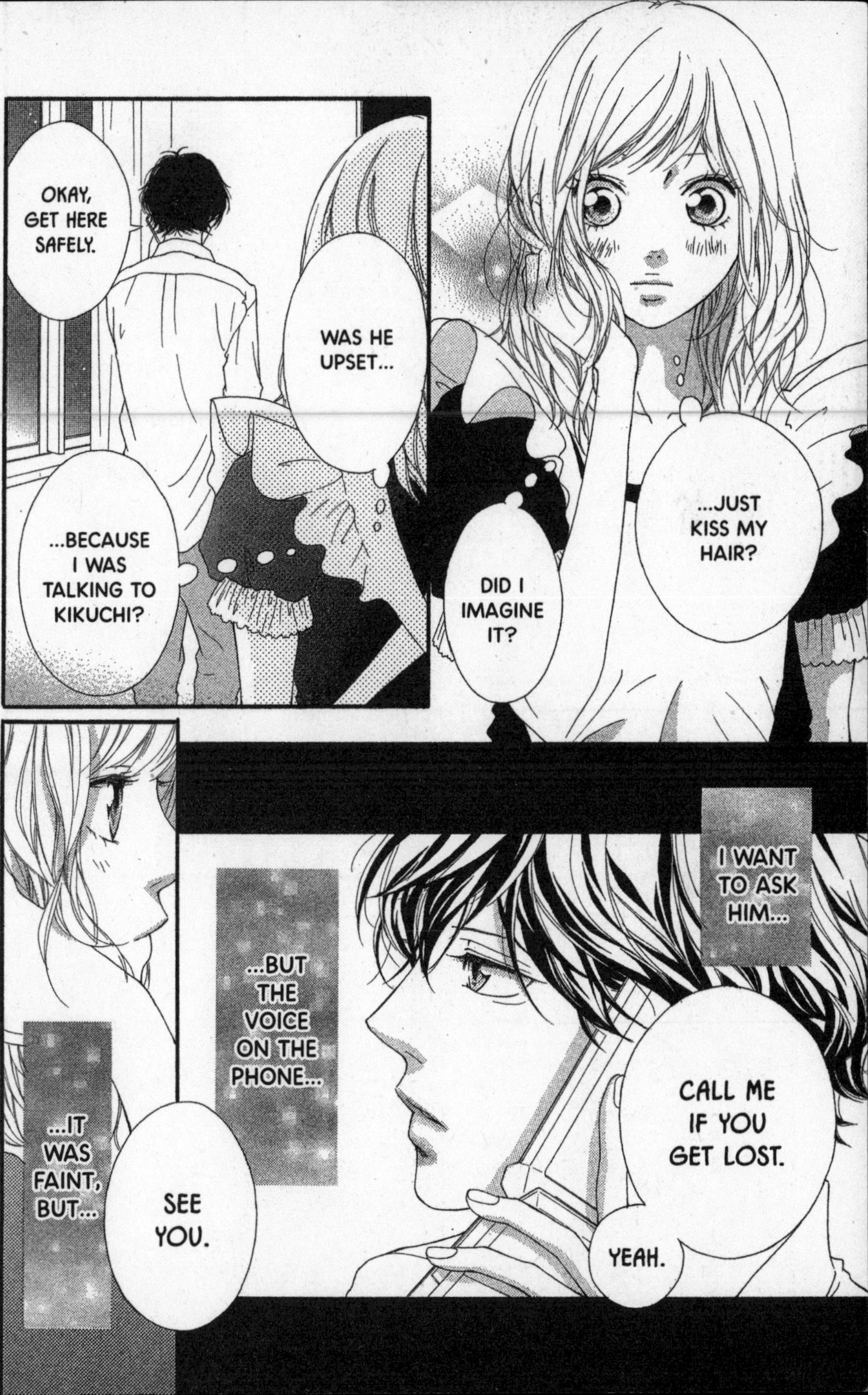
...JUST KISS MY HAIR?
DID I IMAGINE IT?
OKAY, GET HERE SAFELY.
WAS HE UPSET...
...BECAUSE I WAS TALKING TO KIKUCHI?
I WANT TO ASK HIM...
CALL ME IF YOU GET LOST.
YEAH.
...BUT THE VOICE ON THE PHONE...
SEE YOU.
...IT WAS FAINT, BUT...

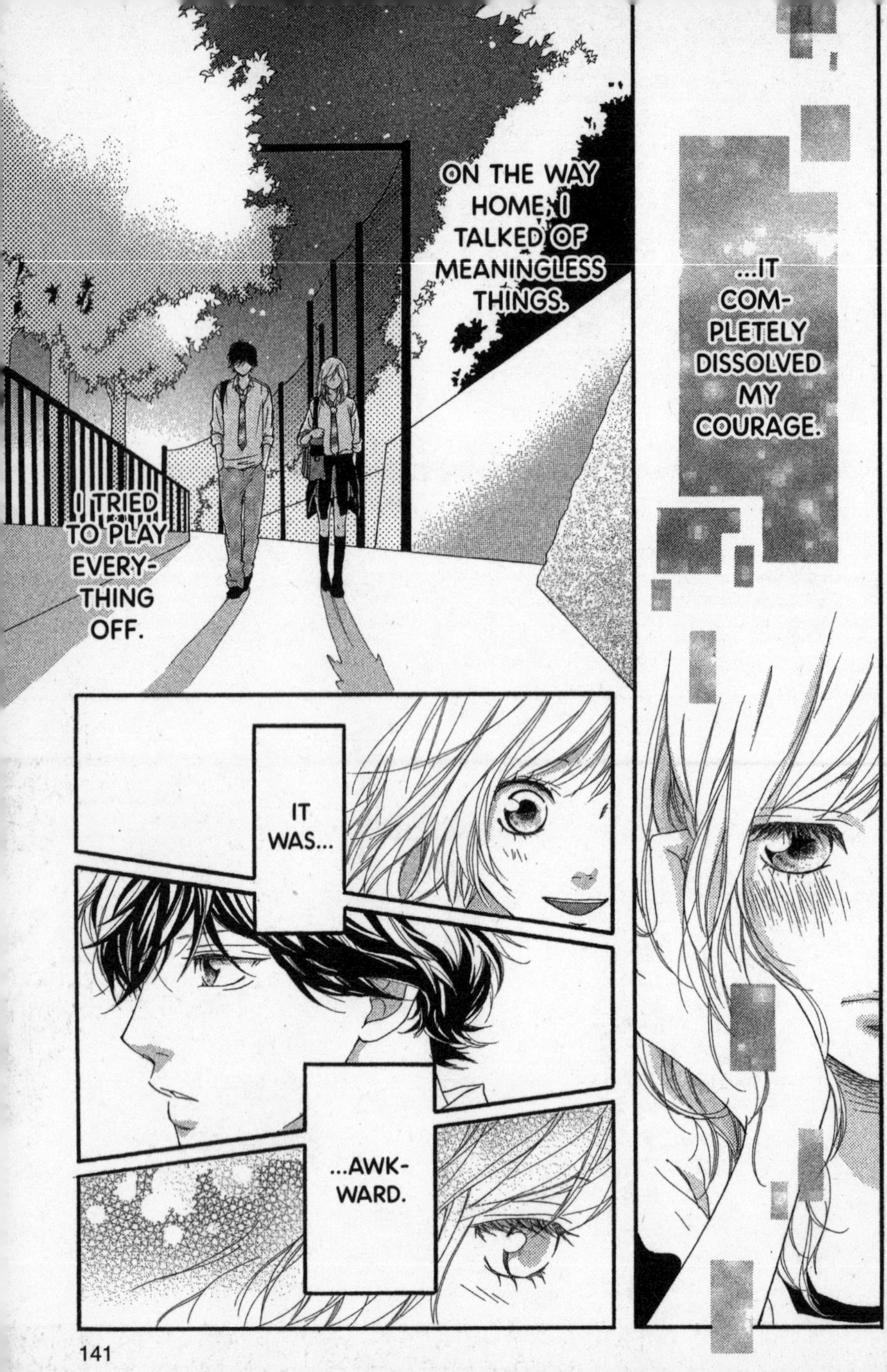

...IT COMPLETELY DISSOLVED MY COURAGE.
ON THE WAY HOME, I TALKED OF MEANINGLESS THINGS.
I TRIED TO PLAY EVERYTHING OFF.
IT WAS...
...AWKWARD.

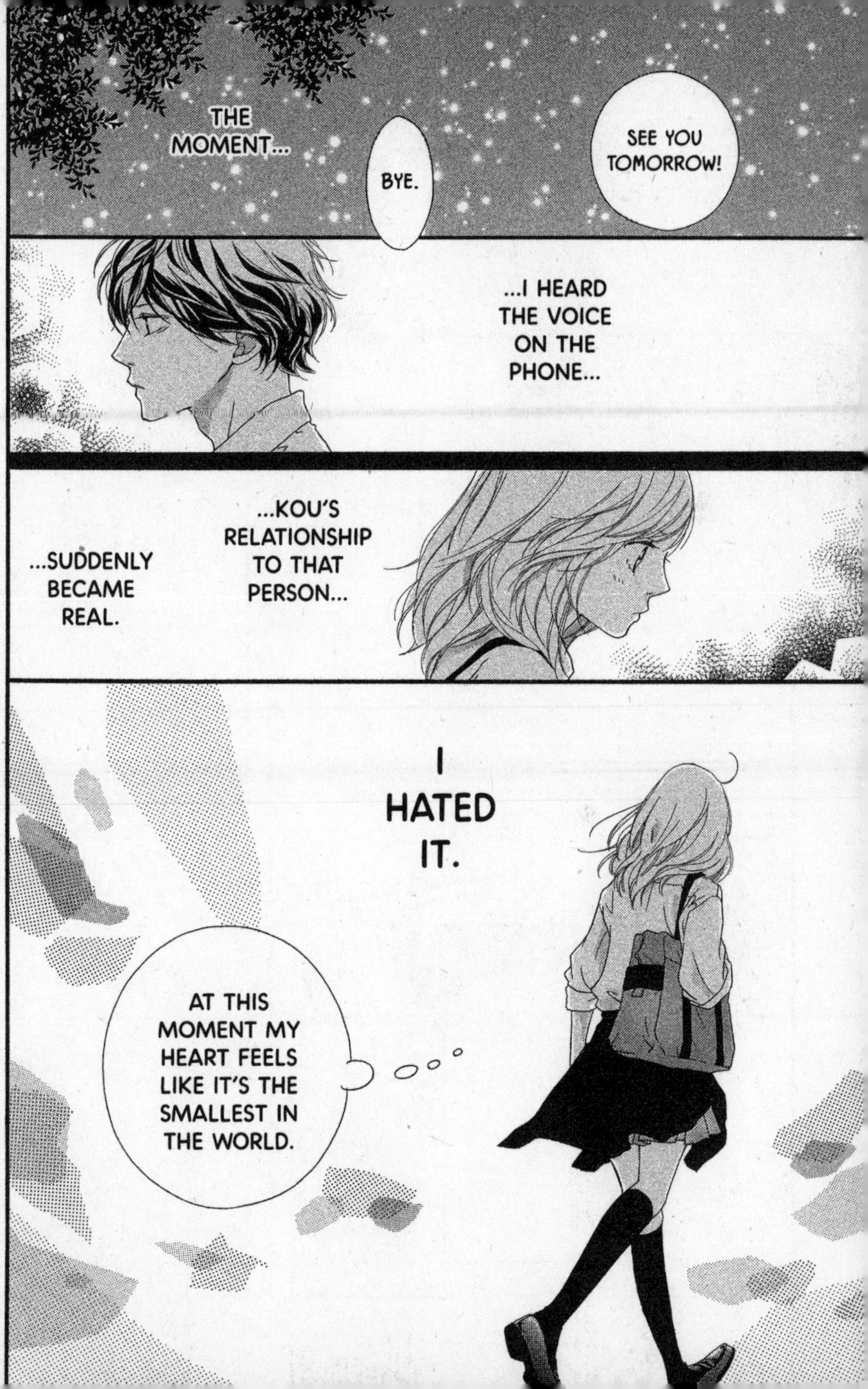
SEE YOU TOMORROW!
BYE.
THE MOMENT...
...I HEARD THE VOICE ON THE PHONE...
...KOU'S RELATIONSHIP TO THAT PERSON...
...SUDDENLY BECAME REAL.
I HATED IT.
AT THIS MOMENT MY HEART FEELS LIKE IT'S THE SMALLEST IN THE WORLD.

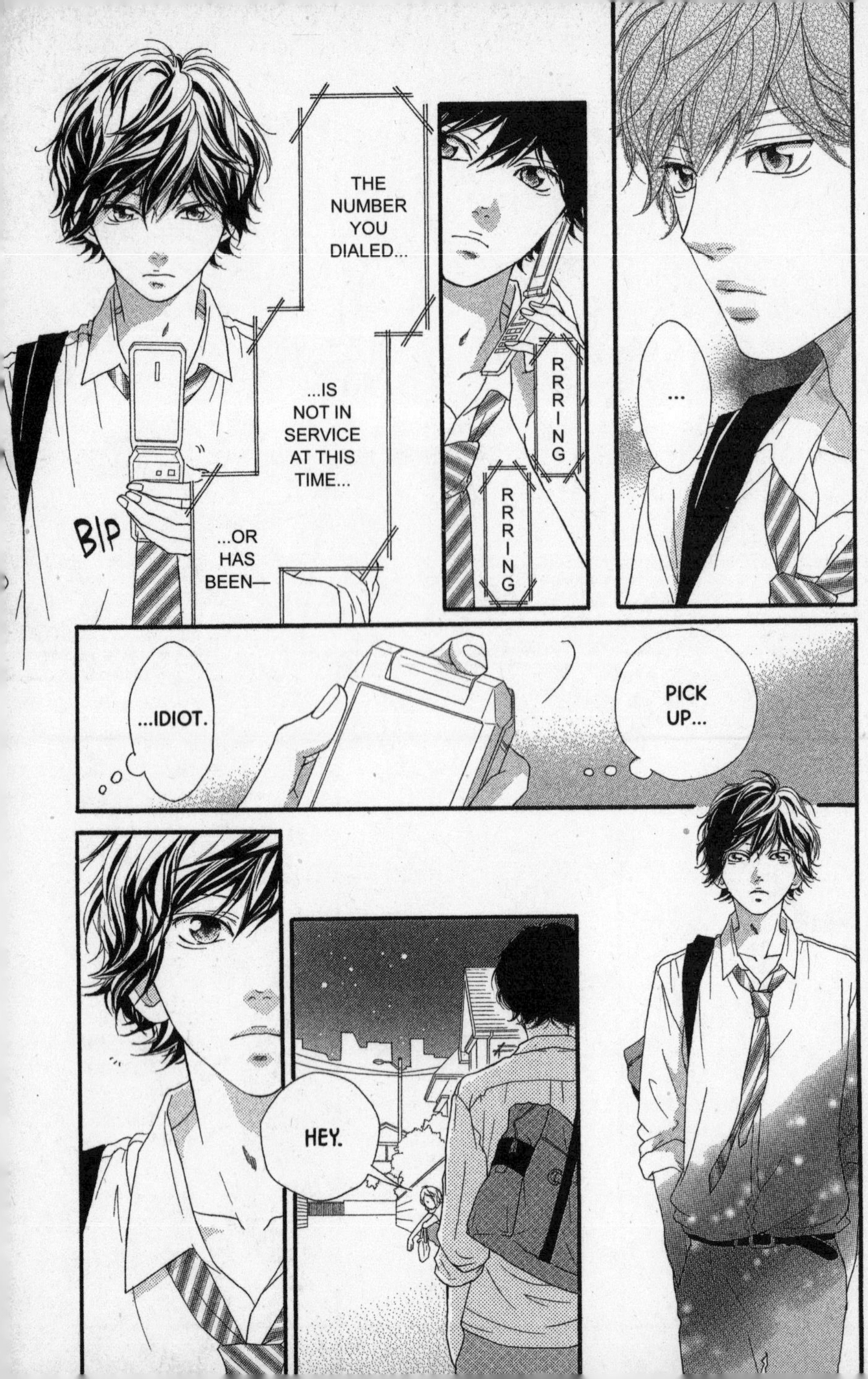
...
RRRING
RRRING
BIP
THE NUMBER YOU DIALED...
...IS NOT IN SERVICE AT THIS TIME...
...OR HAS BEEN—
PICK UP...
...IDIOT.
HEY.

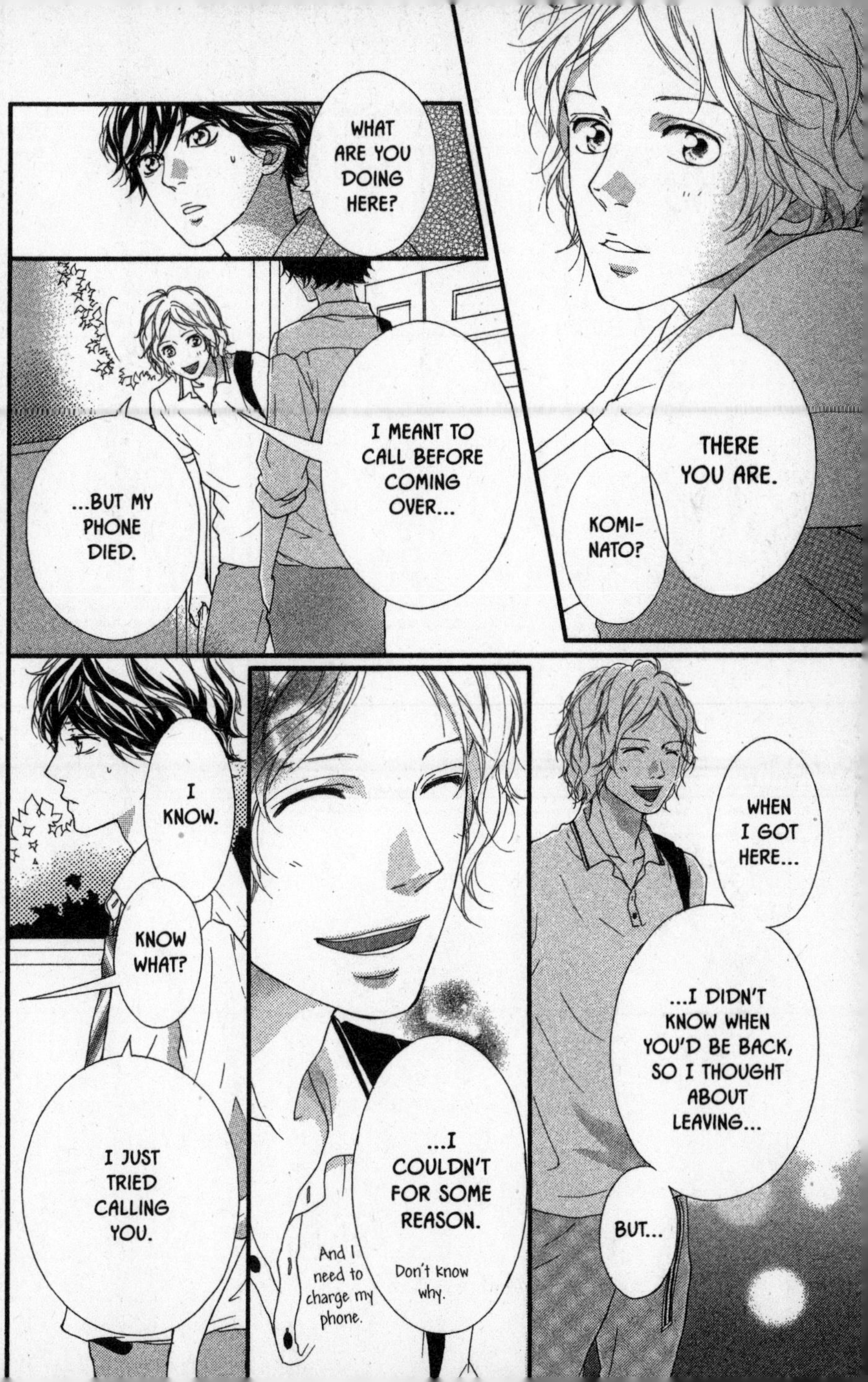
THERE YOU ARE.
KOMINATO?
WHAT ARE YOU DOING HERE?
I MEANT TO CALL BEFORE COMING OVER...
...BUT MY PHONE DIED.
WHEN I GOT HERE...
...I DIDN'T KNOW WHEN YOU'D BE BACK, SO I THOUGHT ABOUT LEAVING...
BUT...
...I COULDN'T FOR SOME REASON.
Don't know why.
And I need to charge my phone.
I KNOW.
KNOW WHAT?
I JUST TRIED CALLING YOU.

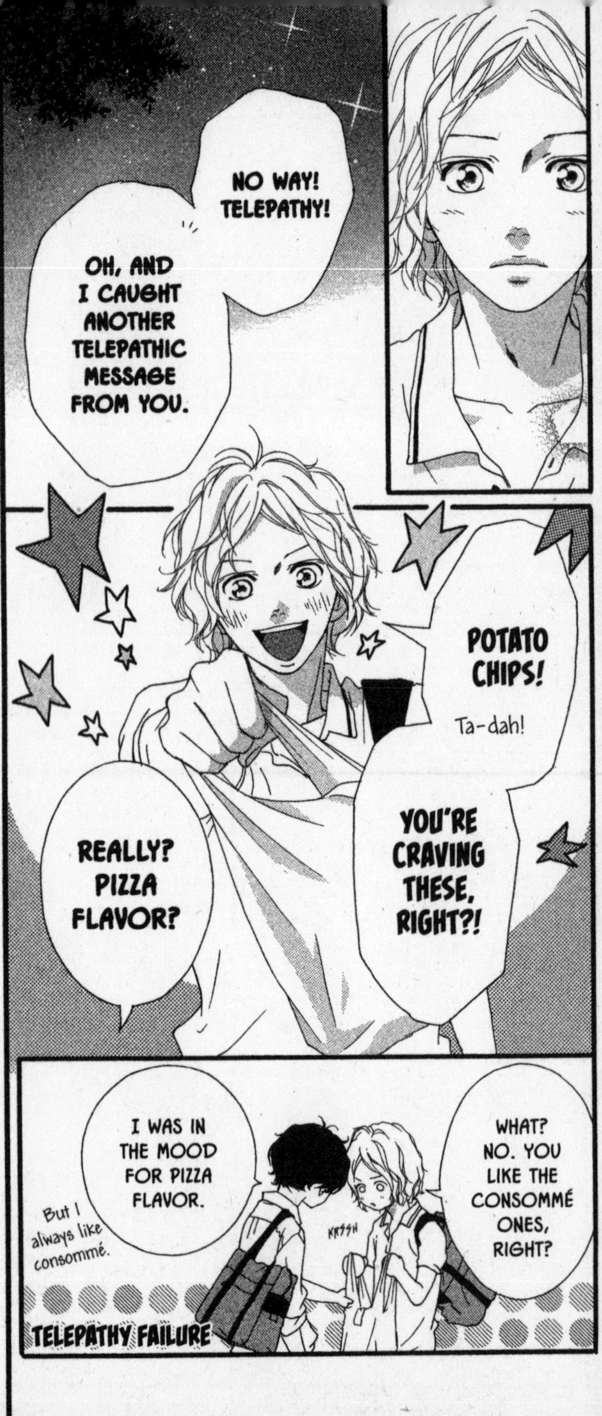
NO WAY! TELEPATHY!
OH, AND I CAUGHT ANOTHER TELEPATHIC MESSAGE FROM YOU.
POTATO CHIPS!
Ta-dah!
YOU'RE CRAVING THESE, RIGHT?!
REALLY? PIZZA FLAVOR?
WHAT? NO. YOU LIKE THE CONSOMMÉ ONES, RIGHT?
KRSSH
I WAS IN THE MOOD FOR PIZZA FLAVOR.
But I always like consommé.
TELEPATHY FAILURE

We first met Toma Kikuchi in volume 4, and his role has gotten bigger starting with this volume. When he first appeared, he was already popular with readers, which made me feel a bit conflicted. On the one hand, I was happy, but he hadn't even done anything yet! Now that he's trying a little harder, I guess it's okay. (*laugh*) Toma does work hard, so I'll forgive him. Heh heh!

He's still a newbie, but I hope you'll support him along with Futaba and the rest of the gang.

And don't forget to check out his profile on one of the earlier pages in this volume. ♡

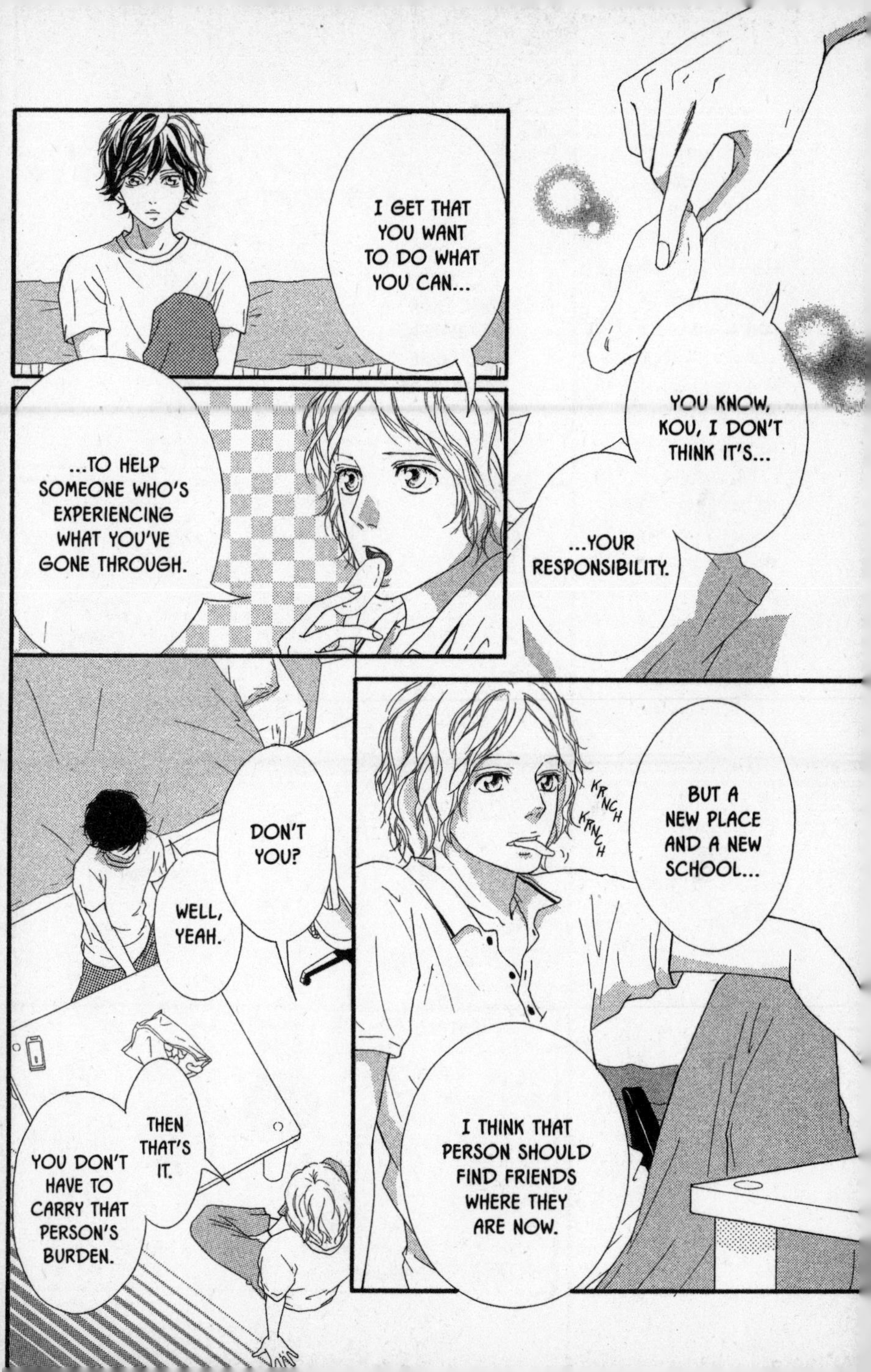
YOU KNOW, KOU, I DON'T THINK IT'S...
...YOUR RESPONSIBILITY.
I GET THAT YOU WANT TO DO WHAT YOU CAN...
...TO HELP SOMEONE WHO'S EXPERIENCING WHAT YOU'VE GONE THROUGH.
BUT A NEW PLACE AND A NEW SCHOOL...
KRNCH KRNCH
I THINK THAT PERSON SHOULD FIND FRIENDS WHERE THEY ARE NOW.
DON'T YOU?
WELL, YEAH.
THEN THAT'S IT.
YOU DON'T HAVE TO CARRY THAT PERSON'S BURDEN.

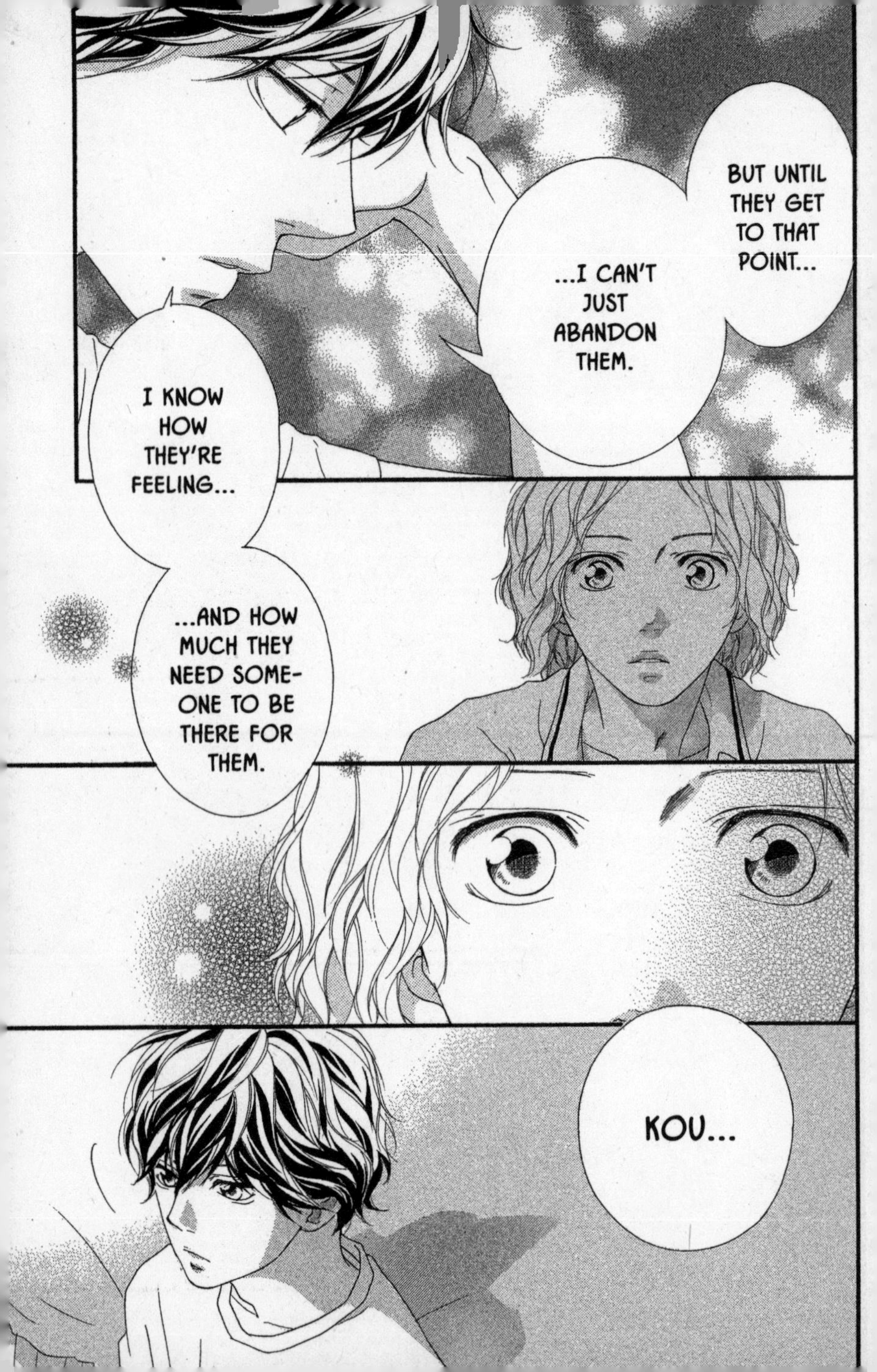
BUT UNTIL THEY GET TO THAT POINT...
...I CAN'T JUST ABANDON THEM.
I KNOW HOW THEY'RE FEELING...
...AND HOW MUCH THEY NEED SOME-ONE TO BE THERE FOR THEM.
KOU...

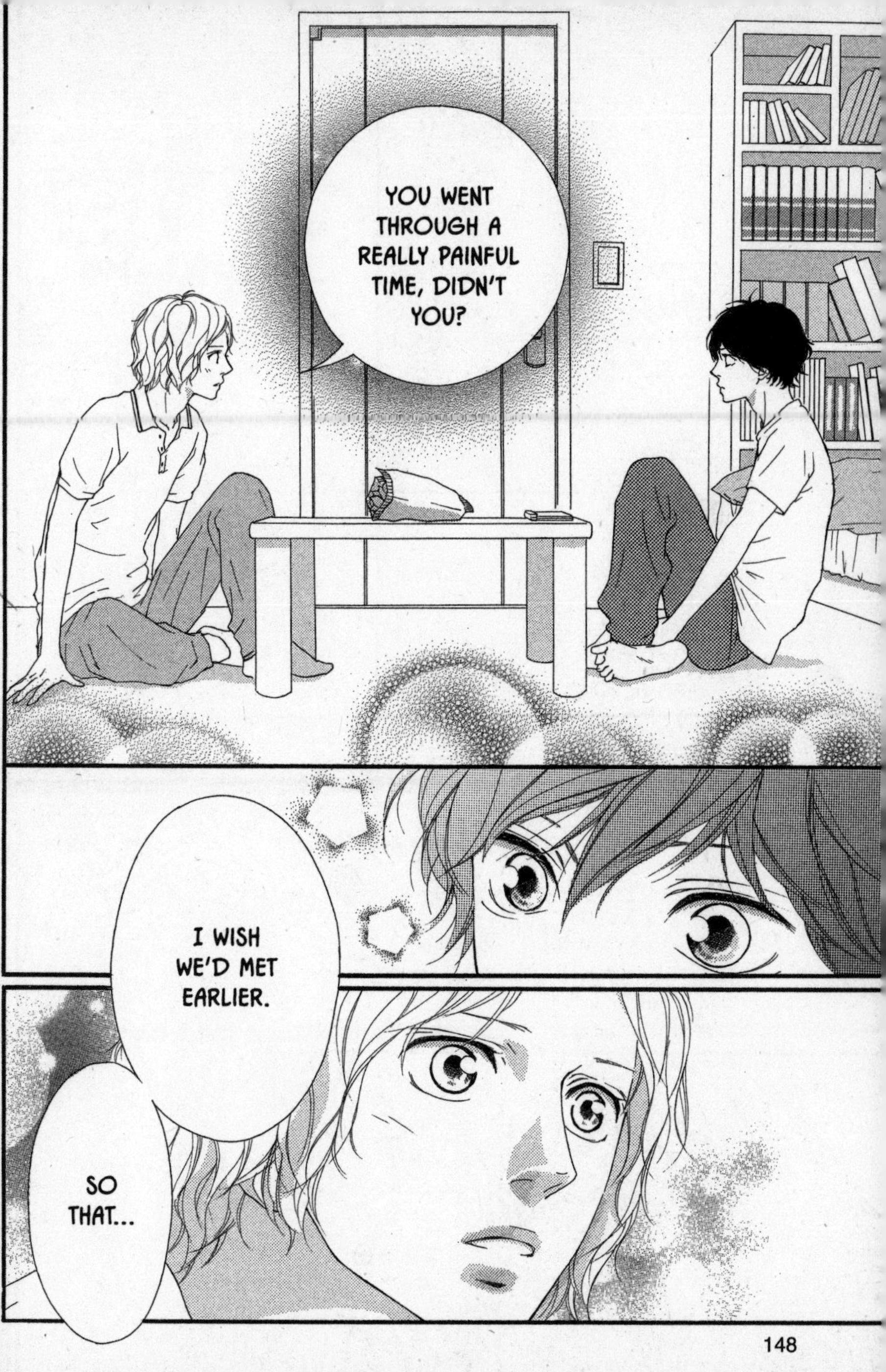

YOU WENT THROUGH A REALLY PAINFUL TIME, DIDN'T YOU?
I WISH WE'D MET EARLIER.
SO THAT...

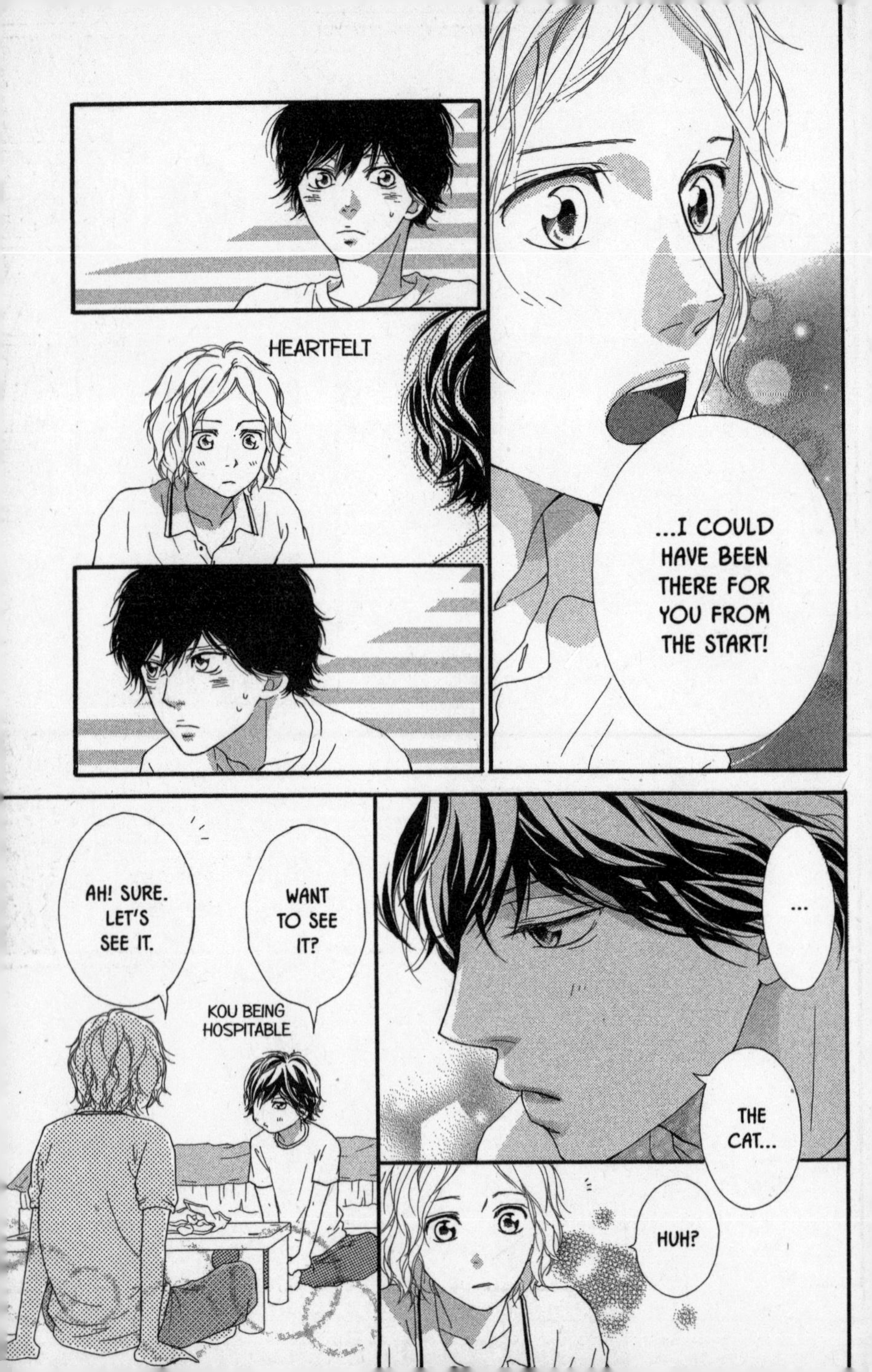
...I COULD HAVE BEEN THERE FOR YOU FROM THE START!
HEARTFELT
...
THE CAT...
HUH?
WANT TO SEE IT?
KOU BEING HOSPITABLE
AH! SURE. LET'S SEE IT.

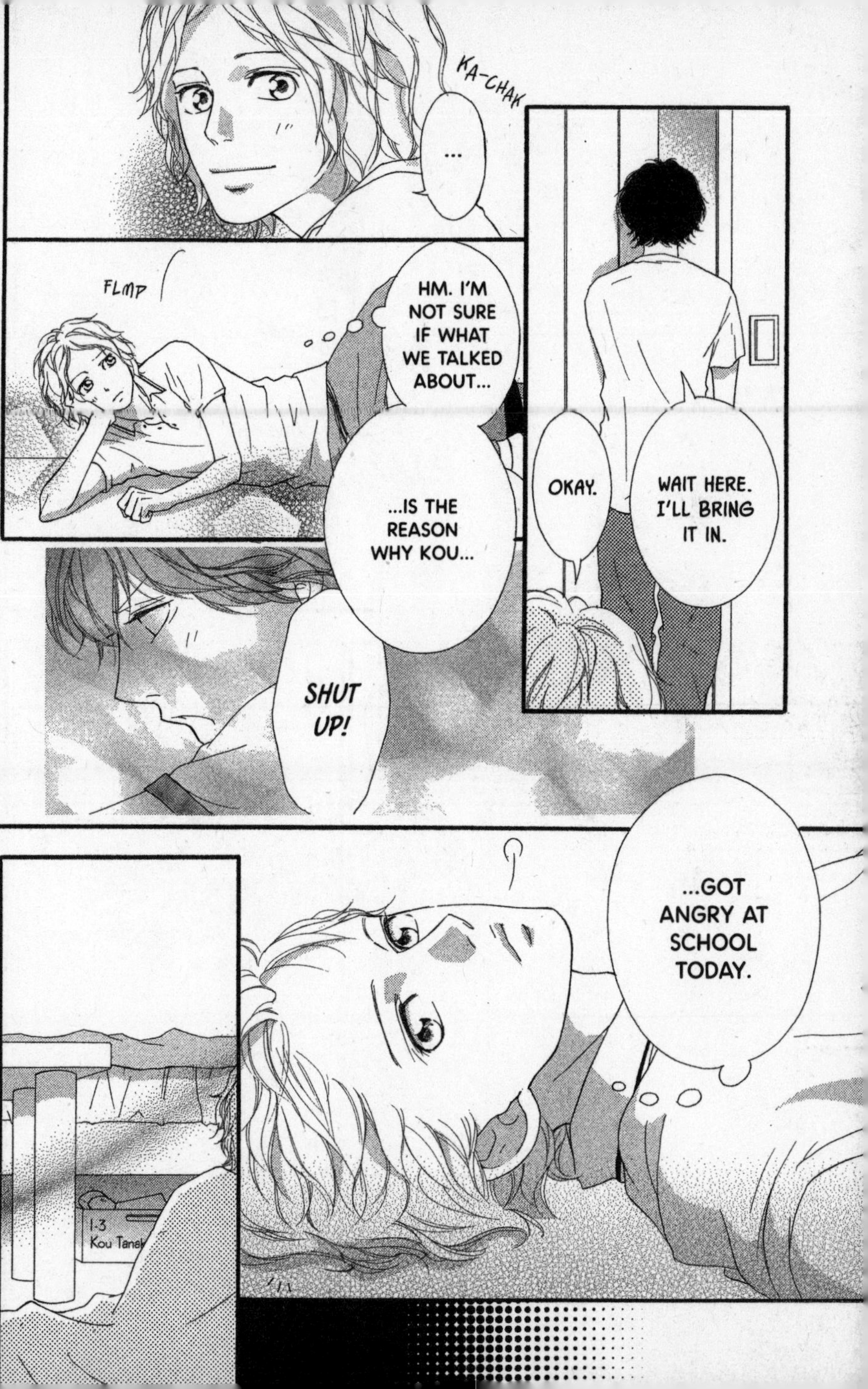
WAIT HERE. I'LL BRING IT IN.
OKAY.
KA-CHAK
...
FLMP
HM. I'M NOT SURE IF WHAT WE TALKED ABOUT...
...IS THE REASON WHY KOU...
SHUT UP!
...GOT ANGRY AT SCHOOL TODAY.
1-3
Kou Tanak

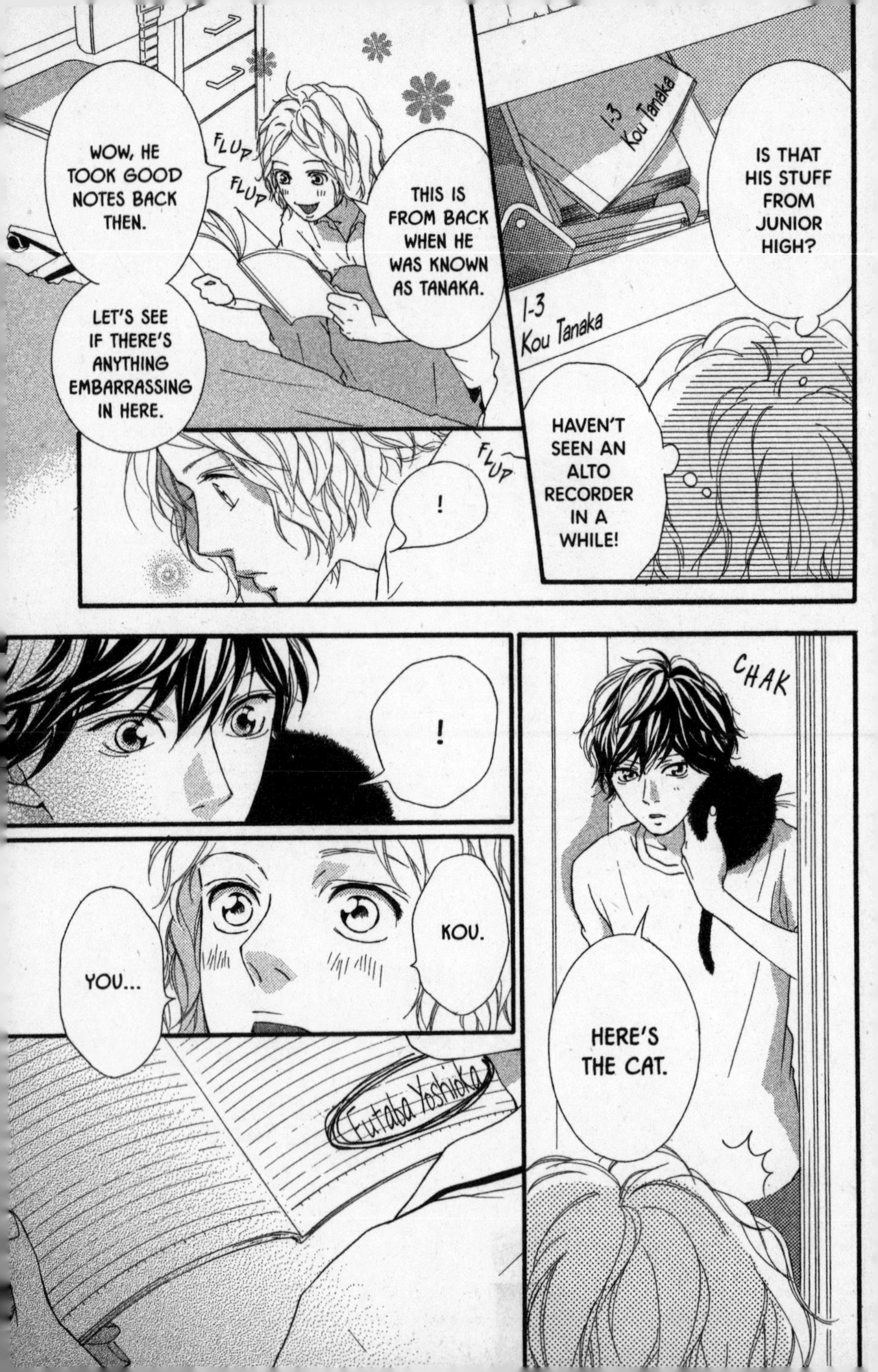
1-3
Kou Tanaka
IS THAT HIS STUFF FROM JUNIOR HIGH?
1-3
Kou Tanaka
HAVEN'T SEEN AN ALTO RECORDER IN A WHILE!
THIS IS FROM BACK WHEN HE WAS KNOWN AS TANAKA.
FLUP
FLUP
WOW, HE TOOK GOOD NOTES BACK THEN.
LET'S SEE IF THERE'S ANYTHING EMBARRASSING IN HERE.
FLUP
!
CHAK
HERE'S THE CAT.
!
KOU.
YOU...
Futaba Yoshioka

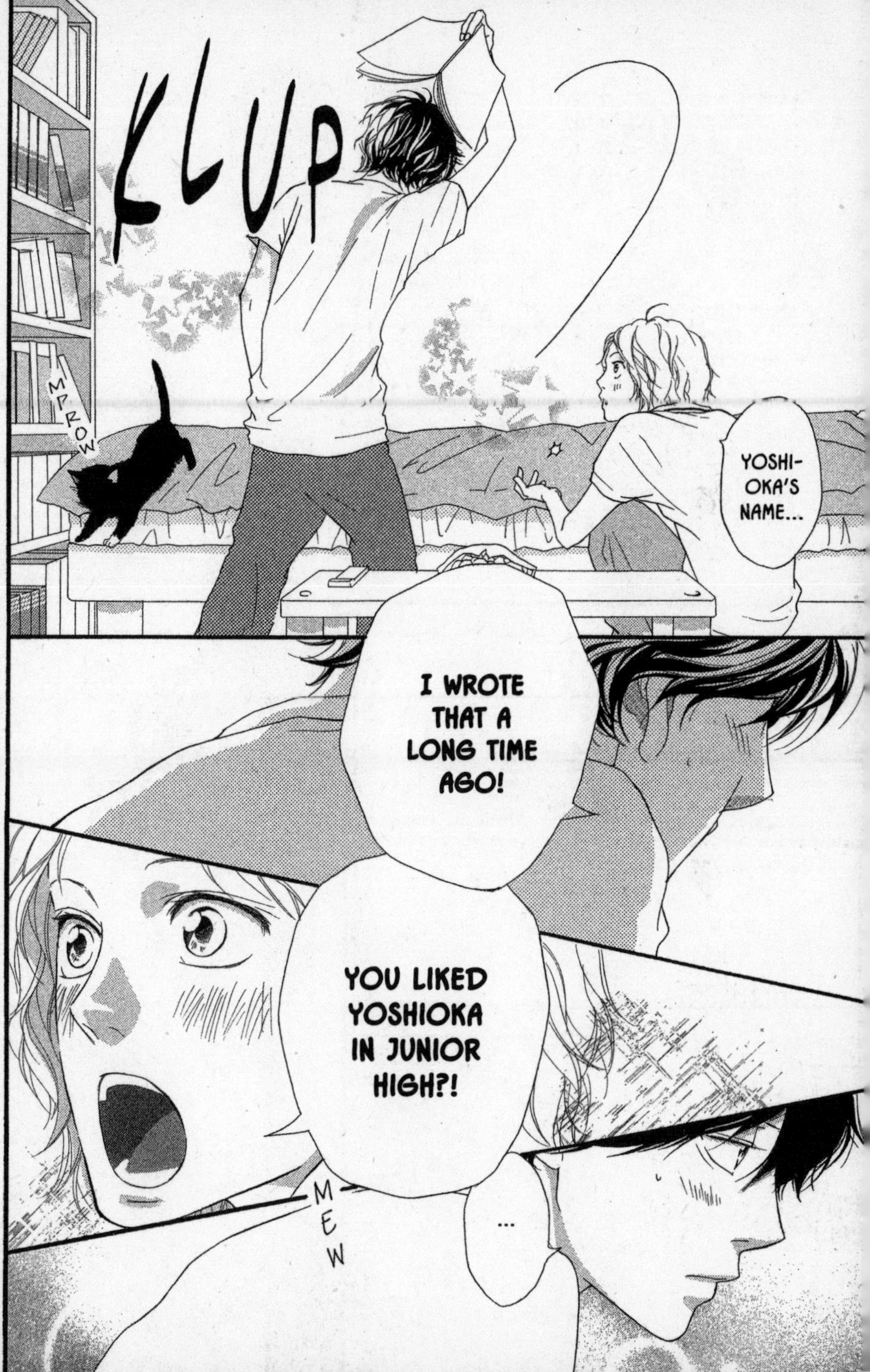
YOSHI-OKA'S NAME...
KLUP
MPROW
I WROTE THAT A LONG TIME AGO!
YOU LIKED YOSHIOKA IN JUNIOR HIGH?!
MEW
...

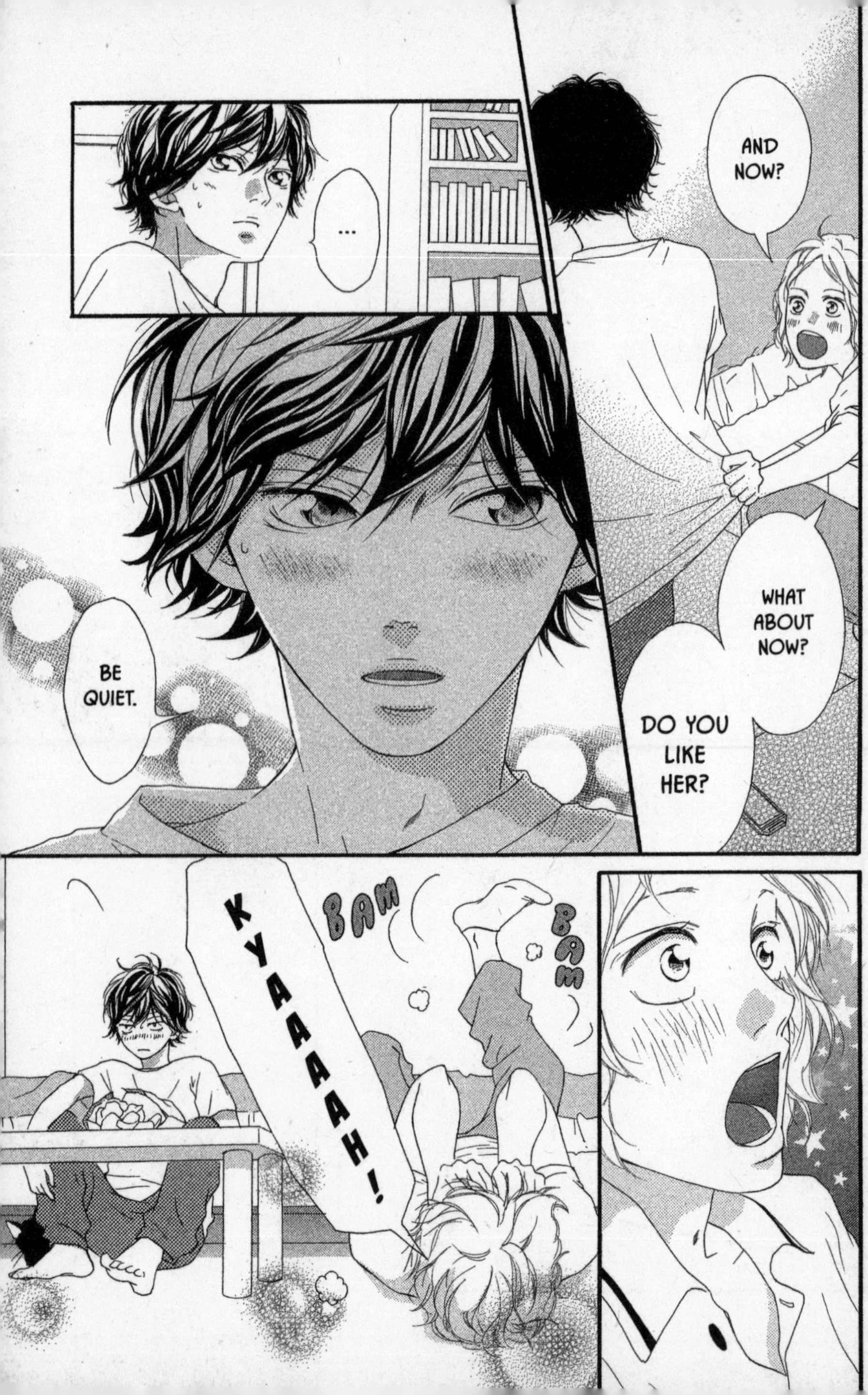
AND NOW?
WHAT ABOUT NOW?
DO YOU LIKE HER?
...
BE QUIET.
KYAAAAH!
BAM
BAM

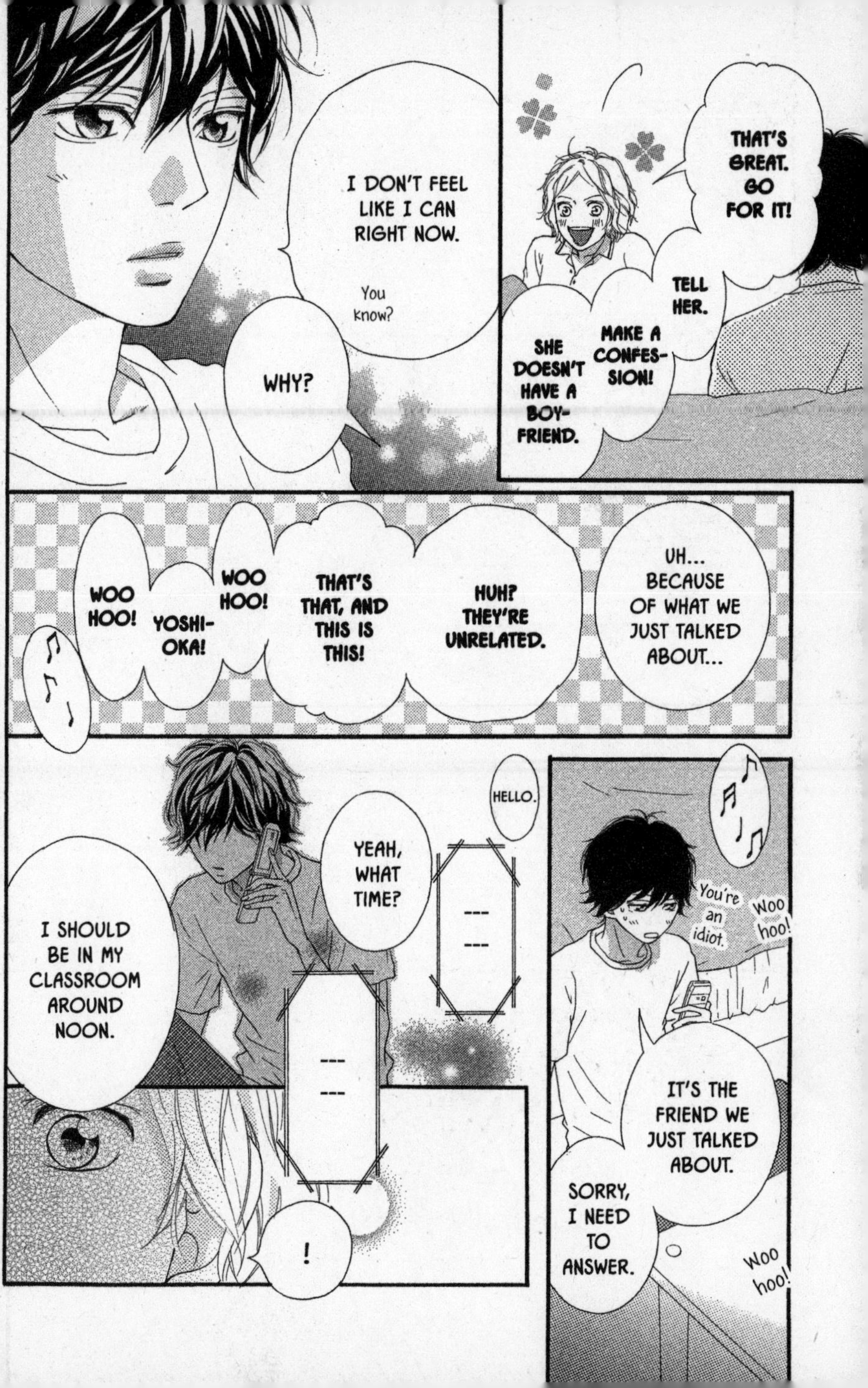
THAT'S GREAT. GO FOR IT!
TELL HER.
MAKE A CONFESSION!
SHE DOESN'T HAVE A BOYFRIEND.
I DON'T FEEL LIKE I CAN RIGHT NOW.
You know?
WHY?
UH... BECAUSE OF WHAT WE JUST TALKED ABOUT...
HUH? THEY'RE UNRELATED.
THAT'S THAT, AND THIS IS THIS!
WOO HOO!
YOSHIOKA!
WOO HOO!
You're an idiot.
Woo hoo!
IT'S THE FRIEND WE JUST TALKED ABOUT.
SORRY, I NEED TO ANSWER.
Woo hoo!
HELLO.
YEAH, WHAT TIME?

I SHOULD BE IN MY CLASSROOM AROUND NOON.

!

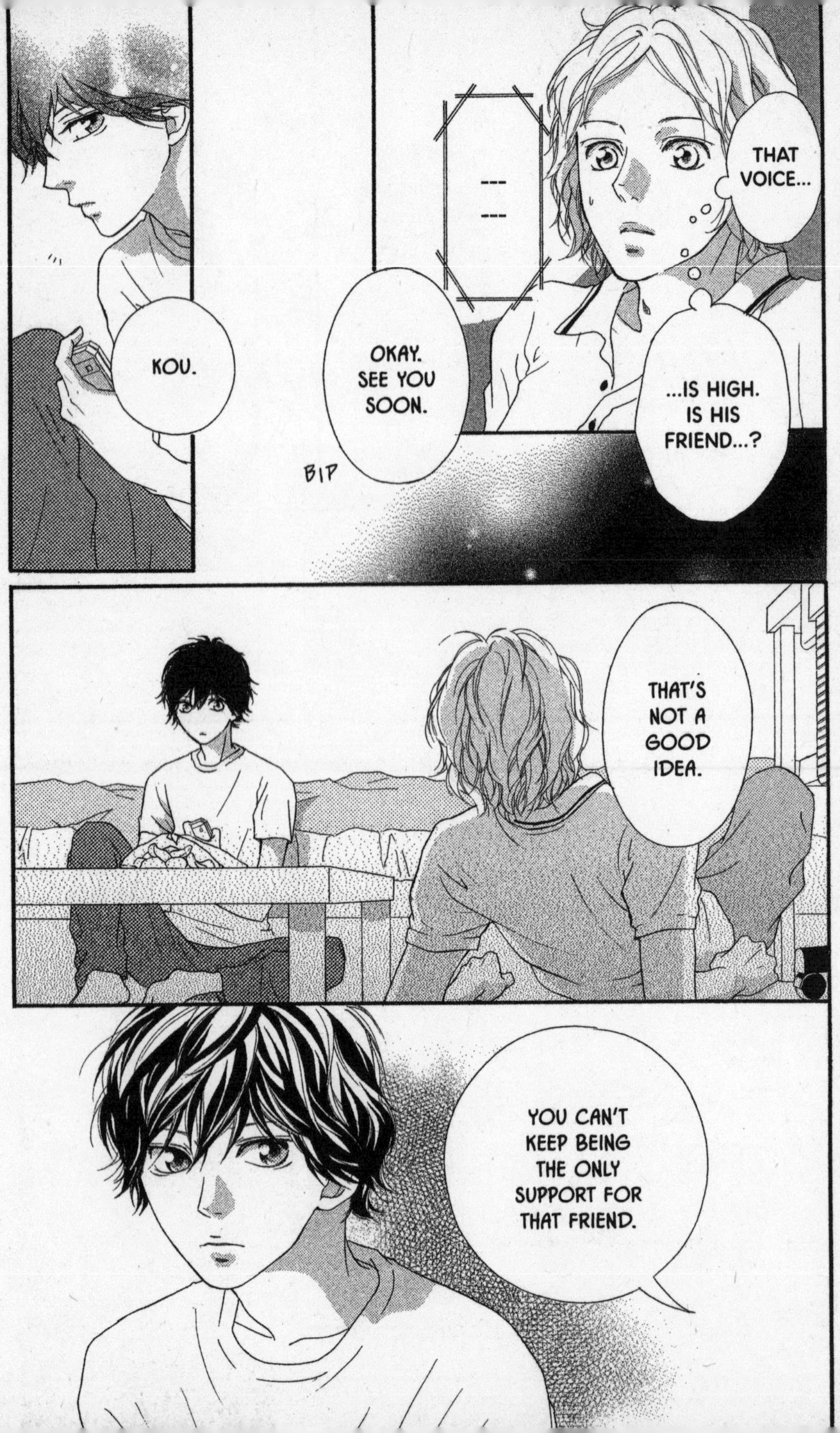
THAT VOICE...
...IS HIGH. IS HIS FRIEND...?

OKAY. SEE YOU SOON.
BIP
KOU.
THAT'S NOT A GOOD IDEA.
YOU CAN'T KEEP BEING THE ONLY SUPPORT FOR THAT FRIEND.

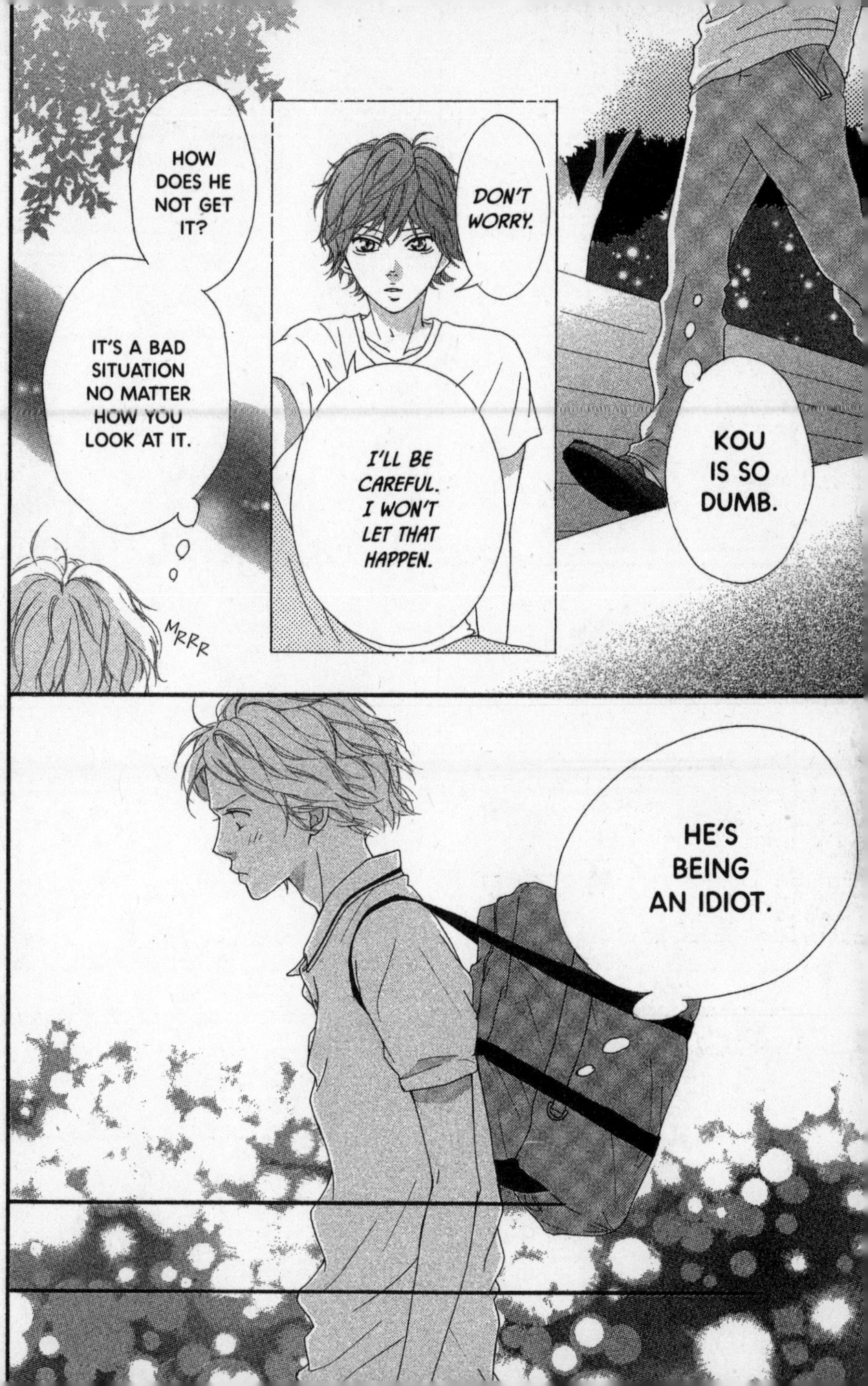
KOU IS SO DUMB.
DON'T WORRY.
I'LL BE CAREFUL. I WON'T LET THAT HAPPEN.
HOW DOES HE NOT GET IT?
IT'S A BAD SITUATION NO MATTER HOW YOU LOOK AT IT.
MRRR
HE'S BEING AN IDIOT.

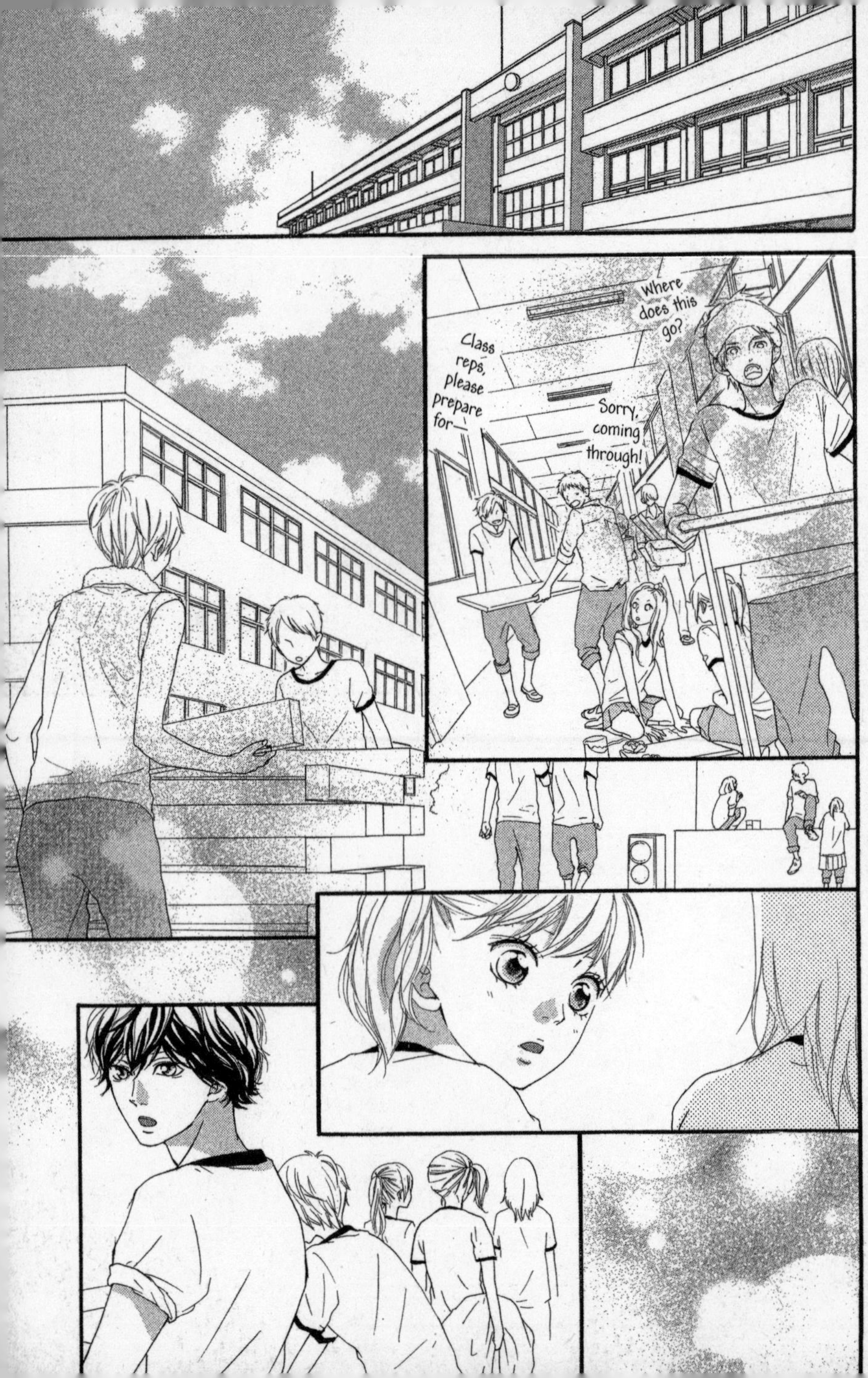
Where does this go?
Sorry, coming through!
Class reps, please prepare for—

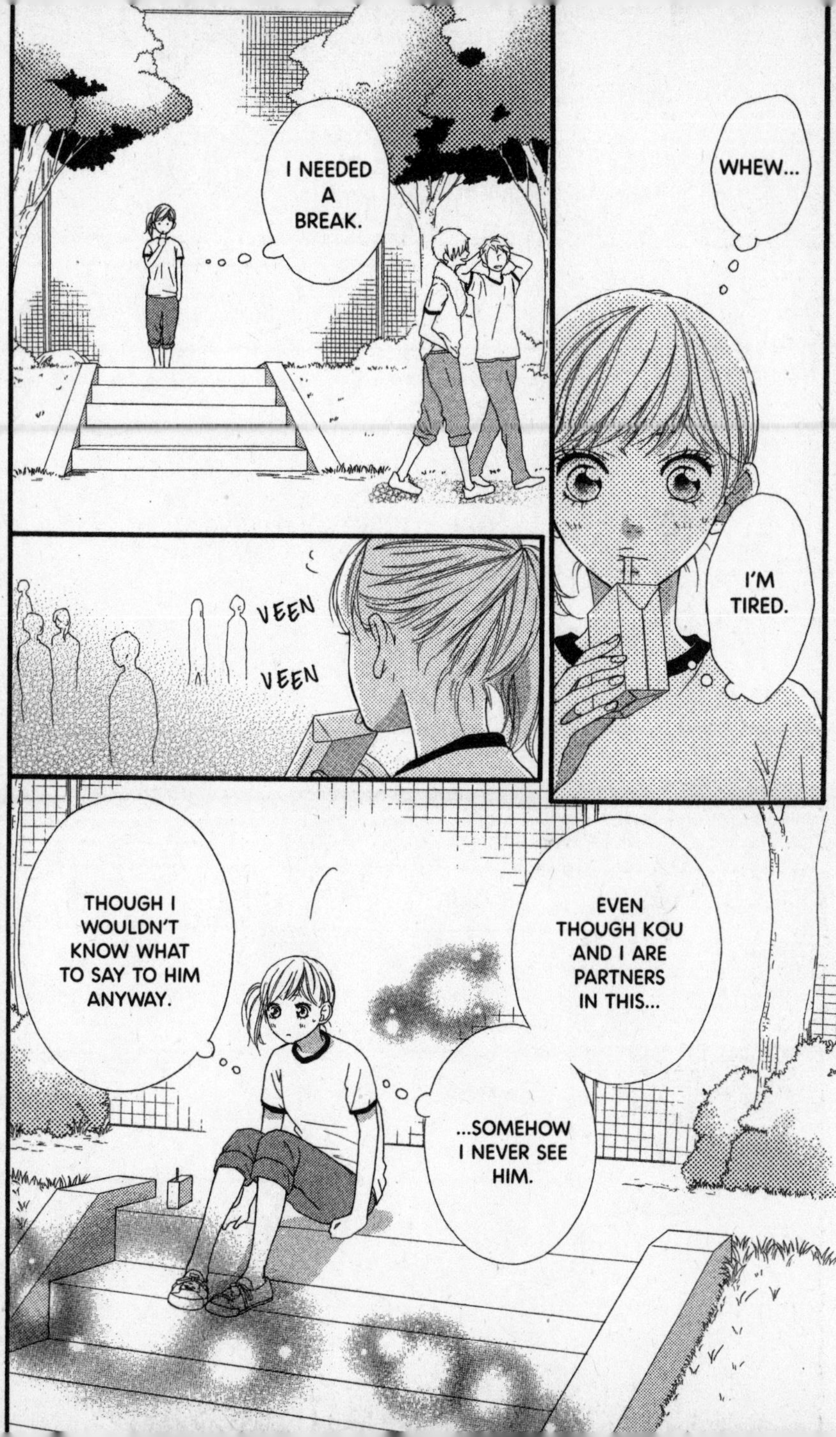
WHEW...
I'M TIRED.
I NEEDED A BREAK.
VEEN
VEEN
EVEN THOUGH KOU AND I ARE PARTNERS IN THIS...
...SOMEHOW I NEVER SEE HIM.
THOUGH I WOULDN'T KNOW WHAT TO SAY TO HIM ANYWAY.

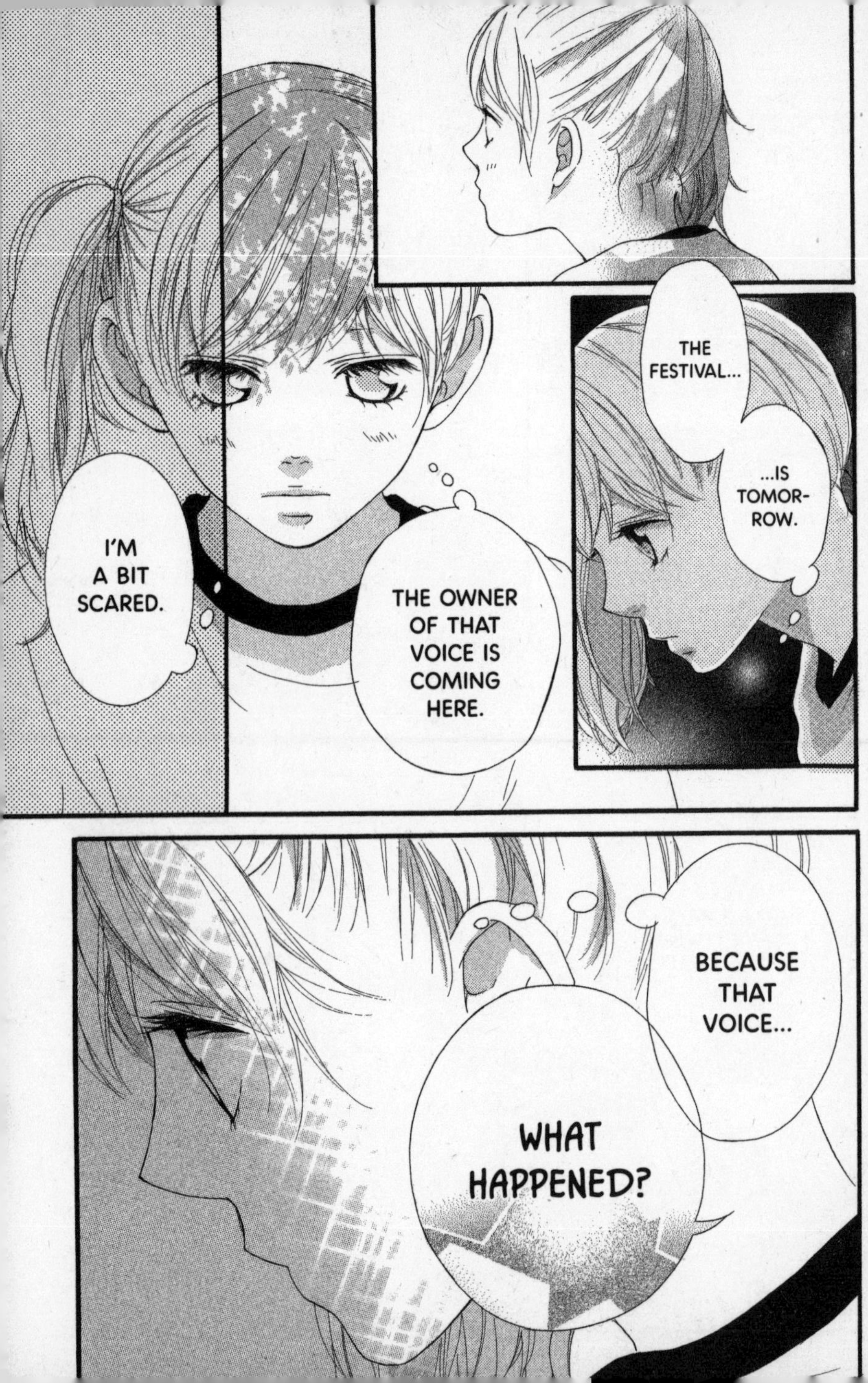
THE FESTIVAL...
...IS TOMORROW.
THE OWNER OF THAT VOICE IS COMING HERE.
I'M A BIT SCARED.
BECAUSE THAT VOICE...
WHAT HAPPENED?

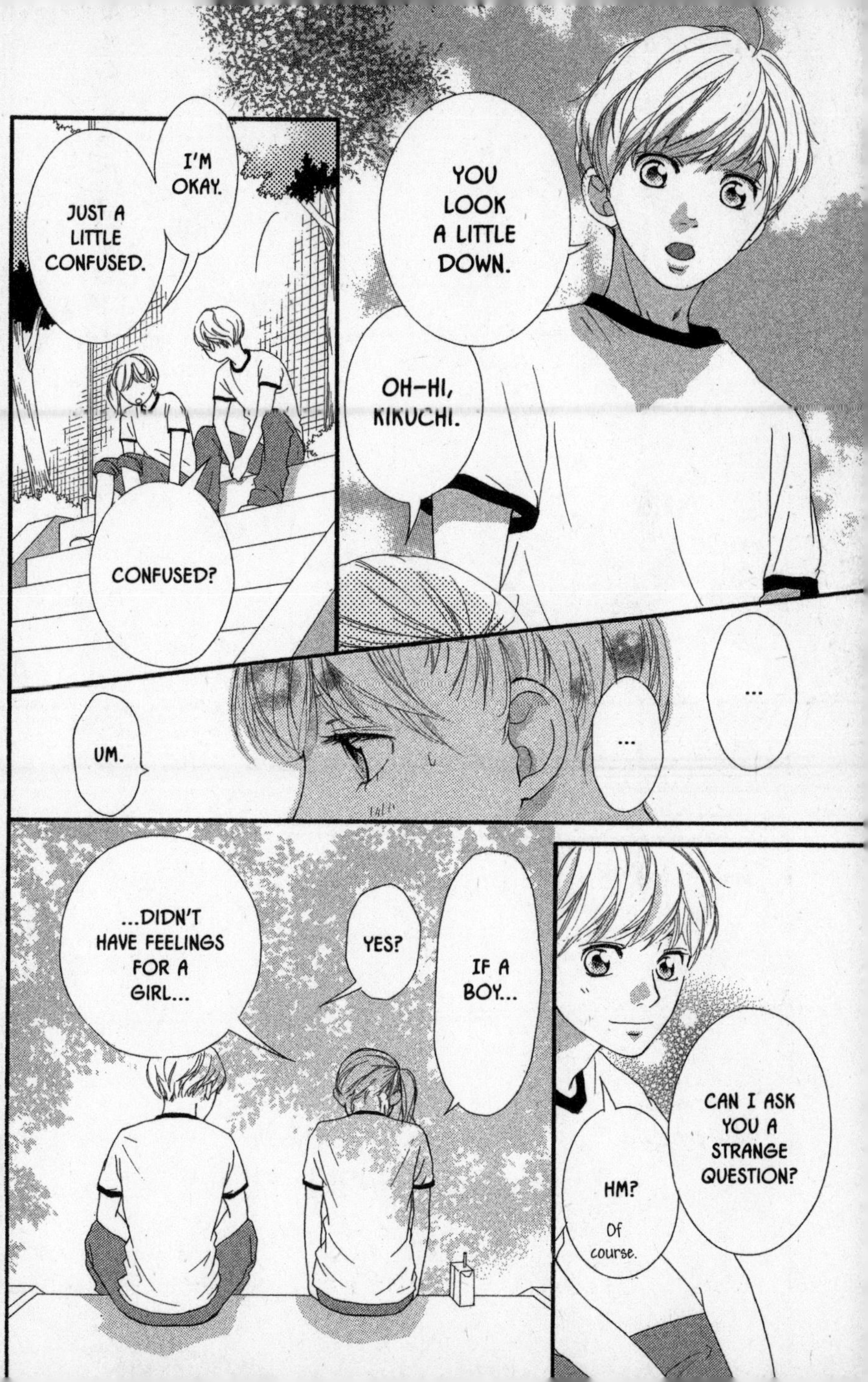
YOU LOOK A LITTLE DOWN.
OH-HI, KIKUCHI.
I'M OKAY.
JUST A LITTLE CONFUSED.
CONFUSED?
...
...
UM.
CAN I ASK YOU A STRANGE QUESTION?
HM?
Of course.
IF A BOY...
YES?
...DIDN'T HAVE FEELINGS FOR A GIRL...

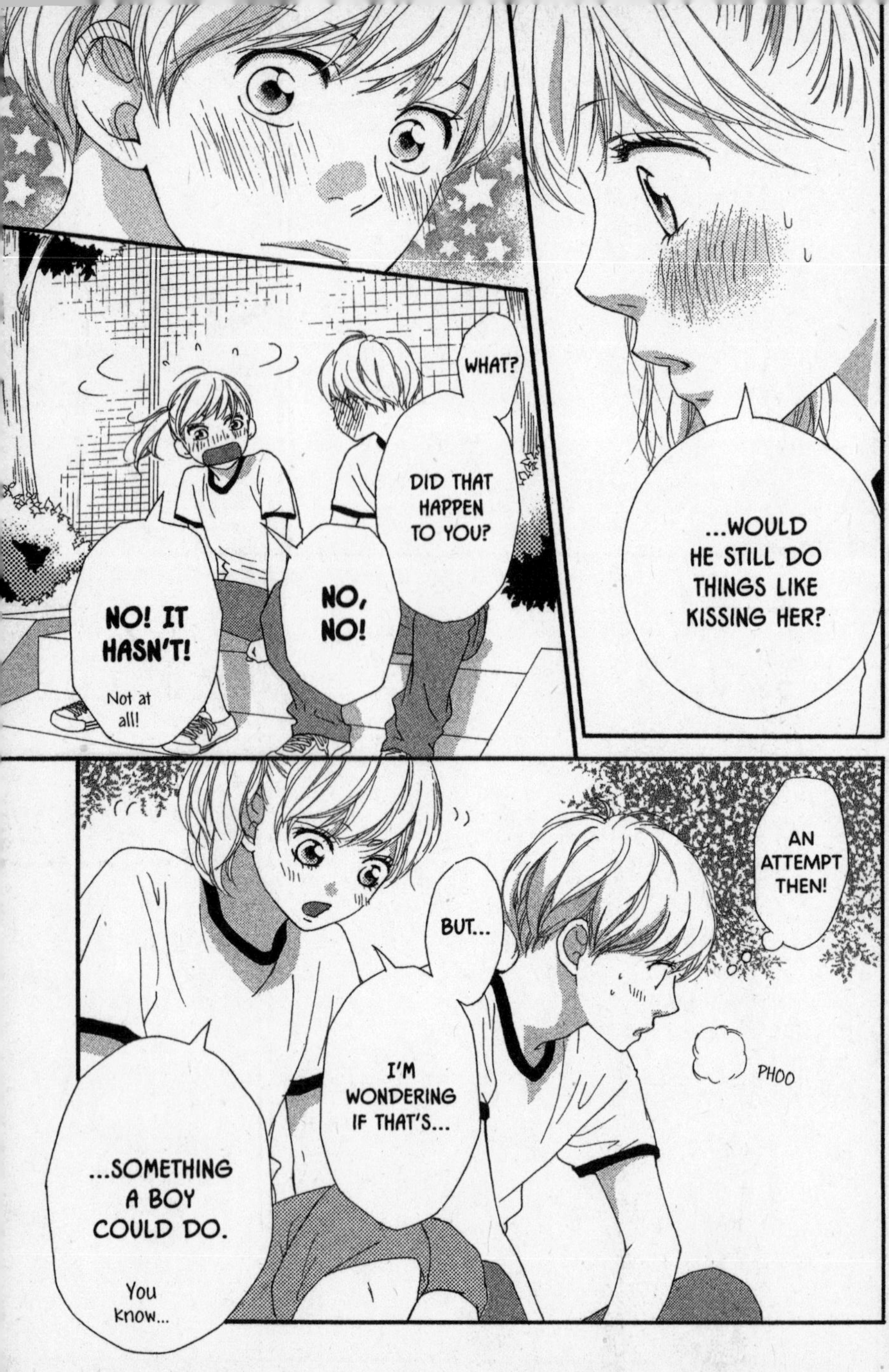
...WOULD HE STILL DO THINGS LIKE KISSING HER?
WHAT?
DID THAT HAPPEN TO YOU?
NO, NO!
NO! IT HASN'T!
Not at all!
AN ATTEMPT THEN!
PHOO
BUT...
I'M WONDERING IF THAT'S...
...SOMETHING A BOY COULD DO.
You know...

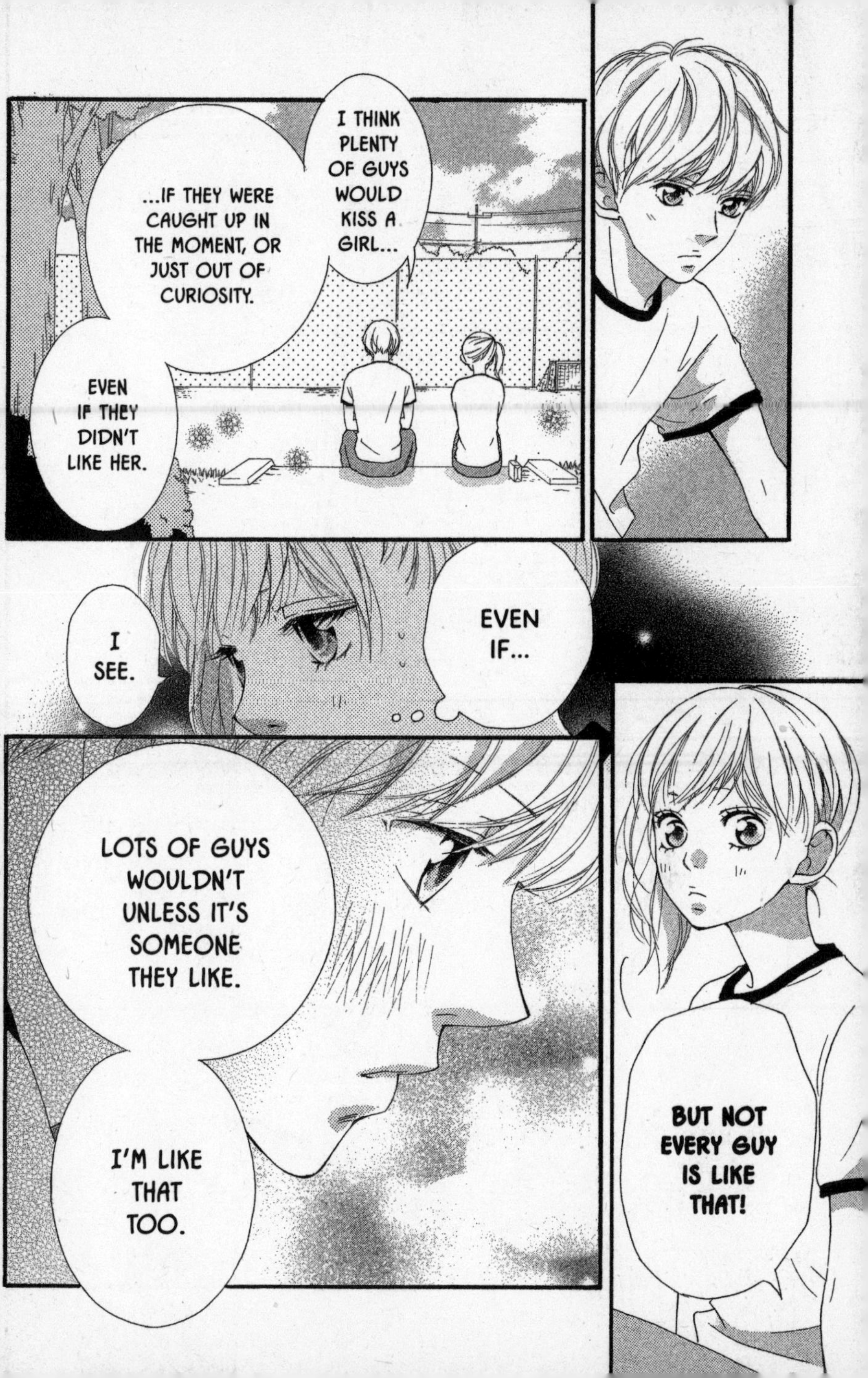
I THINK PLENTY OF GUYS WOULD KISS A GIRL...
...IF THEY WERE CAUGHT UP IN THE MOMENT, OR JUST OUT OF CURIOSITY.
EVEN IF THEY DIDN'T LIKE HER.
EVEN IF...
I SEE.
BUT NOT EVERY GUY IS LIKE THAT!
LOTS OF GUYS WOULDN'T UNLESS IT'S SOMEONE THEY LIKE.
I'M LIKE THAT TOO.

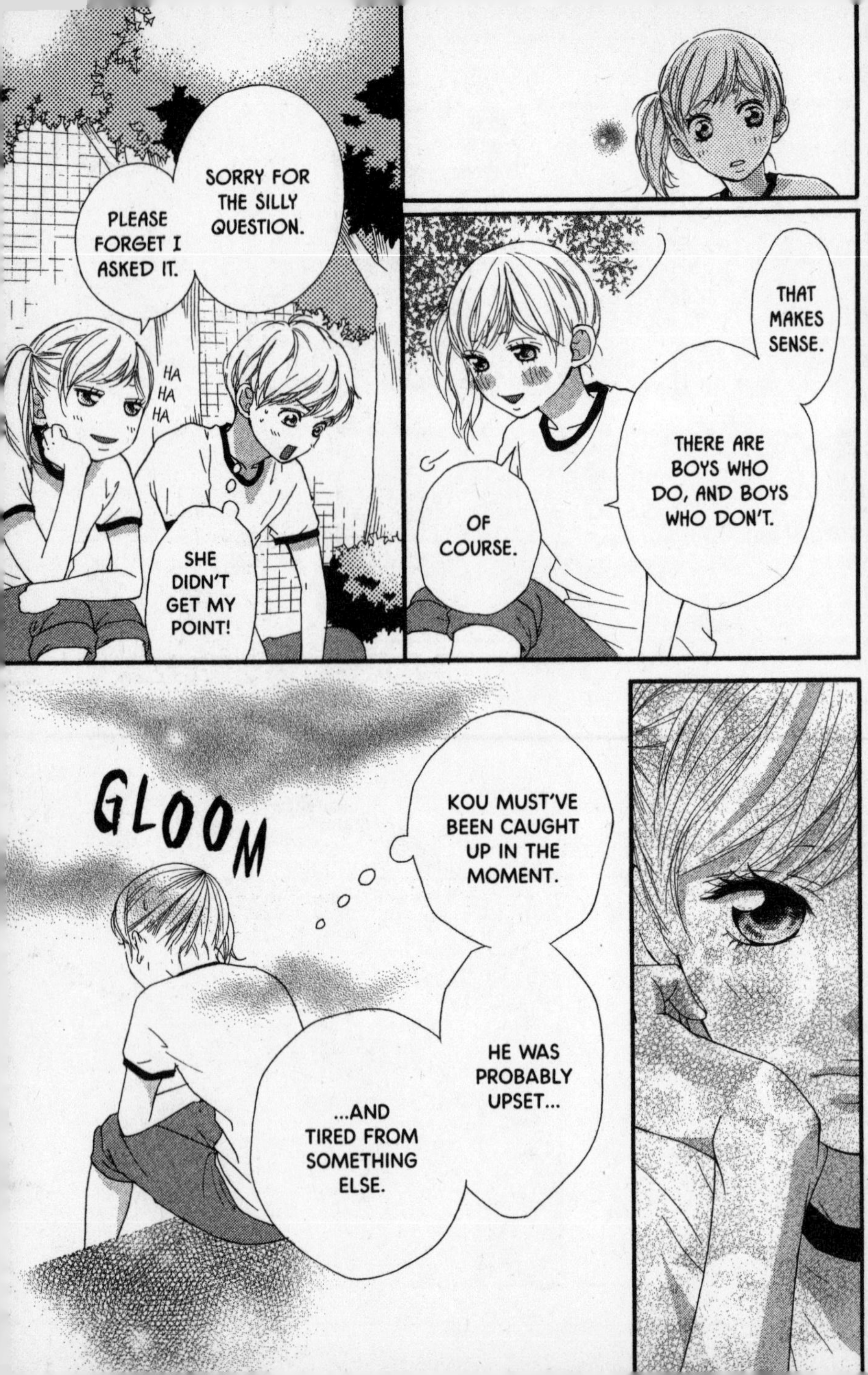
THAT MAKES SENSE.
THERE ARE BOYS WHO DO, AND BOYS WHO DON'T.
OF COURSE.
SORRY FOR THE SILLY QUESTION.
PLEASE FORGET I ASKED IT.
HA HA HA
SHE DIDN'T GET MY POINT!
KOU MUST'VE BEEN CAUGHT UP IN THE MOMENT.
HE WAS PROBABLY UPSET...
...AND TIRED FROM SOMETHING ELSE.
GLOOM

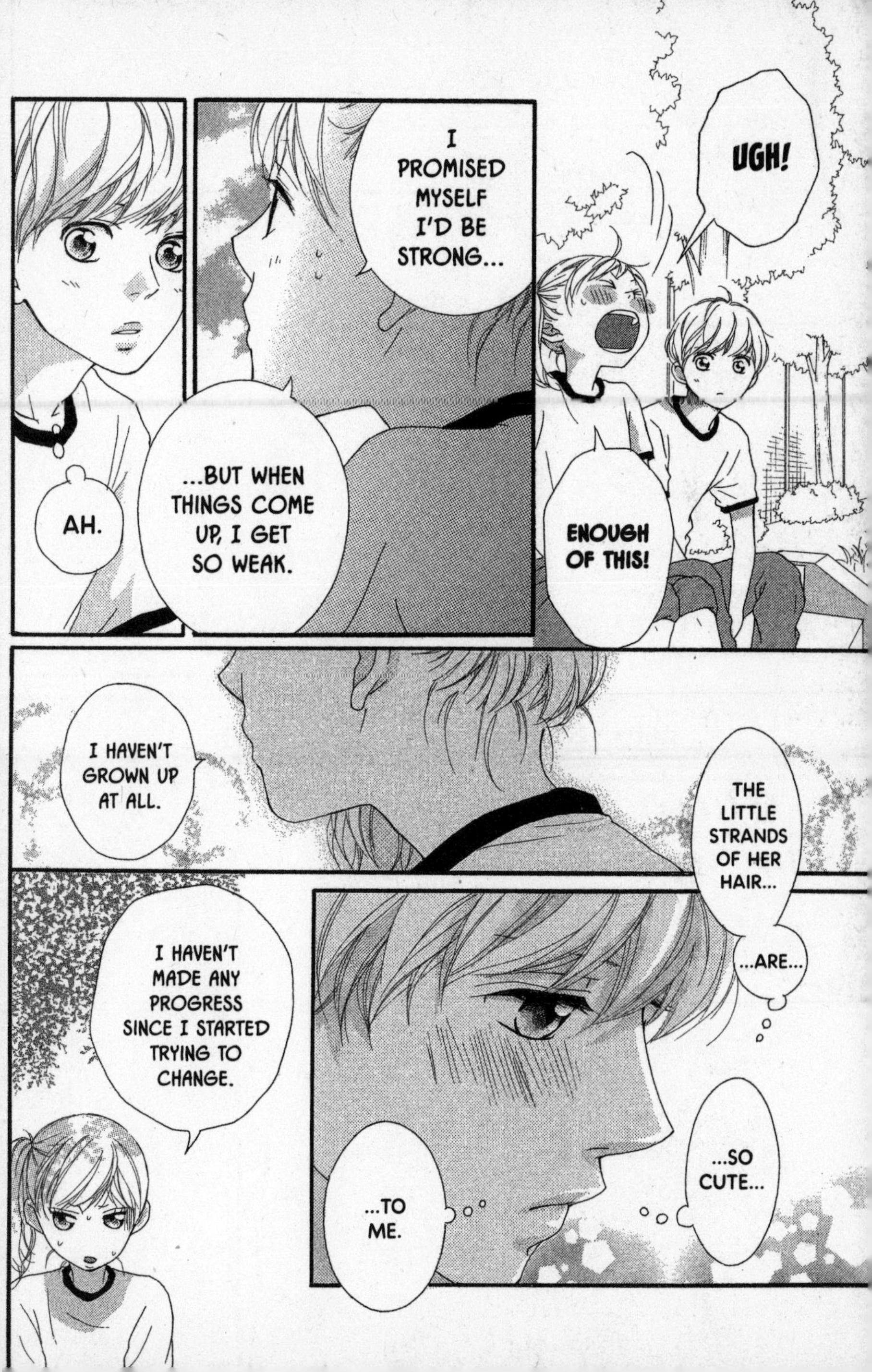
UGH!
ENOUGH OF THIS!
I PROMISED MYSELF I'D BE STRONG...
...BUT WHEN THINGS COME UP, I GET SO WEAK.
AH.
I HAVEN'T GROWN UP AT ALL.
THE LITTLE STRANDS OF HER HAIR...
...ARE...
...SO CUTE...
...TO ME.
I HAVEN'T MADE ANY PROGRESS SINCE I STARTED TRYING TO CHANGE.

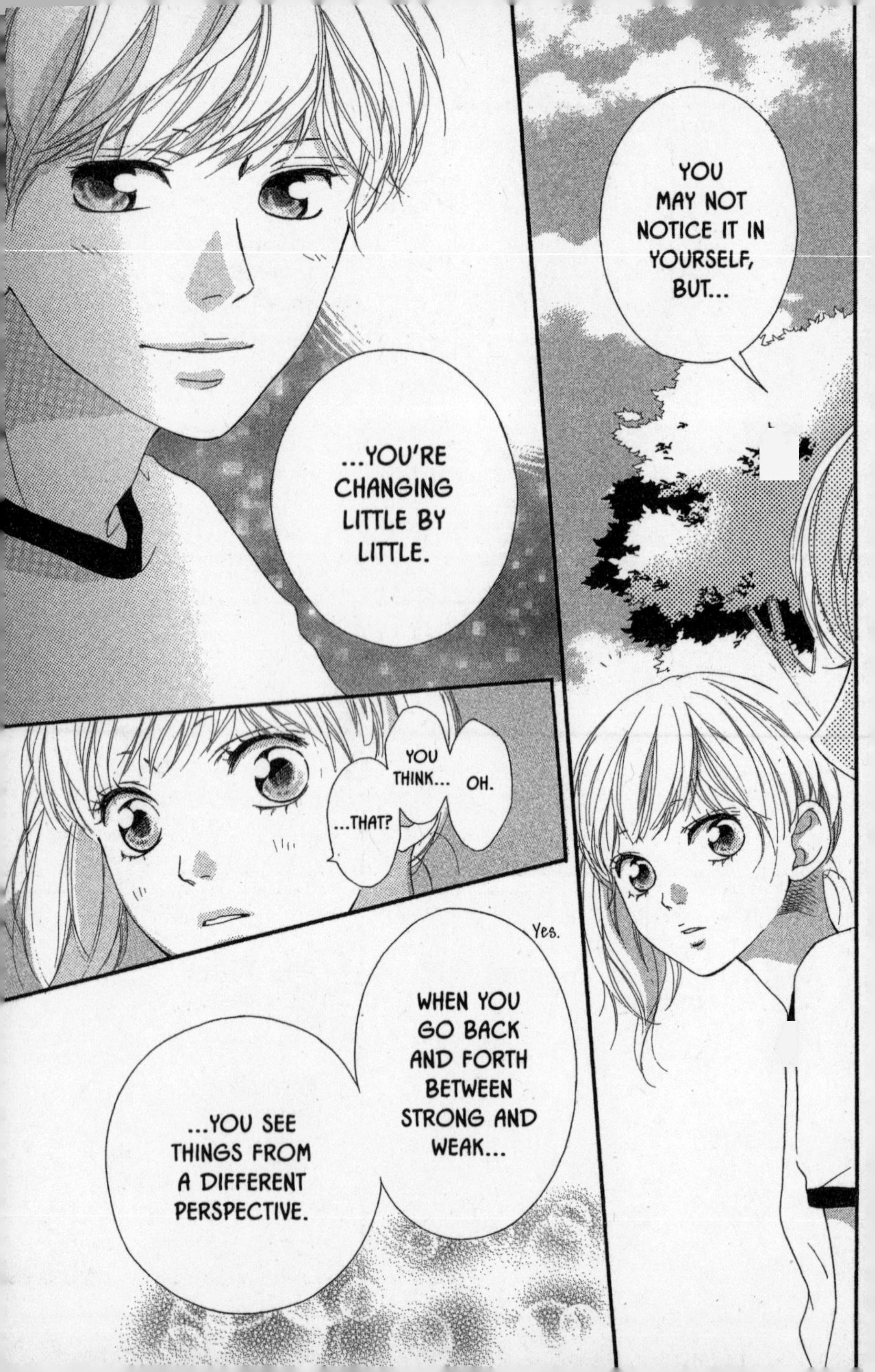
YOU MAY NOT NOTICE IT IN YOURSELF, BUT...
...YOU'RE CHANGING LITTLE BY LITTLE.
OH.
YOU THINK... ...THAT?
Yes.
WHEN YOU GO BACK AND FORTH BETWEEN STRONG AND WEAK...
...YOU SEE THINGS FROM A DIFFERENT PERSPECTIVE.

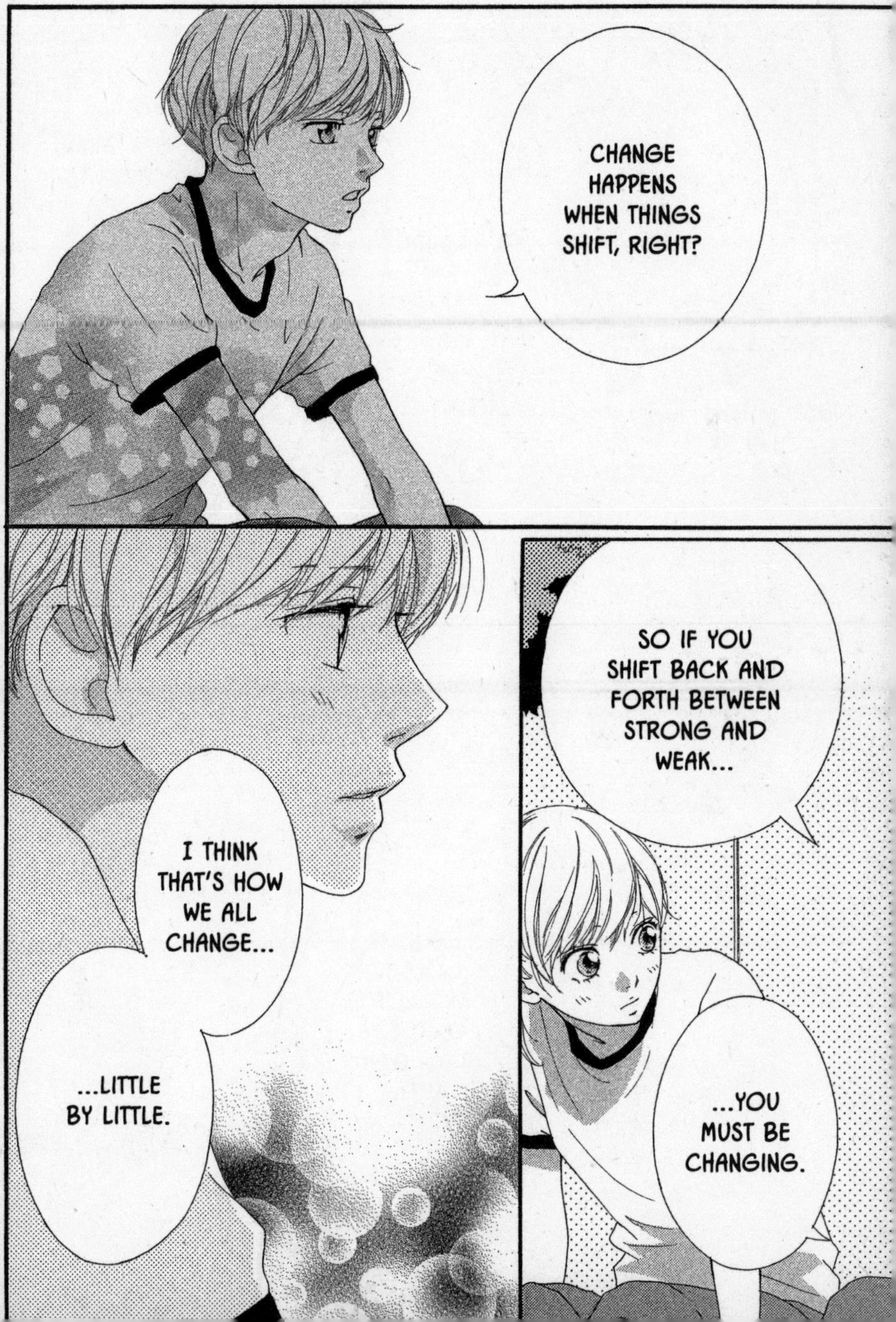
CHANGE HAPPENS WHEN THINGS SHIFT, RIGHT?
SO IF YOU SHIFT BACK AND FORTH BETWEEN STRONG AND WEAK...
...YOU MUST BE CHANGING.
I THINK THAT'S HOW WE ALL CHANGE...
...LITTLE BY LITTLE.

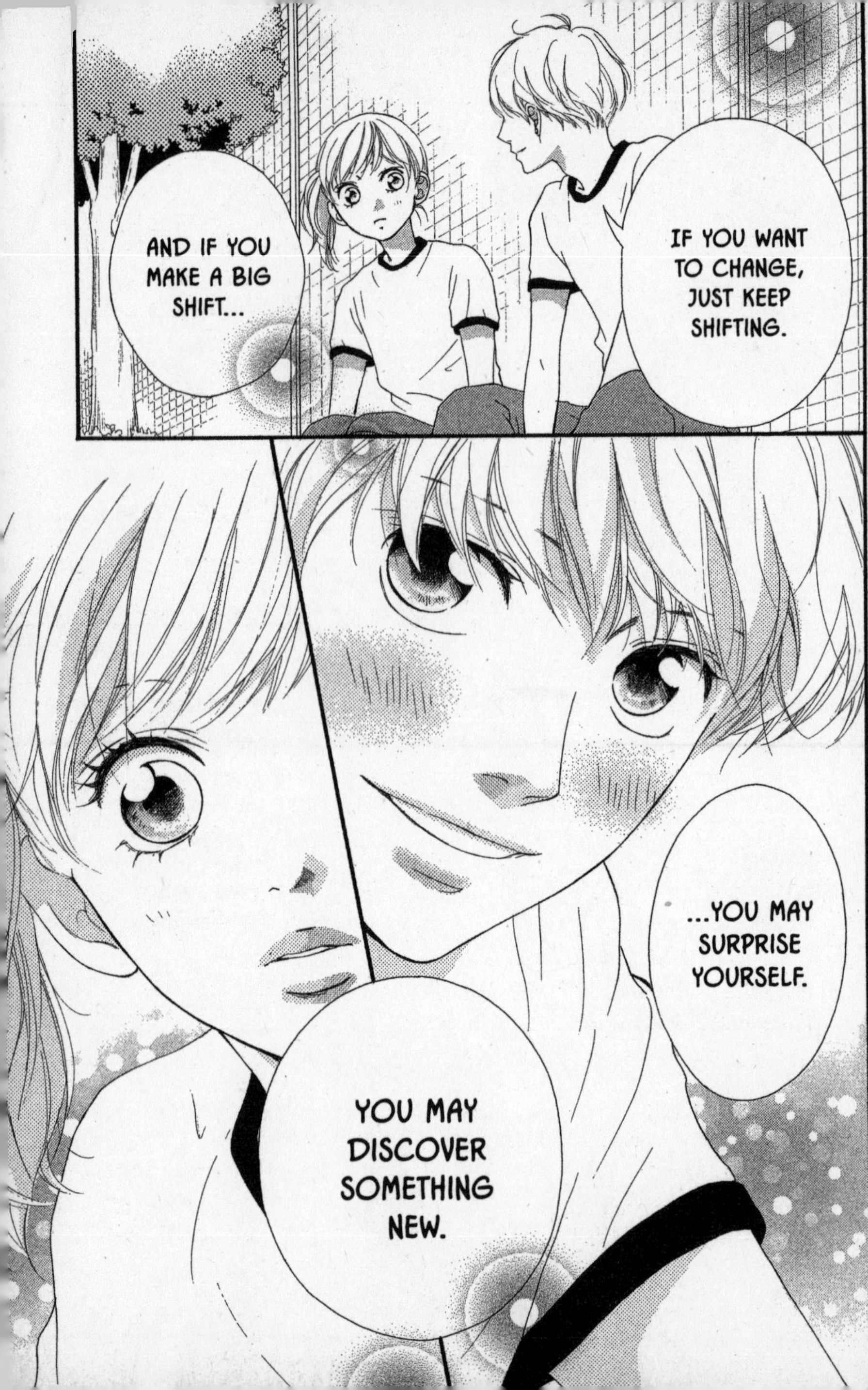
IF YOU WANT TO CHANGE, JUST KEEP SHIFTING.
AND IF YOU MAKE A BIG SHIFT...
...YOU MAY SURPRISE YOURSELF.
YOU MAY DISCOVER SOMETHING NEW.

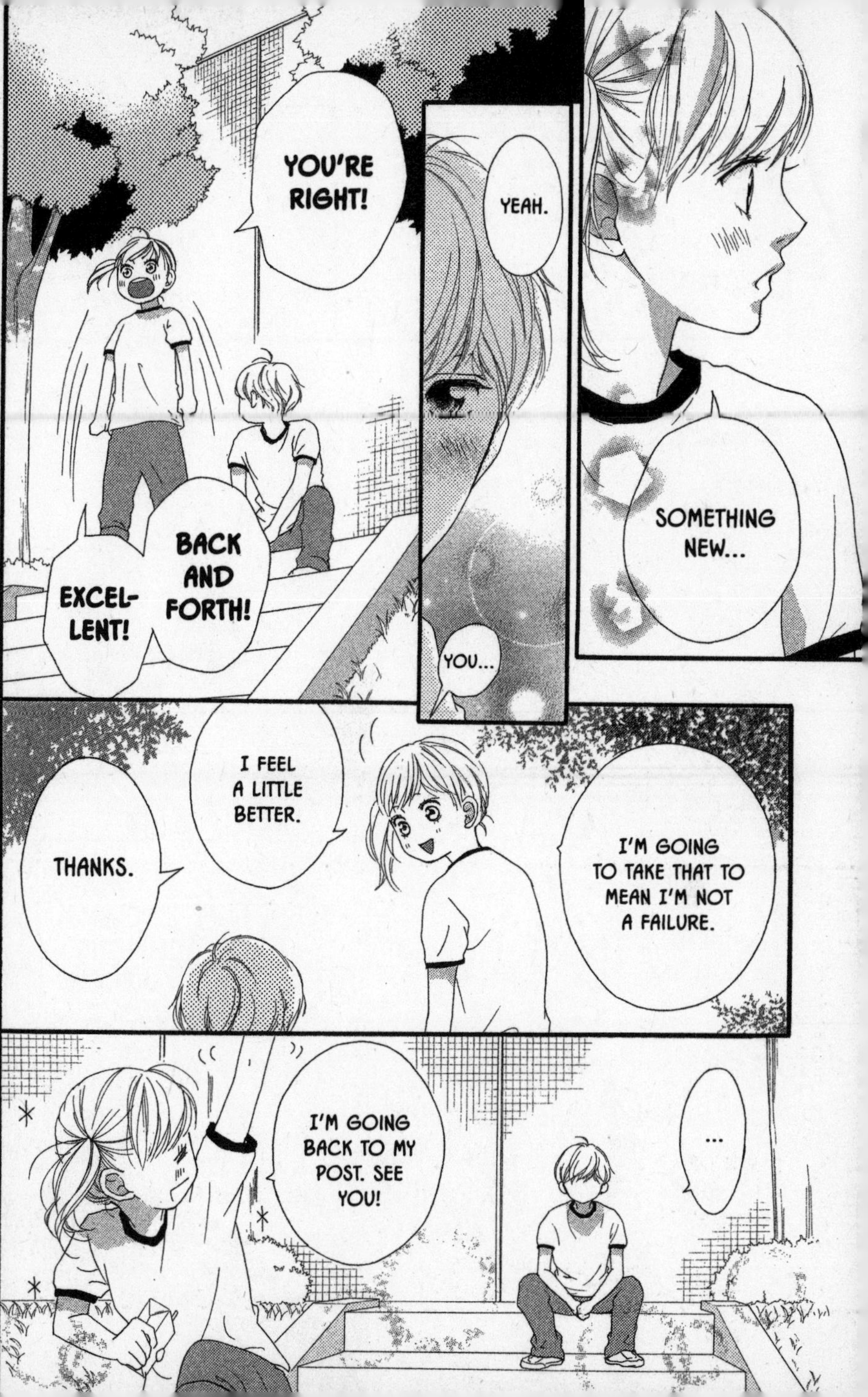
SOMETHING NEW...
YEAH.
YOU...
YOU'RE RIGHT!
BACK AND FORTH!
EXCEL-LENT!
I'M GOING TO TAKE THAT TO MEAN I'M NOT A FAILURE.
I FEEL A LITTLE BETTER.
THANKS.
...
I'M GOING BACK TO MY POST. SEE YOU!

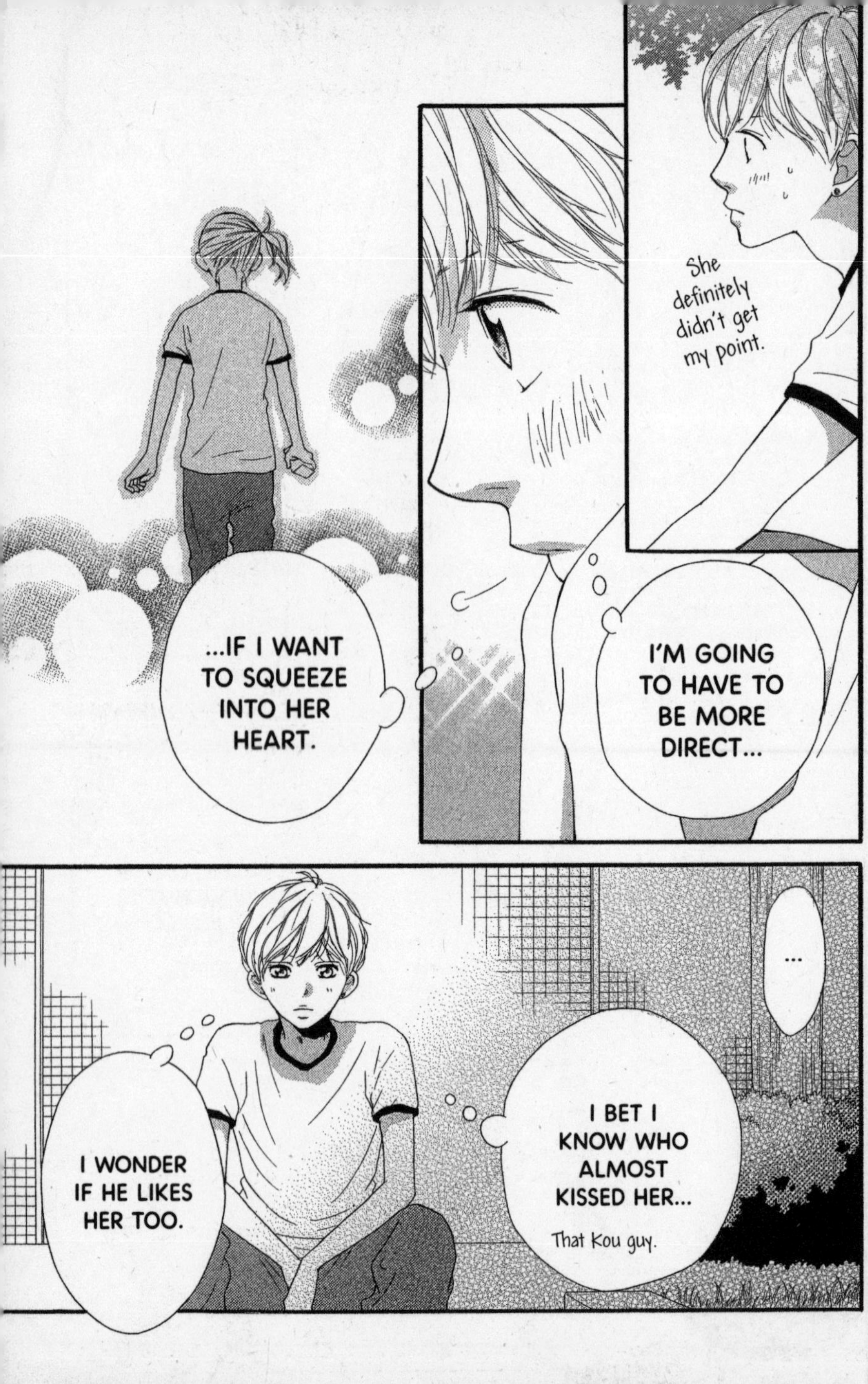
She definitely didn't get my point.
I'M GOING TO HAVE TO BE MORE DIRECT...
...IF I WANT TO SQUEEZE INTO HER HEART.
...
I BET I KNOW WHO ALMOST KISSED HER...
That Kou guy.
I WONDER IF HE LIKES HER TOO.

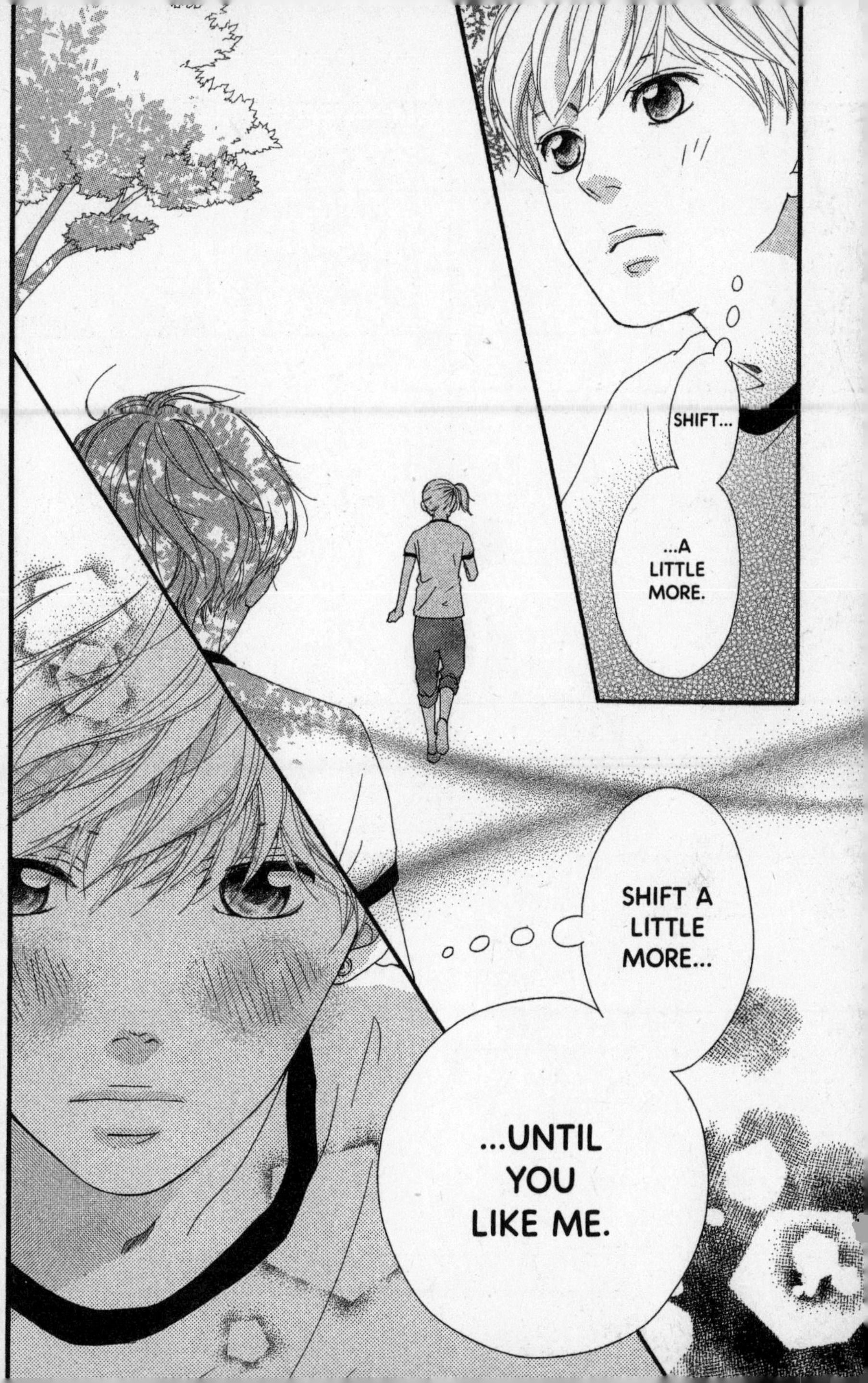
SHIFT...
...A LITTLE MORE.
SHIFT A LITTLE MORE...
...UNTIL YOU LIKE ME.

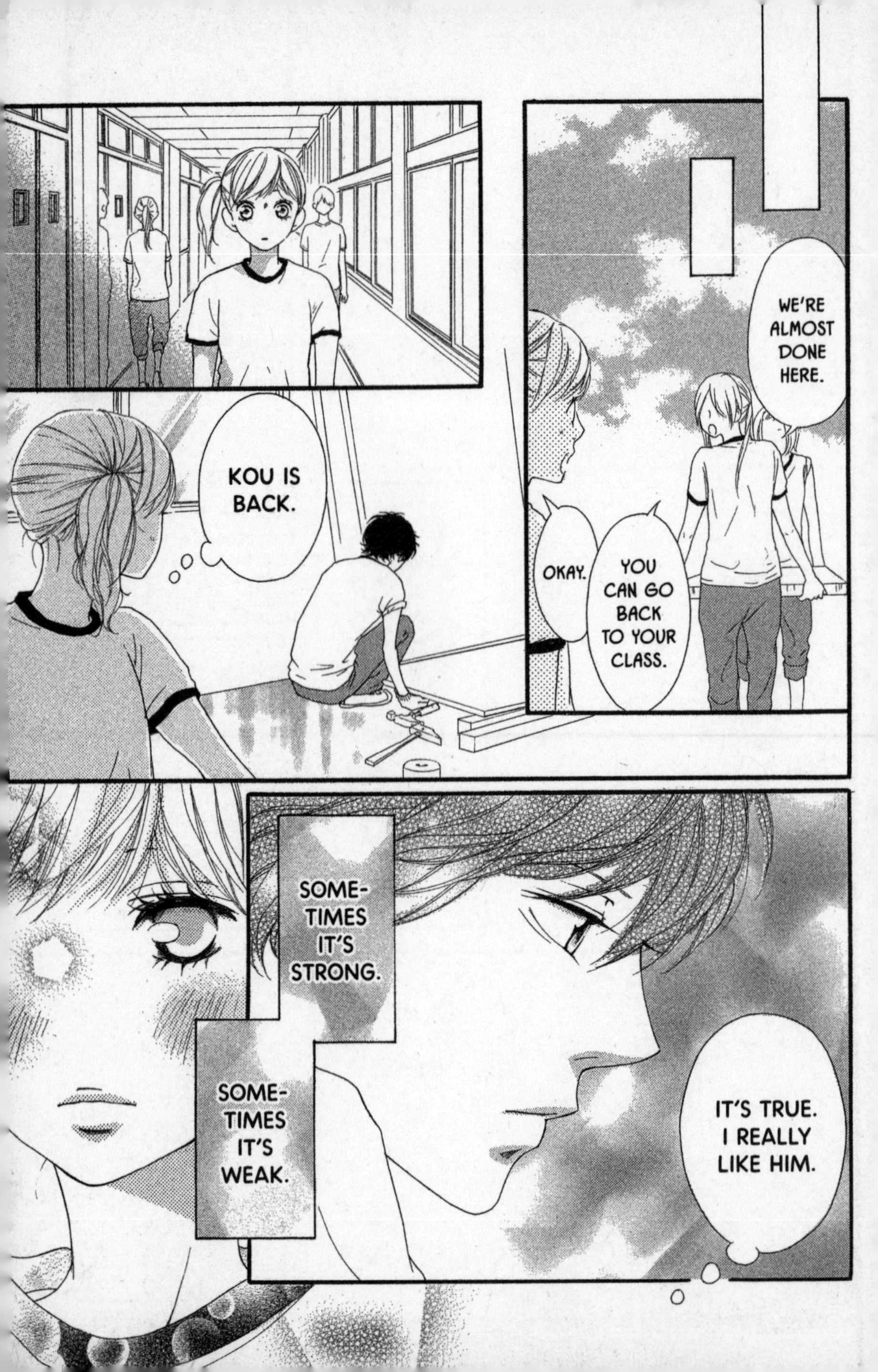
WE'RE ALMOST DONE HERE.
YOU CAN GO BACK TO YOUR CLASS.
OKAY.
KOU IS BACK.
IT'S TRUE. I REALLY LIKE HIM.
SOMETIMES IT'S STRONG.
SOMETIMES IT'S WEAK.

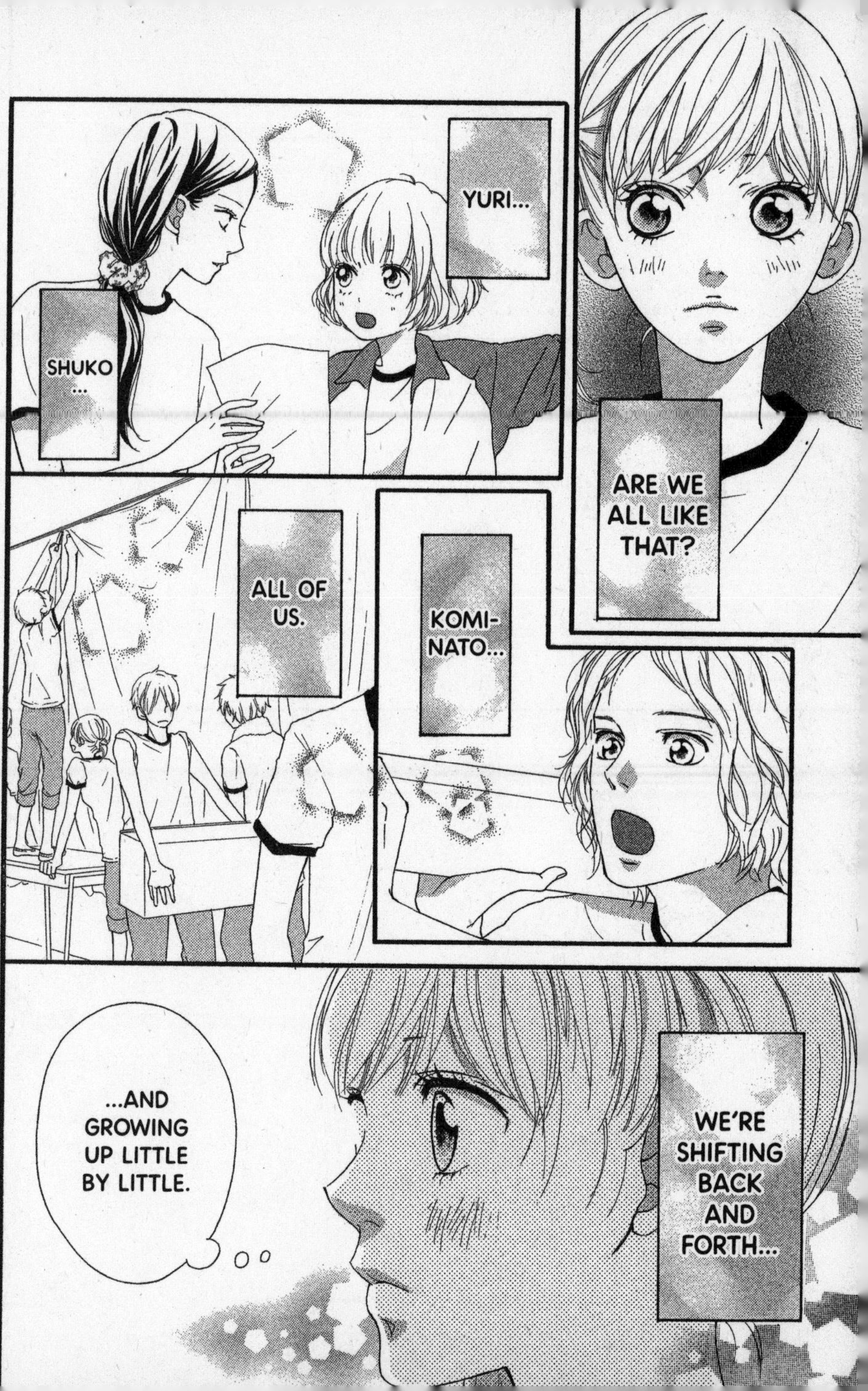
ARE WE ALL LIKE THAT?
YURI...
SHUKO ...
KOMI-NATO...
ALL OF US.
WE'RE SHIFTING BACK AND FORTH...
...AND GROWING UP LITTLE BY LITTLE.

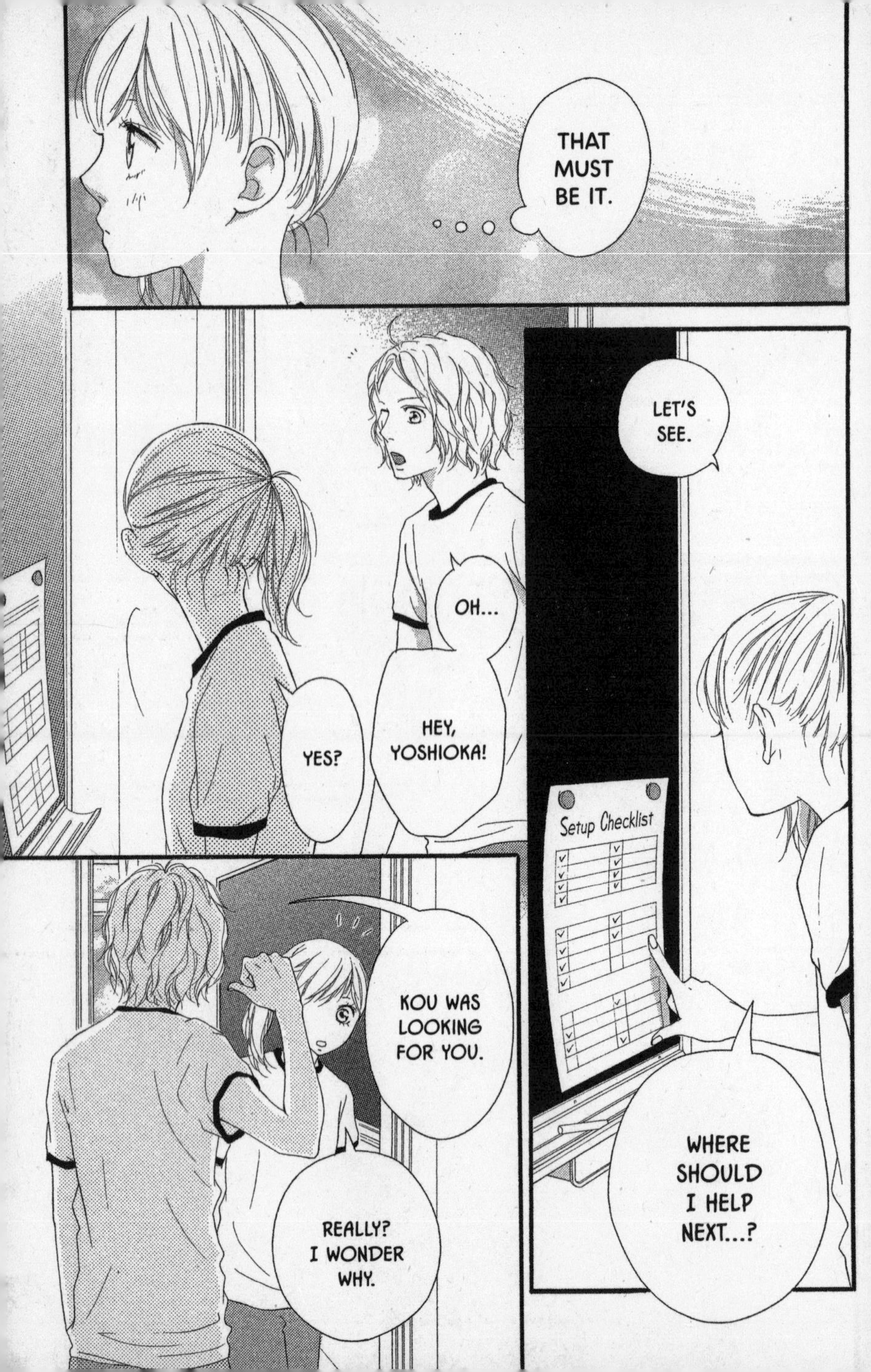
THAT MUST BE IT.
LET'S SEE.
WHERE SHOULD I HELP NEXT...?
Setup Checklist
OH...
HEY, YOSHIOKA!
YES?
KOU WAS LOOKING FOR YOU.
REALLY? I WONDER WHY.

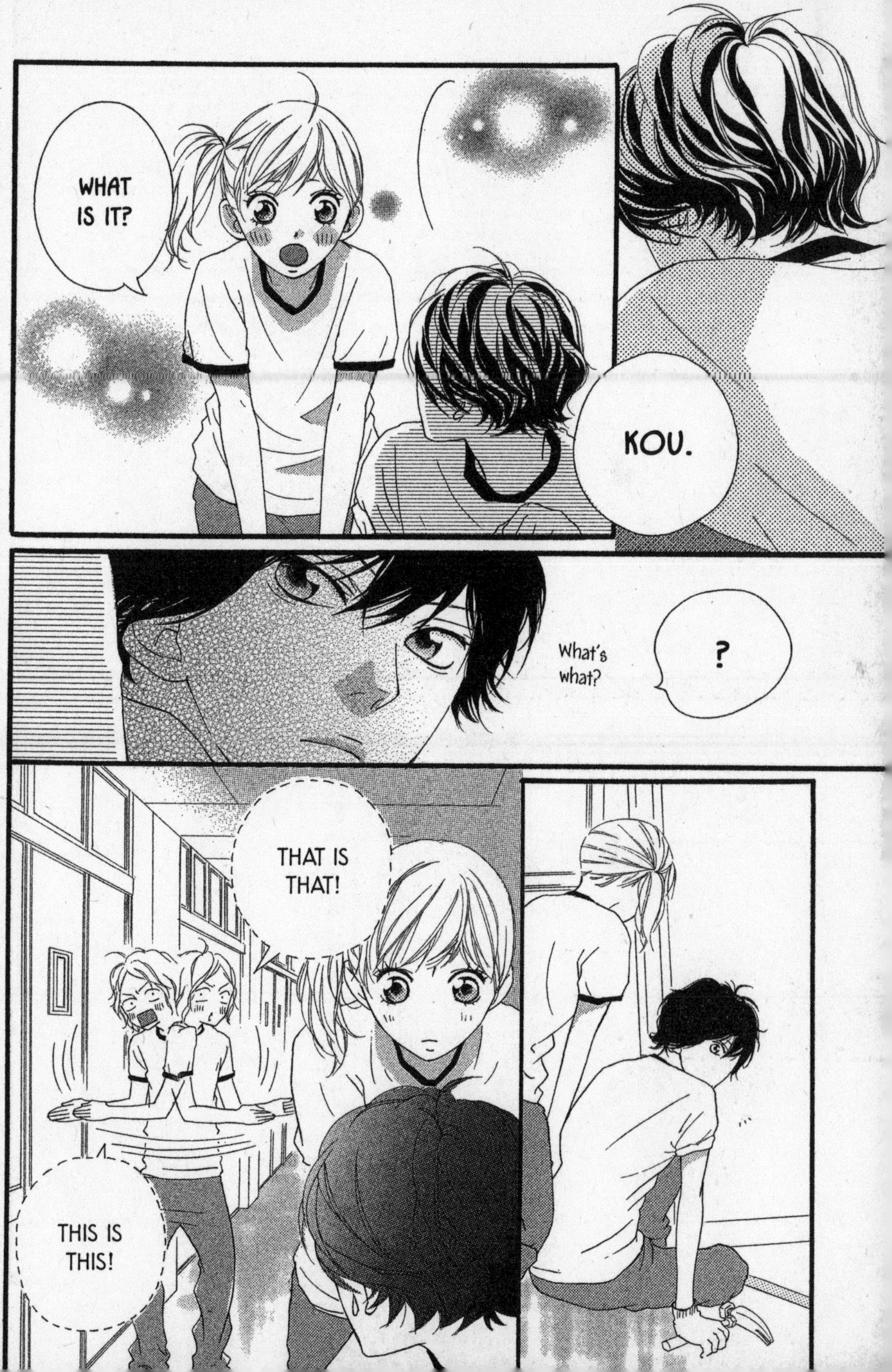
KOU.
WHAT IS IT?
?
What's what?
...
THAT IS THAT!
THIS IS THIS!

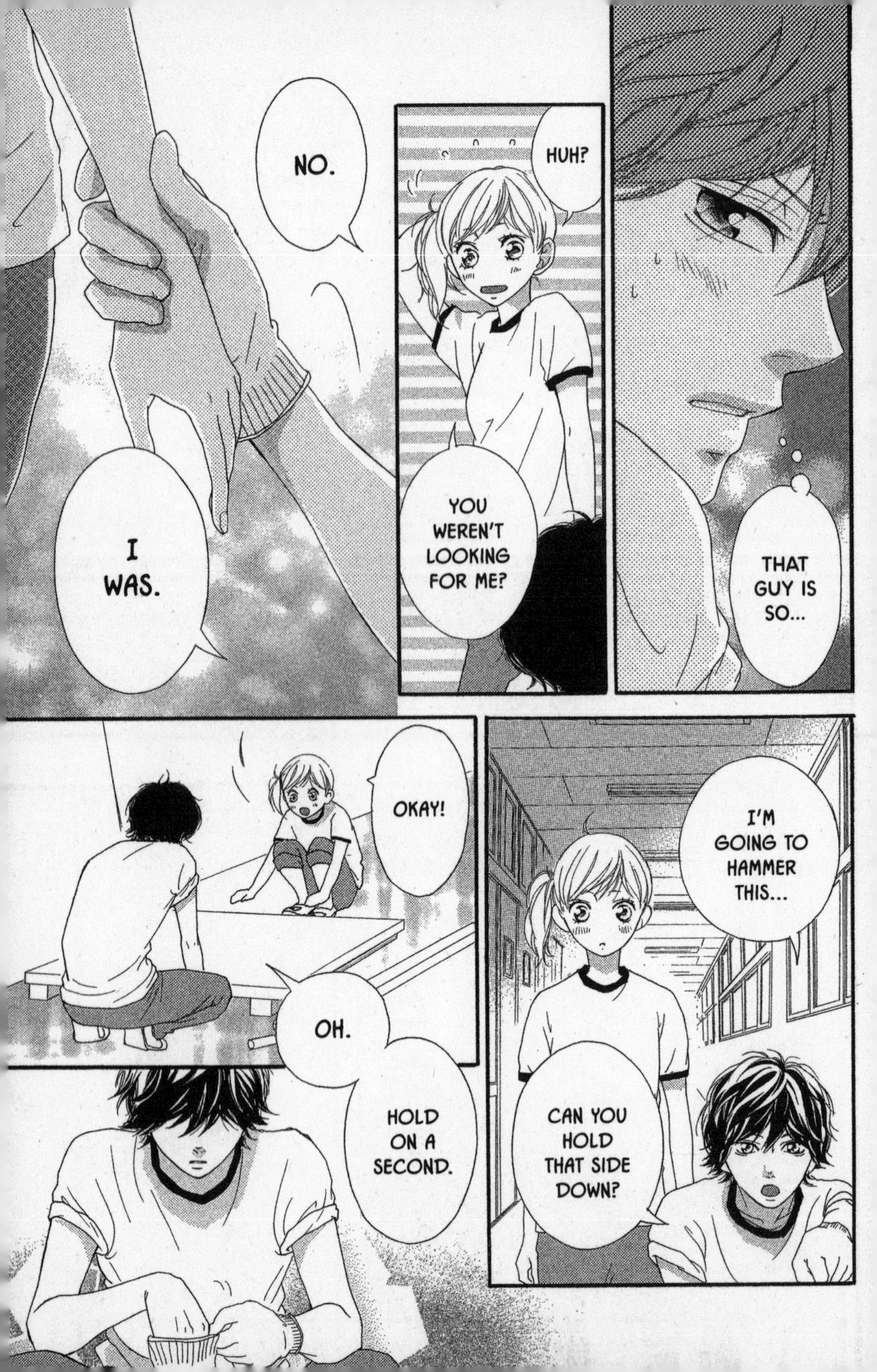
THAT GUY IS SO...
HUH?
YOU WEREN'T LOOKING FOR ME?
NO.
I WAS.
I'M GOING TO HAMMER THIS...
CAN YOU HOLD THAT SIDE DOWN?
OKAY!
OH.
HOLD ON A SECOND.

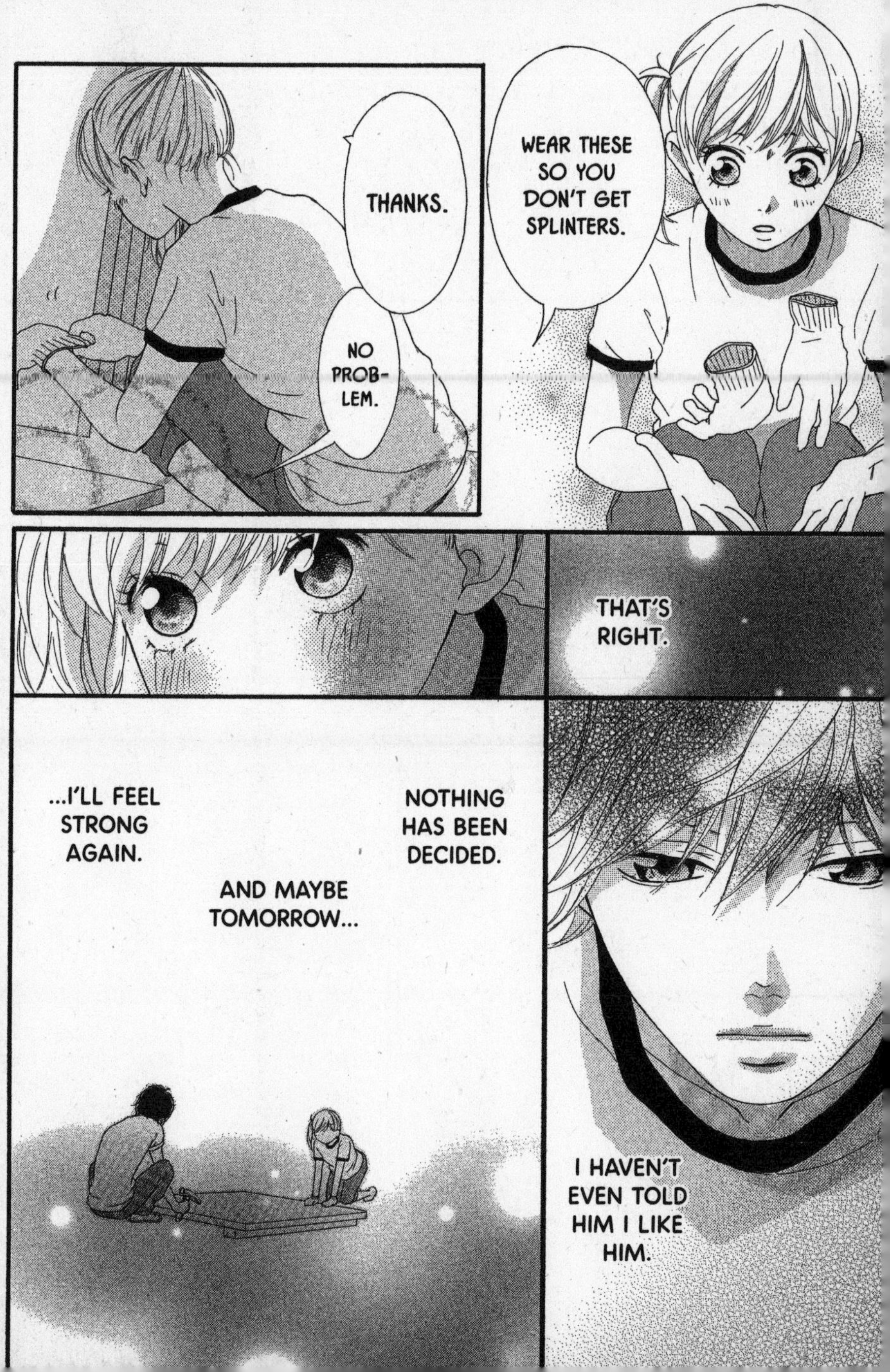
WEAR THESE SO YOU DON'T GET SPLINTERS.
THANKS.
NO PROB-LEM.
THAT'S RIGHT.
I HAVEN'T EVEN TOLD HIM I LIKE HIM.
NOTHING HAS BEEN DECIDED.
AND MAYBE TOMORROW...
...I'LL FEEL STRONG AGAIN.

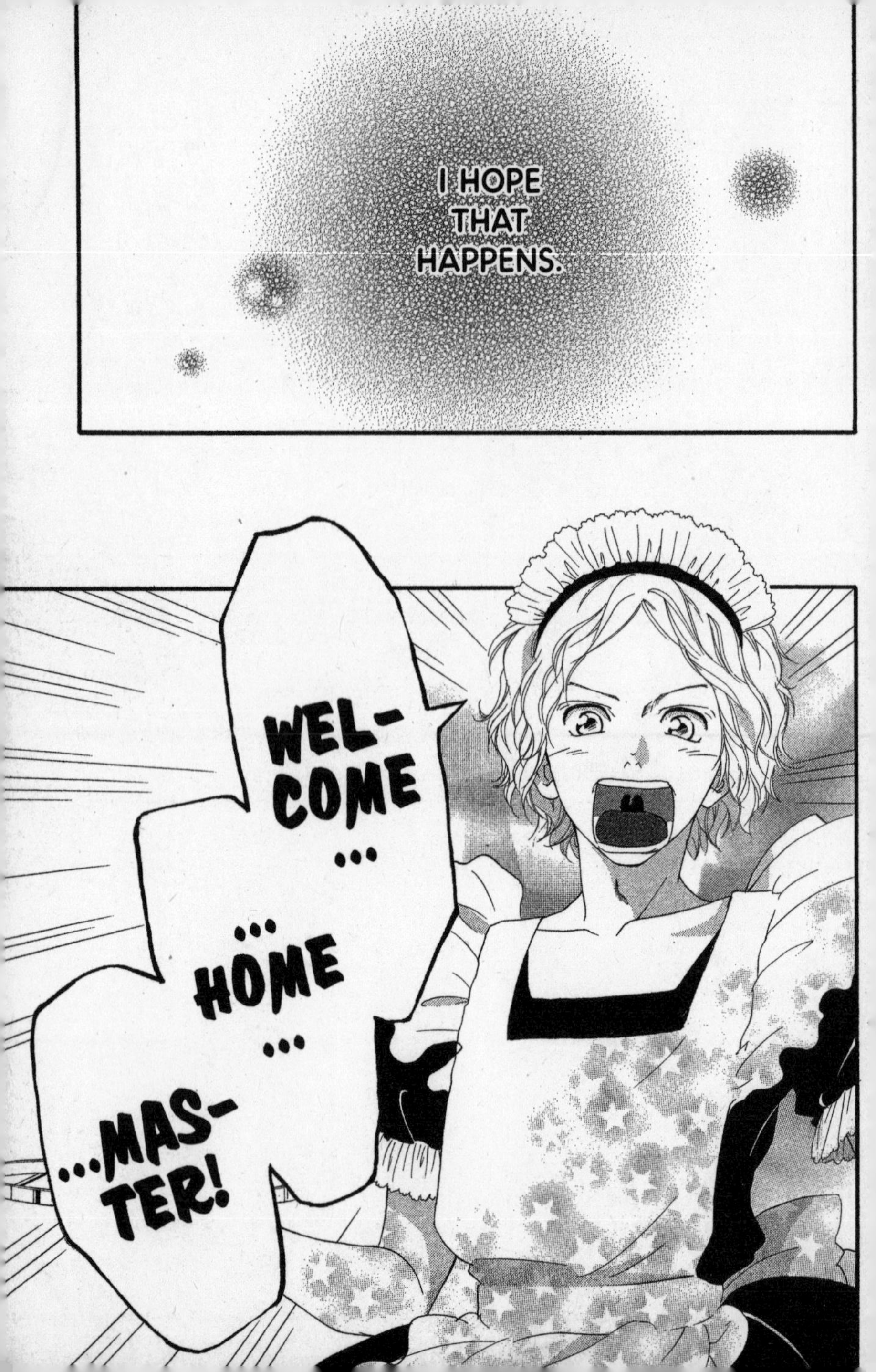
I HOPE THAT HAPPENS.
WEL-COME... ...HOME... ...MAS-TER!

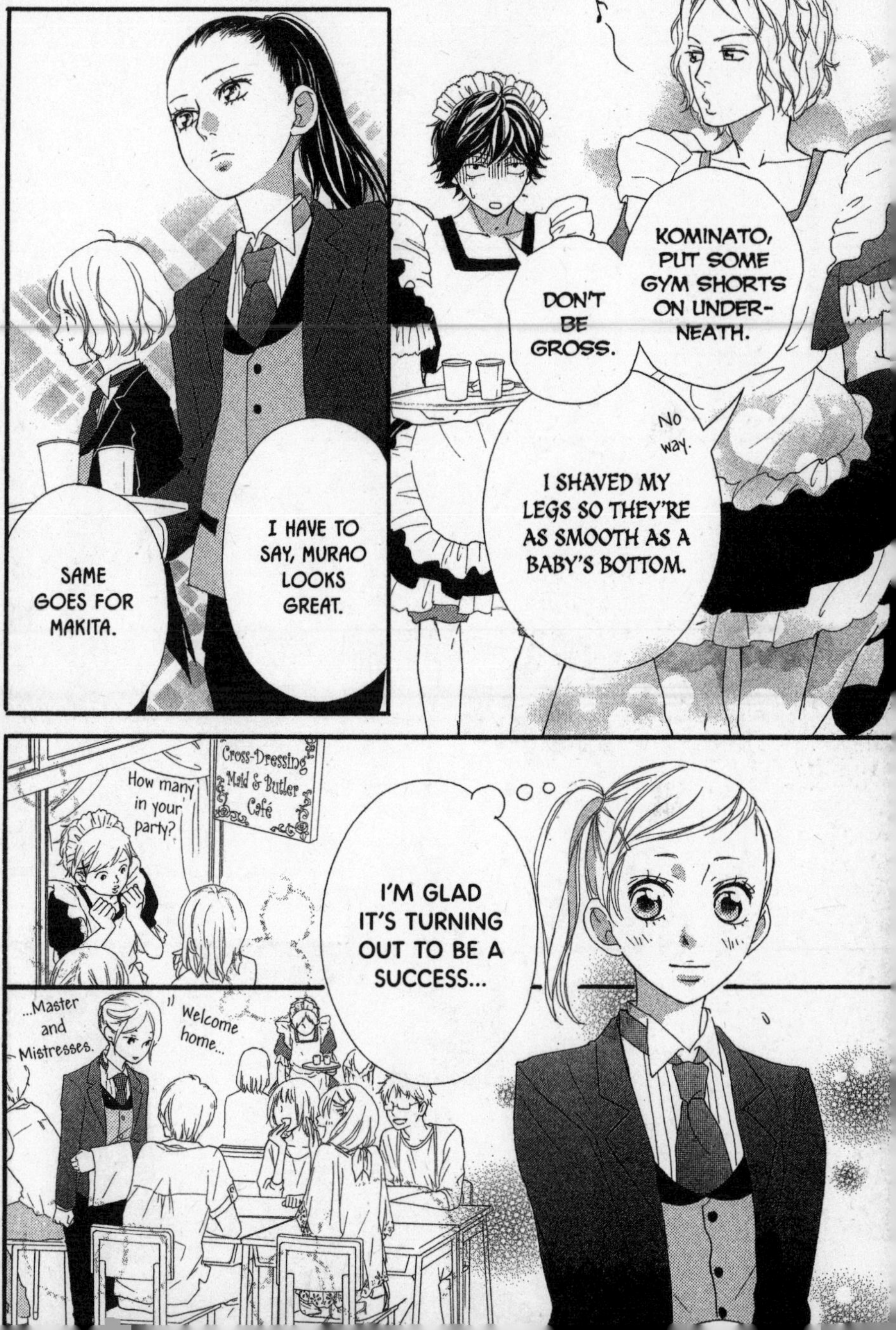
KOMINATO, PUT SOME GYM SHORTS ON UNDERNEATH.
DON'T BE GROSS.
No way.
I SHAVED MY LEGS SO THEY'RE AS SMOOTH AS A BABY'S BOTTOM.
I HAVE TO SAY, MURAO LOOKS GREAT.
SAME GOES FOR MAKITA.
I'M GLAD IT'S TURNING OUT TO BE A SUCCESS...
Cross-Dressing Maid & Butler Café
How many in your party?
Welcome home...
...Master and Mistresses.

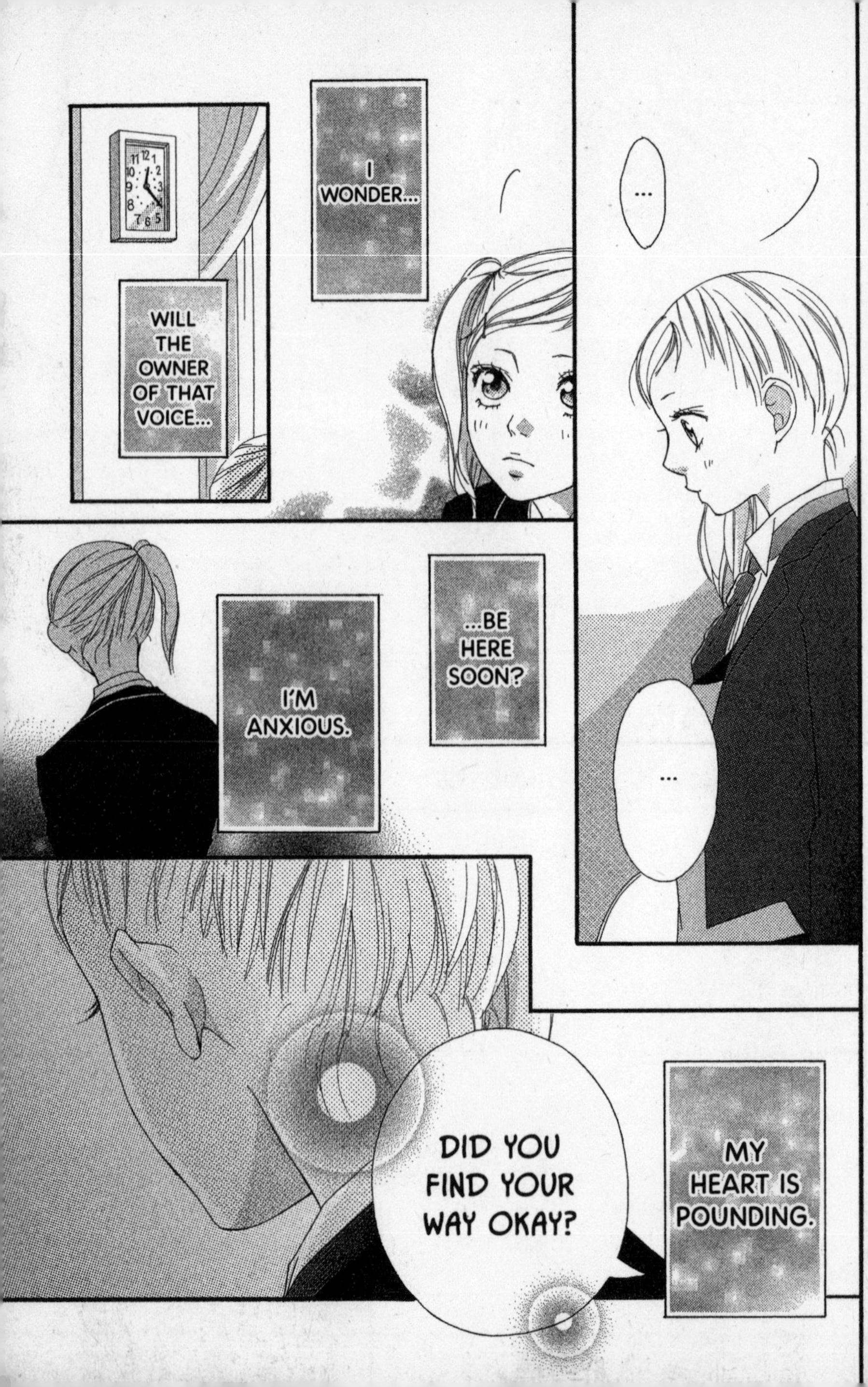
...
...
I WONDER...
WILL THE OWNER OF THAT VOICE...
...BE HERE SOON?
I'M ANXIOUS.
MY HEART IS POUNDING.
DID YOU FIND YOUR WAY OKAY?

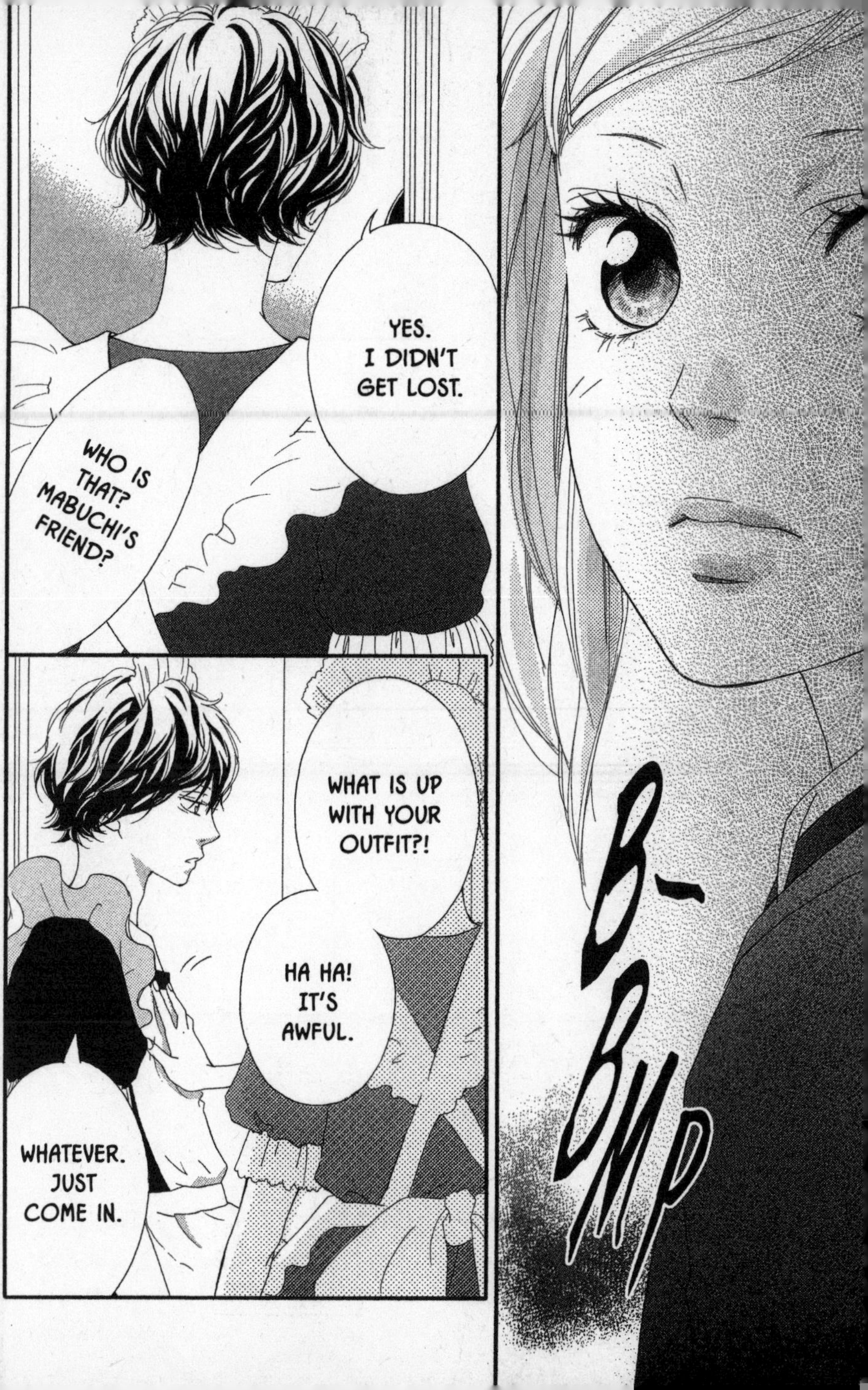
B-BUMP
YES. I DIDN'T GET LOST.
WHO IS THAT? MABUCHI'S FRIEND?
WHAT IS UP WITH YOUR OUTFIT?!
HA HA! IT'S AWFUL.
WHATEVER. JUST COME IN.

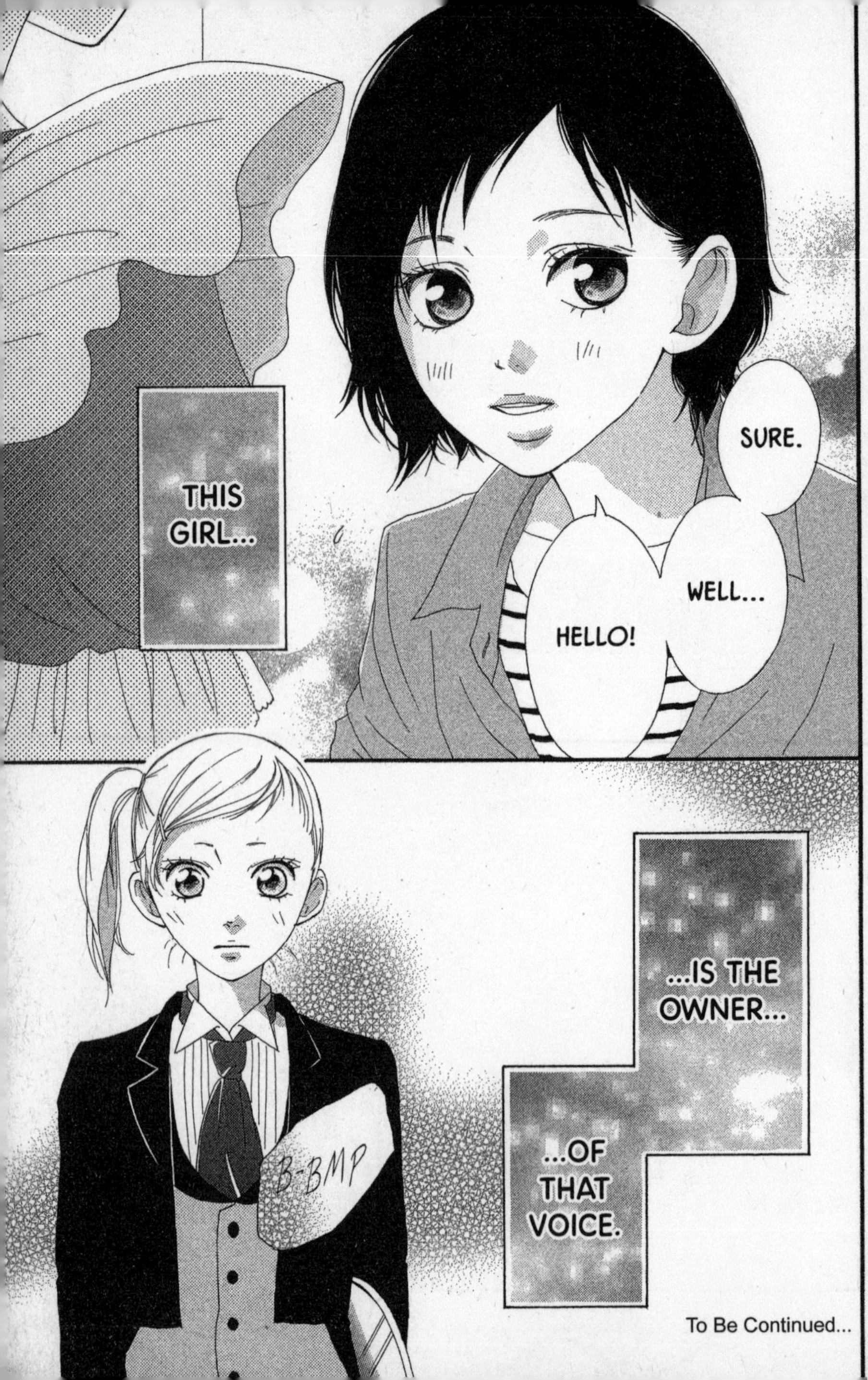
SURE.
WELL...
HELLO!
THIS GIRL...
...IS THE OWNER...
...OF THAT VOICE.
B-BMP
To Be Continued...

Ao Haru Ride

The scent of air after rain...
In the light around us, I felt your heartbeat.

AFTERWORD

Thank you for reading to the end.

I've written about this before, but drawing manga makes me think of my own high school days. Back then I thought I was doing a good job riding the waves of adolescence, but now I think that I didn't work hard enough! I should've done more of those awful, embarrassing things—you know, the stuff that makes you cringe as an adult for being so young and naive that you want to bury your face in your pillow and scream! I firmly believe these kinds of things we can't do as adults have to be done while we're young.

Also, the High School Quiz Championship! I'm an idiot for not participating! Getting together with friends, debating over the answers, getting eliminated after the second or third round, then grabbing food afterwards... The conversation suddenly changes to who likes whom... I wish I had been a part of that! It seems someone I know was on the show when they were a first-year in high school. I'm still jealous.

I want Futaba and the others to do all those things that I can't do now. With that, I hope you'll continue to enjoy *Ao Haru Ride*! See you next time. ♡

 Io Sakisaka

I got braces about two years ago, and my pronunciation has been strange ever since. When I speak, people often respond to me with "Hm?" "Huh?" "What?"

Sometimes I'll force out my words, even though I know they don't sound right. And of course the response is still "Huh?"

"P" sounds are the worst: *pa, pi, pu, pe, po.*

I hope I can get these removed soon!

IO SAKISAKA

Born on June 8, Io Sakisaka made her debut as a manga creator with *Sakura, Chiru.* Her works include *Call My Name, Gate of Planet* and *Blue. Strobe Edge,* her previous work, is also published by VIZ Media's Shojo Beat imprint. *Ao Haru Ride* was adapted into an anime series in 2014. In her spare time, Sakisaka likes to paint things and sleep.

Ao Haru Ride

VOLUME 5
SHOJO BEAT EDITION

STORY AND ART BY **IO SAKISAKA**

TRANSLATION **Emi Louie-Nishikawa**
TOUCH-UP ART + LETTERING **Inori Fukuda Trant**
DESIGN **Shawn Carrico**
EDITOR **Nancy Thistlethwaite**

AOHA RIDE © 2011 by Io Sakisaka
All rights reserved.
First published in Japan in 2011 by SHUEISHA Inc., Tokyo.
English translation rights arranged by SHUEISHA Inc.

Printed in the U.S.A.

Published by VIZ Media, LLC
P.O. Box 77010
San Francisco, CA 94107

10 9 8 7 6 5 4 3 2 1
First printing, June 2019

VIZ MEDIA
viz.com

Shojo Beat
shojobeat.com

Honey
So Sweet

Story and Art by Amu Meguro

Little did Nao Kogure realize back in middle school that when she left an umbrella and a box of bandages in the rain for injured delinquent Taiga Onise that she would meet him again in high school. Nao wants nothing to do with the gruff and frightening Taiga, but he suddenly presents her with a huge bouquet of flowers and asks her to date him—with marriage in mind! Is Taiga really so scary, or is he a sweetheart in disguise?

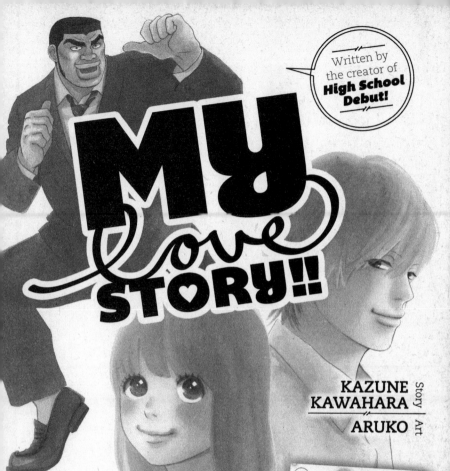

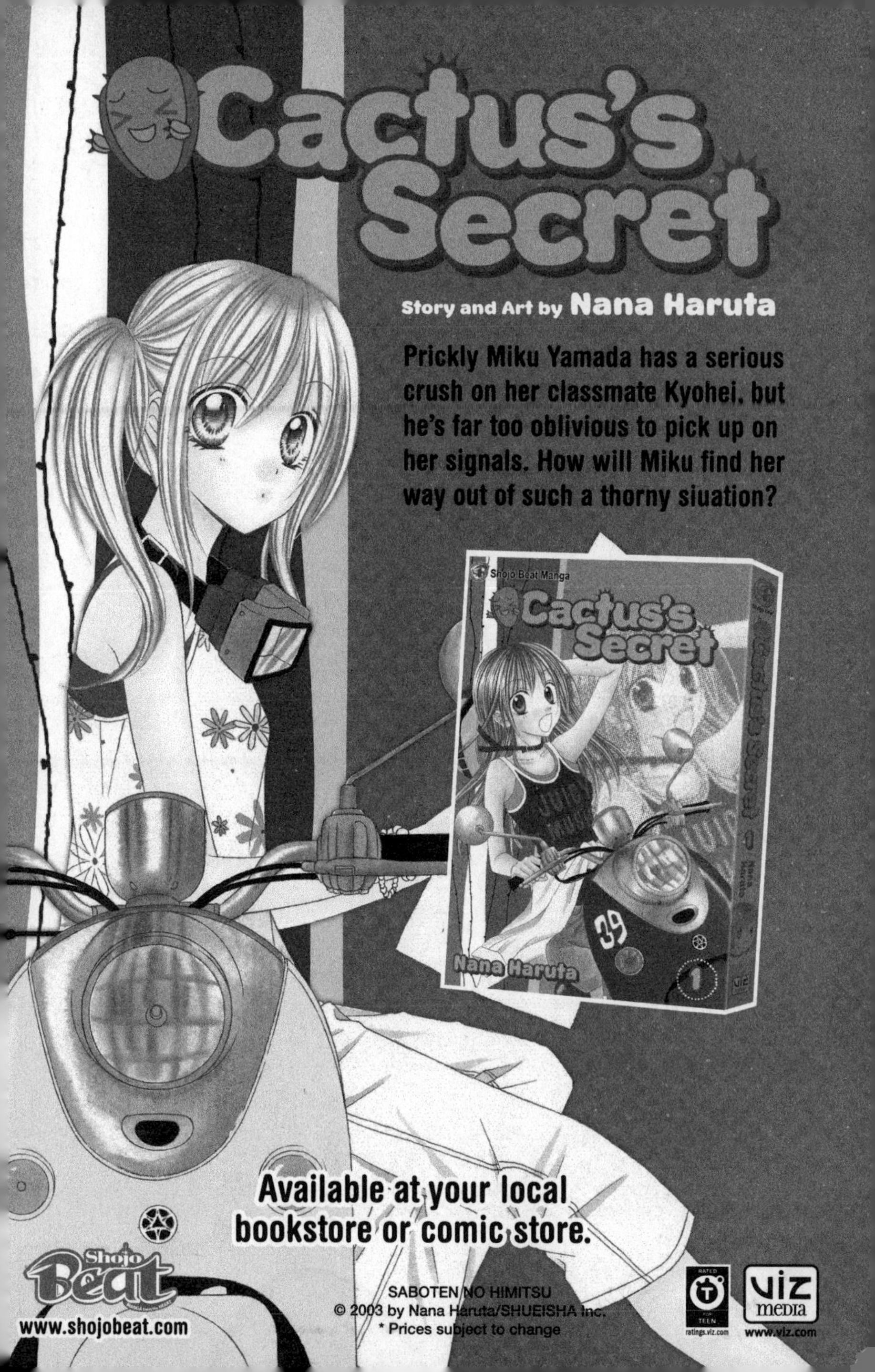
Cactus's Secret
Story and Art by Nana Haruta
Prickly Miku Yamada has a serious crush on her classmate Kyohei, but he's far too oblivious to pick up on her signals. How will Miku find her way out of such a thorny siuation?
Shojo Beat Manga
Cactus's Secret
Nana Haruta
1
Available at your local bookstore or comic store.
Shojo Beat
www.shojobeat.com
SABOTEN NO HIMITSU
© 2003 by Nana Haruta/SHUEISHA Inc.
* Prices subject to change
RATED T FOR TEEN
ratings.viz.com
VIZ media
www.viz.com

STOP!

YOU MAY BE READING THE WRONG WAY.

In keeping with the original Japanese comic format, this book reads from right to left—so action, sound effects and word balloons are completely reversed to preserve the orientation of the original artwork.

P9-DDA-434